D1586768

Empirical Finance

Empirical Finance

for finance and banking

Robert Sollis

A John Wiley & Sons, Ltd., Publication

This edition first published 2012
© 2012 John Wiley & Sons Ltd

Registered office
John Wiley & Sons Ltd, The Atrium, Southern Gate, Chichester, West Sussex, PO19 8SQ,
United Kingdom

For details of our global editorial offices, for customer services and for information about
how to apply for permission to reuse the copyright material in this book please see our
website at www.wiley.com.

The right of Robert Sollis to be identified as the author of this work has been asserted in
accordance with the Copyright, Designs and Patents Act 1988.

All rights reserved. No part of this publication may be reproduced, stored in a retrieval
system, or transmitted, in any form or by any means, electronic, mechanical, photocopying,
recording or otherwise, except as permitted by the UK Copyright, Designs and Patents Act
1988, without the prior permission of the publisher.

Wiley also publishes its books in a variety of electronic formats. Some content that appears
in print may not be available in electronic books.

Designations used by companies to distinguish their products are often claimed as
trademarks. All brand names and product names used in this book are trade names, service
marks, trademarks or registered trademarks of their respective owners. The publisher is not
associated with any product or vendor mentioned in this book. This publication is designed
to provide accurate and authoritative information in regard to the subject matter covered. It
is sold on the understanding that the publisher is not engaged in rendering professional
services. If professional advice or other expert assistance is required, the services of a
competent professional should be sought.

Library of Congress Cataloging-in-Publication Data

Sollis, R.
    Empirical finance : for finance and banking / Robert Sollis.
        p. cm.
    Includes bibliographical references and index.
    ISBN 978-0-470-51289-0
1. Finance. 2. Banks and banking. 3. Investments. I. Title.
    HG173.S65 2011
    332 – dc23

                                    2011034175

A catalogue record for this book is available from the British Library.

Set in 10/13pt Garamond by Laserwords Private Limited, Chennai, India
Printed in Great Britain by TJ International, Padstow, Cornwall

To Clare and Joseph.

Contents

Preface

This book focuses on the use of empirical methods in finance. It is intended for students taking Master's degrees in finance and banking, MBA students and early-stage researchers in these areas. Students and researchers in other related areas, such as economics, might also find it to be useful. After the first three introductory chapters, which outline the structure of the book and review econometric and statistical techniques, the remaining chapters are self-contained discussions of a selection of key topics in finance and banking where empirical methods play an important role. Understanding these topics and methods is important for students interested in working as analysts and researchers in financial institutions.

It is becoming increasingly common that students with relatively non-technical undergraduate degrees switch to finance and banking at the Master's degree level. Therefore, while it is impossible to avoid equations in a book on this subject, I have been selective in the amount of mathematics used in the main text and have tried to write in an "easy-to-read" style. Further technical details on relevant mathematical proofs and the statistical techniques used can be found in the many books and journal articles referenced throughout. The choice of topics covered has been influenced by my own university teaching experience at both undergraduate and postgraduate levels in econometrics, finance and statistics. I have also included some material from practical courses on time series forecasting that I have taught for the Royal Statistical Society to professional economists and statisticians. Note, however, that this book is not intended to be an exhaustive text and there are many interesting topics in finance that are not discussed here.

The 2007–2009 global financial crisis highlighted many weaknesses in orthodox financial modelling and risk management, and some of these weaknesses are discussed in this book. However, I do not attempt to develop any new or improved techniques. Some have already been proposed and no doubt many more will be proposed in White Papers, academic journals and books over the next few years. This book focuses only on existing techniques.

I would like to thank Steve Hardman and Nicole Burnett at Wiley for their patience, support and enthusiasm for this project, and Paul Stringer for his diligent copy-editing. I would also like to thank attendees of my Royal Statistical Society workshops as well as colleagues and students at Newcastle University for helpful comments on much of the material in this book. Most of all, I would like to thank my family for their invaluable support.

Chapter 1
Introduction

1.1 Subject Matter and Structure

1.2 Computer Software

1.3 Data

1.4 References

1.1 Subject Matter and Structure

Chapters 2 and 3 of this book review the main econometric and statistical techniques employed in empirical finance. Chapters 4 to 9 are self-contained discussions of a selection of key topics in finance where empirical methods play an important role. At the end of all the following chapters there are five test questions to help clarify the topics discussed. The questions vary between purely empirical questions and essay-type questions. The empirical questions for Chapters 2 and 3 utilise simulated data; the empirical questions for Chapters 4 to 9 require real-world data. As well as the empirical end of chapter questions, in the penultimate section of the main text for Chapters 4 to 9, selected empirical examples are presented that demonstrate many of the empirical methods discussed. Relevant computer programs and a guide to answering the end of chapter questions will be placed on the companion website: **www.wileyeurope.com/college/sollis**. The computer software MATLAB® is used for all calculations in this book.[1] Statistical tables required for some of the empirical examples are included in an appendix at the end of the book.

Chapter 2 introduces the statistical concepts of random variables and random processes before moving on to discuss **time series models** – an important family of statistical models used in many different subject areas including finance. The parameters of a time series model for a financial asset's price or return can be estimated using sample data on its values over time (**time series data**). The estimated model

---

[1]MATLAB® is a MathWorks product (The MathWorks Inc.: see www.mathworks.com/products/matlab/).

provides important information on the how the price or return randomly evolves over time. Time series models can also be used to compute forecasts of financial variables, which might then be used for financial trading.

Chapter 3 reviews regression modelling. Regression models are the workhorse statistical models for empirical analysis in finance. They can be used to analyse the empirical support for financial theories; they can be employed to compute forecasts of financial variables; they can be used to understand and quantify the risks associated with particular financial assets and combinations of assets. Chapter 3 also covers modelling and forecasting **volatility**. In finance the variance and standard deviation of the return from investing in an asset are used as measures of the asset's risk. The standard deviation is also called the volatility of the return. Accurately modelling and forecasting volatility is particularly important for successful risk management.

Chapter 4 focuses on modern portfolio theory (MPT). MPT has its origins in a seminal journal article on portfolio selection by Markowitz (1952). This article had a significant impact on both financial research and practice. Markowitz (1952) shows formally how the expected return and the variance of the return for a portfolio can be computed as a function of the expected returns, variances and covariances of the returns for the constituent assets. He argues that when constructing portfolios, investors should focus on the performance of different portfolios of assets as measured by combinations of expected portfolio return and portfolio risk, and they should choose from diversified portfolios that maximise expected return for a given level of risk. MPT leads to analytical formulas for optimal asset allocation. The empirical examples in Chapter 4 demonstrate the use of these formulas.

Chapter 5 focuses on asset pricing models and factor models. The capital asset pricing model (CAPM), developed by Sharpe (1964), Lintner (1965) and Mossin (1966), is a theoretical model of the relationship between asset returns and risk under a set of simplifying assumptions. The CAPM is an attractive theoretical model; it is parsimonious and has a clear set of predictions that can be empirically evaluated using statistical techniques; estimated versions of the CAPM can be used for a range of practical tasks. Factor models are a type of asset pricing model that are more general than the CAPM and appear to have greater explanatory power than the CAPM when applied to stock market data. They are widely used by financial institutions to help understand how particular macroeconomic risks affect stock returns. The empirical examples in Chapter 5 include using stock market data to statistically evaluate the empirical support for the CAPM, and estimating and interpreting a factor model.

Chapter 6 focuses on the efficiency of financial markets. In finance the label **efficient market** refers to a financial market (e.g. a stock market, the foreign exchange market) that is informationally efficient, in the sense that current asset prices reflect all relevant information. The **efficient market hypothesis** (EMH) formalised by Fama (1970) states that financial markets are efficient in this way. Chapter 6 begins with a discussion of market efficiency and explains how the EMH can be empirically tested. The EMH implies that **abnormal profits** cannot be generated by trading on forecasts of asset prices or returns computed using historical sample data on prices or returns. Chapter 6 discusses the ability of some particular empirical forecasting techniques to generate abnormal profits. The techniques considered are **econometric forecasting** and **technical analysis**. The empirical examples in Chapter 6 cover testing for stock market efficiency using data on stock market indices for several countries, and forecasting stock index returns using econometric analysis and technical analysis.

Chapter 7 focuses on modelling and forecasting exchange rates. If the foreign exchange market is informationally efficient then certain relationships between current exchange rates, interest rates, forward exchange rates and actual future exchange rates will hold (where the "forward" exchange rate is an exchange rate agreed now for delivery at a future time period). Therefore empirically testing for whether these relationships do hold provides useful empirical evidence on the efficiency of the foreign exchange market. Chapter 7 discusses these relationships and how they can be empirically tested. Chapter 7 also focuses on the relationship between exchange rates and domestic and foreign price levels. In the absence of tariffs, non-tariff barriers and transaction costs, the **law of one price** states that when converted into a common currency the price of a good in different countries should be equal. When applied to the price of a basket of goods (measured using a price index), this law is called the **purchasing power parity** (PPP) hypothesis. The empirical examples in Chapter 7 include empirically testing exchange rate parity conditions and empirically testing the PPP hypothesis. Chapter 7 also considers exchange rate forecasting.

Chapter 8 focuses on modelling and forecasting interest rates, starting with a discussion of the main types of bonds and the traditional formulas for computing bond yields and bond prices. Chapter 8 also introduces an important family of **continuous-time** interest rate models. These models assume that interest rates are time-varying random processes that can be represented using stochastic differential equations. Continuous-time interest rate models can be used to obtain analytical formulas for pricing bonds, bond derivatives, and for describing the term structure of interest rates.

The final topic discussed in Chapter 8 is empirically testing the **expectations hypothesis** of the term structure of interest rates, using econometric tests developed by Campbell and Shiller (1987, 1991). This hypothesis states that the difference between interest rates for bonds with different maturities depends on investors' expectations of future short-term interest rates, where these expectations are formed rationally. If the expectations hypothesis of the term structure of interest rates is correct, the yield curve (a graph of bond yields against time to maturity) contains information on expected future short-term interest rates. Hence a vast amount of research has been undertaken on empirically testing the expectations hypothesis, some of which is discussed in Chapter 8. The empirical examples in Chapter 8 include estimating the parameters of a continuous-time interest rate model, forecasting interest rates and testing the expectations hypothesis using the econometric tests discussed.

Chapter 9 focuses on risk management, in particular the use of statistical techniques to manage **market risk. Value at Risk** (VaR) has for some time been the most popular statistical technique used by banks for managing market risk. VaR is a forecast of a lower quantile of the probability distribution for the change in the value of a portfolio over a particular horizon (e.g. one day). Hence VaR is a monetary measure of downside financial risk. Chapter 9 discusses the main approaches that can be used to compute VaR, including the popular RiskMetrics approach (see for example RiskMetrics, 1996, 2001, 2006). The statistical evaluation of VaR models using **backtesting** is also covered.

Chapter 9 also discusses the role of VaR and backtesting in international financial regulation. Under the Basel II Capital Accord, banks can use VaR to help determine the minimum capital they must hold to cope with potential losses. The performance of their VaR models in backtesting can also have an impact on this minimum capital requirement. In response to the 2007–2009 global financial crisis, a new Capital Accord, Basel III, has been proposed and it appears that VaR will continue to play an important role. VaR is also increasingly popular for risk management in the insurance and re-insurance industries. The empirical examples in Chapter 9 demonstrate how to compute VaR for portfolios containing assets and derivatives using the techniques discussed in the main text. An example of backtesting VaR for a portfolio of stocks is also presented.

1.2 Computer Software

I have chosen to use MATLAB® for all calculations in this book because it is widely used in practice by researchers and analysts in the financial sector. Therefore, it is helpful for students intending to pursue a career in the financial sector that they become familiar with MATLAB®. For some of the empirical examples in Chapters 4 to 9, I have included the MATLAB® program used to compute the empirical results (or a portion of the program). The programs used for all of the empirical examples in Chapters 4 to 9 will be placed on the companion website, www.wileyeurope.com/college/sollis, and further details on the programs are given in an appendix to each of those chapters. All of these programs require a registered version of MATLAB® to run. Note also that some of the programs require a registered version of one of the following **toolboxes** to run: Financial Toolbox®, Statistics Toolbox®, System Identification Toolbox®; or the Oxford MFE Toolbox.[2,3] I have tried to make the programs as simple to understand as possible and have favoured obvious ways of computing relevant estimators and test statistics rather than taking shortcuts that might be less clear (but more efficient). The programs are annotated with instructions.

MATLAB® programs have the extension ".m". A program can be opened by opening MATLAB® and then setting the "Current Directory" (or "Current Folder" depending on the version of MATLAB®) on the toolbar to the directory where the program is saved. The contents of this directory should appear in a separate window. Then double click on the program in the Current Directory and it should open in the "Editor" window. To run the program click the "Run" button on the Editor toolbar, or click "Debug" on the main toolbar and then "Run...". The output goes to the "Workspace" and any relevant graphs will appear in windows.

MATLAB® includes many different built-in functions that users can employ in their programs to simplify certain tasks. For example, the `normpdf` function, which is applied using the command `y=normpdf(X,mu,sigma)`, generates the probability density function (PDF) for a normally distributed random variable X, where mu and sigma are the mean and variance. Users can also write their own MATLAB® functions and save them as separate .m files. If a function has more than one output then when the function is applied, the outputs should be written in square brackets, separated by commas, on the left-hand-side: for instance, `[r1,r2,r3]=functionname(.)`. User-defined functions should be saved in the same directory as the program in which they are being used.

1.3 Data

Virtually all of the external data used in this book has been obtained from publicly accessible sources such as Yahoo! Finance, the Federal Reserve Economic Data (FRED) database at the Federal Reserve Bank of St Louis and the Bank of England Statistics database.[4] Therefore readers should be able

---

[2]Financial Toolbox®, Statistics Toolbox®, and System Identification Toolbox® are MathWorks products (see www.mathworks.com/products/matlab/).

[3]For more information on the Oxford MFE Toolbox, see http://www.kevinsheppard.com/wiki/MFE_Toolbox. I would like to thank Kevin Sheppard for allowing me to use the Oxford MFE Toolbox for computing several results reported in this book.

[4]www.finance.yahoo.com; www.research.stlouisfed.org/fred2/; www.bankofengland.co.uk/statistics

to download these data and use the MATLAB® programs to obtain similar results to many of the results reported in this book.[5] Inputting data into MATLAB® programs is straightforward. For example, to input data from a single Microsoft Excel spreadsheet called "filename.xls", make sure the Excel file is saved in the same directory as the MATLAB® program being used, and then in the program, use the command `Y=xlsread('filename')`, where "filename" is the name of the Excel file without the .xls extension (this assumes the .xls file is an Excel 97–2003 Workbook). The data will be contained in the vector or matrix Y. Further details on the data used in the empirical examples are given in the appendixes to each chapter.[6]

1.4 References

Campbell, J.Y. and R.J. Shiller (1987) Cointegration and tests of present value models, *Journal of Political Economy*, 95, 1062–1088.

Campbell, J.Y. and R.J. Shiller (1991) Interest rate spreads and interest rate movements: a bird's eye view, *Review of Economic Studies*, 58, 495–514.

Fama, E.F. (1970) Efficient capital markets: a review of theory and empirical work, *Journal of Finance*, 25, 383–417.

Lintner, J. (1965) The valuation of risk assets and the selection of risky investments in stock portfolios and capital budgets, *Review of Economics and Statistics*, 47, 13–37.

Markowitz, H.M. (1952) Portfolio selection, *Journal of Finance*, 7, 77–91

Mossin, J. (1966) Equilibrium in a capital asset market, *Econometrica*, 34, 768–783.

RiskMetrics: Technical Document (1996) New York: JP Morgan/Reuters.

RiskMetrics, Return to: The Evolution of a Standard (2001) New York: RiskMetrics Group.

RiskMetrics 2006 Methodology (2006) New York: RiskMetrics Group.

Sharpe, W.F. (1964) Capital asset prices: a theory of market equilibrium under conditions of risk, *Journal of Finance*, 19, 425–442.

---

[5]Thomson Reuters Datastream, which requires a subscription, has been used for a very small proportion of the data employed.

[6]Unfortunately, I cannot guarantee that the exact data used to compute the results in this book will still be available after the book's publication. Whilst every attempt has been made to ensure that the data, text and the MATLAB® programs are free of errors, they cannot be guaranteed to be error-free. Where possible any corrections found subsequent to the book's publication will be placed on the website www.wileyeurope.com/college/sollis. Note also that while the internet links mentioned in this book are currently working, it cannot be guaranteed that they will all continue to work after the book's publication.

Chapter 2
Random Variables and Random Processes

2.1 Introduction

A **random variable** can be formally defined as a variable that has an uncertain numerical value that is determined by the outcome of a random experiment. The uncertainty of random variables can be quantified using the concept of probability. A simple example of a random variable often used in statistics textbooks is the score from rolling a die. We know that for this random variable each of the six possible values has a probability of 1/6, hence they are equally likely. Random variables exist in all aspects of life: for example, the amount of rainfall by the end of today; the waiting time when we arrive at a bus stop; today's closing value for a stock market index.

A **random process** (or **stochastic process**) is a natural extension of the concept of a random variable, being a series of random variables ordered in a particular way. If the ordering is by time then data on the actual values of the random process are called **time series data**, or a **time series**. Many of the variables of interest in finance (e.g. the future value of an exchange rate, interest rate, stock market index) are random variables. Over a period of time these variables can be thought of as random processes, hence this chapter reviews some key econometric and statistical techniques for modelling and forecasting random processes using time series data, focusing in particular on **time series models**.

There are various different types of time series model. A linear univariate time series model for a relevant variable involves modelling the current period's value as a linear function of a zero mean random error term, plus lagged values of the variable, and/or lagged values of the error term. Linear univariate time series models have a simple structure, but they have been shown to be useful tools for modelling and forecasting random processes in many different subject areas, including finance. In addition to linear univariate time series models, this chapter also briefly reviews non-linear univariate time series models and vector time series models. We also discuss how forecasts of future values of a variable can be computed using these models and how the accuracy of the forecasts can be evaluated. First, some basic statistical concepts are reviewed.[1]

2.2 Random Variables and Random Processes

2.2.1 Random Variables

A random variable can be discrete or continuous. For a **discrete random variable** the possible values are countable, hence the variable has a finite number of possible values (e.g. the score from rolling a die). A **continuous random variable** has an infinite number of possible values (e.g. if the variable is a measureable amount like temperature or time). In finance, most relevant random variables (e.g. asset prices, asset returns) can be treated as continuous random variables. Important characteristics of random variables discussed below include the mean, variance, probability density function and cumulative distribution function.

If X is a discrete random variable that can take the values $x_1, x_2, \ldots, x_n$, then the mathematical function

$$f(x) = P(X = x_i), i = 1, 2, \ldots, n \tag{2.1}$$

is the **probability distribution** (PD), where $P(X = x_i)$ denotes the probability that X will equal x_i. Therefore the PD describes the probability of the random variable taking particular values. If X is a continuous random variable then individual values have a probability of zero (since the number of possible values is infinite). The

---

[1]This chapter is a review of the key techniques rather than an exhaustive technical study. If further technical details are required, readers are referred to the following econometrics textbooks: Gujarati and Porter (2009) (intermediate level), Hamilton (1994) and Greene (2008) (advanced level).

probability that a continuous random variable will fall in an interval of values is described by the PDF for the variable. The **probability density function (PDF)** for X is also written $f(x)$, and must satisfy certain mathematical conditions:

(i) $\quad f(x) \geq 0$ $\hspace{7cm}$ (2.2)

(ii) $\quad \displaystyle\int_{x_1}^{x_2} f(x)\, dx = P(x_1 \leq x \leq x_2)$ $\hspace{4cm}$ (2.3)

(iii) $\quad \displaystyle\int_{-\infty}^{\infty} f(x)\, dx = 1$ $\hspace{5.5cm}$ (2.4)

Condition (i) is that $f(x)$ must be zero or positive; condition (ii) can be interpreted as stating that the area under a graph of $f(x)$ against x in the interval $[x_1, x_2]$ is equal to the probability of observing a value for X in the interval $[x_1, x_2]$; condition (iii) can be interpreted as stating that the total area under this graph must be equal to unity. Thus, while in the discrete case the PD describes the probability that a random variable will take particular values, in the continuous case the PDF describes the probability that a random variable will fall in an interval of values.

Most readers of this book will have done a basic course in statistics, and will most likely at some point have been introduced to the normal distribution. To recap, if X is a normally distributed random variable then its PDF has the following mathematical form,

$$f(x) = \frac{1}{\sigma\sqrt{2\pi}} e^{-(x-\mu)^2/(2\sigma^2)} \hspace{4cm} (2.5)$$

where μ and σ^2 are population parameters called the **mean** and **variance**, the mean being a measure of central tendency and the variance being a measure of spread around the mean. (Both mean and variance will be discussed in more detail later in this chapter.)

If X is a normally distributed random variable, then

$$Z = \frac{X - \mu}{\sigma} \hspace{5cm} (2.6)$$

will have a **standard normal distribution**. The standard normal distribution is a normal distribution with a mean of zero and a variance of one. It can be shown that for a normally distributed random variable the probability of observing a value that lies in the interval $[\mu - 2\sigma, \mu + 2\sigma]$ is approximately 95%. Therefore, for a standard normal random variable there is approximately a 95% probability of observing a value between -2 and 2. For a standard normal random variable the probability associated with some defined intervals is given in Table A.1 in the Appendix.

A graph of the PDF for two normally distributed random variables X and Y is given in Figure 2.1. Note that in both cases the PDF is bell-shaped and symmetric around

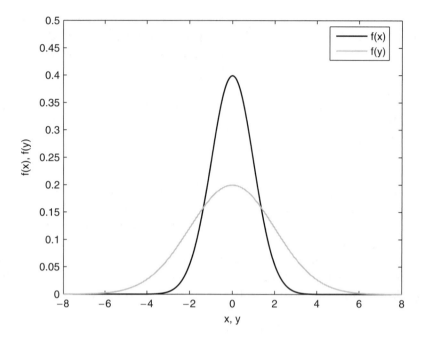

Figure 2.1 Normal distributions.

a central point, which in this case is set at zero for both X and Y. This central point is the mean of the random variable. Note that the variance of the two random variables is different: the variance of X is 1, and the variance of Y is 2. Therefore X is a standard normal random variable.

The **cumulative distribution function** (CDF) for a random variable X describes the probability of X taking a value less than or equal to some particular value x,

$$F(x) = P(X \leq x) = \int_{-\infty}^{x} f(x)\,dx \qquad (2.7)$$

A graph of the CDF for a standard normal random variable is given in Figure 2.2.

The normal distribution is widely used for modelling random variables in finance and in many other subject areas. In finance, typically we do not know the exact form of the true PDF for relevant random variables (the **population** PDF). In many cases the normal PDF will provide a good approximation; however, in some cases it might be inappropriate. For example, a close analysis of sample data might suggest that the PDF has fatter tails than the normal distribution (meaning the probability of extreme values is higher than a normal distribution allows), and/or that it is skewed (meaning that the PDF is asymmetric).

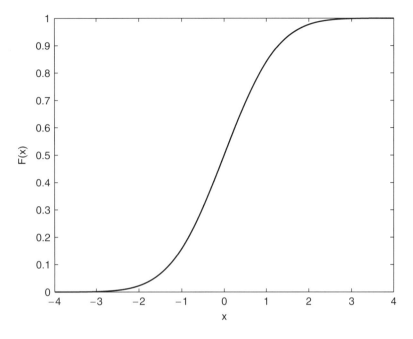

Figure 2.2   Standard normal CDF.

A popular alternative to the normal distribution used in many different subject areas including finance, which has fatter tails than the normal distribution, is **Student's *t*-distribution**. A Student's t random variable with v degrees of freedom can be defined as,

$$t = \frac{Z}{\sqrt{\chi^2(v)/v}} \qquad (2.8)$$

where Z is a standard normal random variable and $\chi^2(v)$ is a **chi-square random variable** with v degrees of freedom, statistically independent of Z. For Student's t and χ^2 random variables the probability of exceeding some defined values is given in the Appendix in Tables A.2 and A.4 respectively. As $v \to 1$ the tails of the t-distribution become fatter relative to the standard normal distribution. As $v \to \infty$ the t-distribution converges to a standard normal distribution. The PDFs for t-distributions with three different values of v are graphed in Figure 2.3. The random variables X, Y and Z have $t(200)$-, $t(5)$- and $t(2)$-distributions respectively, where $t(v)$ denotes a t-distribution with v degrees of freedom.

The **moments** of a random variable are important statistical features of the random variable, the first moment being the mean. The mean of a random variable can be defined mathematically using the expectations operator E. Hence the mean is

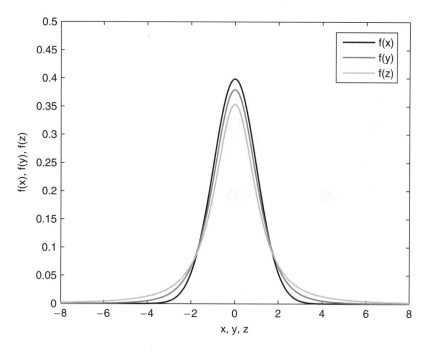

Figure 2.3 *t*-distributions.

also called the **expected value**. If X is a discrete random variable with N possible outcomes then its expected value is calculated by summing the possible outcomes multiplied by their probability,

$$E(X) = \sum_{i=1}^{N} x_i f(x_i) \tag{2.9}$$

If X is a continuous random variable then its expected value can be calculated using,

$$E(X) = \int_{-\infty}^{\infty} x f(x)\, dx \tag{2.10}$$

The second **central moment** (the moment about the mean) is the variance. Let X be a random variable and let $\mu = E(X)$. The variance of X measures the spread of the possible X values around the mean μ. The variance can be written,

$$\sigma^2 = E(X - \mu)^2 \tag{2.11}$$

For a discrete random variable the variance can be calculated using,

$$\sigma^2 = \sum_{i=1}^{N} (x_i - \mu)^2 f(x_i) \tag{2.12}$$

For a continuous random variable the variance can be calculated using,

$$\sigma^2 = \int_{-\infty}^{\infty} (x - \mu)^2 f(x)\, dx \tag{2.13}$$

It has already been mentioned that for some random variables in finance the population PDF might have fatter tails than the normal distribution and/or be skewed. A parameter used as a measure of skewness is,

$$S = \frac{E(X - \mu)^3}{[E(X - \mu)^2]^{3/2}} \tag{2.14}$$

where the numerator is the third central moment of the random variable X (the **skewness**). For a normally distributed random variable $S = 0$. A distribution with a significant positive skewness has a longer right tail than left tail, while a distribution with a significant negative skewness has a longer left tail than right tail. A parameter used as a measure of the peakedness of the distribution (or equivalently how fat the tails are) is,

$$K = \frac{E(X - \mu)^4}{[E(X - \mu)^2]^2} \tag{2.15}$$

The numerator of (2.15) is the fourth central moment of X. For a normally distributed random variable $K = 3$. A PDF that has thinner tails than the normal distribution is leptokurtic (it has positive kurtosis). Platykurtosis (negative kurtosis) refers to a PDF with fatter tails than the normal distribution. The t-distributions graphed in Figure 2.3 are platykurtic, but like the normal distribution they are not skewed. Distributions that allow for both skewness and excess kurtosis have been developed, such as for example a skewed version of Student's t-distribution.

The parameters and moments defined above relate to a single random variable. When analysing the relationships between random variables, **covariance** is a key concept. Let X and Y be two random variables with means μ_x and μ_y. The covariance for X and Y is a parameter that measures their statistical dependence and it can be positive, negative or zero,

$$\sigma_{XY} = E[(X - \mu_x)(Y - \mu_y)] \tag{2.16}$$

For two discrete random variables the covariance can be calculated using,

$$\sigma_{XY} = \sum_{i=1}^{N} \sum_{j=1}^{N} (x_i - \mu_x)(y_j - \mu_y) f(x_i, y_j) \tag{2.17}$$

where $f(x, y)$ is the joint PDF. For two continuous random variables the covariance can be calculated using,

$$\sigma_{XY} = \int_{-\infty}^{\infty} \int_{-\infty}^{\infty} (x - \mu_x)(y - \mu_y) f(x, y)\, dx\, dy \tag{2.18}$$

Note that two random variables are statistically **independent** if $f(x, y) = f(x)f(y)$; that is, the joint PDF is the product of the marginal PDFs. For independent variables,

$\sigma_{XY} = 0$. The **correlation coefficient** is a standardised measure of covariance with limits -1 and 1. For two random variables X and Y the correlation coefficient can be written,

$$\rho_{XY} = \frac{\sigma_{XY}}{\sigma_X \sigma_Y} \tag{2.19}$$

where σ_X and σ_Y are the standard deviation of X and Y; $\rho_{XY} = -1$ indicates perfect negative correlation and $\rho_{XY} = 1$ indicates perfect positive correlation.

In many subject areas including finance, the population parameters and moments for random variables of interest are in most cases unknown, and typically analysts do not have access to the entire population of values on the relevant random variables. Therefore, in practice, sample estimates of the relevant parameters and moments are used. Assume that a sample of N values is available for each of the random variables X and $Y : x_1, x_2, \ldots, x_N$, and $y_1, y_2, \ldots, y_N$. The relevant formulas for the sample mean, variance, skewness, kurtosis, covariance and correlation coefficient are,

$$\bar{x} = N^{-1} \sum_{i=1}^{N} x_i \tag{2.20}$$

$$\hat{\sigma}_X^2 = N^{-1} \sum_{i=1}^{N} (x_i - \bar{x})^2 \tag{2.21}$$

$$\hat{S} = \frac{N^{-1} \sum_{i=1}^{N} (x_i - \bar{x})^3}{\left[N^{-1} \sum_{i=1}^{N} (x_i - \bar{x})^2 \right]^{3/2}} \tag{2.22}$$

$$\hat{K} = \frac{N^{-1} \sum_{i=1}^{N} (x_i - \bar{x})^4}{\left[N^{-1} \sum_{i=1}^{N} (x_i - \bar{x})^2 \right]^{2}} \tag{2.23}$$

$$\hat{\sigma}_{XY} = N^{-1} \sum_{i=1}^{N} (x_i - \bar{x})(y_i - \bar{y}) \tag{2.24}$$

$$\hat{\rho}_{XY} = \frac{\sum_{i=1}^{N} (x_i - \bar{x})(y_i - \bar{y})}{\sqrt{\sum_{i=1}^{N} (x_i - \bar{x})^2 \sum_{i=1}^{N} (y_i - \bar{y})^2}} \tag{2.25}$$

The estimators (2.20)-(2.25) have the property of being **consistent** estimators of the relevant population parameters. In this context consistency is a statistical property which means that as the sample size used increases, the estimator converges to the population parameter. Note that the sample mean (2.20) is an **unbiased** estimator, but (2.21)-(2.25) are **biased** estimators. If an estimator possesses the property of unbiasedness then the expected value of the estimator is equal to the population value, for example $E(\overline{x}) = \mu_x$. Unbiased versions of (2.21)–(2.25) can also be defined: for example, in (2.21), if N is replaced with $N - 1$ then the sample variance is an unbiased and consistent estimator of the population variance. In finance, sample sizes are typically large and so in practice the two types of estimators will give virtually identical estimates.

$\hat{S}$ and $\hat{K}$ can also be used for statistically testing the hypothesis that a variable is normally distributed. The relevant test statistic, proposed by Jarque and Bera (1980, 1987), is,

$$JB = \frac{N}{6}\left[\hat{S}^2 + \frac{1}{4}(\hat{K} - 3)^2\right] \tag{2.26}$$

Under the null hypothesis that the variable is normally distributed the test statistic JB has a $\chi^2(2)$ distribution. When testing statistical hypotheses, to decide whether to accept or reject the null hypothesis at a chosen **significance level** (α) the value of the test statistic is compared with a **critical value** which defines a rejection region. The null hypothesis is rejected if the test statistic lies in the rejection region. The critical value is a value from the null distribution for the test statistic chosen so that the probability of a Type I error (an incorrect rejection) is α. The values for the χ^2 distribution given in the Appendix in Table A.4 can be used to choose a critical value for the JB test statistic (Table A.1 can be used to choose a critical value when a test statistic has a standard normal distribution under the null hypothesis; Table A.2 can be used when a test statistic has a Student's t-distribution under the null hypothesis).

2.2.2 Random Processes

A random process is a natural extension of the concept of a random variable, being a series of random variables ordered in a particular way. If the ordering is by time then the random process can be written Y_t, where the subscript t denotes a value at period (or time) t, so for example Y_1 denotes the value in period one, Y_2 is the value in period two, and so on. The data on this type of random process are called time series data. For brevity, rather than continuously distinguishing between random process and random variable, we will tend to use "variable" to mean either random process or random variable depending on the circumstance, although occasionally it will be necessary to use the original names.

Population parameters and moments for the variable X are defined in Section 2.2.1. Population parameters and moments can also be defined for the variable Y_t, a notable difference being that they might have a subscript t to denote possible time variation. For example, the unconditional mean of Y_t might be written,

$$\mu_t = E(Y_t) \tag{2.27}$$

where E is the expectations operator. The unconditional variance might be written,

$$\sigma_t^2 = E[(Y_t - \mu_t)^2] \tag{2.28}$$

Higher order moments for Y_t follow naturally from the formulas for X given in Section 2.2.1.

When studying random processes a particularly important parameter is the unconditional covariance between Y_t and $Y_{t-\tau}$,

$$\gamma_{\tau,t} = E[(Y_t - \mu_t)(Y_{t-\tau} - \mu_t)] \tag{2.29}$$

where τ is an integer. This parameter quantifies the strength and direction of the relationship between Y at time t and Y at time $t - \tau$. The unconditional covariance between Y_t and $Y_{t-\tau}$ is also called the **autocovariance** (to distinguish it from the covariance of Y_t with some other variable). Note that the autocovariance with $\tau = 0$ is just the variance.

When modelling and forecasting random processes it is important to distinguish between the **unconditional** and the **conditional** distribution, since these can differ. The unconditional mean, variance and autocovariance of Y_t are given above; the conditional mean, variance and autocovariance of Y_t can be written,

$$\mu_t = E(Y_t | \Omega_{t-1}) \tag{2.30}$$

$$\sigma_t^2 = E[(Y_t - \mu_t)^2 | \Omega_{t-1}] \tag{2.31}$$

$$\gamma_{\tau,t} = E[(Y_t - \mu_t)(Y_{t-\tau} - \mu_t) | \Omega_{t-1}] \tag{2.32}$$

where Ω_{t-1} denotes a relevant information set that here includes all previous values of $Y(Y_{t-1}, Y_{t-2}, \ldots)$. Intuitively the parameters (2.30)–(2.32) can be thought of as the mean, variance and autocovariance for Y_t given what is known about the history of the variable. For example, the conditional variance of Y_t can be thought of as the variance of Y at time t given what is known about the values of Y at time $t - 1, t - 2, \ldots$, and so on, whilst the unconditional variance of Y_t can be thought of as the variance of Y at time t, assuming no knowledge of its history.

In some subject areas multiple realisations of a random process might be available, in which case estimating the unconditional mean, variance and autocovariance of the variable at each point in time is straightforward. In finance, multiple realisations on the relevant random processes typically do not exist (since to obtain multiple realisations would require stopping financial markets, going back in time and starting them again). However, an important statistical result is that if the unconditional mean, variance and autocovariance of the variable are constant for all t,

$$E(Y_t) = \mu \tag{2.33}$$

$$Var(Y_t) = \sigma^2 \tag{2.34}$$

$$Cov(Y_t, Y_{t-\tau}) = \gamma_\tau \tag{2.35}$$

then consistent estimates can in most cases be computed using sample data from a single realisation of the variable. The relevant sample estimates are,

$$\overline{Y} = T^{-1} \sum_{t=1}^{T} Y_t \tag{2.36}$$

$$\hat{\sigma}^2 = T^{-1} \sum_{t=1}^{T} (Y_t - \overline{Y})^2 \tag{2.37}$$

$$\hat{\gamma}_\tau = T^{-1} \sum_{t=\tau+1}^{T} (Y_t - \overline{Y})(Y_{t-\tau} - \overline{Y}) \tag{2.38}$$

where T is the sample size, $t = 1, 2, \ldots, T$. Consistent and unbiased estimates of σ^2 and γ_τ can be computed using (2.37) and (2.38) but dividing by $T - 1$ rather than by T. When the unconditional mean, variance and autocovariance for a variable Y_t are constant, it is said to be a **stationary** variable. The implications of a variable being non-stationary are discussed in more detail later in this chapter and in Chapter 3.

When analysing variables in finance the degree to which a variable is correlated with lagged values of itself is of crucial importance for modelling and forecasting. An important standardised measure of this correlation is the **autocorrelation function** (ACF). The unconditional autocovariance divided by the unconditional variance gives the autocorrelation of a variable Y_t,

$$\rho_\tau = \gamma_\tau / \gamma_0 \tag{2.39}$$

The autocorrelations ρ_τ measure the strength of the correlation between Y at time t and Y at a different point in time $t - \tau$, and the ACF refers to the combinations of ρ_τ and $\tau = 0, 1, 2, \ldots$. The population autocorrelations can be estimated using,

$$\hat{\rho}_\tau = \frac{\sum\limits_{t=\tau+1}^{T} (Y_t - \overline{Y})(Y_{t-\tau} - \overline{Y})}{\sum\limits_{t=1}^{T} (Y_t - \overline{Y})^2} \tag{2.40}$$

The **sample autocorrelation function** (SACF) refers to the combinations of $\hat{\rho}_\tau$ and $\tau = 0, 1, 2, \ldots$. In practice, graphs of these combinations are studied.

If the values taken by a variable are assumed to be both normally and independently distributed then the acronym NID might be used (e.g. $Y_t \sim NID(0, \sigma_Y^2)$ indicates that Y_t is normally independently distributed with an unconditional mean of zero and an unconditional variance of σ_Y^2). The more general acronym IID stands for

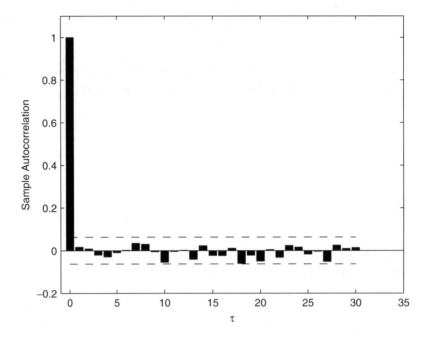

Figure 2.4 SACF for IID variable.

independent and identically distributed. An IID random variable is also referred to as a **white noise** process. Assuming a large sample size, it can be shown that the sample autocorrelations for a white noise process are normally distributed with a mean of zero and standard deviation $T^{-1/2}$ (for example, see Anderson, 1942). It follows that the sample autocorrelations for a variable can be compared with $\pm 2T^{-1/2}$ confidence bands as a test at the 5% significance level of the null hypothesis that a variable is a white noise process (as discussed in Section 2.2.1, we know that for a normally distributed random variable approximately 95% of possible values lie within $\pm 2\sigma$ of the mean). As a simple example the SACF for a simulated IID variable with $\tau = 0, 1, \ldots, 30$ is given in Figure 2.4 along with $\pm 2T^{-1/2}$ confidence bands (the dashed lines). In this case the sample autocorrelations (for $\tau \geq 1$) are within the confidence bands.

2.3 Time Series Models

2.3.1 Autoregressive (AR) and Moving Average (MA) Models

In a univariate time series model the relevant variable Y_t is modelled as a function of a zero mean random error term, plus lagged values of the variable, and/or lagged values of the error term. In finance, Y_t might for example be an exchange rate, interest rate or stock return. Autoregressive (AR) and moving average (MA) models are the simplest types of linear univariate time series model.

The simplest AR model is the AR(1) model,

$$Y_t = \phi_1 Y_{t-1} + \varepsilon_t \tag{2.41}$$

ε_t is a random error term that explains that portion of Y_t not explained by $\phi_1 Y_{t-1}$ where ϕ_1 is a population parameter. Thus the AR(1) model states that Y in period t is a linear function of its value in period $t - 1$ plus a random error term. In finance, the random error term ε_t might be interpretable as the unexpected "news" relevant to a particular variable (e.g. macroeconomic and company news if Y_t is a stock return). Throughout the rest of this chapter assume for simplicity that $\varepsilon_t \sim NID(0, \sigma_\varepsilon^2)$. Throughout the rest of this book the notation σ_ε^2 will be frequently used in different time series and regression models to denote the variance of a random error term. Note that the value of σ_ε^2 can differ across models, even though the same notation is used.

An AR(2) model can be written,

$$Y_t = \phi_1 Y_{t-1} + \phi_2 Y_{t-2} + \varepsilon_t \tag{2.42}$$

More generally an AR(p) model, where p is a positive integer, can be written,

$$Y_t = \phi_1 Y_{t-1} + \phi_2 Y_{t-2} + \cdots + \phi_p Y_{t-p} + \varepsilon_t \tag{2.43}$$

A useful shorthand notation is,

$$\phi(L)Y_t = \varepsilon_t \tag{2.44}$$

where $\phi(L) = 1 - \phi_1 L - \phi_2 L^2 - \cdots - \phi_p L^p$ is a **lag-polynomial** and L is the **lag operator** ($LY_t = Y_{t-1}, L^2 Y_t = Y_{t-2}$, etc.).

If Y_t is generated by the AR(1) model (2.41) and $|\phi_1| < 1$, it can be shown that Y_t is a stationary variable. When graphed against time a stationary variable will appear to fluctuate around its unconditional mean. Hence it is quite common for the terms **stationary** and **mean reverting** to be used interchangeably. As $\phi_1 \to 1$, the deviations of Y_t from its unconditional mean become more persistent. For the AR(1) model an important special case occurs when $\phi_1 = 1$. In this case Y_t is not mean reverting, but wanders randomly. This special case will be discussed in more detail later in this chapter and in Chapter 3.

If Y_t is generated by the AR(1) model (2.41), the unconditional mean of Y_t is zero, $E(Y_t) = 0$. To allow for a non-zero unconditional mean, a separate constant parameter, δ, can be included in the model. For example,

$$Y_t = \delta + \phi_1 Y_{t-1} + \varepsilon_t \tag{2.45}$$

To allow for reversion around a deterministic trend, a trend variable $t = 1, 2, \ldots$ can be included in the model, for example,

$$Y_t = \delta + \gamma t + \phi_1 Y_{t-1} + \varepsilon_t \tag{2.46}$$

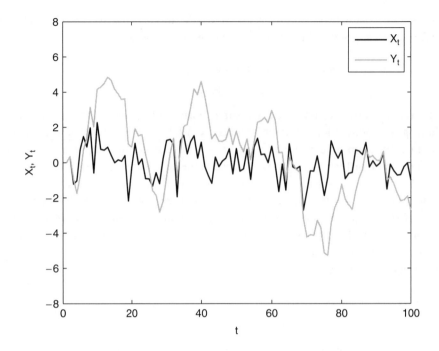

Figure 2.5 AR(1) variables: mean reverting.

where the sign of the parameter γ determines whether the trend is positive or negative. Assuming that $|\phi_1| < 1$, a variable generated by (2.46) is said to be **trend-stationary**. To help clarify, two different AR(1) variables, X_t and Y_t, simulated using (2.41) as the data generation process (DGP) with parameter values $\phi_1 = 0.10, 0.90$, are graphed in Figure 2.5. Two different AR(1) variables, X_t and Y_t, simulated using (2.46) as the DGP with parameter values $\delta = 0.10$, $\gamma = -0.10, 0.10$, $\phi_1 = 0.60$, are graphed in Figure 2.6.

The moving average (MA) model contains no lagged values of the variable, but does contain lagged values of the error term. The simplest MA model is the MA(1),

$$Y_t = \varepsilon_t + \theta_1 \varepsilon_{t-1} \tag{2.47}$$

An MA(2) model can be written,

$$Y_t = \varepsilon_t + \theta_1 \varepsilon_{t-1} + \theta_2 \varepsilon_{t-2} \tag{2.48}$$

More generally, an MA(q) model, where q is a positive integer, can be written,

$$Y_t = \varepsilon_t + \theta_1 \varepsilon_{t-1} + \theta_2 \varepsilon_{t-2} + \cdots + \theta_q \varepsilon_{t-q} \tag{2.49}$$

In this case the shorthand notation is,

$$Y_t = \theta(L)\varepsilon_t \tag{2.50}$$

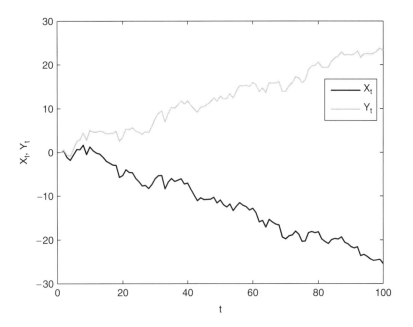

Figure 2.6 AR(1) variables: trend-stationary.

where $\theta(L) = 1 + \theta_1 L + \theta_2 L^2 + \cdots + \theta_q L^q$. Note that visually MA variables will be smoother than white noise if all of the slope parameters are positive, and vice versa. As with the AR model, the MA model can be modified by including a constant and deterministic trend if necessary. MA models tend to be less widely used in finance than AR models.

2.3.2 Autoregressive Moving Average (ARMA) Models

An autoregressive moving average (ARMA) model has both AR and MA components. Therefore in an ARMA model the current value of the variable can be a linear function of both lagged values of the variable and lagged values of the error term. The general notation for ARMA models is ARMA(p, q) where p is the AR order and q is the MA order. An ARMA(1,0) model is therefore the same as an AR(1) model and an ARMA (0,1) model is the same as an MA(1) model. An ARMA(1,1), ARMA(2,1) and ARMA(1,2) model with no constant or deterministic trend can be written,

$$Y_t = \phi_1 Y_{t-1} + \varepsilon_t + \theta_1 \varepsilon_{t-1} \tag{2.51}$$

$$Y_t = \phi_1 Y_{t-1} + \phi_2 Y_{t-2} + \varepsilon_t + \theta_1 \varepsilon_{t-1} \tag{2.52}$$

$$Y_t = \phi_1 Y_{t-1} + \varepsilon_t + \theta_1 \varepsilon_{t-1} + \theta_2 \varepsilon_{t-2} \tag{2.53}$$

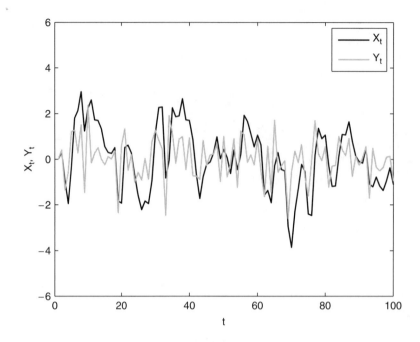

Figure 2.7   ARMA(1,1) variables.

and more generally, an ARMA(p, q) model can be written,

$$Y_t = \phi_1 Y_{t-1} + \phi_2 Y_{t-2} + \cdots + \phi_p Y_{t-p} + \varepsilon_t + \theta_1 \varepsilon_{t-1} + \theta_2 \varepsilon_{t-2} + \cdots + \theta_q \varepsilon_{t-q} \quad (2.54)$$

The shorthand notation is,

$$\phi(L)Y_t = \theta(L)\varepsilon_t \quad\quad\quad (2.55)$$

where $\phi(L)$ and $\theta(L)$ are defined in Section 2.3.1.

Compared with the relevant pure AR model, with a positive MA parameter the deviations of the ARMA variable from its unconditional mean have greater persistence, while with a negative MA parameter they have less persistence. To help clarify, two different ARMA(1,1) variables simulated using (2.51) as the DGP are graphed in Figure 2.7, where the ARMA(1,1) model for X_t has parameter values $\phi_1 = 0.30, \theta_1 = 0.60$ and the ARMA(1,1) model for Y_t has parameter values $\phi_1 = 0.30, \theta_1 = -0.60$.

2.3.3 Non-stationary Time Series

In time series analysis, the term stationary refers to a variable where the unconditional mean, variance and autocovariance are constant over time.[2] If we have a

---

[2]Strictly this is a definition of a **covariance stationary** variable. Stronger forms of stationarity can also be defined but covariance stationarity is sufficient for most theoretical and applied work in finance.

variable Y_t and one or more of the unconditional mean, variance, and autocovariance are time-varying, then the variable is non-stationary.

A simple example of a stationary variable is one that is generated by an AR(1) model with $|\phi_1| < 1$,

$$Y_t = \phi_1 Y_{t-1} + \varepsilon_t \tag{2.56}$$

It is straightforward to show that in this case the unconditional mean, variance and autocovariance of Y_t are,

$$E(Y_t) = 0 \tag{2.57}$$

$$Var(Y_t) = \frac{\sigma_\varepsilon^2}{(1 - \phi_1^2)} \tag{2.58}$$

$$Cov(Y_t, Y_{t-\tau}) = \frac{\phi_1^\tau \sigma_\varepsilon^2}{(1 - \phi_1^2)} \tag{2.59}$$

If the AR(1) model has a constant δ (to capture a non-zero mean) then it can be shown that the unconditional mean of the variable becomes,

$$E(Y_t) = \frac{\delta}{(1 - \phi_1)} \tag{2.60}$$

In both cases the unconditional mean, variance and autocovariance are constant over time and therefore Y_t is stationary.

A simple example of a non-stationary variable is one that is generated by an AR(1) model with a slope parameter of unity,

$$Y_t = \delta + Y_{t-1} + \varepsilon_t \tag{2.61}$$

The model (2.61) is called a **random walk** model, where δ is the **drift** parameter. (A positive (negative) drift parameter generates an upwards (downwards) trend.) It is straightforward to show that if Y_t is generated by a random walk model, the unconditional variance is,

$$Var(Y_t) = t\sigma_\varepsilon^2 \tag{2.62}$$

Therefore the unconditional variance is time-varying, and so in this case Y_t is non-stationary. Three random walks X_t, Y_t and Z_t, simulated using (2.61) as the DGP with $\delta = -0.10, 0, 0.10$, are graphed in Figure 2.8. It can be shown that a variable generated by a higher order AR(p) model will be non-stationary if the slope parameters in the model sum to unity, $\sum_{i=1}^{p} \phi_i = 1$.

If a variable is non-stationary then choosing an appropriate time series model to estimate can be difficult since the sample autocorrelations for that variable will be uninformative of the appropriate model (conversely, for stationary variables these sample autocorrelations can be very informative – see the Box–Jenkins approach

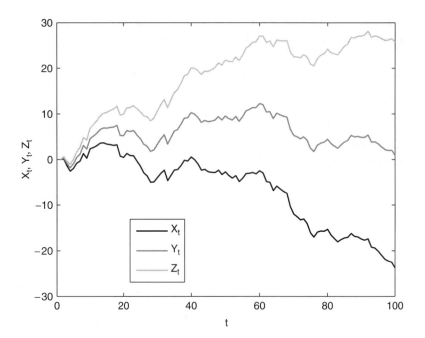

Figure 2.8   Random walks.

discussed in Section 2.3.6). However, in many cases a non-stationary variable can be made stationary by **differencing**. By working with the differenced variable rather than the raw variable conventional techniques can then be applied. This approach is discussed in more detail below. Note also that for statistical models involving non-stationary variables, conventional parameter estimators and inference techniques can have non-standard statistical properties. This issue will be discussed in more detail in Chapter 3.

2.3.4 Autoregressive Integrated Moving Average (ARIMA) Models

In this context, the term integrated refers to the degree to which a variable is non-stationary. More specifically, if a variable Y_t is integrated of order one, or I(1) for short, then the variable is non-stationary, but the first-difference of the variable is stationary (if the variable is Y_t, the first-difference is $\Delta Y_t \equiv Y_t - Y_{t-1}$). If Y_t is stationary, it is I(0). The autoregressive integrated moving average (ARIMA) model is a model for a non-stationary (integrated) variable in differenced form that can involve both AR and MA terms. The general notation for ARIMA models is ARIMA(p, d, q), where p is the AR order, q the MA order and d the degree of differencing required to make the variable stationary. In finance, usually $d = 1$ is sufficient in most applications. An ARIMA($p, 1, q$) model with no constant or deterministic trend can be written,

$$\Delta Y_t = \phi_1 \Delta Y_{t-1} + \phi_2 \Delta Y_{t-2} + \cdots + \phi_p \Delta Y_{t-p} + \varepsilon_t$$
$$+ \theta_1 \varepsilon_{t-1} + \theta_2 \varepsilon_{t-2} + \cdots + \theta_q \varepsilon_{t-q} \tag{2.63}$$

and the shorthand notation is,

$$\phi(L)(1 - L)Y_t = \theta(L)\varepsilon_t \tag{2.64}$$

where $\phi(L)$ and $\theta(L)$ are defined above. The ARIMA($p, 1, q$) model involves modelling the first-difference of the variable ΔY_t, but, as will be shown in Section 2.3.8, it can still be used for forecasting the level of the variable Y_t.

When using a time series model it is important to determine if a variable is stationary or non-stationary. As discussed in more detail in Section 2.3.6, the SACF can be helpful for deciding if a variable is stationary or non-stationary. An alternative approach is to compute a statistical test of the null hypothesis that the variable is non-stationary against the alternative hypothesis it is stationary. A popular test is the Dickey–Fuller (DF) test (Dickey and Fuller, 1979), which is discussed in more detail in Chapter 3.

2.3.5 Parameter Estimation and Inference

If the reader has previously taken a course in basic statistics then he or she will be familiar with ordinary least squares (OLS) as a technique for estimating the parameters of regression models, and the use of OLS in the context of regression modelling with time series data is discussed in Chapter 3. OLS can also be used to estimate the parameters of AR models. OLS involves collecting a sample of data on the relevant variables in the model. The sample size used relative to the number of parameters to be estimated is an important factor in determining the accuracy of the OLS estimator and subsequent test statistics. Assuming a small number of model parameters (say, less than five parameters), then less than 100 time series observations might be deemed to be a "small" sample size, whilst greater than 500 observations might be deemed to be a "large" sample size.

The residual sum of squares (RSS) for an AR(1) model with no constant or deterministic trend is,

$$RSS = \sum_{t=2}^{T} (Y_t - \hat{\phi}_1 Y_{t-1})^2 \tag{2.65}$$

The OLS estimator of ϕ_1 is the value of $\hat{\phi}_1$ that minimises the RSS. This is given by,

$$\hat{\phi}_1 = \left(\sum_{t=2}^{T} Y_{t-1}^2 \right)^{-1} \sum_{t=2}^{T} Y_t Y_{t-1} \tag{2.66}$$

The estimated conditional mean of Y_t is therefore,

$$E(Y_t|\Omega_{t-1}) = \hat{\phi}_1 Y_{t-1} \qquad (2.67)$$

where the information set Ω_{t-1} includes the previous values of Y up to and including period $t - 1$. More generally for an AR(p) model with a constant, the OLS estimator can be concisely written using matrix algebra,

$$\hat{\varphi} = (\mathbf{X}'\mathbf{X})^{-1}\mathbf{X}'\mathbf{Y} \qquad (2.68)$$

where

$$\mathbf{Y} = [Y_{p+1} \; Y_{p+2} \; \cdots \; Y_T]' \qquad (2.69)$$

$$\mathbf{X} = \begin{bmatrix} 1 & Y_p & Y_{p-1} & \cdots & Y_1 \\ 1 & Y_{p+1} & Y_p & \cdots & Y_2 \\ \vdots & \vdots & \vdots & \vdots & \vdots \\ 1 & Y_{T-1} & Y_{T-2} & \cdots & Y_{T-p} \end{bmatrix} \qquad (2.70)$$

$$\hat{\varphi} = [\hat{\delta} \; \hat{\phi}_1 \; \hat{\phi}_2 \; \cdots \; \hat{\phi}_p]' \qquad (2.71)$$

When estimating AR models, OLS is not an unbiased estimator, $E(\hat{\varphi}) \neq \varphi$. In fact for the AR(1) case it can be shown that the OLS slope estimator is biased downwards, $E(\hat{\phi}_1) - \phi_1 < 0$, and that the bias gets worse the closer that the slope parameter is to unity (see e.g. Marriott and Pope, 1954; Kendall, 1954). Fortunately, under weak assumptions, OLS is a consistent estimator for stationary AR models. Therefore, in practice, with a large sample size OLS can be used with confidence to estimate the parameters of AR models. Consistency requires that both the bias and variance of the estimator converge to zero. Here we do not prove this theoretically, but it is illustrated in the following graphs. Each graph is a histogram of 1000 OLS estimates of the slope parameter in the AR(1) model (2.41) where $\phi_1 = 0.90$ and $\varepsilon_t \sim NID(0, 1)$, obtained using simulation. In Figure 2.9a the sample size is $T = 100$; in Figure 2.9b, $T = 200$; in Figure 2.9c, $T = 500$; in Figure 2.9d, $T = 1000$. The negative bias of the OLS estimator $\hat{\phi}_1$ is clear in these graphs. However, it is also clear that as the sample size T gets bigger, both the bias and variance of $\hat{\phi}_1$ get smaller. Hence $\hat{\phi}_1$ is converging towards the relevant population parameter $\phi_1 = 0.90$ as $T \rightarrow \infty$.

Another important parameter of interest when estimating AR models is the population error variance σ_ε^2. An estimate of the error variance is required to test hypotheses regarding the population parameters in the model using t-tests. For the AR(p) model with a constant, the OLS estimator of σ_ε^2 is,

$$\hat{\sigma}_\varepsilon^2 = [T - (2p + 1)]^{-1} \sum_{t=p+1}^{T} (Y_t - \hat{\delta} - \hat{\phi}_1 Y_{t-1} - \hat{\phi}_2 Y_{t-2} - \cdots - \hat{\phi}_p Y_{t-p})^2 \quad (2.72)$$

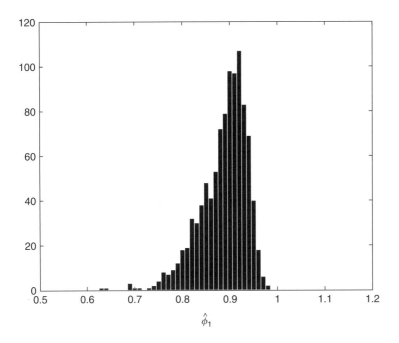

Figure 2.9a   Histogram of OLS estimates, $T = 100$.

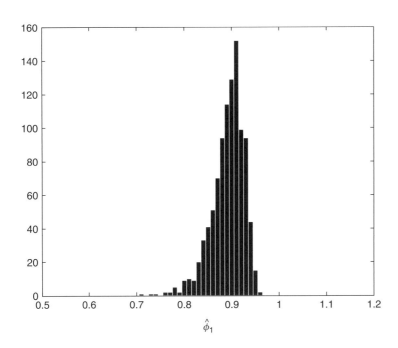

Figure 2.9b   Histogram of OLS estimates, $T = 200$.

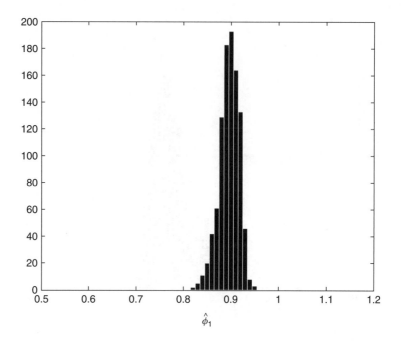

Figure 2.9c   Histogram of OLS estimates, $T = 500$.

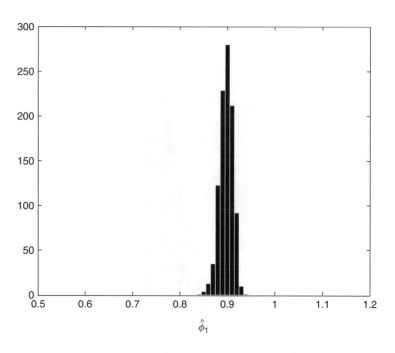

Figure 2.9d   Histogram of OLS estimates, $T = 1000$.

The MA model's parameters can be consistently estimated using the maximum likelihood (ML) technique, where the **likelihood function** refers to the joint conditional PDF for the sample observations given a set of parameter values. Consider the MA(1) model,

$$Y_t = \varepsilon_t + \theta_1 \varepsilon_{t-1} \tag{2.73}$$

If $\varepsilon_t \sim NID(0, \sigma_\varepsilon^2)$, each of the Y_t values is conditionally normally distributed. Therefore the sequence of Y_t values is conditionally normally distributed and it follows that the natural logarithm of the likelihood function (the **log-likelihood**) can be written,

$$\ln L(\theta_1, \sigma_\varepsilon^2) = -\frac{T}{2} \ln 2\pi - \frac{T}{2} \ln \sigma_\varepsilon^2 - \frac{1}{2\sigma_\varepsilon^2} \sum_{t=1}^{T} (Y_t - \theta_1 \varepsilon_{t-1})^2 \tag{2.74}$$

where $\varepsilon_0 = 0$ is assumed. The ML estimates are the parameter values that maximise the log-likelihood function, and hence they maximise the probability of observing the sample data. These parameters can be computed using a numerical optimisation algorithm. The ML technique can also be used to obtain consistent estimates of the parameters in higher order MA models and in AR models, ARMA and ARIMA models.

An attractive property of the OLS and ML estimators of the parameters in AR, MA, ARMA and ARIMA models is that, generally, the estimated parameters are asymptotically normally distributed, meaning that as $T \rightarrow \infty$ they converge in distribution to a normally distributed random variable. In practice this property means that as long as the sample size employed is reasonably large, conventional methods for statistical inference, such as t-tests and F-tests, can be used with confidence to test hypotheses about the population parameters. For example, if we want to test the null hypothesis $H_0 : \phi_1 = 0$ in an AR model against the alternative hypothesis $H_1 : \phi_1 \neq 0$, the relevant t-test statistic is,

$$t = \frac{\hat{\phi}_1}{se(\hat{\phi}_1)} \tag{2.75}$$

where $se(\hat{\phi}_1)$ denotes **standard error** of $\hat{\phi}_1$. Under the null hypothesis this test statistic has a Student's t-distribution with degrees of freedom equal to the sample size minus the number of estimated parameters in the model (Table A.2 can be used to choose a critical value for the test statistic). To decide whether to accept or reject the null hypothesis the absolute value of the t-statistic is compared with the relevant critical value at a chosen significance level, for example 5%. If the absolute value of the t-statistic is greater than the relevant critical value, the null hypothesis is rejected at the chosen significance level and the estimated parameter is said to be **statistically significant**. The absolute value is used here rather than the raw value because the test is two-tailed, since under the alternative hypothesis ϕ_1 can be greater or less than the value assumed under the null hypothesis. Hypotheses involving linear restrictions, for example

$H_0 : \phi_1 = \phi_2$, can be tested using an F-test. The relevant test statistic can be written,

$$F = \frac{(RSS_r - RSS_{ur})/q}{RSS_{ur}/(T - k)} \qquad (2.76)$$

where RSS_r denotes the RSS for a version of the model with the linear restrictions imposed, RSS_{ur} denotes the RSS for the unrestricted model, q is the number of restrictions, T is the sample size and k is the number of estimated parameters in the unrestricted model. Under the null hypothesis this test statistic has an F-distribution (Table A.3 in the Appendix can be used to choose a critical value for the test statistic). Related tests that can be used instead of the F-test include the likelihood ratio (LR) test and the Wald test. Generally, however, these tests and the F-test are asymptotically equivalent, meaning that in practice, if the sample size is large, the tests should lead to the same conclusion regarding whether to accept or reject the null hypothesis.

As well as testing hypotheses about the population parameters in a time series model using t-tests and F-tests, there are other hypotheses that an analyst might be interested in testing using information from the fitted model. For example, the unknown population model can be thought of as the DGP for the variable, and we assume that the errors in this model are a white noise process. Therefore if the chosen model is correctly specified, the errors in the chosen model should be white noise. It can be shown that this hypothesis can be tested using the fitted errors $\hat{\varepsilon}_t$ from the estimated version of the model (this is discussed in more detail in Section 2.3.6). It might also be of interest to assess whether the errors in a time series model are normally distributed. This can be done by applying the Jarque–Bera test discussed in Section 2.2.1 to the fitted errors $\hat{\varepsilon}_t$.

2.3.6 The Box–Jenkins Approach

The **Box–Jenkins approach** (Box and Jenkins, 1970, 1976) is an approach to modelling time series data using time series models that has three steps: (i) identification, (ii) estimation, (iii) diagnostic testing. The first step deals with choosing a model where the choice is made based on the underlying statistical properties of the data being modelled. The main statistical tools used in helping to do this are the sample autocorrelation function (SACF) and the sample partial autocorrelation function (SPACF).

We introduced the ACF and SACF in Section 2.2.2. The kth partial autocorrelation is the autocorrelation between Y_t and Y_{t-k} after accounting for the effects of $Y_{t-1}, Y_{t-2}, \ldots, Y_{t-(k-1)}$ (i.e. the lags in between Y_t and Y_{t-k}). If we assume that Y_t

is an AR(p) variable then it can be shown that the autocorrelations are linked as follows,

$$\rho_\tau = \sum_{j=1}^{p} \phi_j \rho_{\tau-j}, \quad \tau > 0 \tag{2.77}$$

The equations given by (2.77) for different values of τ are called the **Yule–Walker** equations (Yule, 1927; Walker, 1931). The partial autocorrelation at lag k, ϕ_{kk}, is given by solving the set of simultaneous equations,

$$\rho_\tau = \sum_{j=1}^{k} \phi_{kj} \rho_{\tau-j}, \quad \tau = 1, 2, \ldots, k \tag{2.78}$$

The sample partial autocorrelation at lag k, $\hat{\phi}_{kk}$, is given by solving the estimated versions,

$$\hat{\rho}_\tau = \sum_{j=1}^{k} \hat{\phi}_{kj} \hat{\rho}_{\tau-j}, \quad \tau = 1, 2, \ldots, k \tag{2.79}$$

The SPACF refers to the combinations of $\hat{\phi}_{kk}$ and τ obtained from (2.79). Typically these combinations are then studied by graphing them. Note that the sample partial autocorrelation at lag k is equivalent to the estimated slope parameter attached to lag k in an AR(k) model.

If Y_t is a stationary AR(p) variable its autocorrelations are described by the difference equation (2.77), and they will decay with a damped exponential and/or sine wave pattern; furthermore it can be shown that,

$$\phi_{kk} = 0 \quad \text{for all } k > p \tag{2.80}$$

If Y_t is an MA(q) variable then it can be shown that,

$$\rho_\tau = 0 \quad \text{for all } \tau > q \tag{2.81}$$

and its partial autocorrelations will decay after lag q, with a similar pattern of decay to the autocorrelations for a stationary AR variable. If Y_t is a stationary ARMA(p, q) variable with both AR and MA components then its autocorrelations will decay in a similar way to those for a stationary AR(p) variable, and its partial autocorrelations will decay in a similar way to those for an MA(q) variable. If Y_t is an ARIMA($p, 1, q$) variable then its autocorrelations will persist at unity. In practice its sample autocorrelations will decay from unity but only very slowly. Therefore the SACF can be helpful in deciding if a variable is stationary or non-stationary. If it is decided that a variable is non-stationary (so an ARIMA model is appropriate), then after appropriate differencing to achieve an I(0) variable, the rules above can be applied.

It follows from this set of rules that the SACF and SPACF contain information that can be employed to help decide if a variable is best described using a particular AR

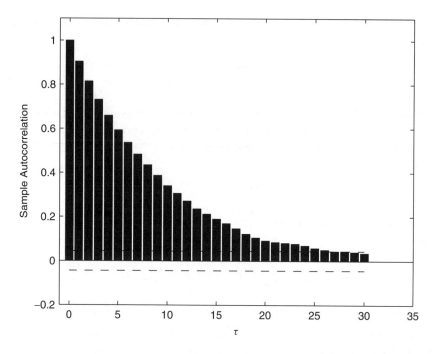

Figure 2.10   SACF for stationary AR(1) variable.

model, MA model or ARMA/ARIMA model. In practice this is done by graphing the SACF and SPACF computed using historical sample data on the relevant variable and then visually assessing which model is suggested. As an example, the SACF for a simulated AR(1) variable with $\phi_1 = 0.90$ is graphed in Figure 2.10 along with $\pm 2T^{-1/2}$ confidence bands (the dashed lines). The SPACF is graphed in Figure 2.11. Clearly the SACF in Figure 2.10 suggests an AR process, and the SPACF in Figure 2.11 indicates that only the first lag is significant, hence the analyst should choose to estimate an AR(1) model.

In practice, model identification using the SACF and SPACF can be difficult, and the results are often not clear-cut. More recently it has become popular to use alternative methods. One approach is to estimate several different competing models and then to choose between them using a measure of fit that penalises for complexity. The most common measures of fit used for this purpose are the Akaike information criterion (AIC) (Akaike, 1969) and the Schwarz information criterion (SIC) (Schwarz, 1978),

$$AIC = \ln(\hat{\sigma}_\varepsilon^2) + 2n/T \tag{2.82}$$

$$SIC = \ln(\hat{\sigma}_\varepsilon^2) + (n/T)\ln(T) \tag{2.83}$$

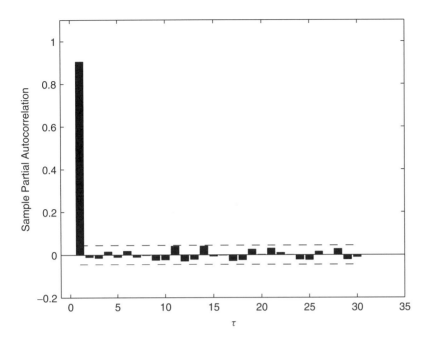

Figure 2.11   SPACF for stationary AR(1) variable.

where $\hat{\sigma}_\varepsilon^2$ is the estimated error variance, n is the total number of estimated parameters and T is the usable sample size. In each case the selection rule is to choose the model that minimises the criterion.

The second step of the Box–Jenkins procedure is parameter estimation using an appropriate estimation technique, as discussed in Section 2.3.5. The final step of the Box–Jenkins procedure is to assess the performance of the model using diagnostic tests, which typically involve analysing the fitted errors. For example, assume that an analyst intends to estimate an AR(1) model,

$$Y_t = \delta + \phi_1 Y_{t-1} + \varepsilon_t \tag{2.84}$$

and assume that if the model is correctly specified then ε_t is white noise. To test this hypothesis the sample autocorrelations for the fitted errors $\hat{\varepsilon}_t$ can be used, where here the fitted errors are,

$$\hat{\varepsilon}_t = Y_t - \hat{\delta} - \hat{\phi}_1 Y_{t-1} \tag{2.85}$$

Following the results in Anderson (1942), the sample autocorrelations for $\hat{\varepsilon}_t$ can be compared with $\pm 2T^{-1/2}$ bands as an approximate test at the 5% level of significance of the null hypothesis that ε_t is white noise.[3] The null hypothesis of correct

---

[3]Note that this test is only approximate because the fitted errors are not the same as the actual errors, which are unknown amounts.

specification is rejected if any of the sample autocorrelations exceed the bands. A related useful diagnostic test is the portmanteau test statistic proposed by Ljung and Box (1978),

$$Q = T(T+2) \sum_{\tau=1}^{M} (T - \tau)^{-1} \hat{\rho}_\tau^2 \tag{2.86}$$

where $\hat{\rho}_\tau^2$ are the squared autocorrelations for the fitted errors. Under the null hypothesis that ε_t is white noise, Q has a $\chi^2(M - p - q)$ distribution (Table A.4 can be used to choose a critical value for the test statistic).[4]

2.3.7 Vector Autoregressive (VAR) Models

Vector autoregressive (VAR) models are a natural extension of autoregressive models to the vector case. A VAR(p) model can be written,

$$\mathbf{Y}_t = \boldsymbol{\varphi}_1 \mathbf{Y}_{t-1} + \boldsymbol{\varphi}_2 \mathbf{Y}_{t-2} + \cdots + \boldsymbol{\varphi}_p \mathbf{Y}_{t-p} + \boldsymbol{\varepsilon}_t \tag{2.87}$$

where there are k variables and k error terms,

$$\mathbf{Y}_t = [Y_{1,t} \quad Y_{2,t} \quad \dots \quad Y_{k,t}]' \tag{2.88}$$

$$\boldsymbol{\varepsilon}_t = [\varepsilon_{1,t} \quad \varepsilon_{2,t} \quad \dots \quad \varepsilon_{k,t}]' \tag{2.89}$$

and $\mathbf{A}_i, i = 1, 2, \dots, p$, are $k \times k$ matrices of parameters. Typically the error terms are assumed to have a mean of zero, to be homoscedastic and uncorrelated,

$$E(\boldsymbol{\varepsilon}_t) = \mathbf{0} \tag{2.90}$$

$$E(\boldsymbol{\varepsilon}_t \boldsymbol{\varepsilon}_t') = \boldsymbol{\Sigma} \tag{2.91}$$

$$E(\boldsymbol{\varepsilon}_t \boldsymbol{\varepsilon}_{t-\tau}') = \mathbf{0} \tag{2.92}$$

As a simple example consider the VAR(1) model with $k = 2$,

$$\mathbf{Y}_t = \boldsymbol{\varphi}_1 \mathbf{Y}_{t-1} + \boldsymbol{\varepsilon}_t \tag{2.93}$$

This model can be written in full as,

$$\begin{bmatrix} Y_{1,t} \\ Y_{2,t} \end{bmatrix} = \begin{bmatrix} \phi_{11} & \phi_{12} \\ \phi_{21} & \phi_{22} \end{bmatrix} \begin{bmatrix} Y_{1,t-1} \\ Y_{2,t-1} \end{bmatrix} + \begin{bmatrix} \varepsilon_{1,t} \\ \varepsilon_{2,t} \end{bmatrix} \tag{2.94}$$

or equation by equation,

$$Y_{1,t} = \phi_{11} Y_{1,t-1} + \phi_{12} Y_{2,t-1} + \varepsilon_{1,t} \tag{2.95}$$

$$Y_{2,t} = \phi_{21} Y_{1,t-1} + \phi_{22} Y_{2,t-1} + \varepsilon_{2,t} \tag{2.96}$$

In standard cases the parameters of VAR(p) models can be consistently estimated using OLS, or using ML.

---

[4]See Box and Jenkins (1970, 1976) and Granger and Newbold (1986) Chapter 3 for further technical details on the Box-Jenkins approach.

VAR models are popular in macroeconomics for analysing how a random shock to a macroeconomic variable transmits through a system of variables (see e.g. Sims, 1980). For example, consider the VAR(1) model (2.93). Assume that the two variables in the system at time $t = 0$ have known values ($Y_{1,0}$ and $Y_{2,0}$), the parameter values are known or have been estimated and that in period 1 ($t = 1$) the first equation is shocked by the error term $\varepsilon_{1,1}$. Clearly, $\varepsilon_{1,1}$ directly affects the first variable in period 1, $Y_{1,1}$; but the second variable is not directly affected. However, in period 2, the second variable $Y_{2,2}$ is indirectly affected by the $\varepsilon_{1,1}$ shock through the lagged value of the first variable $Y_{1,1}$. The specific impact of the shock is $\phi_{21}\varepsilon_{1,1}$. In period 2, $Y_{1,2}$ is also affected by the shock in period 1. The impact is $\phi_{11}\varepsilon_{1,1}$. Clearly, the impact of the shock in periods 3, 4 and so on can be computed, and a graph of how the individual variables respond can be plotted. This graph is called the **impulse response function**.

VAR models can also be used to test the causal relationship between variables. The concept of **causality** in time series analysis refers to whether one variable has information that helps to forecast future values of another variable. The seminal journal article on causality in time series analysis is Granger (1969), and the concept has become known as **Granger causality**. Let $Y_{1,t}$ and $Y_{2,t}$ be the two relevant variables. Let $F(Y_{1,t+h}|\Omega_t)$ denote the conditional CDF for $Y_{1,t+h}$ where Ω_t denotes *all* information. A general definition of Granger causality is that $Y_{2,t}$ does not **Granger-cause** $Y_{1,t}$ if for all $h > 0$,

$$F(Y_{1,t+h}|\Omega_t) = F(Y_{1,t+h}|\Omega_t - Y_{2,t}) \tag{2.97}$$

where $\Omega_t - Y_{2,t}$ denotes all information apart from $Y_{2,t}$. Assuming that a VAR(1) model is appropriate, statistically testing the null hypothesis that $Y_{2,t}$ does not Granger-cause $Y_{1,t}$ can be undertaken using the estimated version of (2.95). The relevant test is the t-test for testing the statistical significance of the estimated slope parameter on $Y_{2,t-1}$. The second equation from the VAR model, (2.96), can be used to test the null hypothesis that $Y_{1,t}$ does not Granger-cause $Y_{2,t}$ in the same way. If a higher order VAR model is more appropriate than a VAR(1) model, to test for Granger causality an F-test would need to be used since there is more than one relevant lag to test.[5]

2.3.8 Forecasting with Time Series Models

Assume that the simple AR(1) model is appropriate for a variable Y_t,

$$Y_t = \phi_1 Y_{t-1} + \varepsilon_t \tag{2.98}$$

---

[5]See Sims (1980) and Lütkepohl (2007) for further technical details on VAR models and multiple time series analysis.

Assume that we have estimated the parameters of the model and now want to compute statistically optimal forecasts of Y_t. Let $\hat{Y}_{t+h}$ denote the h-step ahead forecast made at the current time period t.

A natural measure of forecasting accuracy is the forecast error,

$$\hat{e}_{t+h} = Y_{t+h} - \hat{Y}_{t+h} \tag{2.99}$$

If we assume that positive forecast errors are as undesirable as negative forecast errors then a natural choice for the *optimal* forecast is the forecast that minimises the expected value of the squared forecast error (the mean square error (MSE)),

$$E(\hat{e}_{t+h}{}^2) = E[(Y_{t+h} - \hat{Y}_{t+h})^2] \tag{2.100}$$

It can be shown that this optimal forecast is given by the conditional mean of Y_{t+h} (*i.e.* the conditional expectation), conditioning on the information on Y available at time t,

$$\hat{Y}_{t+h} = E(Y_{t+h}|\Omega_t) \tag{2.101}$$

where Ω_t is the relevant information set.[6] It follows that the optimal forecast from the AR(1) model (2.98) is,

$$\hat{Y}_{t+h} = E(\phi_1 Y_{t+h-1} + \varepsilon_{t+h}|\Omega_t) \tag{2.102}$$

Since we assume that $E(\varepsilon_{t+h}|\Omega_t) = 0$ and because ϕ_1 is a population parameter (hence it is non-stochastic), it follows that,

$$\hat{Y}_{t+h} = \phi_1 E(Y_{t+h-1}|\Omega_t) \tag{2.103}$$

In practice, the population parameters are replaced with estimated values to give the final forecasting function,

$$\hat{Y}_{t+h} = \hat{\phi}_1 E(Y_{t+h-1}|\Omega_t) \tag{2.104}$$

Thus the optimal one-step ahead forecast from the AR(1) model (2.98) is given by,

$$\hat{Y}_{t+1} = \hat{\phi}_1 Y_t \tag{2.105}$$

and more generally,

$$\hat{Y}_{t+h} = \hat{\phi}_1 \hat{Y}_{t+h-1} \tag{2.106}$$

which via repeated substitution can be written as,

$$\hat{Y}_{t+h} = \hat{\phi}_1^h Y_t \tag{2.107}$$

If the relevant model is an AR(1) model with a constant,

$$Y_t = \delta + \phi_1 Y_{t-1} + \varepsilon_t \tag{2.108}$$

---

[6]See, for example, Granger and Newbold (1986) Chapter 4 and Hamilton (1994) Chapter 4 for further technical details on the theory of forecasting.

then the optimal forecast is,

$$\hat{Y}_{t+b} = E(\delta + \phi_1 Y_{t+b-1} + \varepsilon_{t+b} | \Omega_t) = \delta + \phi_1 E(Y_{t+b-1} | \Omega_t) \tag{2.109}$$

Again in practice the population parameters are replaced with estimated values to give the final forecasting function,

$$\hat{Y}_{t+b} = \hat{\delta} + \hat{\phi}_1 E(Y_{t+b-1} | \Omega_t) \tag{2.110}$$

Therefore the optimal one-step ahead forecast is,

$$\hat{Y}_{t+1} = \hat{\delta} + \hat{\phi}_1 Y_t \tag{2.111}$$

and more generally,

$$\hat{Y}_{t+b} = \hat{\delta} + \hat{\phi}_1 \hat{Y}_{t+b-1} \tag{2.112}$$

In this case the forecasting function can also be written,

$$\hat{Y}_{t+b} = (\hat{\phi}_1^{b-1} + \hat{\phi}_1^{b-2} + \cdots + \hat{\phi}_1 + 1)\hat{\delta} + \hat{\phi}_1^b Y_t \tag{2.113}$$

Note an important feature of these forecasts: assuming stationarity, as $b \to \infty$, the forecasts will converge to the estimated unconditional mean of Y_t. As $b \to \infty$, (2.107) converges to $E(Y_t) = 0$. As $b \to \infty$, (2.113) converges to $E(Y_t) = \hat{\delta}/(1 - \hat{\phi}_1)$. The forecasting functions derived here apply to the AR(1) model only, but the forecasting functions for higher order AR models and for MA models can be derived in a similar way and they have similar properties.

For ARMA and ARIMA models, again the optimal forecast is given by the conditional mean. For an ARMA(1,1) model,

$$Y_t = \delta + \phi_1 Y_{t-1} + \varepsilon_t + \theta_1 \varepsilon_{t-1} \tag{2.114}$$

the optimal one-step ahead forecast is,

$$\hat{Y}_{t+1} = \hat{\delta} + \hat{\phi}_1 Y_t + \hat{\theta}_1 \hat{\varepsilon}_t \tag{2.115}$$

and the general forecasting function can be written,

$$\hat{Y}_{t+b} = (\hat{\phi}_1^{b-1} + \hat{\phi}_1^{b-2} + \cdots + \hat{\phi}_1 + 1)\hat{\delta} + \hat{\phi}_1^b Y_t + \hat{\phi}_1^{b-1} \hat{\theta}_1 \hat{\varepsilon}_t \tag{2.116}$$

Since the ARIMA model is a model for ΔY_t, forecasts of Y_t can be obtained by forecasting ΔY_t and then adding these forecasts to the last sample observation on Y_t. For example, assume that an appropriate model for Y_t is an ARIMA(1,1,0),

$$\Delta Y_t = \phi_1 \Delta Y_{t-1} + \varepsilon_t \tag{2.117}$$

In this case the optimal forecast of Y_t is given by,

$$\hat{Y}_{t+b} = \hat{Y}_{t+b-1} + E(\phi_1 \Delta Y_{t+b-1} + \varepsilon_{t+b} | \Omega_t) \tag{2.118}$$

It follows that,

$$\hat{Y}_{t+b} = \hat{Y}_{t+b-1} + \phi_1 E(\Delta Y_{t+b-1} | \Omega_t) \tag{2.119}$$

The population parameters are replaced with estimated values to give the final forecasting function,

$$\hat{Y}_{t+b} = \hat{Y}_{t+b-1} + \hat{\phi}_1 E(\Delta Y_{t+b-1}|\Omega_t) \tag{2.120}$$

The optimal one-step ahead forecast is given by,

$$\hat{Y}_{t+1} = Y_t + \hat{\phi}_1 \Delta Y_t \tag{2.121}$$

and more generally,

$$\hat{Y}_{t+b} = Y_t + \sum_{i=1}^{b} \Delta \hat{Y}_{t+i} \tag{2.122}$$

where

$$\Delta \hat{Y}_{t+i} = \hat{\phi}_1^i \Delta Y_t \tag{2.123}$$

Note that the same general approach is used (taking conditional expectations) when forecasting with higher order ARMA and ARIMA models and with VAR models if the objective is to minimise the expected value of the squared forecast error. Of course in these cases the final forecasting functions will involve more terms.

The forecasts above are conditional mean forecasts of the variable being modelled Y_t, and hence they are also called **point forecasts**. It is also possible to compute a forecast of an interval within which a future value of Y_t will fall. For example, if we assume that the forecast errors are normally distributed, a 95% **interval forecast** is given by,

$$\hat{Y}_{t+b} \pm 1.96\hat{\sigma}_{\hat{e}} \tag{2.124}$$

where $\hat{\sigma}_{\hat{e}}$ is the estimated standard deviation of the forecast error which can be computed using a formula that depends on the forecasting model.[7] As well as computing point and interval forecasts using time series models it is also possible to compute forecasts of the entire conditional PDF for the variable Y_t. A formula for the optimal **density forecast** can be computed theoretically if the distribution of the error terms in the model is assumed to be known. Alternatively, computer simulation techniques can be used. Density forecasting has become increasingly popular in the past decade, with many central banks (such as the Bank of England) producing publicly available density forecasts of key macroeconomic variables.[8]

2.3.9　Evaluating Forecasts

A natural way of evaluating the accuracy of point forecasts from time series models is to use the forecast error $\hat{e}_{t+b}$, defined in (2.99). To choose between competing

---

[7] For more details, see Chatfield (1993), Christoffersen (1998) and Granger and Newbold (1986) Chapter 4.
[8] See Tay and Wallis (2000) and Clements (2004) for more details.

forecasting models the standard approach is to compare the forecasting accuracy of the models on the basis of their forecast errors over a historical period (that is, for a period when the true outcomes are known). In finance, this is typically called **backtesting**. It is popular to compare the mean squared forecast error (MSFE) or the square root of the MSFE (RMSFE) over the sample period for each model. If a series of one-day ahead forecasts are computed over a backtesting period consisting of n days, there are n forecast errors and the MSFE is,

$$MSFE = n^{-1} \sum_{t=1}^{n} \hat{e}_t^2 \tag{2.125}$$

where the subscript t refers to the forecast number. The model with the smallest MSFE (or RSMFE) is deemed to be the preferred forecasting model.

It is important to recognise that if one forecasting model has a smaller MSFE than a competing model for the same variable and the same backtesting period, then it does not necessarily mean it is a superior forecasting model. The MSFEs are functions of random variables and therefore the difference between the MSFEs for different models might be statistically insignificant from zero. Diebold and Mariano (1995) propose a useful test of the null hypothesis that two different models have equal forecast accuracy. Assume that the analyst has computed n, h-step ahead forecasts from two different models over a historical period. There are two sets of forecast errors, $\hat{e}_{1,t}$ and $\hat{e}_{2,t}$, where $t = 1, 2, \ldots, n$. Define the following term,

$$d_t = \hat{e}_{1,t}^2 - \hat{e}_{2,t}^2 \tag{2.126}$$

The null hypothesis of equal forecast accuracy considered by Diebold and Mariano (1995) is $H_0 : E(d_t) = 0$. The sample estimate of $E(d_t)$ is,

$$\bar{d} = n^{-1} \sum_{t=1}^{n} d_t \tag{2.127}$$

The Diebold and Mariano (1995) statistic for testing the null hypothesis of equal forecast accuracy is,

$$DM = [\hat{V}(\bar{d})]^{-1/2} \bar{d} \tag{2.128}$$

where

$$V(\bar{d}) \approx n^{-1} \left(\hat{\gamma}_0 + 2 \sum_{k=1}^{h-1} \hat{\gamma}_k \right) \tag{2.129}$$

and $\hat{\gamma}_k$ can be estimated using,

$$\hat{\gamma}_k = n^{-1} \sum_{t=k+1}^{n} (d_t - \bar{d})(d_{t-k} - \bar{d}), \quad k = 0, 1, \ldots, h - 1 \tag{2.130}$$

Under the null hypothesis of equal forecasting accuracy Diebold and Mariano (1995) show that asymptotically the test statistic DM has a standard normal distribution.

Therefore assuming a large sample size the computed test statistic can be compared with a relevant critical value to decide whether to accept or reject the null hypothesis (Table A.1 in the Appendix can be used to choose a critical value for the test statistic). Monte Carlo simulation experiments in Diebold and Mariano (1995) reveal that the small sample performance of this test statistic is generally good; however, the test can be over-sized in some cases, particularly if the forecasting horizon is greater than one-step ahead.[9]

When forecasting random processes it is important to be aware of the possibility that structural breaks in the underlying DGP can occur. In practice the analyst chooses a time series model that best approximates the unknown DGP. If the correct model is chosen then the forecasts computed as described above will be optimal as defined. A **structural break** can be thought of as a change in the structure of the DGP, for example from an AR(1) model to an AR(2) model. If structural breaks occur but the analyst is unaware of these breaks and they assume a stable model, it is likely that the forecasts computed in the usual way will be sub-optimal. If the analyst is aware of the structural breaks, they have to decide whether to estimate the model using only data from after the structural break, or to include data from before the break. If the post-break sample size is small then even though the pre- and post-break DGPs are different, it can sometimes be optimal to include pre-break data when estimating the parameters of the model used for forecasting.[10]

In finance, as well as point, interval and density forecasting, forecasting the direction of change of variables might also be of interest. For example, investors might want to use direction of change forecasts from a time series model to help them decide whether to invest in a particular portfolio of risky assets, or to invest in a government bond. Let Y_t be the difference between the monthly return from investing in the portfolio and the bond (the **excess return**). Assume an investor believes that the DGP for Y_t is an AR(p) model and they intend to invest over time on the basis of the sign of one-month ahead forecasts of the excess return $\hat{Y}_{t+1}$ computed from recursively estimated AR(p) models: if $\hat{Y}_{t+1} > 0$ they will invest in the portfolio; if $\hat{Y}_{t+1} \leq 0$ they will switch their funds into the bond. Before putting this investment strategy into action it is sensible for the investor to investigate how successful the AR(p) model is for forecasting the sign of Y_t in backtesting. Henriksson and Merton (1981) and Pesaran and Timmermann (1992) have developed tests that can be used to help determine how successful a model is at forecasting the sign of a variable. The Pesaran and Timmermann (1992) test can be computed as

---

[9]Here **size** is a statistical property meaning the probability of incorrectly rejecting a true null hypothesis, or the probability of a Type I error. Harvey, Leybourne and Newbold (1997) propose a modified version of the *DM* test with improved small sample properties.

[10]These issues are discussed in detail by Pesaran and Timmermann (2005, 2007).

follows.[11] Let $x_t = E(y_t|\Omega_{t-1})$ be a forecast of the relevant variable y_t obtained from a particular model over a backtesting period (e.g. an AR(p) model), and assume that n forecasts are available. Define the following indicator functions,

$$Y_t = 1 \text{ if } y_t > 0$$
$$= 0 \text{ otherwise} \tag{2.131}$$
$$X_t = 1 \text{ if } x_t > 0$$
$$= 0 \text{ otherwise} \tag{2.132}$$
$$Z_t = 1 \text{ if } y_t x_t > 0$$
$$= 0 \text{ otherwise} \tag{2.133}$$

and define the following probability terms,

$$P_y = P(y_t > 0) \tag{2.134}$$
$$P_x = P(x_t > 0) \tag{2.135}$$
$$\hat{P} = n^{-1} \sum_{t=1}^{n} Z_t = \overline{Z} \tag{2.136}$$
$$\hat{P}_y = n^{-1} \sum_{t=1}^{n} Y_t = \overline{Y} \tag{2.137}$$
$$\hat{P}_x = n^{-1} \sum_{t=1}^{n} X_t = \overline{X} \tag{2.138}$$
$$\hat{P}_* = \hat{P}_y \hat{P}_x + (1 - \hat{P}_y)(1 - \hat{P}_x) \tag{2.139}$$

Under the null hypothesis that y_t and x_t are independently distributed (x_t has no directional forecasting power), Pesaran and Timmermann (1992) show that the following test statistic is asymptotically distributed as a standard normal random variable,

$$PT = \frac{\hat{P} - \hat{P}^*}{[Var(\hat{P}) - Var(\hat{P}_*)]^{1/2}} \tag{2.140}$$

where

$$Var(\hat{P}) = n^{-1} \hat{P}_*(1 - \hat{P}_*) \tag{2.141}$$
$$Var(\hat{P}_*) = n^{-1}(2\hat{P}_y - 1)^2 \hat{P}_x(1 - \hat{P}_x) + n^{-1}(2\hat{P}_x - 1)^2 \hat{P}_y(1 - \hat{P}_y)$$
$$+ 4n^{-2} \hat{P}_y \hat{P}_x(1 - \hat{P}_y)(1 - \hat{P}_x) \tag{2.142}$$

Therefore the null hypothesis that x_t has no directional forecasting power can be tested by computing the Pesaran and Timmermann (1992) test and comparing with a relevant critical value (Table A.1 can be used to choose a critical value for the test statistic).

---

[11] Note that for the purposes of this explanation we switch to lower case letters to be consistent with the notation in Pesaran and Timmermann (1992).

2.3.10 Non-linear Time Series Models

The time series models discussed so far in this chapter are all linear, and, in practice, linear time series models are more widely used in finance than non-linear time series models. Recently, however, the latter have become more popular, particularly in academic research. Two popular types of non-linear univariate time series model are threshold autoregressive (TAR) models and smooth transition autoregressive (STAR) models. Both models are a type of **regime-switching** model. TAR models allow for parameter shifts (regime switches) depending on the value of a lag of the variable being modelled relative to a threshold level. For example, a two-regime, first-order TAR model (a TAR(1) model) can be written,

$$Y_t = (\delta_1 + \phi_{11} Y_{t-1}) I_t + (\delta_2 + \phi_{12} Y_{t-1})(1 - I_t) + \varepsilon_t \qquad (2.143)$$

where $I_t = 1$ if $Y_{t-d} > \tau$ and 0 otherwise, and d is a positive integer. This TAR(1) model allows for a different constant and AR(1) parameter depending on a previous value of the variable Y_{t-d} relative to a threshold τ. Note that the TAR(1) model can be easily extended to allow for higher order lags. For example, a TAR(p) model can be written,

$$
\begin{aligned}
Y_t = {} & (\delta_1 + \phi_{11} Y_{t-1} + \phi_{21} Y_{t-2} + \cdots + \phi_{p1} Y_{t-p}) I_t \\
& + (\delta_2 + \phi_{12} Y_{t-1} + \phi_{22} Y_{t-2} + \cdots + \phi_{p2} Y_{t-p})(1 - I_t) + \varepsilon_t \qquad (2.144)
\end{aligned}
$$

TAR models were developed in the specialist statistics literature on time series analysis (see e.g. Tong, 1978, 1983; Tong and Lim, 1980). Estimating the parameters of TAR models is less straightforward than with linear time series models; however, an OLS-type estimator can be used, called conditional least squares (CLS), which involves estimating the parameters using OLS conditional on a grid-search over all feasible values of τ and d.

In the TAR models above there are two regimes. Allowing for multiple regimes is possible and choosing the number of regimes is straightforward although it can be computationally expensive. To decide on the number of regimes there are two main approaches: either fit several different models with different numbers of regimes and choose between them using information criteria and/or F-tests; or, use a specification-test (e.g. see Tsay, 1989). The optimal value of d can be determined using an information criterion (e.g. AIC, SIC). When TAR models are used for macroeconomic and financial data, in practice a low value for d is often found to be optimal. Prior to estimating a TAR model it is sensible to pre-test data to determine whether non-linearity is present in the data. Numerous tests are available: for example, see Tsay (1989) and Granger and Teräsvirta (1993) Chapter 6 for further details.

In TAR models regime switching is discrete, in the sense that it takes place in a single period. STAR models are extensions of TAR models that allow for gradual regime switching between different parameter values, whilst also allowing for rapid regime switching. For example, a first-order logistic-STAR model can be written,

$$Y_t = (\delta_1 + \phi_{11} Y_{t-1})F(Y_{t-d}) + (\delta_2 + \phi_{12} Y_{t-1})[1 - F(Y_{t-d})] + \varepsilon_t \qquad (2.145)$$

$$F(Y_{t-d}) = [1 + \exp -\gamma(Y_{t-d} - \tau)]^{-1}, \gamma \geq 0 \qquad (2.146)$$

Therefore rather than using a discrete indicator function I_t to define the regime switch, a CDF is used, $F(Y_{t-d})$. In (2.145) the logistic CDF is used, hence the model is known as a logistic-STAR or LSTAR model. Since it is a first-order model, we call it an LSTAR(1) model. The parameter γ controls the speed of the regime switch and τ is the threshold parameter. Assuming that γ is positive, for $Y_{t-d} - \tau \to -\infty$, $F(Y_{t-d}) \to 0$, while for $Y_{t-d} - \tau \to \infty$, $F(Y_{t-d}) \to 1$. Hence the transition function moves between 0 and 1 depending on the value of Y_{t-d} relative to a threshold. For small values of γ the transition takes place gradually, while for large values it takes place rapidly. Hence, for large values of γ an LSTAR model closely approximates the equivalent TAR model. The LSTAR(1) model can be easily extended to deal with higher order lags in the same way as the TAR(1) model. A popular alternative to the LSTAR model is the exponential-STAR (ESTAR) model in which the exponential CDF is employed to model the regime switch,

$$F(Y_{t-d}) = 1 - \exp[-\gamma(Y_{t-d} - \tau)^2] \qquad (2.147)$$

The parameters of LSTAR and ESTAR models, including γ and τ, can be estimated by ML, or equivalently by non-linear least squares (NLS), and subject to weak assumptions the estimates are consistent and asymptotically normally distributed.[12]

Optimal forecasts from TAR and STAR models can be computed using the same general approach as for linear time series models. Thus the optimal forecast is given by the conditional mean. So for example in the case of the TAR(1) model (2.143) with $d = 1$, the optimal one-step ahead forecast is,

$$\hat{Y}_{t+1} = (\hat{\delta}_1 + \hat{\phi}_{11} Y_t)I_{t+1} + (\hat{\delta}_2 + \hat{\phi}_{12} Y_t)(1 - I_{t+1}) \qquad (2.148)$$

where $I_{t+1} = 1$ if $Y_t > \hat{\tau}$ and 0 otherwise. Forecasting for horizons greater than d is less straightforward. For example, if $d = 1, h = 2$, then,

$$\hat{Y}_{t+2} = (\hat{\delta}_1 + \hat{\phi}_{11} \hat{Y}_{t+1})I_{t+2} + (\hat{\delta}_2 + \hat{\phi}_{12} \hat{Y}_{t+1})(1 - I_{t+2}) \qquad (2.149)$$

where $I_{t+2} = 1$ if $Y_{t+1} > \hat{\tau}$ and 0 otherwise. Note, however, that Y_{t+1} is unobserved at time t since it is a future value, and so I_{t+2} is undefined. A solution is to use $\hat{Y}_{t+1}$ to define when $I_{t+2} = 1$, and Monte Carlo simulation-based approaches have also been proposed (see e.g. Clements and Smith, 1997).

---

[12]See Granger and Teräsvirta (1993), Teräsvirta (1994) and van Dijk, Teräsvirta and Franses (2002) for further technical details on smooth transition models.

There are many economic and financial variables where the autoregressive dynamics might be expected to switch depending on whether a previous value of the variable is above or below a threshold. For example, the evolution of time series data on industrial production growth might be expected to depend on whether last period's value was negative or positive; the evolution of time series data on stock returns might be expected to depend on the size and sign of the return last period. Hence the TAR and STAR models discussed here have been used in academic research on various topics in macroeconomics and finance, and in some cases they can be very informative (for example, see Koop and Potter, 1999; Michael, Nobay and Peel, 1997; Taylor, Sarno and Peel, 2001). Note, however, that the empirical evidence on forecasting macroeconomic and financial variables suggests that when compared with linear models any improvements in forecasting accuracy from using a non-linear model are likely to be relatively small (e.g. see Stock and Watson, 1999).

2.4　Summary

This chapter has reviewed some key econometric and statistical techniques for modelling and forecasting financial data, focusing in particular on techniques that can be applied to time series data. We have discussed random variables, probability distributions and random processes, and progressed to linear time series models, vector time series models, and non-linear time series models. We have also discussed how to compute optimal forecasts of a variable from a time series model and how these forecasts can be evaluated. Many of the techniques covered in this chapter will be referred to in subsequent chapters and used in the empirical examples throughout this book.

2.5　End of Chapter Questions[13]

> **Q1.** Simulate 1000 independent values for a normally distributed random variable with $\mu = 0$ and $\sigma = 3$. Assume these are the values of a stationary random process Y_t.

---

[13]A guide to answering these questions and relevant MATLAB® programs are given on the companion website (www.wileyeurope.com/college/sollis).

(a) Compute the sample autocorrelations for $\tau = 0, 1, 2, \ldots, 30$ and graph the SACF.

(b) Use the SACF to test the null hypothesis that the variable is a white noise process.

Q2. Simulate 1000 values for two AR(1) variables using the following DGPs with the same random error terms for each variable,

$$X_t = 0.90 + 0.10X_{t-1} + \varepsilon_t$$

$$Y_t = 0.90 + 0.90Y_{t-1} + \varepsilon_t$$

$$\varepsilon_t \sim NID(0, 1)$$

(a) Graph X_t and Y_t and comment on the persistence of each variable.

(b) Estimate the parameters of AR(1) and AR(2) models for X_t and Y_t including a constant.

(c) For each estimated model test the statistical significance of the estimated slope parameters using t-tests and comment on your results in the light of the true DGPs.

Q3. Simulate 1000 values for two ARMA(1,1) variables using the following DGPs with the same random error terms for each variable,

$$X_t = 0.10X_{t-1} + \varepsilon_t + 0.30\varepsilon_{t-1}$$

$$Y_t = 0.90Y_{t-1} + \varepsilon_t - 0.30\varepsilon_{t-1}$$

$$\varepsilon_t \sim NID(0, 1)$$

(a) Graph X_t and Y_t and compare with your graphs for Question 2.

(b) Graph the SACF and the SPACF for X_t and Y_t and comment on the differences and similarities.

(c) Estimate the parameters of ARMA(2,1) and ARMA(1,1) models for X_t and Y_t. Test the statistical significance of the estimated slope parameters using t-tests. Comment on your results in the light of the true DGPs.

Q4. Simulate 2000 values for the I(1) variable Y_t from the following DGP,

$$\Delta Y_t = 0.25\Delta Y_{t-1} + \varepsilon_t + 0.50\varepsilon_{t-1}$$

$$\varepsilon_t \sim NID(0, 1)$$

Assume that Y_t is a variable that you want to model and that you do not know the true DGP. Use the Box–Jenkins approach to model Y_t.

Q5. (a) Write out the forecasting function for computing optimal h-step ahead forecasts of Y_t in Question 2.

(b) Write out the forecasting function for computing optimal h-step ahead forecasts of Y_t in Question 3.

(c) Write out the forecasting function for computing optimal h-step ahead forecasts of Y_t in Question 4.

(d) Critically discuss some of the different approaches that can be used to evaluate the accuracy of point forecasts from time series models.

2.6 References

Akaike, H. (1969) Fitting autoregressive models for prediction, *Annals of the Institute of Statistical Mathematics*, 21, 243–247.

Anderson, L.R. (1942) The distribution of the serial correlation coefficient, *The Annals of Mathematical Statistics*, 13, 1–13.

Box, G.E.P. and G. Jenkins (1970) *Time Series Analysis: Forecasting and Control*. San Francisco: Holden-Day.

Box, G.E.P. and G. Jenkins (1976) *Time Series Analysis: Forecasting and Control*, rev. edn. San Francisco: Holden-Day.

Chatfield, C. (1993) Calculating interval forecasts, *Journal of Business and Economic Statistics*, 11, 121–135.

Christoffersen, P.F. (1998) Evaluating interval forecasts, *International Economic Review*, 39, 841–862.

Clements, M.P. (2004) Evaluating the Bank of England density forecasts of inflation, *Economic Journal*, 114, 844–866.

Clements, M.P. and J. Smith (1997) The performance of alternative forecasting methods for SETAR models, *International Journal of Forecasting*, 13, 463–475.

Dickey, D.A. and W.A. Fuller (1979) Distribution of the estimators for autoregressive time series with a unit root, *Journal of the American Statistical Association*, 74, 427–431.

Diebold, F.X. and R. Mariano (1995) Comparing predictive accuracy, *Journal of Business and Economic Statistics*, 13, 253–262.

Granger, C.W.J. (1969) Investigating causal relations by econometric models and cross-spectral methods, *Econometrica*, 37, 424–438.

Granger, C.W.J. and P. Newbold (1986) *Forecasting Economic Time Series*, 2nd edn. San Diego: Academic Press.

Granger, C.W.J. and T. Teräsvirta (1993) *Modeling Nonlinear Economic Relationships*. Oxford: Oxford University Press.

Greene, W. (2008) *Econometric Analysis*, 6th edn. New Jersey: Pearson Education.

Gujarati, D.N. and D.C. Porter (2009) *Basic Econometrics*, 5th edn. New York: McGraw-Hill Higher Education.

Hamilton, J.G. (1994) *Time Series Analysis*, Princeton: Princeton University Press.

Harvey, D., Leybourne, S.J. and P. Newbold (1997) Testing the equality of prediction mean squared errors, *International Journal of Forecasting*, 13, 281–291.

Henriksson, R.D. and R.C. Merton (1981) On market timing and investment performance. II. Statistical procedures for evaluating forecasting skills, *Journal of Business*, 54, 513–533.

Jarque, C.M. and A.K. Bera (1980) Efficient tests for normality, homoscedasticity and serial independence of regression residuals, *Economics Letters*, 6, 255–259.

Jarque, C.M. and A.K. Bera (1987) A test for normality of observations and regression residuals, *International Statistical Review*, 55, 163–172.

Kendall, M.G. (1954) Note on the bias in the estimation of autocorrelation, *Biometrika*, 41, 403–404.

Koop, G. and S. Potter (1999) Dynamic asymmetries in US unemployment, *Journal of Business and Economic Statistics*, 17, 298–312.

Ljung, G.M. and G.E.P. Box (1978) On a measure of a lack of fit in time series models, *Biometrika*, 65, 297–303.

Lütkepohl, H. (2007) *New Introduction to Multiple Time Series Analysis*. New York: Springer.

Marriott, F.H.C. and J.A. Pope (1954) Bias in the estimation of autocorrelations, *Biometrika*, 41, 390–402.

Michael, P., Nobay A.R. and D.A. Peel (1997) Transactions costs and nonlinear adjustment in real exchange rates: an empirical investigation, *Journal of Political Economy*, 105, 862–879.

Pesaran, M.H. and A. Timmermann (1992) A simple non-parametric test of predictive performance, *Journal of Business and Economic Statistics*, 10, 461–465.

Pesaran, M.H. and A. Timmermann (2005) Small sample properties of forecasts from autoregressive models under structural breaks, *Journal of Econometrics*, 129, 183–217.

Pesaran, M.H. and A. Timmermann (2007) Selection of estimation window in the presence of breaks, *Journal of Econometrics*, 137, 134–161.

Schwarz, G. (1978) Estimating the dimension of a model, *Annals of Statistics*, 6, 461–464.

Sims, C. (1980) Macroeconomics and reality, *Econometrica*, 48, 1–48.

Stock, J.H. and M.H. Watson (1999) A comparison of linear and nonlinear univariate models for forecasting macroeconomic time series. In Engle, R.F. and H. White (eds) *Cointegration, Causality and Forecasting: A Festschrift in Honour of Clive W.J. Granger*. Oxford: Oxford University Press, pp. 1–44.

Tay, A.S. and K.F. Wallis (2000) Density forecasting: a survey, *Journal of Forecasting*, 19, 235–254

Taylor, M.P., Sarno, L. and D. Peel (2001) Nonlinear mean reversion in real exchange rates: towards a solution to the purchasing power parity puzzles, *International Economic Review*, 42, 1015–1042.

Teräsvirta, T. (1994) Specification, estimation and evaluation of smooth transition autoregressive models, *Journal of the American Statistical Association*, 89, 208–218.

Tong, H. (1978) On a threshold model. In Chen, C.H. (ed.) *Pattern Recognition and Signal Processing*. Amsterdam: Sijtho & Noordho.

Tong, H. (1983) *Threshold Models in Non-Linear Time Series Analysis*, Lecture Notes in Statistics, No. 21. New York: Springer-Verlag.

Tong, H. and K.S. Lim (1980) Threshold autoregression, limit cycles and cyclical data, *Journal of the Royal Statistical Society, Series B*, 42, 245–292.

Tsay, R.S. (1989) Testing and modeling threshold autoregressive processes, *Journal of the American Statistical Association*, 84, 231–240.

van Dijk, D., Teräsvirta, T. and P.H. Franses (2002) Smooth transition autoregresive models – a survey of recent developments, *Econometric Reviews*, 21, 1–47.

Walker, G. (1931) On periodicity in series of related terms, *Proceedings of the Royal Society of London A*, 131, 518–532.

Yule, G.U. (1927) On a method for investigating periodicities in disturbed series with special reference to Wolfer's sunspot numbers, *Philosophical Transactions of the Royal Society of London A*, 226, 267–298.

Chapter 3
Regression and Volatility

3.1 Introduction

Regression models are the workhorse statistical models for empirical analysis in finance. They are widely used in research to analyse the empirical support for financial theories. Regression models can be employed to compute forecasts of financial variables which might then be used for financial trading. Regression models can also be used to help estimate the covariance matrix for multiple asset returns, providing important information for portfolio managers and risk managers. This chapter begins with a review of conventional regression techniques, assuming the variables being modelled are time-indexed random processes. We then discuss the implications for regression modelling if the relevant variables are non-stationary random processes; in particular, the possibility that non-stationarity can lead to the discovery of spurious statistical relationships between unrelated variables. The cointegration methodology for modelling non-stationary variables is covered and we briefly discuss forecasting with regression models. This chapter also reviews modelling and forecasting **conditional volatility**. In finance, the variance and standard deviation of an asset return are used as measures of the risk associated with investing in the asset. The standard deviation is also called the **volatility** of the return. Accurately modelling and forecasting volatility is particularly important for successful portfolio management and risk management. The *conditional* volatility of a variable is the volatility at a point in time conditional on an information set that includes the history of the variable. In finance, conditional volatility is often time-varying and accurately modelling and forecasting conditional volatility requires specialist statistical techniques.[1]

3.2 Regression Models

3.2.1 Linear Regression

The bivariate linear regression model can be written,

$$Y_t = \beta_0 + \beta_1 X_t + \varepsilon_t \tag{3.1}$$

and the multiple linear regression model,

$$Y_t = \beta_0 + \beta_1 X_{1,t} + \beta_2 X_{2,t} + \cdots + \beta_k X_{k,t} + \varepsilon_t \tag{3.2}$$

where Y_t is the dependent variable (the regressand), $X_{i,t}$ ($i = 1, 2, \ldots, k$) are the independent variables (the regressors) and ε_t is a random error term. Therefore, the regressand is a linear function of the regressor; the error terms capture what cannot be explained by the regressors. The subscript t indicates that here we are assuming that Y_t is a time-indexed random process, implying that the actual values of Y_t over a particular time period are time series data. The regressors $X_{i,t}$ can be random processes or non-random processes. Linear regression models can also be used for modelling cross-sectional data (observations for different units at a single point in time) and panel data (observations for different cross-sectional units over time). The models and parameters given in (3.1) and (3.2) are **population** models and parameters, in the sense that we assume they apply to the entire population of data on the relevant variables. Typically in most applications of linear regression models the population parameters are unknown and we do not have access to the entire population of data. Hence, in practice, population parameters are estimated using a sample of data.

The **Classical Linear Regression Model** (CLRM) model refers to a linear regression model when the following assumptions are made:

   (i) ε_t has a mean of zero, $E(\varepsilon_t) = 0$ (3.3)

   (ii) ε_t has a constant variance, $Var(\varepsilon_t) = \sigma^2$ (3.4)

   (iii) The ε_t are statistically independent, $E(\varepsilon_t \varepsilon_{t-j}) = 0$ where $j \neq 0$ (3.5)

   (iv) The regressors are not random (they are **non-stochastic**)   (3.6)

---

[1]As in Chapter 2, this chapter is a review of the key techniques rather than an exhaustive technical study. If further technical details are required, readers are referred to the following econometrics textbooks: Gujarati and Porter (2009) (intermediate level), Hamilton (1994) and Greene (2008) (advanced level).

(v) The regressors are not perfectly linearly correlated with each other   (3.7)

(vi) ε_t is normally distributed   (3.8)

A well-known result formalised in the **Gauss–Markov theorem** is that under assumptions (i)-(v), the ordinary least squares (OLS) estimator of the parameters in a linear regression model is the minimum variance unbiased estimator from the class of linear estimators (or the best, linear, unbiased (BLUE) estimator). In this context "linear" refers to the fact that the OLS estimator is a linear function of the sample data on the regressand. Recall from Chapter 2 that an estimator $\hat{\beta}$ is **unbiased** if $E(\hat{\beta}) = \beta$. Note that OLS will also be the BLUE estimator if the regressors are random but statistically independent of the errors. If assumption (iv) is true, the regressors will be independent of the errors, but this can also be true for some random processes. It can also be shown that under assumptions (i)-(v) the OLS estimator is **consistent** (it converges asymptotically to the population parameter).

In empirical applications in finance assumption (iv) is typically not satisfied; in practice it is often the case that the regressors will be random processes. In this case, if the other assumptions are satisfied and the regressors and the error terms are independent then the OLS estimator will be the BLUE estimator. However, if the regressors and the error terms are contemporaneously correlated then the OLS estimator will be biased and inconsistent. In this case an alternative **instrumental variables** (IV) estimator can usually be employed to obtain consistent estimates.[2] If the regressors involve lagged values of the dependent variable then the OLS estimator will be biased, although it will be consistent (assuming no regressors are contemporaneously correlated with the error terms).

We have already briefly reviewed OLS when discussing time series models in Chapter 2. For the bivariate linear regression model, the OLS estimates of β_0 and β_1 are the parameters that minimise the following **residual sum of squares** (RSS),

$$\sum_{t=1}^{T} \hat{\varepsilon}_t^2 = \sum_{t=1}^{T} (Y_t - \hat{\beta}_0 - \hat{\beta}_1 X_t)^2 \tag{3.9}$$

which can be computed using,

$$\hat{\beta} = (\mathbf{X}'\mathbf{X})^{-1}\mathbf{X}'\mathbf{Y} \tag{3.10}$$

where

$$\mathbf{Y} = [Y_1 \ \ Y_2 \ \ \ldots \ \ Y_T]' \tag{3.11}$$

---

[2]See Greene (2008) Chapter 12 for further technical details.

$$\mathbf{X} = \begin{bmatrix} 1 & X_1 \\ 1 & X_2 \\ \vdots & \vdots \\ 1 & X_T \end{bmatrix} \tag{3.12}$$

$$\hat{\boldsymbol{\beta}} = [\hat{\beta}_0 \ \hat{\beta}_1]' \tag{3.13}$$

The same approach can be used to estimate the parameters of multiple linear regression models, where

$$\mathbf{X} = \begin{bmatrix} 1 & X_{1,1} & X_{2,1} & \cdots & X_{k,1} \\ 1 & X_{1,2} & X_{2,2} & \cdots & X_{k,2} \\ \vdots & \vdots & \vdots & \cdots & \vdots \\ 1 & X_{1,T} & X_{2,T} & \cdots & X_{k,T} \end{bmatrix} \tag{3.14}$$

$$\hat{\boldsymbol{\beta}} = [\hat{\beta}_0 \ \hat{\beta}_1 \ \cdots \ \hat{\beta}_k]' \tag{3.15}$$

Note that the parameters of the CLRM can also be estimated by maximum likelihood (ML) and it can be shown that if the errors ε_t are normally distributed, the ML estimator is equivalent to the OLS estimator.

The OLS **fitted** bivariate and multiple linear regression models can be written,

$$\hat{Y}_t = \hat{\beta}_0 + \hat{\beta}_1 X_t \tag{3.16}$$

$$\hat{Y}_t = \hat{\beta}_0 + \hat{\beta}_1 X_{1,t} + \hat{\beta}_2 X_{2,t} + \cdots + \hat{\beta}_k X_{k,t} \tag{3.17}$$

$\hat{Y}_t$ is the estimated conditional mean of Y_t (e.g. in the bivariate case the estimated value of $E(Y_t|X_t)$). For the bivariate model the OLS estimation method can be interpreted as finding the line that provides the best fit to the data. To clarify, it is helpful to consider graphs for the bivariate case. In Figures 3.1 and 3.2, graphs of the scatter plot and fitted OLS regression line are given for Y_t and X_t simulated using the following data generation process (DGP),

$$Y_t = \beta_0 + \beta_1 X_t + \varepsilon_t \tag{3.18}$$

$$\varepsilon_t \sim NID(0, \sigma_\varepsilon^2) \tag{3.19}$$

$$X_t \sim NID(0, 1) \tag{3.20}$$

where $Cov(X_t, \varepsilon_t) = 0$. In Figure 3.1, $\beta_0 = 1$, $\beta_1 = 1.50$, $\sigma_\varepsilon^2 = 1$ and in Figure 3.2, $\beta_0 = 1$, $\beta_1 = -1.50$, $\sigma_\varepsilon^2 = 5$.

In practice, having estimated a regression model an analyst will be interested in how well the model fits the data. The coefficient of determination R^2 is a useful numerical measure for assessing how well an estimated linear regression model

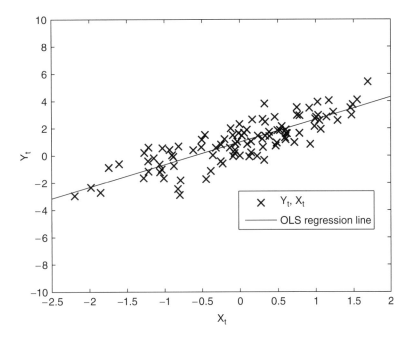

Figure 3.1   Scatter plot with OLS regression line.

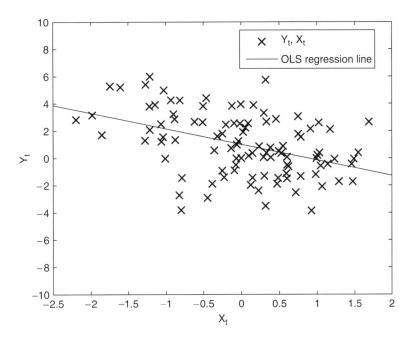

Figure 3.2   Scatter plot with OLS regression line.

explains variation in the regressand. Define the following variation terms,

$$TSS = \sum_{t=1}^{T} (Y_t - \overline{Y})^2 \tag{3.21}$$

$$ESS = \sum_{t=1}^{T} (\hat{Y}_t - \overline{Y})^2 \tag{3.22}$$

$$RSS = \sum_{t=1}^{T} \hat{\varepsilon}_t^2 \tag{3.23}$$

where TSS is the **total sum of squares** (the total variation of Y_t around its sample mean), ESS is the **explained sum of squares**, and RSS is the residual sum of squares. $\overline{Y}$ is the sample mean of the Y_t values ($\overline{Y} = T^{-1} \sum_{t=1}^{T} Y_t$). It follows straightforwardly that $TSS = ESS + RSS$,

$$\sum_{t=1}^{T} (Y_t - \overline{Y})^2 = \sum_{t=1}^{T} (\hat{Y}_t - \overline{Y})^2 + \sum_{t=1}^{T} \hat{\varepsilon}_t^2 \tag{3.24}$$

Consequently,

$$\left(\sum_{t=1}^{T} (Y_t - \overline{Y})^2 \right)^{-1} \sum_{t=1}^{T} (\hat{Y}_t - \overline{Y})^2 + \left(\sum_{t=1}^{T} (Y_t - \overline{Y})^2 \right)^{-1} \sum_{t=1}^{T} \hat{\varepsilon}_t^2 = 1 \tag{3.25}$$

which can be rearranged to give,

$$R^2 = 1 - \left(\sum_{t=1}^{T} (Y_t - \overline{Y})^2 \right)^{-1} \sum_{t=1}^{T} \hat{\varepsilon}_t^2, \quad 0 \le R^2 \le 1 \tag{3.26}$$

Therefore, R^2 measures the proportion of the variation in the regressand that is explained by the regressors. If a large proportion of the variation is explained by the regressors, R^2 will be close to 1. Conversely, if only a small proportion of the variation is explained, R^2 will be closer to zero.

R^2 is a useful guide to the explanatory power of a model. However, it has a fundamental weakness; it can be shown that adding regressors to the model will increase the R^2 value obtained, suggesting greater explanatory power, even if the regressors actually have *no* explanatory power. An alternative measure of fit that corrects for this problem is the **Adjusted-R^2** (also called $\overline{R}^2$),

$$\text{Adjusted-}R^2 = 1 - \frac{(T-k)^{-1} \sum_{t=1}^{T} \hat{\varepsilon}_t^2}{(T-1)^{-1} \sum_{t=1}^{T} (Y_t - \overline{Y})^2} \tag{3.27}$$

where k denotes the number of estimated parameters. Therefore Adjusted-R^2 penalises for additional explanatory variables (as do the AIC and SIC measures discussed in Chapter 2). Note that Adjusted-R^2 is not an exact measure of the *proportion* of the variation of the regressand explained by the regressors, and in practice while its upper limit is one, negative values can be obtained.

The CLRM assumption (vi) means that the OLS estimates, $\hat{\beta}_i$, $i = 1, 2, \ldots, k$, obtained from a sample of data will be normally distributed. It can then be shown that the t-statistic,

$$t = \frac{\hat{\beta}_i - \beta_i}{se(\hat{\beta}_i)},\qquad (3.28)$$

has a Student's t-distribution. Hence t-tests can be used for testing hypotheses about the population parameters (Table A.2 in the Appendix can be used to choose a critical value for the test statistic). For example, it is standard practice to test the null hypothesis $H_0 : \beta_i = 0$ against the alternative hypothesis $H_1 : \beta_i \neq 0$ for each of the population parameters using a t-test (if the null hypothesis is rejected, the estimated parameter is said to be **statistically significant**). Similarly it follows from assumption (vi) that the following statistic has an F-distribution,

$$F = \frac{(RSS_r - RSS_{ur})/q}{RSS_{ur}/(T - k)}\qquad (3.29)$$

where RSS_r denotes the RSS for a version of the model with linear restrictions imposed, RSS_{ur} denotes the RSS for the unrestricted model, q is the number of restrictions, and k is the number of estimated parameters in the unrestricted model. Hence F-tests can be used to test hypotheses involving linear restrictions (Table A.3 can be used to choose a critical value for the test statistic). Note that even if ε_t is not normally distributed, then under weak assumptions the OLS estimates will be asymptotically normally distributed.

If the CLRM assumptions (i)–(v) are not satisfied then the OLS estimator will not be the BLUE estimator. If the error variance is time-varying ($Var(\varepsilon_t) = \sigma_t^2$), there is **heteroscedasticity**, and if the errors are correlated ($E(\varepsilon_t\varepsilon_{t-j}) \neq 0$), there is **autocorrelation**. In both of these cases it can be shown that the OLS estimator is not the minimum variance estimator. Popular statistical tests for the presence of heteroscedasticity are the Breusch–Pagan test (Breusch and Pagan, 1979) and the White test (White, 1980). Popular statistical tests for the presence of autocorrelation are the Durbin–Watson test (1950, 1951), and the Breusch–Godfrey test (Breusch, 1978; Godfrey, 1978). Alternative estimation techniques exist that are minimum variance under heteroscedasticity and autocorrelation. The generalised least squares (GLS) estimator is BLUE in these cases.[3] In practice, a viable alternative to using GLS in these cases might be to use OLS (which is still an unbiased

---

[3]See Greene (2008) Chapter 8 for further technical details.

and consistent estimator if the remaining CLRM assumptions are satisfied), but to employ robust standard errors for inference.[4]

In the linear regression models defined in (3.1) and (3.2), both models assume that Y_t can be explained by contemporaneous values of explanatory variables. In some empirical applications there might be reasons to include lagged values of the explanatory variable(s) and/or lagged values of the dependent variable as additional regressors. A general dynamic version of the bivariate linear regression model can be written,

$$Y_t = \beta_0 + \beta_1 X_t + \beta_2 X_{t-1} + \cdots + \beta_p X_{t-p}$$
$$+ \lambda_1 Y_{t-1} + \lambda_2 Y_{t-2} + \cdots + \lambda_q Y_{t-q} + \varepsilon_t \tag{3.30}$$

or using appropriately defined lag polynomials $\beta(L)$ and $\lambda(L)$,

$$Y_t = \beta_0 + \beta(L)X_t + \lambda(L)Y_t + \varepsilon_t \tag{3.31}$$

This type of model is called an autoregressive distributed lag (ADL) model and it can be extended to include multiple explanatory variables. Assuming that the regressors are not contemporaneously correlated with the error term, the parameters of ADL models can be consistently estimated using OLS, although the OLS estimator is biased. ADL models have been shown to be useful for analysing the effects of economic policy changes, where X_t is a policy variable (e.g. an interest rate) and Y_t is a macroeconomic variable (e.g. inflation), and for modelling economic expectations. There are also strong theoretical links between ADL models and an important type of dynamic model discussed in more detail in Section 3.2.4, called an error correction model (ECM).

Although linear regression modelling with time series data was well-established by the 1970s, serious problems with the application of regression models to non-stationary variables were highlighted in a seminal journal article by Granger and Newbold (1974). These problems are discussed in more detail in the next section.

3.2.2 Spurious Regression

Granger and Newbold (1974) show in simulation experiments that if the regressand and regressors in a linear regression model are non-stationary but unrelated, then conventional regression techniques (e.g. OLS, t-tests, F-tests, R^2) will tend to lead the analyst to conclude that statistically significant relationships exist. More specifically, Granger and Newbold (1974) show using simulations that if statistically independent random walks are regressed on each other, the t-statistic for testing the significance of the regression slope will suggest a statistically significant

---

[4]For example, see White (1980) and Newey and West (1987).

relationship with a high probability, and the R^2 value for the regression will be close to one with a high probability, spuriously suggesting strong explanatory power. Granger and Newbold's simulations reveal that if a random walk of 50 observations in length is regressed on another independent random walk, conventional hypothesis tests will reject the null hypothesis of no relationship with a probability of around 75%. This probability rises with the number of unrelated independent random walk regressors. With five random walk regressors (all independent of the random walk regressand), the null hypothesis of no relationship will almost certainly be rejected using conventional tests.[5]

Granger and Newbold (1974) argue that signs of a spurious regression are statistically significant t-statistics and high R^2 values, combined with the Durbin–Watson test indicating strong autocorrelation. They suggest that to avoid the problem of spurious regression the first-differences of potentially non-stationary variables should be used rather than the levels of the variables. Recall from Chapter 2 that if a variable Y_t is integrated of order one, or I(1) for short, then the variable is non-stationary, but the first-difference of the variable is stationary (it is I(0)).

Prior to the work of Granger and Newbold (1974) these types of problems were not widely recognised. However, following this journal article it was clear that in the context of regression models, non-stationary variables should not be treated the same as stationary variables when carrying out statistical inference. These findings ultimately led to the development of new techniques and methodologies to deal with the particular subtleties of regression involving non-stationary variables, including the **cointegration** methodology proposed by Engle and Granger (1987), which is discussed in more detail in Section 3.2.4.

3.2.3 Unit Root Tests

The simulation results in Granger and Newbold (1974) highlight that orthodox regression and inference techniques do not always have their orthodox statistical properties when variables are non-stationary. A full understanding of the theoretical reasons for their simulation results took some time to emerge. This was provided by Phillips (1986) who proves theoretically that for a regression model consisting of independent random walks, the OLS estimates and R^2 converge to random variables.

In practice, prior to estimating a regression model it is important to determine whether the relevant variables are stationary or non-stationary. As discussed in Chapter 2, if the mean, variance and autocovariance for a variable are constant then

---

[5]See Granger and Newbold (1974) Table 2.

the variable is stationary. It can be shown that if Y_t is generated by a random walk model it is non-stationary,

$$Y_t = Y_{t-1} + \varepsilon_t \tag{3.32}$$

where we assume that $\varepsilon_t \sim IID(0, \sigma_\varepsilon^2)$. Conversely, if Y_t is generated by the AR(1) model,

$$Y_t = \phi_1 Y_{t-1} + \varepsilon_t, \quad |\phi_1| < 1 \tag{3.33}$$

then it is stationary. Therefore a test of the null hypothesis $H_0 : \phi_1 = 1$ in (3.33) is a test of the null hypothesis that Y_t is a particular type of non-stationary process. Dickey and Fuller (1979) consider testing this null hypothesis against the alternative hypothesis $H_1 : \phi_1 < 1$ using a t-test. They show that under the null hypothesis $H_0 : \phi_1 = 1$, the t-test for testing this null hypothesis does not converge asymptotically to a random variable with a Student's t-distribution, but in fact converges to a random variable with a non-standard distribution which is shifted to the left of the t-distribution. The statistical form of this distribution can be derived (see e.g. Dickey and Fuller, 1979; Phillips 1987).

The practical implications of Dickey and Fuller's (1979) findings are that if the critical values associated with Student's t-distribution are used when testing the null hypothesis $H_0 : \phi_1 = 1$, then empirically the test will be **over-sized**. In this context "size" is a statistical property meaning the probability of a false rejection of a true null hypothesis, or alternatively the probability of a Type I error. Consequently, in repeated trials of the test, the null hypothesis $H_0 : \phi_1 = 1$ would be incorrectly rejected too often if Student's t-distribution critical values were used. The t-test of the null hypothesis $H_0 : \phi_1 = 1$ in the AR(1) model against the alternative hypothesis $H_1 : \phi_1 < 1$ has become known as the Dickey–Fuller (DF) test. Fuller (1976) provides bespoke critical values for this test statistic, given here in Table A.5 in the Appendix, which we will refer to as "DF critical values".

The DF test and various extensions of it are popular in many different subject areas, including finance. The test is typically computed using a modified version of the AR(1) model,

$$\Delta Y_t = \phi_1^* Y_{t-1} + \varepsilon_t \tag{3.34}$$

where $\phi_1^* = (\phi_1 - 1)$. Thus the null hypothesis $H_0 : \phi_1^* = 0$ is equivalent to the null hypothesis $H_0 : \phi_1 = 1$, and the relevant test statistic is,

$$\tau = \frac{\hat{\phi}_1^*}{se(\hat{\phi}_1^*)} \tag{3.35}$$

The model (3.34) can be extended to allow for a constant and deterministic trend if necessary,

$$\Delta Y_t = \mu + \gamma t + \phi_1^* Y_{t-1} + \varepsilon_t \tag{3.36}$$

The DF test statistic is usually denoted by τ_μ if just a constant is included in the model, and τ_τ if both a constant and deterministic trend are included.

The DF test allows for first-order autoregressive dynamics; however, in practice some variables might contain higher order dynamics. For these cases the DF test is inappropriate and the augmented Dickey–Fuller (ADF) test proposed by Said and Dickey (1984) should instead be used, the general model being,

$$\Delta Y_t = \mu + \gamma t + \phi_1^* Y_{t-1} + \sum_{i=1}^{k} \beta_i \Delta Y_{t-i} + \varepsilon_t \tag{3.37}$$

Again the relevant test statistic is simply the t-statistic for testing $H_0 : \phi_1^* = 0$ which should be compared with the DF critical values. In practice, to decide on the value of k, a general-to-specific approach can be employed where k is set equal to a positive integer ($k^* \geq 1$), and then repeated estimation is carried out with decreasing values of k ($k = k^*, k^* - 1, k^* - 2, \ldots, 0$), computing an information criterion (e.g. AIC, SIC) for each model. The final ADF test statistic chosen is the one associated with the model that is chosen on the basis of the information criterion.

For both DF and ADF tests it is important to include a constant and/or deterministic trend if required. However, if a constant and/or trend is included when in fact it is not needed then the power of the test will be reduced compared with a correctly specified model. In this context **power** is a statistical term meaning the probability of correctly rejecting a false null hypothesis. Perron (1988) develops a testing procedure that helps when there is uncertainty regarding whether to include a constant and/or trend when carrying out a DF or ADF test. In practice, however, a decision is often made by visually analysing a graph of the variable.

In the DF and ADF models, under the null hypothesis $H_0 : \phi_1^* = 0$, the relevant AR lag-polynomial contains a root of unity, hence the DF and ADF tests are collectively referred to as **unit root** tests. Other popular unit root tests include those developed by Phillips and Perron (1988) and Kwiatkowski *et al.* (1992). Since the early literature on unit testing, this area has become hugely popular with academic econometricians and there are vast numbers of academic journal articles suggesting different unit root tests and extensions of the original DF and ADF tests to allow for structural breaks and non-linearity.[6]

3.2.4 Cointegration

The simulation results in Granger and Newbold (1974), discussed here in Section 3.2.2, ultimately led to the development of new techniques and methodologies for modelling non-stationary variables – the most important development being the cointegration methodology. We previously introduced the I(1) and I(0) notation in Chapter 2. To explain cointegration it is helpful to use this notation. If a

---

[6]For further details on many of the modified tests, see Maddala and Kim (1998).

variable must be differenced d times before it becomes stationary then it contains d unit roots and is said to be integrated of order d, denoted I(d) (where $d \geq 0$). Consider two variables Y_t and X_t, which are both I(d), where $d > 0$. If a vector β exists, such that $\varepsilon_t = Y_t - \beta X_t$ is of a lower order of integration, I($d - b$), where $b > 0$, then Engle and Granger (1987) define Y_t and X_t as cointegrated of order (d, b), denoted by CI(d, b). Thus, if Y_t and X_t are both I(1), and ε_t is I(0), then the two variables are CI(1,1). This is a simple example of cointegration and, as will be discussed in more detail below, the concept can be extended to more advanced single-equation models (e.g. including constants, deterministic trends and multiple regressors), and to multivariate models.

Cointegrated variables can be interpreted as being in a long-run equilibrium relationship, defined by a regression model. In contrast to spurious regressions between unrelated I(1) variables, cointegrated I(1) variables are genuinely statistically related to each other, and recognising cointegration can be extremely helpful for modelling and forecasting using regression models. To help clarify, two CI(1,1) variables Y_t and X_t are simulated and graphed in Figure 3.3. The following DGP is used,

$$Y_t = \beta_0 + \beta_1 X_t + \varepsilon_t \tag{3.38}$$

$$X_t = X_{t-1} + u_t \tag{3.39}$$

where $\beta_0 = 1, \beta_1 = 1, \varepsilon_t \sim NID(0, 1), u_t \sim NID(0, 1), E(\varepsilon_t u_t) = 0$. Here the long-run equilibrium model is $Y_t = 1 + X_t$.

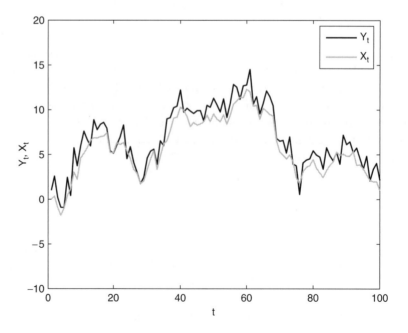

Figure 3.3   Cointegrated variables.

Note in Figure 3.3 how the variables Y_t and X_t seem to follow each other through time. This is a feature of variables that are cointegrated. The difference between the variables is not constant since in the short-run they deviate from the equilibrium model, but they eventually return to this equilibrium because the error term is stationary.

Engle and Granger (1987) propose a number of different tests for cointegration. One of the most popular tests in practice is a two-step approach that involves estimating the parameters of the appropriate regression model using OLS and then testing for a unit root in the fitted errors. Consider two variables Y_t and X_t and assume that both have been found to be I(1) using a DF or ADF test. If they are both I(1) then they can be cointegrated. The two-step test can be computed as follows.

Step (i)   Estimate a regression of Y_t on X_t using OLS for parameter estimation,

$$Y_t = \beta_0 + \beta_1 X_t + \varepsilon_t \tag{3.40}$$

and save the fitted errors,

$$\hat{\varepsilon}_t = Y_t - \hat{\beta}_0 - \hat{\beta}_1 X_t \tag{3.41}$$

Step (ii) Test for a unit root in the fitted errors $\hat{\varepsilon}_t$, taking care not to include a constant (or deterministic trend) if these terms were deemed necessary to be included in the long-run model (3.40). The DF or ADF test can be used. For example, if the DF test is used then the model employed for testing can be written,

$$\Delta\hat{\varepsilon}_t = \psi\hat{\varepsilon}_{t-1} + v_t \tag{3.42}$$

where we assume that $v_t \sim IID(0, \sigma_v^2)$. The relevant null and alternative hypotheses are,

$H_0 : \psi = 0$ no cointegration
$H_1 : \psi < 0$ cointegration

The test statistic is,

$$\tau = \frac{\hat{\psi}}{se(\hat{\psi})} \tag{3.43}$$

The relevant critical values are not the usual DF critical values and they depend on the number of regressors in the long-run model. The critical values for a test at the $p\%$ significance level can be computed using the following formula,

$$C(p) = \phi_\infty + \phi_1 T^{-1} + \phi_2 T^{-2} \tag{3.44}$$

where the values of $\phi_\infty, \phi_1, \phi_2$, which depend on the long-run model, have been computed by MacKinnon (1991) (a selection are given in the Appendix in Table A.6). If cointegration is found, a vector containing the estimated parameters in (3.41) is called the estimated **cointegrating vector**.

Engle and Granger (1987) show that if two variables are cointegrated then a dynamic **error correction model** (ECM) exists. This model links ΔY_t to ΔX_t and the lagged fitted error $\hat{\varepsilon}_{t-1}$ (the disequilibrium),

$$\Delta Y_t = \gamma \Delta X_t + \theta \hat{\varepsilon}_{t-1} + \eta_t \qquad (3.45)$$

The θ parameter is the **speed-of-adjustment** parameter in the ECM, as it measures the rate at which Y_t adjusts to the disequilibrium $\hat{\varepsilon}_{t-1}$ (for cointegrated variables, $\theta < 0$). A more general ECM often used in practice includes lags of ΔX_t and ΔY_t on the right-hand side rather than ΔX_t.

As a simple example, the fitted errors from the OLS regression of the Y_t in Figure 3.3 on the X_t in Figure 3.3 are graphed in Figure 3.4. Clearly in Figure 3.4 the fitted errors appear visually to be stationary. A DF test with no constant applied to the Y_t and X_t in Figure 3.3 gives -1.113 and -0.695, meaning that in both cases the null hypothesis of a unit root cannot be rejected at conventional significance levels using the DF critical values. A DF test with no constant applied to the fitted errors in Figure 3.4 gives $\tau = -11.939$, which on the basis of the relevant MacKinnon (1991) critical values means that the null hypothesis of no cointegration is rejected at the 1% level of significance.

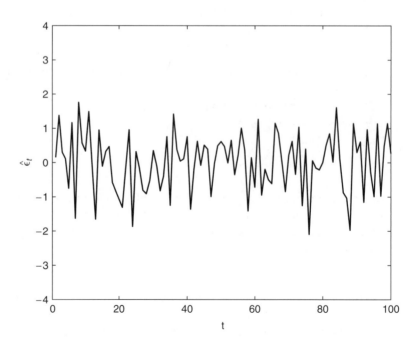

Figure 3.4   Fitted errors from cointegrating regression.

An attractive feature of the ECM when variables are CI(1,1) is that all of the variables in the ECM are stationary, since the I(1) variables enter in first-differenced form (ΔY_t and ΔX_t) and the lagged fitted error $\hat{\varepsilon}_{t-1}$ is by definition stationary if the variables are cointegrated. This means that when applied to a correctly specified ECM the popular inference techniques and diagnostic tests will have their standard statistical properties (e.g. t-tests, F-tests, and tests for heteroscedasticity and autocorrelation).

Extending cointegration to multiple regression models is less straightforward than one might imagine. The two-step approach to testing can be used starting with the OLS estimation of a multiple linear regression model. However, if the variables are cointegrated the estimated long-run model and ECM are not entirely informative since it can be shown that if there are more than two variables being considered, there can be more than one cointegrating vector; that is, there can be more than one set of parameters that, when attached to the variables, generates a stationary variable. In fact, with n variables up to $n-1$ independent cointegrating vectors can exist. Therefore if $n > 2$, the cointegrating vector obtained by estimating a multiple linear regression model by OLS might be some linear combination of the possible $n-1$ cointegrating vectors.

The single equation ECMs can be extended to the vector autoregressive (VAR) framework to allow for multiple cointegrating vectors. For example, in the case of three variables, define a vector,

$$\mathbf{Y}_t = [Y_{1,t} \ \ Y_{2,t} \ \ Y_{3,t}]' \tag{3.46}$$

Define the VAR model,

$$\mathbf{Y}_t = \boldsymbol{\varphi}_1 \mathbf{Y}_{t-1} + \boldsymbol{\varphi}_2 \mathbf{Y}_{t-2} + \cdots + \boldsymbol{\varphi}_p \mathbf{Y}_{t-p} + \boldsymbol{\varepsilon}_t \tag{3.47}$$

where $\boldsymbol{\varepsilon}_t$ denotes a vector of zero mean, IID random errors. This VAR model can be reformulated into a vector error-correction model (VECM),

$$\Delta \mathbf{Y}_t = \boldsymbol{\Gamma}_1 \Delta \mathbf{Y}_{t-1} + \boldsymbol{\Gamma}_2 \Delta \mathbf{Y}_{t-2} + \cdots + \boldsymbol{\Gamma}_{p-1} \Delta \mathbf{Y}_{t-p+1} + \boldsymbol{\Pi} \mathbf{Y}_{t-1} + \boldsymbol{\varepsilon}_t \tag{3.48}$$

$$\boldsymbol{\Pi} = \boldsymbol{\alpha}\boldsymbol{\beta}' \tag{3.49}$$

where here $\boldsymbol{\alpha}$ represents a matrix of speed-of-adjustment parameters and $\boldsymbol{\beta}$ is a matrix that contains the cointegrating vectors. For the case of $p = 2$ and two cointegrating vectors we can write the model out in full as,

$$
\begin{bmatrix} \Delta Y_{1,t} \\ \Delta Y_{2,t} \\ \Delta Y_{3,t} \end{bmatrix}
=
\begin{bmatrix} \Gamma_{11} & \Gamma_{12} & \Gamma_{13} \\ \Gamma_{21} & \Gamma_{22} & \Gamma_{23} \\ \Gamma_{31} & \Gamma_{32} & \Gamma_{33} \end{bmatrix}
\begin{bmatrix} \Delta Y_{1,t-1} \\ \Delta Y_{2,t-1} \\ \Delta Y_{3,t-1} \end{bmatrix}
$$

$$
+
\begin{bmatrix} \alpha_{11} & \alpha_{12} \\ \alpha_{21} & \alpha_{22} \\ \alpha_{31} & \alpha_{32} \end{bmatrix}
\begin{bmatrix} \beta_{11} & \beta_{21} & \beta_{31} \\ \beta_{12} & \beta_{22} & \beta_{32} \end{bmatrix}
\begin{bmatrix} Y_{1,t-1} \\ Y_{2,t-1} \\ Y_{3,t-1} \end{bmatrix}
+
\begin{bmatrix} \varepsilon_{1,t} \\ \varepsilon_{2,t} \\ \varepsilon_{3,t} \end{bmatrix}
\tag{3.50}
$$

The two cointegrating vectors are,

$$\begin{bmatrix} \beta_{11} & \beta_{21} & \beta_{31} \end{bmatrix} \qquad (3.51)$$

$$\begin{bmatrix} \beta_{12} & \beta_{22} & \beta_{32} \end{bmatrix} \qquad (3.52)$$

Therefore, rather than have a single ECM as in the bivariate case, in this case there are three ECMs, one for each variable in the system. These individual ECMs can be written,

$$\begin{aligned} \Delta Y_{1,t} = {} & \Gamma_{11}\Delta Y_{1,t-1} + \Gamma_{12}\Delta Y_{2,t-1} + \Gamma_{13}\Delta Y_{3,t-1} \\ & + \alpha_{11}(\beta_{11}Y_{1,t-1} + \beta_{21}Y_{2,t-1} + \beta_{31}Y_{3,t-1}) \\ & + \alpha_{12}(\beta_{12}Y_{1,t-1} + \beta_{22}Y_{2,t-1} + \beta_{32}Y_{3,t-1}) + \varepsilon_{1,t} \qquad (3.53) \end{aligned}$$

$$\begin{aligned} \Delta Y_{2,t} = {} & \Gamma_{21}\Delta Y_{1,t-1} + \Gamma_{22}\Delta Y_{2,t-1} + \Gamma_{23}\Delta Y_{3,t-1} \\ & + \alpha_{21}(\beta_{11}Y_{1,t-1} + \beta_{21}Y_{2,t-1} + \beta_{31}Y_{3,t-1}) \\ & + \alpha_{22}(\beta_{12}Y_{1,t-1} + \beta_{22}Y_{2,t-1} + \beta_{32}Y_{3,t-1}) + \varepsilon_{2,t} \qquad (3.54) \end{aligned}$$

$$\begin{aligned} \Delta Y_{3,t} = {} & \Gamma_{31}\Delta Y_{1,t-1} + \Gamma_{32}\Delta Y_{2,t-1} + \Gamma_{33}\Delta Y_{3,t-1} \\ & + \alpha_{31}(\beta_{11}Y_{1,t-1} + \beta_{21}Y_{2,t-1} + \beta_{31}Y_{3,t-1}) \\ & + \alpha_{32}(\beta_{12}Y_{1,t-1} + \beta_{22}Y_{2,t-1} + \beta_{32}Y_{3,t-1}) + \varepsilon_{3,t} \qquad (3.55) \end{aligned}$$

The parameters α_{ij} $(i = 1, 2, 3, j = 1, 2)$ measure the speed of adjustment of variable $Y_{i,t}$ to the equilibrium error associated with the jth cointegrating vector.

If variables are cointegrated then the OLS estimator of the parameters in a single-equation regression model for those variables (e.g. the static model in step (i) of the Engle and Granger (1987) approach) is consistent. Furthermore, the convergence of the estimated parameters to the population parameters with increases in the sample size will be faster than for regressions involving stationary variables. For this reason the OLS estimator in cointegrating regressions is said to be **superconsistent**. However, for small sample sizes, in practice the OLS estimator will often be affected by bias due to autocorrelation and because the regressors are endogenous. In this case a solution is to use a modified version of OLS for parameter estimation: for example, the fully modified OLS (FM-OLS) estimator of Phillips and Hansen (1990). It can be shown that t-tests computed in the usual way employing the FM-OLS estimator are asymptotically normal.

When dealing with more than two variables ML is usually employed to estimate the parameters of the VECM, and assuming the VECM is correctly specified, typically the ML results do not suffer from the small sample problems that affect OLS. Note that rather than just focus on testing the null hypothesis of no cointegration against the alternative hypothesis of cointegration, in the multivariate case the null hypothesis of no cointegration can be tested against the alternative hypothesis that a specific number of cointegrating vectors exist (see e.g. Johansen, 1988; Johansen and Juselius, 1992).

3.2.5 Forecasting with Regression Models

Forecasting with time series models is discussed in Chapter 2. For regression models involving time series data the forecasting theory is similar to that discussed in Chapter 2. Hence it can be shown that under certain assumptions the optimal forecast is given by the conditional mean. In the case of a bivariate linear regression model with stationary variables,

$$Y_t = \beta_0 + \beta_1 X_t + \varepsilon_t \tag{3.56}$$

the optimal b-step ahead forecast can be written,

$$\hat{Y}_{t+b} = \hat{\beta}_0 + \hat{\beta}_1 X_{t+b} \tag{3.57}$$

where $\hat{\beta}_0$ and $\hat{\beta}_1$ are the OLS estimates. Therefore, in order to compute a forecast of the regressand Y_t, we need to compute a forecast of the regressor X_t (assuming the future value of X_t is unknown). If we assume that the DGP for the regressor is a stationary AR variable, for example an AR(1) variable,

$$X_t = \delta + \phi_1 X_{t-1} + \varepsilon_t, \quad |\phi_1| < 1 \tag{3.58}$$

then the forecasting procedures discussed in Chapter 2 can be used. In this case it follows that the relevant forecasting function for X_t is,

$$\hat{X}_{t+b} = (\hat{\phi}_1^{b-1} + \hat{\phi}_1^{b-2} + \cdots + \hat{\phi}_1 + 1)\hat{\delta} + \hat{\phi}_1^b X_t \tag{3.59}$$

and so the optimal b-step ahead forecast of Y_t is,

$$\hat{Y}_{t+b} = \hat{\beta}_0 + \hat{\beta}_1 \hat{X}_{t+b} \tag{3.60}$$

This approach can be extended to multiple regression models and to different DGPs for the regressor(s).

If the regressand and regressors are non-stationary variables then the optimal forecasting model depends on whether the variables are cointegrated or not. In the case of bivariate cointegration the relevant forecasting model is the ECM. So, for example, if the appropriate ECM is,

$$\Delta Y_t = \gamma \Delta X_t + \theta \hat{\varepsilon}_{t-1} + \eta_t \tag{3.61}$$

where $\eta_t \sim NID(0, \sigma_\eta^2)$, the forecasting function for ΔY_t is,

$$\Delta \hat{Y}_{t+b} = \hat{\gamma} \Delta X_{t+b} + \hat{\theta} \varepsilon_{t+b-1} \tag{3.62}$$

A one-step ahead forecast of ΔY_t is computed using,

$$\Delta \hat{Y}_{t+1} = \hat{\gamma} \Delta \hat{X}_{t+1} + \hat{\theta} \hat{\varepsilon}_t \tag{3.63}$$

where $\Delta \hat{X}_{t+1}$ is a forecast of ΔX_{t+1}. The forecast of Y_{t+1} can then be obtained by adding the forecast of ΔY_{t+1} to the last value Y_t. Similarly, in the case of multivariate cointegration the relevant forecasting model is the VECM. The backtesting techniques discussed in Chapter 2 can be used to evaluate the forecasting accuracy of regression models.

3.3 Modelling and Forecasting Conditional Volatility

3.3.1 Univariate Conditional Volatility

The regression models discussed above are conditional mean models, in the sense that they give an estimate of the mean of the regressand conditional on the regressor(s). In finance, the variance and standard deviation of the return for an asset are used as a measure of the risk associated with investing in the asset. Hence the variance and standard deviation of asset returns are important inputs for many investment decisions. Rather than employ the unconditional variance and standard deviation of returns, in many areas of finance (e.g. risk management) it has become popular to use the conditional variance and the conditional standard deviation. **Conditional volatility** refers to the conditional standard deviation (the square root of the conditional variance), hence this area is called **conditional volatility modelling**. These amounts explicitly condition on the history of the asset return and in finance they are likely to be time-varying. Accurately modelling and forecasting conditional volatility requires specialist statistical techniques.[7]

For most variables of interest in finance, including asset returns, the conditional volatility of the variable is unobserved, since we typically only have a single observation on the variable at each time period. A simple way of estimating the conditional volatility of a variable Y_t at time t, σ_t, is to use a sample standard deviation,

$$\hat{\sigma}_t = \sqrt{\frac{\sum_{i=1}^{T}(Y_{t-i} - \overline{Y})^2}{T - 1}} \tag{3.64}$$

where T is the sample size and $\overline{Y}$ is the sample mean. In practice when producing estimates over time, T can be a fixed value or can expand with each additional observation. The conditional volatility estimated in this way using a fixed T is also called a **moving average** (MA) estimate of the conditional volatility. Note that if σ_t is time-varying then this estimate might be slow to capture changes in its value because the T historical observations used are equally weighted. In this case, using smaller samples to compute $\hat{\sigma}_t$ will often help.

---

[7]See Chapter 2 for a formal definition of the conditional variance.

The exponentially weighted moving average (EWMA) estimate of the conditional volatility of a variable Y_t is usually more successful than the MA approach if σ_t is time-varying. The EWMA estimate can be computed using,

$$\hat{\sigma}_t = \sqrt{(1 - \lambda) \sum_{i=1}^{T} \lambda^{i-1}(Y_{t-i} - \overline{Y})^2} \qquad (3.65)$$

In (3.65), historical observations are weighted with an exponentially decaying weight determined by λ ($0 < \lambda < 1$). The lower λ is, the less weight will be given to older observations relative to recent observations, which helps to capture changes in σ_t. However, if there is little or no variability in σ_t, then a low value for λ will produce an overly noisy estimate. Usually in finance λ is set to a number in the range 0.940–0.999.

The autoregressive conditional heteroscedasticity (ARCH) model introduced by Engle (1982) is an alternative way of estimating the conditional variance of a variable (and so the conditional volatility) that is more flexible than the MA or EWMA approaches. The simplest ARCH model can be written,

$$Y_t = \sigma_t \varepsilon_t \qquad (3.66)$$

$$\varepsilon_t \sim NID(0, 1) \qquad (3.67)$$

$$\sigma_t = (\alpha_0 + \alpha_1 Y_{t-1}^2)^{1/2} \qquad (3.68)$$

Assume that $\alpha_0 > 0, 0 \leq \alpha_1 < 1$, which ensures a positive and stationary conditional variance. It can be shown that the unconditional mean and variance of Y_t are,

$$E(Y_t) = 0 \qquad (3.69)$$

$$Var(Y_t) = \frac{\alpha_0}{(1 - \alpha_1)} \qquad (3.70)$$

and the conditional mean and variance of Y_t are,

$$E(Y_t|\Omega_{t-1}) = 0 \qquad (3.71)$$

$$Var(Y_t|\Omega_{t-1}) = \alpha_0 + \alpha_1 Y_{t-1}^2 \qquad (3.72)$$

where Ω_{t-1} contains the information on previous values of Y_t. Note therefore that the unconditional variance of Y_t is constant, but the conditional variance σ_t^2 is a function of Y_{t-1}^2, and will therefore be time-varying. It can be shown that for a conditionally normally distributed ARCH variable, the unconditional distribution of the variable will be non-normal. More specifically, the variable will have a fat-tailed unconditional distribution. Hence the ARCH model is particularly useful for analysing variables in finance where the unconditional distribution is thought to be fat-tailed.

The ARCH model given by (3.66)–(3.68) is a first-order model (an ARCH(1) model), and it can be extended to an ARCH(q) model with a constant as follows,

$$Y_t = \mu + \sigma_t \varepsilon_t \qquad (3.73)$$

$$\varepsilon_t \sim NID(0, 1) \tag{3.74}$$

$$\sigma_t = (\alpha_0 + \alpha_1(Y_{t-1} - \mu)^2 + \alpha_2(Y_{t-2} - \mu)^2 + \cdots + \alpha_q(Y_{t-q} - \mu)^2)^{1/2} \tag{3.75}$$

Note also that the conditional mean model (3.73) can be augmented with lags of Y_t (to make an AR-ARCH model) or with explanatory variables (to make a regression-ARCH model).

Although an iterative OLS approach can be shown to produce consistent estimates of the parameters in ARCH models (see e.g. Engle, 1982), ML estimation has superior asymptotic performance and is usually preferred in practice. The log-likelihood function for the ARCH(q) model above can be written,

$$\ln L(\alpha) = -\frac{1}{2} \sum_{t=q+1}^{T} \ln(\sigma_t^2) - \frac{1}{2} \sum_{t=q+1}^{T} \frac{(Y_t - \mu)^2}{\sigma_t^2} \tag{3.76}$$

This function can be numerically maximised with respect to the vector of relevant parameters to give a set of ML estimates of these parameters, and the estimated model can then be used to compute an estimate of the conditional volatility at each t. For example, in the case of the ARCH(q) model (3.73)–(3.75), the estimated conditional volatility can be written,

$$\hat{\sigma}_t = (\hat{\alpha}_0 + \hat{\alpha}_1(Y_{t-1} - \hat{\mu})^2 + \hat{\alpha}_2(Y_{t-2} - \hat{\mu})^2 + \cdots + \hat{\alpha}_q(Y_{t-q} - \hat{\mu})^2)^{1/2} \tag{3.77}$$

Rather than estimate an ARCH model only to find that the ARCH effect is statistically insignficant, it is sensible to pre-test the variable for ARCH and then only estimate an ARCH model if the test suggests that the ARCH effects are statistically significant. Engle (1982) proposes a simple Lagrange Multiplier (LM) test for ARCH. If the relevant variable is assumed to have a conditional mean of zero, then the test can be computed by estimating the following regression by OLS,

$$Y_t^2 = \alpha_0 + \alpha_1 Y_{t-1}^2 + \alpha_2 Y_{t-2}^2 + \cdots + \alpha_q Y_{t-q}^2 + u_t \tag{3.78}$$

where u_t is a zero mean IID error. If ARCH is not present, the estimated parameters $\hat{\alpha}_1, \hat{\alpha}_2, \ldots, \hat{\alpha}_q$ should be statistically insignificant from zero. To test the null hypothesis of no ARCH, $H_0 : \alpha_1 = \alpha_2 = \ldots = \alpha_q = 0$, a standard F-test can be used. If the variable is thought to have a non-zero conditional mean, then the test is essentially the same but with the Y_t^2 and lagged Y_t^2 terms replaced by the squared fitted errors and squared lagged fitted errors from the conditional mean equation.

The generalised ARCH (GARCH) model introduced by Bollerslev (1986) extends the ARCH model by including lags of the conditional variance in the model for the conditional variance. For example, a GARCH(p, q) model assuming a conditional mean of zero can be written,

$$Y_t = \sigma_t \varepsilon_t \tag{3.79}$$

$$\varepsilon_t \sim NID(0, 1) \tag{3.80}$$

$$\sigma_t = (\alpha_0 + \alpha_1 Y_{t-1}^2 + \alpha_2 Y_{t-2}^2 + \cdots + \alpha_q Y_{t-q}^2 + \beta_1 \sigma_{t-1}^2$$
$$+ \beta_2 \sigma_{t-2}^2 + \cdots + \beta_p \sigma_{t-p}^2)^{1/2} \tag{3.81}$$

where

$$\alpha_0 > 0, \alpha_i \geq 0, i = 1, 2, \ldots, q \tag{3.82}$$

$$\beta_j \geq 0, j = 1, 2, \ldots, p \tag{3.83}$$

It can be shown that a GARCH(p, q) model is theoretically equivalent to an infinite-order ARCH model, and therefore in practice the appropriate GARCH model will usually involve fewer terms than if an ARCH model is used. In finance, the model most often used in practice is the GARCH(1,1) model. Note that, for a GARCH(1,1) model, if $\alpha_1 + \beta_1 < 1$, the conditional variance reverts around the unconditional variance. If $\alpha_1 + \beta_1 = 1$, this is not the case and the GARCH model is called an integrated GARCH (IGARCH) model. In Figure 3.5 a simulated GARCH(1,1) variable is graphed, where $\alpha_0 = 0.10, \alpha_1 = 0.30$ and $\beta_1 = 0.60$. In Figure 3.6 the relevant conditional volatility is graphed.

In Figure 3.5 it can be seen that this degree of GARCH generates "spikes" in the data and clusters of extreme values. This is also a feature of ARCH models, hence the usefulness of ARCH and GARCH models in finance, where such features are often observed in data on asset returns. The ARCH and GARCH models discussed

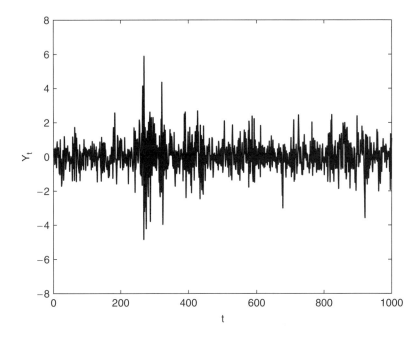

Figure 3.5   GARCH(1,1) variable.

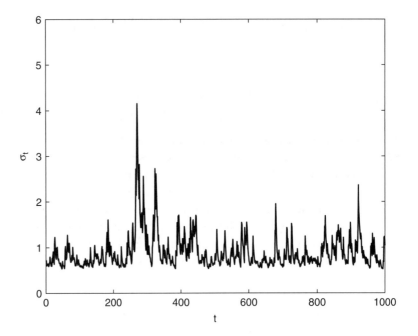

Figure 3.6   GARCH(1,1) conditional volatility.

above assume that Y_t is conditionally normally distributed (since ε_t is assumed to be normally distributed). Under this assumption, parameter estimation by ML is straightforward. For many variables conditional normality might be a reasonable assumption. However, if required, the parameters of ARCH and GARCH models can also be estimated using ML, explicitly allowing for conditional non-normality by assuming a particular non-normal distribution for ε_t (e.g. a Student's t-distribution might be assumed).

ARCH and GARCH models have proved to be hugely popular in finance, particularly for modelling and forecasting the conditional volatility of asset returns, and numerous extensions have been suggested. For example, Engle, Lilien and Robins (1987) suggest the model,

$$Y_t = \mu_t + \varepsilon_t \tag{3.84}$$

$$\varepsilon_t \sim NID(0, \sigma_t^2) \tag{3.85}$$

$$\sigma_t^2 = \alpha_0 + \sum_{i=1}^{q} \alpha_i \varepsilon_{t-i}^2 \tag{3.86}$$

$$\mu_t = \beta + \delta \sigma_t \tag{3.87}$$

This model is called the **ARCH-in-mean**, or ARCH-M model, since the conditional volatility is present in the conditional mean. A GARCH-M model could be similarly defined. Further extensions of ARCH and GARCH models have been proposed to allow for the asymmetric impact of financial and macroeconomic news on the conditional variance of the returns for financial assets (e.g. see Glosten, Jagannathan and Runkle, 1993).

In addition to ARCH and GARCH models, there are other parametric models that can be used to estimate the conditional volatility for a variable. For example, stochastic volatility (SV) models are an alternative approach in which the conditional volatility is modelled as a stochastic process. The standard SV model proposed by Taylor (1986) is,

$$Y_t = \mu + \sigma_t \varepsilon_t \qquad (3.88)$$

$$\varepsilon_t \sim NID(0, 1) \qquad (3.89)$$

$$\ln(\sigma_t) - \alpha = \phi \ln(\sigma_{t-1} - \alpha) + \eta_t \qquad (3.90)$$

$$\eta_t \sim NID(0, \sigma_\eta^2) \qquad (3.91)$$

Therefore in SV models the equation for the conditional volatility has an additive random error η_t, making it fundamentally different to ARCH/GARCH models, and considerably more flexible. However, estimating the parameters of SV models is more involved than for ARCH/GARCH models.[8]

Forecasts of conditional volatility can be computed easily using the MA and EWMA techniques and ARCH/GARCH models. For example the MA formula employing data up to time t can be used to compute a one-step ahead conditional volatility forecast. Similarly, the EWMA formula employing data up to time t can be used to compute a one-step ahead forecast. In practice, for high-frequency data on asset returns (e.g. daily data or higher), the sample mean return is often so small that when computing the conditional variance it can be assumed to be zero. In the EWMA case, and assuming $\overline{Y} = 0$, it can be shown that recursive one-step ahead forecasts of the conditional variance can be computed using the formula,

$$\hat{\sigma}_{t+1|t}^2 = \lambda \hat{\sigma}_{t|t-1}^2 + (1 - \lambda) Y_t^2 \qquad (3.92)$$

where $\hat{\sigma}_{t|t-1}^2$ denotes the EWMA conditional variance computed using the data up to time $t - 1$.

We have previously discussed that in time series models and regression models, when forecasting a variable Y_{t+b} the optimal b-step ahead forecast is given by the conditional expectation of the variable, with the population parameters replaced by estimates. The same approach can be used with ARCH/GARCH models to obtain the optimal forecast of the conditional variance (and therefore an optimal forecast of the conditional volatility). For example, the optimal one-step ahead forecast of the conditional volatility from a GARCH(1,1) model assuming a conditional mean of zero is,

$$\hat{\sigma}_{t+1} = (\hat{\alpha}_0 + \hat{\alpha}_1 Y_t^2 + \hat{\beta}_1 \hat{\sigma}_t^2)^{1/2} \qquad (3.93)$$

---

[8]See Taylor (2005) Chapter 11 for technical details.

where $\hat{\alpha}_0$, $\hat{\alpha}_1$ and $\hat{\beta}_1$, are consistent parameter estimates obtained using ML.[9] It can be shown that for optimal multi-step ahead forecasts the relevant forecasting function is,

$$\hat{\sigma}_{t+b} = \left[\hat{\alpha}_0 \sum_{i=1}^{b-1} (\hat{\alpha}_1 + \hat{\beta}_1)^{i-1} + (\hat{\alpha}_1 + \hat{\beta}_1)^{b-1} \hat{\sigma}_{t+1}^2 \right]^{1/2} \tag{3.94}$$

An important difference between the EWMA conditional volatility and ARCH/GARCH conditional volatility is that in the latter, under certain parameter values, the conditional volatility is mean reverting around the unconditional volatility. For example, in the GARCH(1,1) model this is true if $\alpha_1 + \beta_1 < 1$. Consequently, when computing conditional volatility forecasts the ARCH/GARCH forecasts will converge to the unconditional volatility as $b \to \infty$. EWMA forecasts do not have this feature. In finance, in practice the EWMA and GARCH conditional volatility forecasts are typically quite similar for short forecasting horizons, but they can differ more substantially for longer horizons.

In Chapter 2, evaluating the forecasts of a variable Y_t using backtesting is discussed and we showed how the forecast errors computed over a historical sample period (the backtesting period) play an important role. Evaluating conditional volatility forecasts is more difficult because the true conditional volatility σ_t is unobserved. One possible approach is to use a proxy for the true conditional volatility over the backtesting period. The conditional volatility forecasts can then be compared with this proxy to compute forecast errors which can be evaluated in the usual way (e.g. using RMSFE). For example, assuming a conditional mean of zero, as a proxy for the conditional variance of Y_t over the backtesting period, the squared value Y_t^2 might be used, since it can be shown that for ARCH/GARCH models Y_t^2 is an unbiased estimator of σ_t^2 (e.g. see Figlewski, 1997). This implies that the absolute value of the variable be used as a proxy for the conditional volatility. An alternative approach is to estimate the conditional volatility for each time period using high-frequency data over the time period (the **realised volatility**), and then use this as a proxy for the unknown true conditional volatility (e.g. see Anderson and Bollerslev, 1998). For example, for daily asset returns, use intra-daily data on returns to estimate the realised volatility. In finance, conditional volatility forecasts are often used as inputs to produce some other final forecast (e.g. in risk management when computing a forecast of potential loss), and other methods for evaluating this final forecast might be available. The evaluation of potential loss forecasts is discussed in more detail in Chapter 9.

3.3.2 Conditional Covariance Matrices

In finance and, in particular, risk management, the conditional covariances between variables such as asset returns will often be of interest, as well as the conditional

---

[9]Note that the log-likelihood function for the GARCH(1,1) model has the same general form as (3.76).

volatilities. Let $\mathbf{Y}_t$ be a vector of N variables,

$$\mathbf{Y}_t = [Y_{1,t} \quad Y_{2,t} \quad \cdots \quad Y_{N,t}]' \tag{3.95}$$

the conditional covariance matrix for $\mathbf{Y}_t$ is the $N \times N$ matrix,

$$\Sigma_t = \begin{bmatrix} \sigma_{1,t}^2 & \sigma_{12,t} & \cdots & \sigma_{1N,t} \\ \sigma_{21,t} & \sigma_{2,t}^2 & \cdots & \sigma_{2N,t} \\ \vdots & \vdots & \ddots & \vdots \\ \sigma_{N1,t} & \sigma_{N2,t} & \cdots & \sigma_{NN,t}^2 \end{bmatrix} \tag{3.96}$$

where the diagonal elements of Σ_t are the conditional variances for the variables in $\mathbf{Y}_t$ and the off-diagonal elements of Σ_t are the conditional covariances. The techniques and models discussed in Section 3.3.1 can be extended to estimate and forecast conditional covariance matrices. For example, assume that a sample of historical time series data on the N relevant variables is available, and for each variable there are T observations. Let $\mathbf{M}$ be the $T \times N$ matrix of this data in mean-deviation form,

$$\mathbf{M} = \begin{bmatrix} y_{1,t-1} & y_{2,t-1} & \cdots & y_{N,t-1} \\ y_{1,t-2} & y_{2,t-2} & \cdots & y_{N,t-2} \\ \vdots & \vdots & \ddots & \vdots \\ y_{1,t-T} & y_{2,t-T} & \cdots & y_{N,t-T} \end{bmatrix} \tag{3.97}$$

where $y_{i,t} = Y_{i,t} - \overline{Y}_i, i = 1, 2, \ldots, N$. A simple way of estimating the conditional covariance matrix is to use the sample covariance matrix,

$$\hat{\Sigma}_t = (T - 1)^{-1}(\mathbf{M}'\mathbf{M}) \tag{3.98}$$

When producing estimates over time, if T is a fixed value, (3.98) is called an MA estimate; the square root of the diagonal elements are the estimated conditional volatilities and the off-diagonal elements are the estimated conditional covariances. Similarly to the univariate case in (3.64), if the population conditional covariance matrix is time-varying then (3.98) might not be a particularly good estimator to use. It can be slow to capture changes in the population conditional covariance matrix due to the fact that the historical sample data employed is equally weighted. In this case a matrix version of the EWMA approach is likely to be more successful. The EWMA estimate of the conditional covariance matrix can be computed using,

$$\hat{\Sigma}_t = \tilde{\mathbf{M}}'\tilde{\mathbf{M}} \tag{3.99}$$

where

$$\tilde{\mathbf{M}} = \sqrt{\frac{1 - \lambda}{1 - \lambda^T}} \begin{bmatrix} y_{1,t-1} & y_{2,t-1} & \cdots & y_{N,t-1} \\ \sqrt{\lambda}y_{1,t-2} & \sqrt{\lambda}y_{2,t-2} & \cdots & \sqrt{\lambda}y_{N,t-2} \\ \vdots & \vdots & \ddots & \vdots \\ \sqrt{\lambda^{T-1}}y_{1,t-T} & \sqrt{\lambda^{T-1}}y_{2,t-T} & \cdots & \sqrt{\lambda^{T-1}}y_{N,t-T} \end{bmatrix} \tag{3.100}$$

and where $0 < \lambda < 1$.

Conditional covariance matrices can also be estimated using multivariate ARCH and GARCH models. As in the univariate case, there are many different types of multivariate ARCH/GARCH model. A seminal journal article on multivariate ARCH by Engle, Granger and Kraft (1984) introduces the bivariate ARCH model. Engle and Kroner (1995) discuss various multivariate GARCH models including the **VEC** model proposed by Bollerslev, Engle and Wooldridge (1988). This model utilises the *vech* matrix operator. For a symmetric matrix the *vech* operator stacks the lower triangular elements into a column. Assume that the vector $\mathbf{Y}_t$ contains N variables, each of which has a conditional mean of zero. A VEC multivariate GARCH model for the elements of the conditional covariance matrix can be written,

$$vech(\Sigma_t) = \alpha_0 + \sum_{i=1}^{q} \alpha_i vech(\mathbf{Y}_{t-i}\mathbf{Y}'_{t-i}) + \sum_{j=1}^{p} \beta_j vech(\Sigma_{t-j}) \qquad (3.101)$$

where α_0 is an $N(N+1)/2 \times 1$ vector, and α_i and β_j are $\left[\dfrac{N(N+1)}{2} \times \dfrac{N(N+1)}{2} \right]$ matrices of parameters. In the case of $N=2$ with $p=q=1$, the VEC multivariate GARCH(1,1) model for the elements of the conditional covariance matrix can be written,

$$
\begin{bmatrix} \sigma_{1,t}^2 \\ \sigma_{12,t} \\ \sigma_{2,t}^2 \end{bmatrix}
=
\begin{bmatrix} \alpha_{0,11} \\ \alpha_{0,21} \\ \alpha_{0,31} \end{bmatrix}
+
\begin{bmatrix} \alpha_{1,11} & \alpha_{1,12} & \alpha_{1,13} \\ \alpha_{1,21} & \alpha_{1,22} & \alpha_{1,23} \\ \alpha_{1,31} & \alpha_{1,32} & \alpha_{1,33} \end{bmatrix}
\begin{bmatrix} Y_{1,t-1}^2 \\ Y_{1,t-1}Y_{2,t-1} \\ Y_{2,t-1}^2 \end{bmatrix}
$$

$$
+
\begin{bmatrix} \beta_{1,11} & \beta_{1,12} & \beta_{1,13} \\ \beta_{1,21} & \beta_{1,22} & \beta_{1,23} \\ \beta_{1,32} & \beta_{1,32} & \beta_{1,33} \end{bmatrix}
\begin{bmatrix} \sigma_{1,t-1}^2 \\ \sigma_{12,t-1} \\ \sigma_{2,t-1}^2 \end{bmatrix}
\qquad (3.102)
$$

As in the univariate case, in practice typically the parameter vectors and matrices in multivariate GARCH models can be consistently estimated by ML. The estimated parameters can then be used to compute estimates of the conditional variance and covariance terms, and hence the conditional covariance matrix. A weakness of this type of model is that restrictive conditions need to be imposed to ensure that the estimated covariance matrix is positive-definite. If the estimated covariance matrix is not positive-definite this can be problematic if it is to be used in portfolio optimisation and/or risk management. Another practical weakness is the large number of parameters to be estimated.

Several alternative multivariate GARCH models have been proposed that have fewer parameters than the equivalent VEC model: see, for example, Bollerslev (1990). In Bollerslev (1990) a simplified conditional covariance matrix is used,

$$\Sigma_t = diag(\sigma_{1,t}, \dots, \sigma_{N,t})\rho diag(\sigma_{1,t}, \dots, \sigma_{N,t}) \qquad (3.103)$$

where $diag(\sigma_{1,t}, \ldots, \sigma_{N,t})$ denotes a diagonal matrix with GARCH(p, q) conditional volatilities as the main diagonal and,

$$\boldsymbol{\rho} = \begin{bmatrix} 1 & \rho_{12} & \cdots & \rho_{1N} \\ \rho_{21} & 1 & \cdots & \rho_{2N} \\ \vdots & \vdots & \ddots & \vdots \\ \rho_{N1} & \rho_{N2} & \cdots & 1 \end{bmatrix} \tag{3.104}$$

where ρ_{ij} is the correlation coefficient measuring the correlation of variable i with variable j.

In the case of $N = 2$ and $p = q = 1$,

$$\boldsymbol{\Sigma}_t = \begin{bmatrix} \sigma_{1,t} & 0 \\ 0 & \sigma_{2,t} \end{bmatrix} \begin{bmatrix} 1 & \rho_{12} \\ \rho_{21} & 1 \end{bmatrix} \begin{bmatrix} \sigma_{1,t} & 0 \\ 0 & \sigma_{2,t} \end{bmatrix} \tag{3.105}$$

where $\sigma_{1,t}$ and $\sigma_{2,t}$ are individual GARCH(1,1) conditional volatilities. In this case, the estimated conditional covariance matrix $\hat{\boldsymbol{\Sigma}}_t$ will be positive-definite under the usual GARCH restrictions and the model has significantly fewer parameters than the equivalent VEC model. In fact, with $N = 2, p = q = 1$, there are only seven parameters to be estimated (three GARCH parameters for each variable and the correlation coefficient ρ_{12}). A further extension of this type of multivariate GARCH model by Engle (2002), called the Dynamic Conditional Correlation (DCC) model, has also become popular in empirical work. This model relaxes the assumption of constant correlations and allows $\boldsymbol{\rho}$ to be time-varying. Forecasts of the conditional covariance matrix can be computed using the techniques and models discussed in this section. For example, the MA or EWMA techniques employing data up to time t can be used, or a forecast can be computed from one of the multivariate GARCH models by applying the conditional expectations rule previously discussed.

3.4 Summary

This chapter has reviewed regression modelling and volatility modelling. We have discussed classical linear regression and the importance of recognising if the variables being modelled are non-stationary. Ignoring possible non-stationarity can result in spurious conclusions being drawn from regression models about the strength of the relationships between variables. Testing for non-stationarity using unit root tests has been discussed, as has the cointegration methodology for modelling non-stationary variables. In finance, the conditional volatilities and the conditional covariance matrix for variables such as asset returns contain important information for analysts. This information is particularly important for effective risk management. Hence this chapter has reviewed the main approaches to modelling and forecasting conditional volatility and conditional covariance matrices.

3.5 End of Chapter Questions[10]

Q1. Simulate 100 values for Y_t and X_t using the following DGP,

$$Y_t = 2 + 2.5X_t + \varepsilon_t$$
$$\varepsilon_t \sim NID(0, 1)$$
$$X_t = 0.30X_{t-1} + u_t$$
$$u_t \sim NID(0, 1)$$

(a) Using the simulated data, estimate the parameters of a bivariate linear regression model for Y_t and X_t employing OLS and test the statistical significance of the estimated parameters using t-tests.

(b) Graph a scatterplot of Y_t and X_t and the fitted regression line.

(c) Compute the R^2 and Adjusted-R^2 for the estimated model.

Q2. Simulate 100 values for Y_t from each of the following DGPs, and in each case test for a unit root using the appropriate DF test or ADF test.

(a)

$$Y_t = Y_{t-1} + \varepsilon_t$$
$$\varepsilon_t \sim NID(0, 1)$$

(b)

$$Y_t = 0.30Y_{t-1} + \varepsilon_t$$
$$\varepsilon_t \sim NID(0, 1)$$

(c)

$$Y_t = 0.50 + 0.30Y_{t-1} + 0.30\Delta Y_{t-1} + 0.15\Delta Y_{t-2} + \varepsilon_t$$
$$\varepsilon_t \sim NID(0, 1)$$

(d)

$$Y_t = 0.50 + 0.50t + 0.30Y_{t-1} + 0.30\Delta Y_{t-1} + 0.15\Delta Y_{t-2} + \varepsilon_t$$
$$\varepsilon_t \sim NID(0, 1)$$

Q3. Simulate 300 values for Y_t and X_t using the following DGP:

$$Y_t = 2 + 0.50X_t + 0.25X_{t-1} + 0.25Y_{t-1} + \varepsilon_t$$
$$\varepsilon_t \sim NID(0, 1)$$
$$X_t = X_{t-1} + u_t$$
$$u_t \sim NID(0, 1)$$

---

[10]A guide to answering these questions and relevant MATLAB® programs are given on the companion website (www.wileyeurope.com/college/sollis).

Use the Engle–Granger two-step approach to test for whether Y_t and X_t are cointegrated.

Q4. Write out the forecasting function for computing an optimal one-step ahead forecast of Y_t in Question 3 from the appropriate ECM.

Q5. Simulate 1000 values for Y_t using the following DGP,

$$Y_t = \sigma_t \varepsilon_t$$
$$\varepsilon_t \sim NID(0, 1)$$
$$\sigma_t = (0.10 + 0.30 Y_{t-1}^2 + 0.60 \sigma_{t-1}^2)^{1/2}$$

(a) Using the first 900 simulated values for Y_t, estimate the parameters of a GARCH(1,1) model and graph the estimated conditional volatility obtained.

(b) Compute and graph one-step ahead forecasts of the final 100 values of the conditional volatility σ_t.

(c) Evaluate the accuracy of your GARCH(1,1) forecasts for part (b).

3.6 References

Anderson, T.G. and T. Bollerslev (1998) Answering the skeptics: yes, standard volatility models do provide accurate forecasts, *International Economic Review*, 39, 885–905.

Bollerslev, T. (1986) Generalized autoregressive conditional heteroscedasticity, *Journal of Econometrics*, 31, 307–327.

Bollerslev, T. (1990) Modeling the coherence in short-run nominal exchange rates: a multivariate generalized ARCH approach, *Review of Economics and Statistics*, 72, 498–505.

Bollerslev, T., Engle, R.F. and J.M. Wooldridge (1988) A capital asset pricing model with time varying covariances, *Journal of Political Economy*, 96, 116–131.

Breusch, T.S. (1978) Testing for autocorrelation in dynamic linear models, *Australian Economic Papers*, 17, 334–355.

Breusch, T.S. and A.R. Pagan (1979) A simple test for heteroscedasticity and random coefficient variation, *Econometrica*, 47, 1287–1294.

Dickey, D.A. and W.A. Fuller (1979) Distribution of the estimators for autoregressive time series with a unit root, *Journal of the American Statistical Association*, 74, 427–431.

Durbin, J. and G.S. Watson (1950) Testing for serial correlation in least squares regression, I, *Biometrika*, 37, 409–428.

Durbin, J. and G.S. Watson (1951) Testing for serial correlation in least squares regression, II, *Biometrika*, 38, 159–179.

Engle, R.F. (1982) Autoregressive conditional heteroscedasticity with estimates of the variance of United Kingdom inflation, *Econometrica*, 50, 987–1007.

Engle, R. (2002) Dynamic conditional correlation – a simple class of multivariate GARCH models, *Journal of Business and Economic Statistics*, 20, 339–350.

Engle, R. and C.W.J. Granger (1987) Co-integration and error correction: representation, estimation and testing, *Econometrica*, 55, 251–276.

Engle, R.F. and K.F. Kroner (1995) Multivariate simultaneous generalized ARCH, *Econometric Theory*, 11, 122–150.

Engle, R.F., Granger, C.W.J. and D. Kraft (1984) Combining competing forecasts of inflation using a bivariate ARCH Model, *Journal of Economic Dynamics and Control*, 8, 151–165.

Engle, R.F., Lilien, D.M. and R.P. Robins (1987) Estimating time-varying risk premia in the term structure: the ARCH-M model, *Econometrica*, 55, 391–407.

Figlewski, S. (1997) Forecasting volatility, *Financial Markets, Institutions and Instruments*, 6, 1–88.

Fuller, W.A. (1976) *Introduction to Statistical Time Series*, New York: John Wiley & Sons.

Glosten, L.R., Jagannathan, R. and D. Runkle (1993) Relationship between the expected value and the volatility of the nominal excess return on stocks, *Journal of Finance*, 48, 1779–1801.

Godfrey, L. (1978) Testing against general autoregressive and moving average error models when the regressors include lagged dependent variables, *Econometrica*, 46, 1293–1302.

Granger, C.W.J. and P. Newbold (1974) Spurious regressions in econometrics, *Journal of Econometrics*, 2, 111–120.

Greene, W. (2008) *Econometric Analysis*, 6th edn. New Jersey: Pearson Education.

Gujarati, D.N. and D.C. Porter (2009) *Basic Econometrics*, 5th edn. New York: McGraw-Hill Higher Education.

Hamilton, J.G. (1994) *Time Series Analysis*. Princeton: Princeton University Press.

Johansen, S. (1988) Statistical analysis of cointegrating vectors, *Journal of Economic Dynamics and Control*, 12, 231–254.

Johansen, S. and K. Juselius (1992) Testing structural hypotheses in a multivariate cointegration analysis of PPP and the UIP for UK, *Journal of Econometrics*, 53, 211–244.

Kwiatkowski, D, Phillips, P.C.B., Schmidt, P. and Y. Shin (1992) Testing the null hypothesis of stationarity against the alternative of a unit root, *Journal of Econometrics*, 54, 159–178.

MacKinnon, J.G. (1991) Critical values for cointegration tests. In Engle, R.F. and C.W.J. Granger (eds) *Long-Run Economic Relationships: Readings in Cointegration*. Oxford: Oxford University Press.

Maddala, G.S. and I.-M. Kim (1988) *Unit Roots, Cointegration and Structural Change*. Cambridge: Cambridge University Press.

Newey, W.K. and K.D. West (1987) A simple, positive-definite, heteroskedasticity and autocorrelation consistent covariance matrix, *Econometrica*, 55, 703–708.

Perron, P. (1988) Trends and random walks in macroeconomic time series: further evidence from a new approach, *Journal of Economic Dynamics and Control*, 12, 297–332.

Phillips, P.C.B. (1986) Understanding spurious regressions in econometrics, *Journal of Econometrics*, 33, 311–340.

Phillips, P.C.B. (1987) Time series regression with a unit root, *Econometrica*, 55, 277–301.

Phillips, P.C.B. and B.E. Hansen (1990) Statistical inference in instrumental variables regression with I(1) processes, *Review of Economic Studies*, 57, 99–125.

Phillips, P.C.B and P. Perron (1988) Testing for a unit root in time series regression, *Biometrika*, 75, 335–346.

Said, E. and D.A. Dickey (1984) Testing for unit roots in autoregressive moving average models of unknown order, *Biometrika*, 71, 599–607.

Taylor, S.J. (1986) *Modelling Financial Time Series*. Chichester: John Wiley & Sons.

Taylor, S.J. (2005) *Asset Price Dynamics, Volatility, and Prediction*. Princeton: Princeton University Press.

White, H. (1980) A heteroscedasticity-consistent covariance matrix estimator and a direct test for heteroscedasticity, *Econometrica*, 48, 817–838.

Chapter 4
Portfolio Theory and Asset Allocation

4.1 Introduction

This chapter discusses the empirical application of modern portfolio theory (MPT) to compute optimal portfolios of financial assets. MPT has its origins in a seminal journal article on portfolio selection by Markowitz (1952). Prior to this article popular advice when constructing portfolios of risky assets was that investors should focus primarily on analysing the assets' discounted expected future returns, since it was widely believed that portfolio risk could be driven to zero through sufficient diversification (see e.g. Williams, 1938; Rubinstein 2002). Markowitz (1952) argues that because of the interrelationships between asset returns, diversification cannot eliminate all portfolio risk. He investigates the simple normative rule that investors view expected return as desirable and risk, measured by the variance of returns, as undesirable (the expected return-variance (E-V) rule). Markowitz (1952) shows formally how the expected return and the variance of the return for a portfolio can be computed as a function of the expected returns, variances and covariances of the returns for the constituent assets. He shows that when constructing portfolios the E-V rule implies that investors should focus on the performance of different portfolios of assets as measured by combinations of expected portfolio return and portfolio risk, and they should choose from diversified portfolios that maximise expected return for a given level of risk. Markowitz (1952) labels these portfolios **efficient**. Tobin (1958) and Markowitz (1959) build on these ideas and introduce a risk-free asset into the asset allocation problem. The importance of this body of work cannot be overstated. It forms the foundations of MPT and much of modern financial theory.[1]

Prior to focusing on MPT in more detail, we begin this chapter by explaining how to compute the rates of return for assets (the asset **returns**). We also briefly discuss the **dividend discount model** (DDM), which can be used to value individual stocks. The penultimate section of the main text presents six empirical examples in which MPT is applied to US stock market data to compute optimal portfolios.

4.2 Returns

Let P_t denote the asset price at time t (e.g. a stock price), and let p_t denote the natural logarithm of this price, $p_t \equiv \ln(P_t)$ (the log-price). Asset returns can be computed in two different ways. The **simple return** from period $t-1$ to period t is defined as,

$$r_t \equiv \frac{P_t - P_{t-1}}{P_{t-1}} \qquad (4.1)$$

This amount will be a decimal value, so if a percentage return is required, multiply r_t by 100. Dividends (D_t) can be incorporated as follows,

$$r_t \equiv \frac{P_t - P_{t-1} + D_t}{P_{t-1}} \qquad (4.2)$$

The return computed using (4.1) or (4.2) can also be called the **holding period return**. In empirical work in finance, rather than use the simple return, the return computed by taking the first-difference of the log-price is often used,

$$r_t \equiv p_t - p_{t-1} \qquad (4.3)$$

---

[1]See Markowitz (1999) and Rubinstein (2002) for further details on the history and impact of the ideas expressed in Markowitz (1952), and Fabozzi, Gupta and Markowitz (2002) for further details on the legacy of MPT. There are many established textbooks on investment analysis that provide a comprehensive coverage of MPT and the links between MPT and other areas of financial theory: for example, see Elton and Gruber (1995), Sharpe, Alexander and Bailey (1998), Reilly and Brown (2006) and Bodie, Kane and Marcus (2009).

The return computed using (4.3) is called the **log-return** and is equal to the **continuously compounded return**. For small values, r_t computed using (4.3) is approximately equal to r_t computed using (4.1).

The primary reason why the log-return is often preferred in empirical work is that under standard assumptions it has some convenient statistical properties that help simplify empirical analysis. For example, it can be shown that log-returns are additive over time. Therefore, the log-return for a horizon of n-periods, $r_{t+1:t+n}$, can be computed by summing the one-period log-returns,

$$r_{t+1:t+n} = \sum_{i=1}^{n} r_{t+i} \tag{4.4}$$

Furthermore, if the log-return is IID, the variance of the n-period log-return $\sigma^2_{t+1:t+n}$ can be computed by multiplying the variance of the one-period log-return σ^2_{t+1} by n,

$$\sigma^2_{t+1:t+n} = n\sigma^2_{t+1} \tag{4.5}$$

Similarly the covariance of the n-period log-return with another log-return can be computed by multiplying the one-period covariance by n.

In MPT, the return for a portfolio of assets is assumed to be equal to the appropriately weighted sum of the returns for the individual assets. Log-returns do not have this property but simple returns do. Therefore if log-returns are used in an empirical application of MPT rather than simple returns there will be an associated approximation error. Note, however, that this approximation error might be quite small, and in practice log-returns are often employed.

The standard statistical model in financial economics for the log-price is the random walk model,

$$p_t = \mu + p_{t-1} + \varepsilon_t \tag{4.6}$$

where typically it is assumed either that $\varepsilon_t \sim IID(0, \sigma^2_\varepsilon)$, or $\varepsilon_t \sim NID(0, \sigma^2_\varepsilon)$, or that ε_t is a more general GARCH process; for the moment, assume that $\varepsilon_t \sim NID(0, \sigma^2_\varepsilon)$.[2] μ is the **drift** parameter – a constant parameter that can be positive or negative (or zero). A positive (negative) drift is consistent with an upwards (downwards) trend in prices.[3]

The random walk model is a popular statistical model for the log-price because under certain assumptions it can be shown to be consistent with an informationally efficient financial market (this point will be discussed in more detail in Chapter 6).

---

[2] See Chapter 3 for a recap on GARCH models.
[3] The statistical properties of a variable generated by a random walk are discussed in Chapters 2 and 3. Recall that such a variable is non-stationary.

Working with the random walk model for the log-price is also convenient from a methodological point of view because it is consistent with the fact that in practice raw prices are always positive. It follows from (4.6) that raw prices are generated by,

$$P_t = P_{t-1}e^{(\mu + \varepsilon_t)} \tag{4.7}$$

and so if $P_0 > 0$ then $P_t > 0$. Under the assumption that ε_t is normally distributed, it follows from (4.7) that P_t is log-normally distributed. Note also that since ε_t is assumed to be normally distributed, (4.6) implies that the log-return is a normally distributed random variable, which simplifies empirical work involving quantiles of the probability density function (PDF) for returns. To see this more clearly rearrange (4.6) to get,

$$r_t = \mu + \varepsilon_t \tag{4.8}$$

where r_t is the log-return. It follows, therefore, that $r_t \sim NID(\mu, \sigma_\varepsilon^2)$. It is important to note that if the data generation process (DGP) for p_t is (4.6), then although p_t is non-stationary, the log-return r_t is stationary. It is straightforward to show this by computing the mean, variance and autocovariance of r_t, as defined by (4.8),

$$E(r_t) = \mu \tag{4.9}$$

$$Var(r_t) = E[r_t - E(r_t)]^2 = \sigma^2 \tag{4.10}$$

$$Cov(r_t, r_{t-\tau}) = E[(r_t - E(r_t))(r_{t-\tau} - E(r_t))] = 0, \tau \neq 0 \tag{4.11}$$

Clearly none of these is time-varying, which satisfies the criterion for stationarity discussed in Chapter 2. To help clarify, a simulated random walk Y_t with $\varepsilon_t \sim NID(0, 1)$ and a starting value of zero ($Y_0 = 0$) is graphed in Figure 4.1. A simulated log-normal price series obtained using (4.7) as the DGP is graphed in Figure 4.2. The first-difference of the log of the price series given in Figure 4.2 is graphed in Figure 4.3 (a series of simulated log-returns). In all cases $\mu = 0$.

Note that in Figure 4.1 the simulated random walk contains negative values, but that in Figure 4.2, as expected, all of the values are positive. In Figure 4.3 the returns fluctuate between positive and negative values around an unconditional mean of zero (since $\mu = 0$).

In the model used above we have assumed that the conditional variance is constant. However, for many financial assets, data suggest that the conditional variance of the returns is time-varying and that extreme returns cluster. In Figures 4.4–4.6 the daily log-returns for three popular stocks are graphed over the sample period 02/01/98–31/12/08 (Exxon Mobil Corporation, General Electric Company, Microsoft Corporation).

There is an obvious visual difference in the general pattern of the returns in Figures 4.4–4.6 and the simulated returns in Figure 4.3. In Figures 4.4–4.6

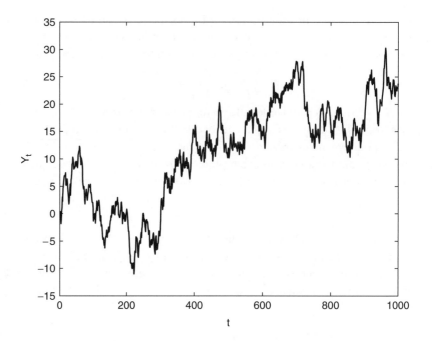

Figure 4.1 Simulated random walk.

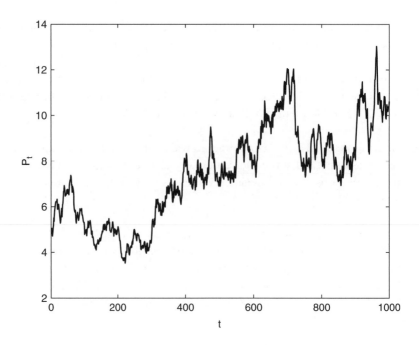

Figure 4.2 Simulated log-normal prices.

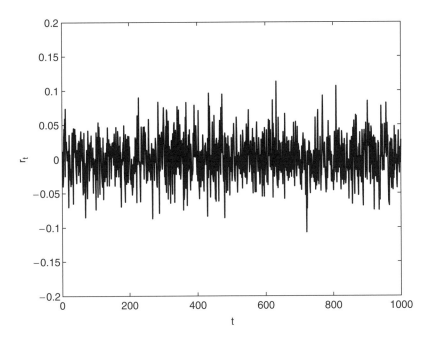

Figure 4.3 Simulated returns.

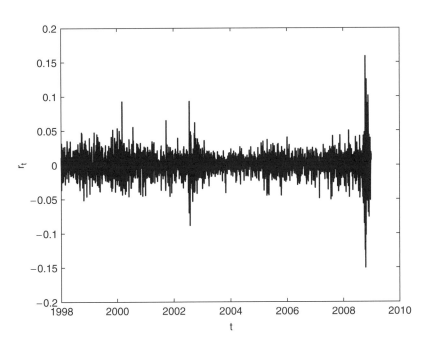

Figure 4.4 Exxon returns, 02/01/98–31/12/08.

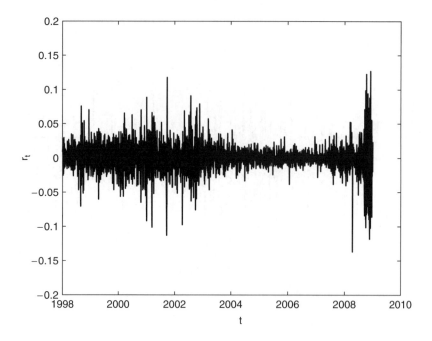

Figure 4.5 General Electric returns, 02/01/98–31/12/08.

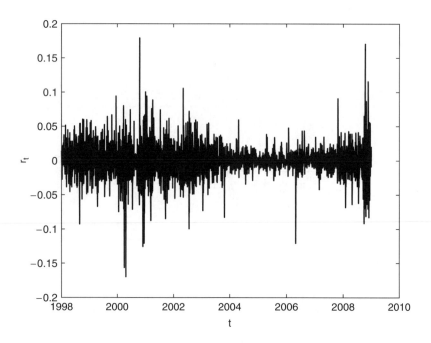

Figure 4.6 Microsoft returns, 02/01/98–31/12/08.

the graphs strongly suggest that the conditional variance of the returns is time-varying (there is conditional heteroscedasticity). For General Electric and Microsoft, there are clusters of very large positive and negative returns from early 2000 through to the end of 2001 – coinciding with the peak of the dot-com bubble and subsequent crash. For all three stocks, there are significantly fewer extreme returns between 2004 and 2006, and there is a dramatic increase in extreme returns in 2008 corresponding to the global financial crisis.

The variance and standard deviation of asset returns are fundamentally important concepts in finance. In orthodox financial theory, investors are assumed to quantify the risk of an investment using the variance of the return associated with that investment (or the standard deviation).[4] As discussed in more detail below, MPT suggests that investors should seek to maximise the risk-adjusted expected excess portfolio return. Therefore a high-risk portfolio might be preferred to a low-risk portfolio if the expected return associated with the former is sufficiently higher than the expected return associated with the latter to compensate for the additional risk.

The random walk model for p_t can be extended to allow for a time-varying conditional variance as follows,

$$p_t = \mu + p_{t-1} + \sigma_t \varepsilon_t \qquad (4.12)$$

where $\varepsilon_t \sim NID(0, 1)$. σ_t^2 is the conditional variance of the log-returns r_t. We could let σ_t^2 evolve according to a GARCH model. For example, in the GARCH(1,1) case,

$$\sigma_t^2 = \alpha_0 + \alpha_1 (r_{t-1} - \mu)^2 + \beta_1 \sigma_{t-1}^2 \qquad (4.13)$$

where $\alpha_0 > 0, \alpha_1 > 0, \beta_1 > 0, \alpha_1 + \beta_1 < 1$, and the unconditional mean and variance of r_t are,

$$E(r_t) = \mu \qquad (4.14)$$

$$Var(r_t) = \frac{\alpha_0}{(1 - \alpha_1 - \beta_1)} \qquad (4.15)$$

Therefore, although in this case r_t is conditionally heteroscedastic, it is unconditionally homoscedastic. It can be shown that the unconditional distribution of r_t in this case is non-normal; more specifically, it is leptokurtic meaning that it has a higher peak than the normal distribution and fatter tails. Note however that conditional on σ_t, r_t is normally distributed.

---

[4]In MPT, and more generally in financial economics, the variance and standard deviation of the return for an asset/portfolio are often both referred to as the risk of the asset/portfolio.

4.3 Dividend Discount Model

In financial economics the **intrinsic value** of an asset is defined as the present value of the future cash flows associated with the asset. A formula for computing the present value of a series of annual cash-flows is,

$$V_t = \sum_{i=1}^{N} \left[\frac{CF_{t+i}}{(1+k)^i} \right] \tag{4.16}$$

where here we assume that CF_{t+i} denotes the cash-flow for year $t+i$, k is an appropriate annual discount rate (assume this is constant over time), and N is the number of annual cash-flows. The discount rate k can be thought of as the **required rate of return** for investing in the asset, which will depend on the risk-free rate of return available to investors, and a **risk premium** for bearing any additional risk associated with the asset relative to a risk-free asset. Note that as k increases, the present value of the cash flows falls, and vice versa. The model given by (4.16) is a type of present value model (PVM) (also called a discounted cash flow model (DCF)). Whilst the random walk model is a statistical model and not an explanatory model like the PVM, Samuelson (1973) shows that these two models can be reconciled under certain assumptions.

PVMs have a long history in finance (e.g. see Williams, 1938) and they are popular tools for investment analysis. In the case of stocks, the relevant cash flows are the dividends over the investment horizon D_t and the price of the stock at the end of the investment horizon P_N. Therefore we can write,

$$V_t = \sum_{i=1}^{N} \left[\frac{D_{t+i}}{(1+k)^i} \right] + \frac{P_N}{(1+k)^N} \tag{4.17}$$

An obvious practical difficulty with this PVM is that in practice the final stock price is unknown and a random variable, and the dividend values into the future are usually unknown random variables. Therefore, to use this PVM it appears that forecasts of these amounts are required. Note, however, that we do not actually have to compute forecasts if some simplifying assumptions are made. If future prices are assumed to be equal to the discounted value of the relevant future dividends, then after substitution the formula becomes,

$$V_t = \sum_{i=1}^{\infty} \left[\frac{D_{t+i}}{(1+k)^i} \right] \tag{4.18}$$

If dividends are assumed to grow at rate g, then future dividends can be written as a function of the current dividend,

$$D_{t+i} = D_t(1+g)^i \tag{4.19}$$

Substituting (4.19) into (4.18) and simplifying gives,

$$V_t = \frac{D_t(1+g)}{k-g} \tag{4.20}$$

Therefore, under these assumptions, the intrinsic value of the stock can be computed just using the current dividend, the required rate of return and the growth rate of dividends. This particular model, proposed by Gordon (1959), is called the constant growth dividend discount model (DDM), and also the **Gordon model**.

The basic DDM assumes a constant discount rate and a constant dividend growth rate. However, more realistic versions of the DDM have been developed to allow for a time-varying discount rate and time-varying dividend growth rates. A more general DDM for valuing stock prices can be written,

$$V_t = \sum_{i=1}^{\infty} \left[\frac{D_{t+i}}{(1+k_{t+1})\ldots(1+k_{t+i})} \right] \tag{4.21}$$

where $k_{t+1}, k_{t+2}, \ldots$ are time-varying discount rates (i.e. time-varying required rates of return).

A stock's intrinsic value is also called its **fundamental value**. Analysing a stock's intrinsic value using the DDM is a type of **fundamental analysis**. Advocates of fundamental analysis believe that if a stock is undervalued, in the sense that the current stock price is less than the current fundamental value of the stock, $P_t < V_t$, then, since eventually the stock's price will converge to its fundamental value, a long position should be taken in the stock. Conversely, if a stock is overvalued then a short position should be taken.

Fundamental analysis is popular in practice. In addition to the DDM, investors using fundamental analysis might also employ valuation ratios such as the price/earnings ratio to try to identify undervalued stocks. For example, if a company has a very low price/earnings ratio relative to other companies with the same underlying characteristics then this suggests that its stock is undervalued. Large financial institutions typically do not make investment decisions on the basis of single equity valuation ratios or the prescriptions of basic DDMs. However, such tools might be used as inputs into a wider fundamental valuation approach, or as a filtering tool prior to a more detailed fundamental analysis. Present value models like the DDM are important tools for investment analysis and for comparing individual assets. However, computing optimal combinations of assets requires MPT, which is discussed below.

4.4 Modern Portfolio Theory

4.4.1 Basic Theory

Consider the simple example of risk-neutral investors with a one-period horizon facing the choice between two risky assets and assume that they can only invest their funds in one of the assets. If the investor knows with certainty what the one-period return is going to be, the choice of which asset to invest in is obvious. However, in practice future returns for risky assets are unknown at the present (time t) because risky asset prices are random variables; thus, for each asset the future price P_{t+1} is uncertain, and therefore the return between time t and time $t+1$, r_{t+1}, which depends on the future price, is uncertain. (Note that in this section r_{t+1} refers to the simple return.) The range of possible values for the returns and the associated probability of obtaining values within particular intervals are described by the relevant PDF.

Since future returns are uncertain, a sensible investment strategy is to choose the asset that has the highest expected return, $E(r_{t+1})$. This implicitly assumes that the investors' **utility** is a positive function of expected return – a reasonable assumption to make for rational investors. If for each asset the investors have data on the historical returns then assuming stationarity they can consistently estimate the expected returns using the sample mean returns.

Expand this simple example by assuming that investors are risk-averse (their utility is a positive function of expected return but a negative function of risk), and assume that the risk associated with an asset can be quantified using the variance of the return. It follows that when deciding which asset to invest in, the investors will not just be concerned with the estimated expected return for each asset, but also with the estimated variance of the return for each asset. Assuming stationarity, the variance can be consistently estimated using the sample variance formula. Depending on the investors' degree of risk aversion, an asset with a low expected return might be preferred to an asset with a high expected return if the variance of the former is lower than the variance of the latter. If the estimated expected returns for the two assets are equal, then in this simple example the investors should invest in the asset with the lowest estimated variance. If the estimated variances are equal, then the investors should invest in the asset with the highest estimated expected return. If neither are equal, then the investors should decide which asset's combination of estimated expected return and risk generates the highest utility, and invest in that asset. MPT deals with the more realistic case of many assets, where investors can invest in different combinations (i.e. portfolios) of the assets and in risk-free assets (with a zero return variance), but the logic is the same as for the simple example above.

Traditional MPT makes the following assumptions:

 (i) Investors have a one-period horizon.
 (ii) Investors are risk-averse and they maximise utility, which is positive function of expected return.
(iii) Investors quantify the risk of an asset using the variance of the return.
(iv) Investors can invest and borrow at a risk-free rate of interest.
 (v) There are no taxes or transaction costs.

Under these assumptions investors' preferred combinations of risky assets are the combinations that for the different portfolio variances available (i.e. the different levels of risk), σ_P^2, maximise expected portfolio return, $E(r_P)$.[5] Equivalently, the preferred combinations of risky assets are the combinations that, for the different expected portfolio returns available, minimise the portfolio variance. Recall that the expected value of a random variable is the population mean of the random variable. Hence the expected portfolio return in this case is also called the *ex ante* mean portfolio return (as opposed to the *ex post* mean portfolio return – the sample mean portfolio return computed from historical data).[6]

Assuming that the choice is between risky assets and a single risk-free asset, in practice MPT suggests that optimal asset allocation for an investor can be split into two main steps, each with several sub-steps.

Step (i) Estimate the expected returns, variances and covariances of the returns for the risky assets being considered. Using these inputs compute the different preferred risky portfolios. From these portfolios and using information on the risk-free rate, choose the optimal risky portfolio (ORP) weights, which are the weights for the constituent assets that maximise the slope of the **capital allocation line** (CAL),

$$CAL_{slope} = \frac{E(r_P) - r_f}{\sigma_P} \tag{4.22}$$

where r_f denotes the risk-free rate (the return on the risk-free asset). The slope of the CAL is the risk-adjusted expected excess return.

Step (ii) Using information on the investor's individual characteristics (e.g. their degree of risk aversion), compute the proportion of their total funds to be allocated to the risky portfolio and the risk-free asset. Call this final portfolio the optimal final portfolio (OFP).

---

[5]To simplify notation, here and in the rest of this chapter we drop the subscript $t + 1$. For more details on the theory covered in this section, see Elton and Gruber (1995) Chapters 4–12 and Bodie, Kane and Marcus (2009) Chapters 6–8.

[6]In applications of MPT, traditionally estimates of the unconditional means, variances and covariances of returns are used as inputs. However, in practice, more recently it has become popular to use estimates of the conditional means, variances and covariances to capture the changing statistical properties of the returns: see Section 4.4.2 for further details.

Each of these steps will now be analysed in more detail for the simple example of a portfolio of two risky assets, and one risk-free asset. Let the risky asset returns be denoted by r_1 and r_2 respectively, and the risk-free rate by r_f.

Optimal asset allocation: Step (i)

Step (i) involves computing the preferred risky portfolios, which can be represented graphically as an **efficient frontier**, and then the ORP. Typically, the expected returns, variances and covariances of the returns for the risky assets will need to be estimated as discussed previously. For simplicity, assume here that the population values for these parameters are known. More specifically, assume that the expected returns, variance and covariance for the two risky assets (in per cent) are,

$$E(r_1) = 15 \tag{4.23}$$

$$E(r_2) = 10 \tag{4.24}$$

$$\sigma_1^2 = E[r_1 - E(r_1)]^2 = 500 \tag{4.25}$$

$$\sigma_2^2 = E[r_2 - E(r_2)]^2 = 250 \tag{4.26}$$

$$\sigma_{12} = E[(r_1 - E(r_1))(r_2 - E(r_2))] = 100 \tag{4.27}$$

For a portfolio of these two risky assets the expected portfolio return and portfolio variance for a given combination of asset weights w_1 and w_2 can be computed using,

$$E(r_P) = w_1 E(r_1) + w_2 E(r_2)$$
$$= w_1 15 + w_2 10 \tag{4.28}$$

$$\sigma_P^2 = w_1^2 \sigma_1^2 + w_2^2 \sigma_2^2 + 2 w_1 w_2 \sigma_{12}$$
$$= w_1^2 500 + w_2^2 250 + 2 w_1 w_2 100 \tag{4.29}$$

The general formulas for the portfolio mean and variance in the case of N assets are,

$$E(r_P) = \sum_{i=1}^{N} w_i E(r_i) \tag{4.30}$$

$$\sigma_P^2 = \sum_{i=1}^{N} \sum_{j=1}^{N} w_i w_j \sigma_{ij} \tag{4.31}$$

where for $i = j, \sigma_{ij} = \sigma_i^2$. Clearly the size of the portfolio variance will depend on the asset weights, the size of the variance terms (which will always be positive), and the size of the covariance terms (which can be positive or negative).

Diversifying a portfolio typically reduces the portfolio variance relative to a less diversified portfolio (thus, diversification typically reduces portfolio risk). Consider the example here with $w_1 = 0.50, w_2 = 0.50$. It follows from (4.31) that the portfolio variance is,

$$\sigma_P^2 = 0.25 \times 500 + 0.25 \times 250 + 2 \times 0.25 \times 100 = 237.5 \qquad (4.32)$$

Therefore relative to an investment of all funds in either asset 1 or asset 2, this degree of diversification has reduced risk. Whilst diversification often reduces portfolio risk relative to a less diversified portfolio this is not always true and it depends on the values of the relevant inputs, particularly on the size and sign of the covariance. For the example here, if the covariance is increased to 150 then,

$$\sigma_P^2 = 0.25 \times 500 + 0.25 \times 250 + 2 \times 0.25 \times 150 = 262.50 \qquad (4.33)$$

Therefore, relative to investing all funds in asset 2 (with variance 250), this degree of diversification has not reduced risk. Risk reduction through diversification is largest if the covariance of asset returns is negative. It can be shown theoretically that, in some circumstances, by increasing the number of assets in a portfolio to a very large number the portfolio variance can be reduced virtually to zero. However, these circumstances rarely occur and there is a natural lower bound on the portfolio variance. In practice, all risky assets are affected by common risk factors and this common risk cannot be diversified away. Hence two types of financial risk can be defined: systematic risk (i.e. common risk) and non-systematic risk (i.e. specific risk).

The combinations of expected portfolio return and portfolio standard deviation that can be created by combining the assets in different proportions is called the **portfolio opportunity set**. In practice, the portfolio opportunity set can be computed by varying the asset weights, subject to the constraint that the weights sum to unity. The portfolio opportunity set can be represented graphically by a line in the expected portfolio return and portfolio standard deviation space. For portfolios consisting of two risky assets the set is given by points on this line; for portfolios consisting of more than two risky assets this line represents the boundary of the set. The preferred risky portfolios can be represented graphically as a segment of the portfolio opportunity set called the **efficient frontier**. The portfolio opportunity set is graphed for the example here in Figure 4.7. The efficient frontier is the segment of the portfolio opportunity set from the minimum variance portfolio upwards.

The ORP is the portfolio from the different preferred risky portfolios on the efficient frontier that maximises the slope of the CAL, as defined in (4.22). Graphically, the

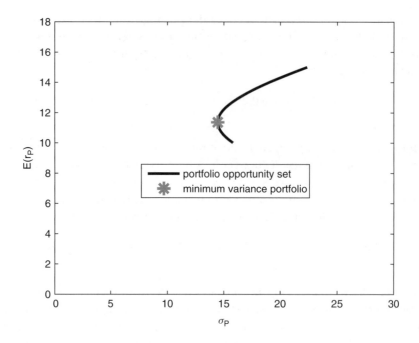

Figure 4.7   Portfolio opportunity set.

CAL is a line in the expected portfolio return – portfolio standard deviation space from r_f. Therefore, the ORP is the portfolio given by the point of tangency between the CAL and the efficient frontier.

In the case of two risky assets and a single risk-free asset it is straightforward to derive formulas for the asset weights associated with the ORP by solving the following maximisation problem using differential calculus,

$$\underset{w_i}{Max} \; CAL_{slope} = \frac{E(r_P) - r_f}{\sigma_P} \tag{4.34}$$

$$\text{subject to} \sum_{i=1}^{2} w_i = 1 \tag{4.35}$$

The solutions are,

$$w_1 = \frac{[E(r_1) - r_f]\sigma_2^2 - [E(r_2) - r_f]\sigma_{12}}{[E(r_1) - r_f]\sigma_2^2 + [E(r_2) - r_f]\sigma_1^2 - [E(r_1) - r_f + E(r_2) - r_f]\sigma_{12}} \tag{4.36}$$

$$w_2 = 1 - w_1 \tag{4.37}$$

A graph of the ORP for the example here is given in Figure 4.8 assuming that the risk-free rate is 6%.

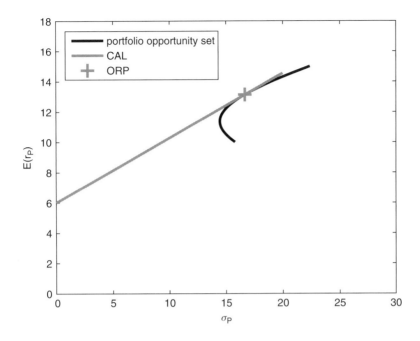

Figure 4.8   Optimal risky portfolio.

In this case it can be shown that the asset weights associated with the ORP are $w_1 = 0.627$ and $w_2 = 0.373$, and the expected return and standard deviation of the ORP are $E(r_{ORP}) = 13.136$, and $\sigma_{ORP} = 16.678$.

Optimal asset allocation: Step (ii)

The next step is to use information on an individual investor's degree of risk aversion to choose the optimal proportion of funds to split between the ORP and the risk-free asset, thus giving an OFP for that investor. It is assumed that investors seek to maximise their utility, which is a function of the expected portfolio return and risk, and therefore this OFP can be interpreted as a tangency point with an indifference curve.[7] A formula for the optimal proportion of funds allocated to the ORP, p, can be derived. To illustrate, assume the following quadratic utility function,

$$U = E(r_P) - 0.005\alpha\sigma_P^2 \qquad (4.38)$$

where α is the coefficient of risk aversion which measures an investor's sensitivity to risk (if $\alpha = 0$, the investor is risk-neutral). Here we assume that $\alpha = 4$ (typically

---

[7]In this context the **indifference curve** is a curve that describes different combinations of expected portfolio return and portfolio standard deviation between which an investor is indifferent (the different combinations generate the same level of utility).

α is set to a value between 2 and 5). The maximisation problem can be written,

$$\underset{p}{Max}\, U = E(r_{OFP}) - 0.005\alpha\sigma_{OFP}^2$$
$$= r_f + p[E(r_{ORP}) - r_f] - 0.005\alpha p^2\sigma_{ORP}^2 \qquad (4.39)$$

For the example here, the solution is,

$$p = \frac{E(r_{ORP}) - r_f}{0.01\alpha\sigma_{ORP}^2} = \frac{13.136 - 6}{0.01 \times 4 \times 16.678^2} = 0.641 \qquad (4.40)$$

Therefore, in this example, the investor would invest 64.1% of their funds in the ORP and 35.9% in the risk-free asset. The OFP and indifference curve in this case are graphed in Figure 4.9.

The fact that, under MPT, asset allocation can be split into the two steps discussed above has become known as the **separation principle**. It implies that a portfolio manager using MPT only has to compute one set of ORP asset weights for all clients (assuming those clients are content with the portfolio manager selecting from the same base set of risky assets). In practice, portfolio rebalancing, transaction costs and client-specific objectives mean that portfolio management is typically more

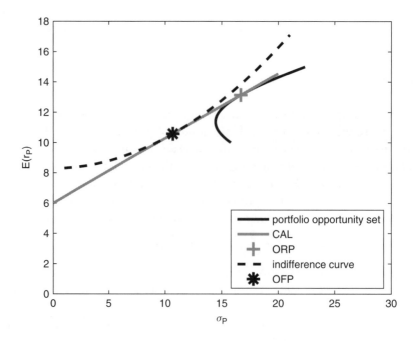

Figure 4.9 Optimal final portfolio.

involved than suggested in this section. However, many of these issues can be dealt with using MPT with appropriate extensions of the traditional underlying theory.

4.4.2 Generalisations

The simple numerical example in Section 4.4.1 involves just two assets. In practice portfolio managers would typically invest in a much larger number of assets so as to exploit the benefits of diversification discussed above. Although the relevant theory discussed in Section 4.4.1 also applies to larger portfolios, computing the ORP asset weights does become more difficult when there are large numbers of assets. In practice the solutions are typically obtained using quadratic programming algorithms on a computer.

In the example in Section 4.4.1, the OFP does not involve borrowing. However, recall from the assumptions listed in Section 4.4.1 that investors are able to borrow (at the risk-free rate). By investing the borrowed money in the ORP, this opens up the possibility of OFPs to the right of the ORP. Whether borrowing is optimal depends on the values taken by the various inputs and the investors' coefficient of risk aversion.

In the example in Section 4.4.1 we have implicitly imposed the restriction of no **short sales**; however, it is easy to extend MPT to allow for short selling. If an asset is sold it will have a negative weight in the portfolio ($w_i < 0$), allowing for other assets to have weights greater than unity.

In applications of MPT, traditionally the sample means, variances and covariances of the returns for the constituent assets are used as inputs; assuming stationarity, these are consistent estimates of the unconditional means, variances and covariances. However, in practice it might be argued that estimates of the *conditional* means, variances and covariances of the returns should be used to capture time-variation. For example, if the asset returns are stationary multivariate-GARCH variables (see Chapter 3 for more details), then the conditional variances and covariances of the returns will be time-varying and in the short-run they will fluctuate around the relevant unconditional variances and covariances. In this case, therefore, the ORP and OFP at a particular point in time computed using estimates of the conditional variances and covariances as inputs might be quite different than if the traditional inputs are used. Note that in the empirical examples in this chapter the traditional sample means, variances and covariances are used as inputs.[8]

---

[8]See Cumby, Figlewski and Hasbrouck (1994) and Flavin and Wickens (2003) for empirical evidence on the benefits of using conditional inputs in applications of MPT.

4.4.3 Strengths and Weaknesses

MPT is an elegant theory that provides analytical results for optimal asset allocation. However, MPT is sometimes criticised on the grounds that the assumptions on which it is based are unrealistic. For example, assumptions (iv) and (v) will typically be unrealistic in practice. Critics might also claim that MPT is invalid because of sample evidence suggesting that the probability distributions for asset returns are skewed. (MPT assumes that only the mean and variance of returns matters, not the skewness.) Whilst it is undoubtedly true that sample evidence suggests that for some assets the distribution of returns is skewed, when such evidence is assessed there is always a non-zero probability that a Type I error has occurred and that in fact the null hypothesis of a symmetric distribution has been incorrectly rejected. Therefore, MPT cannot be invalid *with certainty* on the basis of such evidence. If strong sample evidence is found suggesting that the distribution of asset returns is skewed, then this suggests that the outcome from applying MPT might best be viewed as an approximation of the optimal solution. However, all solutions to asset allocation problems are essentially approximations of an unknown optimal solution. Therefore, even though some of the MPT assumptions are unrealistic, the MPT solutions might still be the best approximation of those available to the portfolio manager.

In the example in Section 4.4.1 we assume that the inputs (the expected returns, variances and covariances) are known. In practice this will not be the case and they will need to be estimated. Assuming that the asset returns are stationary processes, these inputs can be consistently estimated using the sample formulas discussed in Chapters 2 and 3. For example, the unconditional covariance matrix for the returns on N assets can be written,

$$
\Sigma = \begin{bmatrix} \sigma_1^2 & \sigma_{12} & \cdots & \sigma_{1N} \\ \sigma_{21} & \sigma_2^2 & \cdots & \sigma_{2N} \\ \vdots & \vdots & \ddots & \vdots \\ \sigma_{N1} & \sigma_{N2} & \cdots & \sigma_N^2 \end{bmatrix}
\tag{4.41}
$$

Let $\mathbf{R}$ be a $T \times N$ matrix of data on the one-period returns for the N assets over T periods in mean-deviation form (i.e. subtracting the relevant sample mean from each return). The unconditional covariance matrix for the returns can be consistently estimated using the sample covariance matrix,

$$
\hat{\Sigma} = (T - 1)^{-1}(\mathbf{R}'\mathbf{R})
\tag{4.42}
$$

Define a $N \times 1$ vector of portfolio weights,

$$
\mathbf{w} = [w_1 \ w_2 \ \cdots \ w_N]'
\tag{4.43}
$$

The sample portfolio variance is,

$$
\hat{\sigma}_P^2 = \mathbf{w}'\hat{\Sigma}\mathbf{w}
\tag{4.44}
$$

In practice, one potential problem with this approach is that for large numbers of assets the number of terms in the covariance matrix becomes extremely large, making the approach computationally expensive. Another potential problem is that the estimated covariance matrix (4.42) is not guaranteed to be positive-definite. If the estimated covariance matrix is not positive-definite then the estimated portfolio variance is not guaranteed to be non-negative. Another potential problem with estimating the relevant inputs using the sample means and sample covariance matrix is the possibility that the asset returns could be non-stationary processes (e.g. due to structural breaks). If they are, the estimates obtained that ignore this feature will be biased.

There are numerous possible solutions to these problems. Possible solutions to the first two problems are to impose restrictions that simplify the covariance matrix, making it less costly to estimate, and restrictions to force the covariance matrix to be positive-definite. Another possible solution to these problems is to use a factor model to estimate the covariance matrix. This approach is discussed in more detail in Chapter 5. Factor model-based estimates of the covariance matrix usually involve computing fewer terms and usually are more likely to be positive-definite. Note also that methods can be used to improve the traditional sample covariance matrix. The most popular of these is the shrinkage method: see Ledoit and Wolf (2004) for further details. One possible solution to the third problem is to reduce the sample size used to estimate the inputs, so that only data from the most recent stationary time period are employed.

The next section discusses the empirical examples for this chapter, which involve small portfolios of Conglomerate stocks and a single risk-free asset. These portfolios are not supposed to be representative of portfolios constructed by professional portfolio managers, and are kept deliberately simple for pedagogic reasons. In practice, professional portfolio managers using MPT would typically invest in large numbers of assets across different asset classes and possibly different countries so as to exploit the benefits of diversification. Further details on the MATLAB® programs and the data used are given in Section 4.8. Note that these empirical examples require estimates of the expected returns and covariance matrix for the annual simple returns as inputs. Rather than compute these directly using annual data, monthly data on log-returns are used to estimate the sample means and sample covariance matrix for the log-returns, which are then converted to the simple return values.[9]

---

[9]For brevity, the conversion formulas are not given in the text, but they are labelled in the MATLAB® programs used: see Meucci (2001) for further technical details. Note that the programs used here employ the MATLAB® Financial Toolbox, which requires the relevant inputs to be in decimal form. Further details on using the Financial Toolbox for asset allocation can be obtained from the ''Help'' facility within MATLAB®.

4.5 Empirical Examples

Example 4.1: Asset allocation I

Using monthly data on the price of General Electric Company (GE) and United Technologies Corporation (UTX) stock for 1997:12–2007:12 and an annual risk-free rate of 4%, compute the ORP and OFP assuming a one-year investment horizon, a quadratic utility function with $\alpha = 4$, no borrowing and no short sales.

The relevant MATLAB® program is given in the file E41.m and a portion of E41.m is given in Box 4.1. The results are graphed in Figure 4.10. The estimated expected returns and the returns covariance matrix for the two stocks are given in Tables 4.1 and 4.2 respectively.

Box 4.1   E41.m

```
%Compute the efficient frontier.
[PortRisk,PortReturn,PortWts]=portopt(ExpReturn,...
ExpCovariance,100);
%Compute the optimal risky portfolio and optimal complete portfolio.
RisklessRate=0.04;
BorrowRate=NaN;
RiskAversion=4;
[RiskyRisk,RiskyReturn,RiskyWts,RiskyFraction,OverallRisk,...
OverallReturn]=portalloc(PortRisk,PortReturn,PortWts,...
RisklessRate,BorrowRate, RiskAversion);
%Draw the graph.
set(gcf,'color','white','DefaultAxesColorOrder',...
[0 0 0;0.5 0.5 0.5;0 0 0;0.5 0.5 0.5],'PaperPositionMode','auto');
plot(PortRisk,PortReturn,RiskyRisk,RiskyReturn,'*',...
OverallRisk,OverallReturn,'*',[0;RiskyRisk],...
[RisklessRate;RiskyReturn],'LineWidth',2,'MarkerSize',13);
title({'Figure 4.10 Asset allocation I: two stocks and a risk-'...
'free asset'},'FontSize',14,'FontName','Times New Roman');
ylabel('E(r_P)','FontSize',14,'FontName','Times New Roman');
xlabel('\sigma_P','FontSize',14,'FontName','Times New Roman');
ylim([0 0.4]);
xlim([0 0.4]);
legend('efficient frontier','ORP','OFP','CAL',...
'Location','Best');
print -depsc2 Figure 410.eps;
```

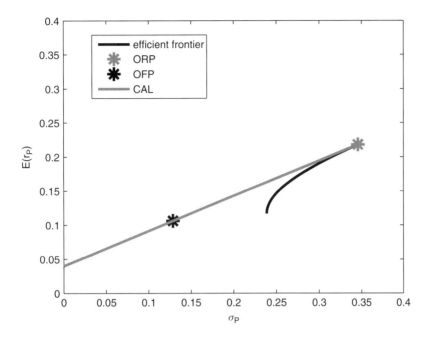

Figure 4.10   Asset allocation I: two stocks and a risk-free asset.

Table 4.1   Estimated expected returns

GE	UTX
0.092	0.218

Table 4.2   Estimated returns covariance matrix

0.061	0.042
0.042	0.119

From Table 4.1 it can be seen that the estimated expected return is much larger for UTX than for GE. From Table 4.2 it can be seen that the estimated variance for UTX is larger than the estimated variance for GE and that the covariance of the returns is positive.

The expected return and standard deviation of the ORP are $E(r_{ORP}) = 0.218$, $\sigma_{ORP} = 0.346$. The asset weights for the ORP are given in Table 4.3.

Table 4.3   Asset weights for ORP

w_{GE}	w_{UTX}
0	1

Therefore the ORP involves investing in only one of the stocks, UTX. This result can be explained by the very high estimated expected return for UTX relative to its risk and the inputs for GE. The OFP involves investing 37.2% of funds in the ORP and the remainder in the risk-free asset. The expected return and standard deviation of the OFP are $E(r_{OFP}) = 0.106$, $\sigma_{OFP} = 0.129$.

Example 4.2:   Asset allocation II

Using monthly data on the price of GE and UTX stock for 1997:12–2007:12 and an annual risk-free rate of 2.5%, compute the ORP and OFP assuming a one-year investment horizon, a quadratic utility function with $\alpha = 2$, no borrowing and no short sales.

The relevant MATLAB® program is given in the file E42.m. The results are graphed in Figure 4.11.

In this case the ORP is the same as in Example 4.1 – invest in UTX only. However, the combination of a reduction in the risk-free rate (from 0.055 to 0.025) and a reduction in the investor's degree of risk aversion (from 4 to 2) means that the OFP involves investing a lower proportion of funds in the risk-free asset, and a higher proportion of funds in the ORP. Specifically, the OFP now involves investing 80.7% of funds in the ORP and the remainder in the risk-free asset. The expected return and standard deviation of the OFP are $E(r_{OFP}) = 0.181$, $\sigma_{OFP} = 0.279$.

Example 4.3:   Asset allocation III

Using monthly data on the price of GE, UTX, 3M Company (MMM), Danaher Corporation (DHR) and PPG Industries Inc. (PPG) stock for 1997:12–2007:12 and an annual risk-free rate of 4%, compute the ORP and OFP assuming a one-year investment horizon, a quadratic utility function with $\alpha = 4$, no borrowing and no short sales.

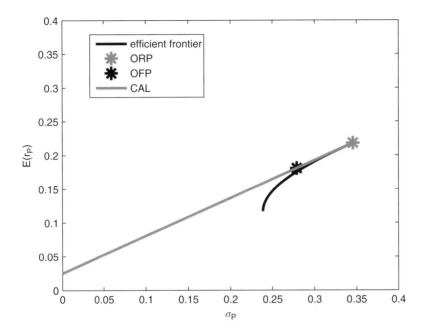

Figure 4.11   Asset allocation II: two stocks and a risk-free asset.

The relevant MATLAB® program is given in the file E43.m. The results are graphed in Figure 4.12. The estimated expected returns and the returns covariance matrix for the five stocks are given in Tables 4.4 and 4.5.

The expected return and standard deviation of the ORP are $E(r_{ORP}) = 0.207$, $\sigma_{ORP} = 0.266$. Compared with Figures 4.10 and 4.11, it can be seen that the efficient frontier in Figure 4.12 gets closer to the y-axis, demonstrating the effects of diversification. The asset weights for the ORP are given in Table 4.6.

It can be seen from Table 4.6 that DHR has the largest weight and that GE and PPG have zero weights. The OFP involves investing 58.9% of funds in the ORP and the remainder in the risk-free asset. The expected return and standard deviation of the OFP are $E(r_{OFP}) = 0.138$, $\sigma_{OFP} = 0.157$.

In the empirical examples above, some of the assets have a weight of zero for the ORP. In practice, it might be desirable to impose a constraint that restricts the asset weights to have a minimum (non-zero) value and a maximum value, so as to guard against insufficient diversification. Using the Financial Toolbox for MATLAB®, minimum and maximum constraints can be imposed on the asset weights. This is demonstrated in Example 4.4.

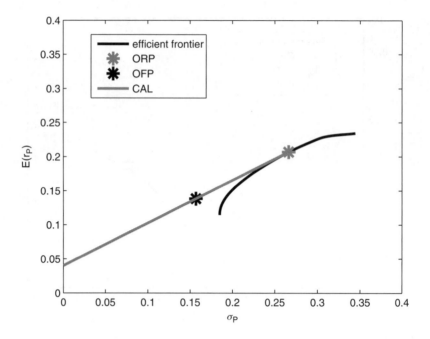

Figure 4.12   Asset allocation III: five stocks and a risk-free asset.

Table 4.4   Estimated expected returns

GE	UTX	MMM	DHR	PPG
0.092	0.218	0.125	0.234	0.088

Table 4.5   Estimated returns covariance matrix

0.061	0.042	0.011	0.025	0.020
0.042	0.119	0.034	0.063	0.048
0.011	0.034	0.060	0.027	0.039
0.025	0.063	0.027	0.119	0.044
0.020	0.048	0.039	0.044	0.069

Table 4.6   Asset weights for ORP

w_{GE}	w_{UTX}	w_{MMM}	w_{DHR}	w_{PPG}
0	0.321	0.201	0.478	0

Example 4.4:   Asset allocation IV

Using monthly data on the price of GE, UTX, MMM, DHR and PPG stock for 1997:12–2007:12 and an annual risk-free rate of 4%, compute the ORP and OFP assuming a one-year investment horizon, a quadratic utility function with $\alpha = 4$, no borrowing and no short sales. Constrain the minimum asset weight to be 0.10 and the maximum asset weight to be 0.50.

The relevant MATLAB® program is given in the file E44.m. The results are graphed in Figure 4.13.

The expected return and standard deviation of the ORP are $E(r_{ORP}) = 0.190$, $\sigma_{ORP} = 0.252$. The asset weights for the ORP are given in Table 4.7.

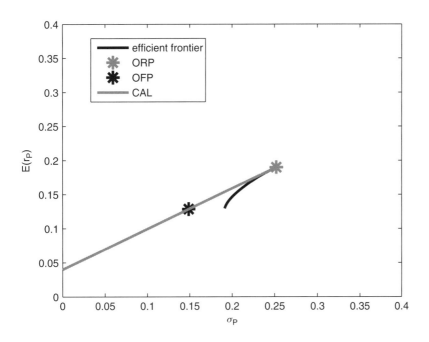

Figure 4.13   Asset allocation IV: five stocks and a risk-free asset.

Table 4.7   Asset weights for ORP

w_{GE}	w_{UTX}	w_{MMM}	w_{DHR}	w_{PPG}
0.100	0.257	0.103	0.440	0.100

It can be seen from Table 4.7 that the largest weight is for DHR, and the minimum possible weights are assigned to GE and PPG. The expected return and standard deviation of the OFP are $E(r_{OFP}) = 0.129, \sigma_{OFP} = 0.149$.

Example 4.5: Asset allocation V

Using monthly data on the price of GE, UTX, MMM, DHR and PPG stock for 1997:12–2007:12 and an annual risk-free rate of 2.5%, compute the ORP and OFP assuming a one-year investment horizon, a quadratic utility function with $\alpha = 2$, no short sales and borrowing at the risk-free rate.

The relevant MATLAB® program is given in the file E45.m. The results are graphed in Figure 4.14.

The expected return and standard deviation of the ORP are $E(r_{ORP}) = 0.202, \sigma_{ORP} = 0.258$. The OFP involves borrowing at the risk-free rate and investing an amount equal to 132.8% of funds in the ORP. The expected return and standard deviation of the OFP are $E(r_{OFP}) = 0.259, \sigma_{OFP} = 0.342$. The asset weights for the ORP are given in Table 4.8.

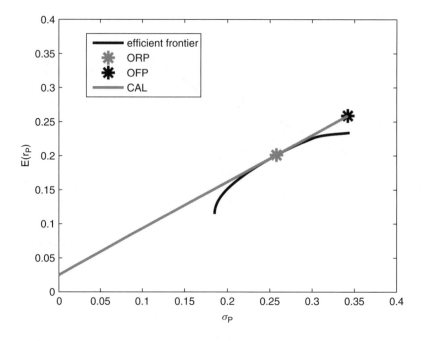

Figure 4.14   Asset allocation V: five stocks and a risk-free asset.

Table 4.8 Asset weights for ORP

w_{GE}	w_{UTX}	w_{MMM}	w_{DHR}	w_{PPG}
0	0.298	0.255	0.447	0

In practice, the rate at which funds can be borrowed is typically higher than the risk-free rate by an amount sufficient to compensate the lender for the credit risk of the borrower. Consequently, if investors borrow at the risk-free rate plus a premium, but can invest only at the risk-free rate, then the CAL will be kinked at the ORP.

Example 4.6: Asset allocation VI

Using monthly data on the price of GE, UTX, MMM, DHR and PPG stock for 1997:12–2007:12 and an annual risk-free rate of 2.5%, compute the ORP and OFP assuming a one-year investment horizon, a quadratic utility function with $\alpha = 2$ and borrowing at the risk-free rate. Allow for short sales, setting a minimum asset weight of −0.50 and a maximum asset weight of 1.5.

The relevant MATLAB® program is given in the file E46.m. The results are graphed in Figure 4.15.

Compared with the previous examples involving these five stocks, allowing for short sales generates an efficient frontier that includes portfolios with significantly greater expected return and risk. The asset weights for the ORP are given in Table 4.9.

The ORP involves short selling PPG. The expected return and standard deviation of the ORP are $E(r_{ORP}) = 0.238$, $\sigma_{ORP} = 0.287$. The OFP involves borrowing at the risk-free rate and investing an amount equal to 129.3% of funds in the ORP. The expected return and standard deviation of the OFP are $E(r_{OFP}) = 0.300$, $\sigma_{OFP} = 0.371$.

4.6 Summary

This chapter has focused on the empirical application of MPT to compute optimal portfolios of financial assets. For risk-averse investors wanting to allocate funds between a group of risky assets in an optimal way, a sensible portfolio

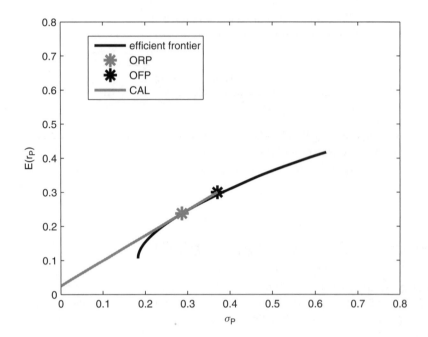

Figure 4.15   Asset allocation VI: five stocks and a risk-free asset.

Table 4.9   Asset weights for ORP

w_{GE}	w_{UTX}	w_{MMM}	w_{DHR}	w_{PPG}
0.044	0.386	0.523	0.548	−0.500

investment strategy is to choose from between portfolios that for the different portfolio variances available maximise expected portfolio return. This is the essence of MPT. The fundamentals of MPT were developed in a seminal journal article by Markowitz (1952). MPT implies that if different investors consider allocating their funds between the same set of risky assets and a risk-free asset, and they use the same inputs, then the optimal combination of the risky assets will be the same for all investors. These investors' optimal final portfolios will only differ in terms of the proportion of their funds split between the optimal risky portfolio and the risk-free asset. Therefore, in practice, optimal asset allocation between risky assets and risk-free assets can in many cases be clearly separated into two tasks: (i) compute the optimal risky portfolio weights; (ii) decide how to split the total funds between the optimal risky portfolio and risk-free assets. MPT has had a profound impact on portfolio management in practice, and on many other areas of finance.

4.7 End of Chapter Questions[10]

Q1. Download monthly data on the prices of five financial sector stocks for the period 1997:12 – 2010:12.[11]

  (a) Graph the log-prices and comment on any notable fluctuations in the graphs obtained.

  (b) Compute the sample means and sample covariance matrix for the log-returns and simple returns, then briefly discuss your results.

  (c) For each returns series compute the sample skewness, sample kurtosis and the Jarque – Bera test and briefly discuss your results.

Q2. Using the data from Question 1 for the period 1997:12 – 2007:12 and an annual risk-free rate of 0.025, compute the ORP and OFP assuming a one-year investment horizon, a quadratic utility function with α set to 2, 3, or 4, no borrowing and no short sales. Graph your results.

Q3. Investigate the impact on the ORP and OFP in Question 2 of the following:

  (a) Reducing the sample size used to compute the inputs.

  (b) Allowing for borrowing.

  (c) Allowing for borrowing and short sales.

Q4. Download monthly data on the prices of five stocks from five different sectors (excluding the financial sector) for the period 1997:12 – 2007:12.[12] Using this data and an annual risk-free rate of 0.025, compute the ORP and OFP assuming a one-year investment horizon, a quadratic utility function with the same α as in your answer to Question 2, no borrowing and no short sales. Graph your results and compare your results with those obtained for Question 2.

Q5. **(a)** Compute the ORP and OFP for a portfolio of the five financial sector stocks used in Questions 1 – 3 and the five stocks used in Question 4 employing the data for 1997:12 – 2007:12 and an annual risk-free rate of 0.025. Assume a one-year investment horizon, a quadratic utility function with the same α as in your answer to Question 2, no borrowing and no short sales. Graph your results.

  (b) Discuss the weaknesses of asset allocation using MPT in the light of your previous answers and the additional MATLAB® output from running the relevant programs.

---

[10]A guide to answering these questions and relevant MATLAB® programs are given on the companion website (www.wileyeurope.com/college/sollis).

[11]Yahoo! Finance is one possible source of these data (www.finance.yahoo.com).

[12]Yahoo! Finance is one possible source of these data (www.finance.yahoo.com).

4.8 Appendix

4.8.1 Data

Figures 4.4, 4.5, 4.6

xom.xls, ge.xls, msft.xls

Daily data on the price of Exxon Mobil Corporation (XOM), General Electric Company (GE) and Microsoft Corporation (MSFT) stock for 31/12/97–31/12/08 from Yahoo! Finance (www.finance.yahoo.com).

Example 4.1

Columns one and two of C4stocks.xls

C4stocks.xls: monthly data on the price of General Electric Company (GE), United Technologies Corporation (UTX), 3M Company (MMM), Danaher Corporation (DHR) and PPG Industries Inc. (PPG) stock for 1997:12–2007:12 from Yahoo! Finance (www.finance.yahoo.com).

Example 4.2

Columns one and two of C4stocks.xls

See above.

Example 4.3

C4stocks.xls

See above.

Example 4.4

C4stocks.xls

See above.

Example 4.5

C4stocks.xls

See above.

Example 4.6

C4stocks.xls

See above.

4.8.2 MATLAB® Programs and Toolboxes[13]

Example 4.1

E41.m, MATLAB® Financial Toolbox

Example 4.2

E42.m, MATLAB® Financial Toolbox

Example 4.3

E43.m, MATLAB® Financial Toolbox

Example 4.4

E44.m, MATLAB® Financial Toolbox

Example 4.5

E45.m, MATLAB® Financial Toolbox

Example 4.6

E46.m, MATLAB® Financial Toolbox

---

[13]See www.wileyeurope.com/college/sollis for the programs E##.m.

4.9 References

Bodie, Z., Kane, A. and A.J. Marcus (2009) *Investments*, 8th edn. New York: McGraw-Hill.

Cumby, R.E., Figlewski S. and J. Hasbrouck (1994) International asset allocation with time varying risk: an analysis and implementation, *Japan and the World Economy*, 6, 1-25.

Elton, E.J. and M.J. Gruber (1995) *Modern Portfolio Theory and Investment Analysis*, 5th edn. New York: John Wiley & Sons.

Fabozzi, F.J., Gupta, F. and H.M. Markowitz (2002) The legacy of modern portfolio theory, *The Journal of Investing*, Fall, 7-22.

Flavin, T.J. and M.R. Wickens (2003) Macroeconomic influences on optimal asset allocation, *Review of Financial Economics*, 12, 207-231.

Gordon, M.J. (1959) Dividends, earnings and stock prices, *Review of Economics and Statistics*, 41, 99-105.

Ledoit, O. and M. Wolf (2004) Honey, I shrunk the sample covariance matrix, *Journal of Portfolio Management*, 30, 110-119.

Markowitz, H.M. (1952) Portfolio selection, *Journal of Finance*, 7, 77-91.

Markowitz, H.M. (1959) *Portfolio Selection: Efficient Diversification of Investments*. New York: John Wiley & Sons.

Markowitz, H.M. (1999) The early history of portfolio theory: 1600-1960, *Financial Analysts Journal*, 55, 5-16.

Meucci, A. (2001) A common pitfall in mean-variance asset allocation, Wilmott Technical Article, Wilmott.com, October 2001.

Reilly, F.K. and K.C. Brown (2006) *Investment Analysis and Portfolio Management*, 8th edn. Ohio: Thomson South-Western.

Rubinstein, M. (2002) Markowitz's "portfolio selection": a fifty-year retrospective, *Journal of Finance*, 57, 1041-1045.

Samuelson, P.A. (1973) Proof that properly discounted present values of assets vibrate randomly, *Bell Journal of Economics, The RAND Corporation*, 4, 369-374.

Sharpe, W.F., Alexander, G.J. and J.V. Bailey (1998) *Investments*, 6th edn. Englewood Cliffs, NJ: Prentice Hall.

Tobin, J. (1958) Liquidity preference as behavior towards risk, *Review of Economic Studies*, 25, 65-86.

Williams, J.B. (1938) *The Theory of Investment Value*. Cambridge, MA: Harvard University Press.

Chapter 5

Asset Pricing Models and Factor Models

5.1 Introduction

Empirical methods play an important role in the analysis and application of asset pricing models and factor models. The **capital asset pricing model** (CAPM) developed by Sharpe (1964), Lintner (1965a, 1965b) and Mossin (1966) is a theoretical model of the relationship between asset returns and risk under a set of simplifying assumptions. The CAPM shows that under this set of assumptions an equilibrium will exist where all investors will invest their funds in a portfolio containing each of the risky assets available, where the proportion of funds invested in each asset (the asset weight) is given by the asset's total market value as a proportion of the total market value of all risky assets. This portfolio is called the **market portfolio**. The CAPM also shows that the risk premium for an individual asset depends on the asset's contribution to the risk of the market portfolio (the risk premium is defined as the expected return in excess of the risk-free rate of return). Differences in the risk premium for individual assets can be explained entirely by differences in the covariance of their returns with the return for the market portfolio. The CAPM is an attractive theoretical model; it is parsimonious and has a clear set of predictions that can be empirically evaluated using standard statistical techniques discussed in Chapter 3. Furthermore, empirical versions of the CAPM can be used for practical applications of the underlying theory.

Factor models are a type of asset pricing model that are more general than the CAPM and appear to have greater explanatory power than the CAPM when applied to stock market data. They are widely used by analysts in financial institutions for a range of practical tasks associated with investing in stocks. For example, they can be used to understand how particular types of systematic macroeconomic risk affect expected returns. This information can then be used by portfolio managers to inform stock selection. Factor models can also be used to estimate and forecast the covariance matrix for a group of stock returns, which might then be used as an input for portfolio optimisation and for risk management. Factor model estimates of covariance matrices for large numbers of assets usually involve computing fewer terms than orthodox estimates.

This chapter begins with a brief review of the main theoretical results involving the CAPM before discussing some of its applications and how to empirically test the CAPM. The strengths and weaknesses of the CAPM and the empirical tests are discussed before we focus on factor models. The penultimate section of the main text presents three empirical examples. The first example involves empirically testing the CAPM using stock market data; the second involves estimating a factor model; the third involves using a factor model to estimate the unconditional covariance matrix for a group of stock returns, which is then used as an input for portfolio optimisation.

5.2 CAPM

5.2.1 Main Results

The CAPM is a theoretical model derived under a set of simplifying assumptions that explains what *ex ante* expected returns for assets will be given their risk.[1] This expected return can be interpreted as the required rate of return for discounting the future cash flows associated with an asset so as to compute a *fair* price (a price consistent with the CAPM assumptions). The key CAPM assumptions are:

(i) All risky assets can be publicly traded.
(ii) There are multiple investors and no individual investor can affect asset prices.

---

[1]Assume in this chapter that "return" refers to the simple return.

(iii) Investors can borrow or lend unlimited amounts at a risk-free rate of interest.

(iv) All investors have the same single-period investment horizon.

(v) There are no taxes or transaction costs.

(vi) Investors employ modern portfolio theory (MPT).[2]

(vii) Investors are homogenous; so, for example, they use the same inputs in their application of MPT.

Under these assumptions, several important results can be mathematically proved. For example, it can be shown that all investors will choose to invest in the market portfolio and that, in the terminology of MPT (see Chapter 4), this portfolio is the optimal risky portfolio (ORP) for each investor; hence, it will be the portfolio given by the tangency of each investor's capital allocation line (CAL) with their efficient frontier. This CAL is called the **capital market line** (CML). Furthermore, let r_i be the return for asset i, r_m the return for the market portfolio, and r_f the risk-free rate of interest. Under the CAPM assumptions it can be shown that the risk premium for asset i, $E(r_i) - r_f$, is given by the product of the risk premium for the market portfolio and the asset's **beta**,

$$\beta_i = \frac{Cov(r_i, r_m)}{\sigma_m^2} \tag{5.1}$$

where σ_m^2 denotes the variance of the return for the market portfolio. This key result of the CAPM is summarised in the following expected return-beta equation,

$$E(r_i) - r_f = \beta_i \left[E(r_m) - r_f \right] \tag{5.2}$$

Therefore the CAPM tells us that investors are rewarded for bearing **systematic risk**, where an asset's systematic risk is measured by its contribution to the risk of the market portfolio, as measured by its beta (β_i). Assets with a large positive beta have a larger risk premium than assets with a small positive beta (or small or large negative beta). If $\beta_i = 1$, asset i will have the same risk premium as the market portfolio.[3]

Equation (5.2) can be represented graphically by a line in the expected return beta space called the **security market line** (SML). An example is graphed in Figure 5.1

---

[2]This assumption means that all investors employ Markowitz's expected return-variance rule, discussed in Chapter 4 (see Markowitz, 1952, 1959). It is important to recognise that whilst the CAPM requires MPT, MPT does not depend on the validity of the CAPM (see Fabozzi, Gupta and Markowitz, 2002).

[3]We have briefly discussed the main CAPM results here but do not focus on mathematically proving these results. This is covered in the original journal articles mentioned and is discussed in many established textbooks on investment analysis: for example, see Elton and Gruber (1995); Sharpe, Alexander and Bailey (1998); Reilly and Brown (2006); Bodie, Kane and Marcus (2009).

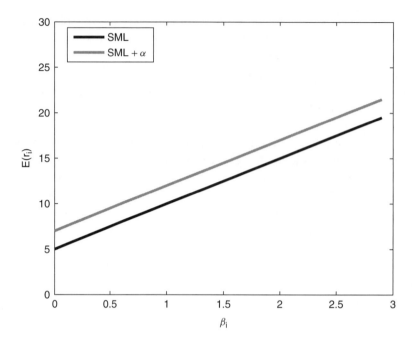

Figure 5.1   Security market line.

where the expected return on the market portfolio is assumed to be 10% and the risk-free rate is assumed to be 5%.

The CAPM expected return-beta equation can be rearranged into the familiar $y = a + bx$ form,

$$E(r_i) = r_f + \left[E(r_m) - r_f\right]\beta_i \tag{5.3}$$

Note, therefore, that the slope of the SML is the market risk premium, $E(r_m) - r_f$. The grey line in Figure 5.1 is a graph of the following augmented SML,

$$E(r_i) = \alpha + r_f + \left[E(r_m) - r_f\right]\beta_i \tag{5.4}$$

where $\alpha = 2$ (labelled SML $+ \alpha$). If an empirical analysis suggests that a particular asset falls on SML $+ \alpha$, then clearly under the assumptions of the CAPM this suggests that the asset is **underpriced** in the sense that the current price is too low to be consistent with the CAPM expected return (because the expected return is too high). Underpriced assets might be considered to be attractive investments because they provide higher expected returns than the return consistent with the assumptions of the CAPM, and one might argue that their price will rise when this is widely recognised. If the assumptions of the CAPM are all perfectly satisfied, there should be no underpriced assets since all assets will fall on the SML.

5.2.2 CAPM Applications

The CAPM is a theoretical model; however, it can also be used for empirical appli-cations. Most obviously the CAPM can be used to estimate the expected return for an asset that is consistent with the CAPM assumptions. This expected return can be interpreted as a required rate of return to invest in the asset. Therefore, it can be used as the discount rate for computing an asset's intrinsic value (e.g. using the dividend discount model discussed in Chapter 4). For example, if we assume that $r_f = 5\%, E(r_m) = 10\%$ and $\beta_i = 0.5$, then it follows from (5.2) that the expected return for asset i is,

$$E(r_i) = 5\% + 0.5\,[10\% - 5\%] = 7.5\% \tag{5.5}$$

Since the expected return on the market portfolio and the beta for an asset are unknown population parameters, in practice they would need to be estimated from sample data. Hence in practice the following sample version of (5.2) would typically be used to estimate the expected return,

$$E(r_i) = \bar{r}_f + \hat{\beta}_i\left[\bar{r}_m - \bar{r}_f\right] \tag{5.6}$$

where $\hat{\beta}_i$ is the estimated beta and $\bar{r}_m$ and $\bar{r}_f$ are the sample mean values for the market portfolio return and the risk-free rate computed from time series data over the same sample period. As well as being an integral part of the CAPM, the estimated beta for an asset provides a simple measure of systematic risk that might be used by a portfolio manager for stock selection.

Other CAPM applications include determining the prices that public utility com-panies can charge for their goods and services. Since the CAPM expected return can be interpreted as a **fair return**, a public utility might be required to set prices so that it generates a return equal to the CAPM expected return. In practice, (5.6) would be used with an estimated beta obtained using sample data on stock returns for the utility company. The CAPM has also become popular as a tool to help com-pute a company's **cost of capital**, which can be used to decide whether capital investment projects should proceed. Consider a company proposing to invest share-holders' money to develop a new product. Assuming that a beta for the product can be estimated, the CAPM can be used to compute a required rate of return on the investment to help determine whether it should go ahead.

The CAPM also provides a useful benchmark model for measuring the performance of portfolio managers. Consider again the augmented SML given by (5.4). If *ex post* a particular portfolio manager can be shown to have generated a positive alpha, then conditional on the CAPM this suggests that the portfolio manager has identified underpriced assets. Hence a popular measure for evaluating portfolio performance is **Jensen's alpha** (Jensen, 1968), which is just the *ex post* estimated alpha,

$$\hat{\alpha}_P = \bar{r}_P - \bar{r}_f - \hat{\beta}_P(\bar{r}_m - \bar{r}_f) \tag{5.7}$$

where a subscript P denotes a portfolio amount and a bar above a term denotes its sample mean computed using time series data. Since $\hat{\alpha}_P$ estimates the expected return in excess of the value predicted by the CAPM, portfolio managers with high values of $\hat{\alpha}_P$ are regarded as more successful than those with low values. Other popular portfolio evaluation measures related to the CAPM include the **Sharpe ratio** (Sharpe, 1966, 1994),

$$SR_p = \frac{\bar{r}_P - \bar{r}_f}{\hat{\sigma}_P} \tag{5.8}$$

which is just the sample equivalent of the risk-adjusted expected excess return, and the **Treynor ratio** (Treynor, 1965) which is given by (5.8) with $\hat{\sigma}_P$ replaced by $\hat{\beta}_P$.

If an empirical analysis reveals consistently positive alphas then one possible explanation is that the asset market is inefficient, in the sense that asset prices do not incorporate all relevant information. It is tempting to interpret such empirical evidence as a rejection of the efficient market hypothesis (EMH) (Roberts, 1967; Fama, 1970). Note, however, that any conclusions regarding the EMH from an empirical version of an asset pricing model such as the CAPM are conditional on the implicit assumption that the asset pricing model is appropriate (including that its assumptions are a true description of reality). Therefore, a rejection of the hypothesis that the EMH is true could be due to the asset pricing model being false; a stock market might be strongly efficient but an empirical analysis reveals positive alpha stocks simply because the CAPM is incorrect in some way. This **joint-hypothesis problem** is discussed in detail by Fama (1991) and here in Chapter 6.

5.2.3 Empirically Testing the CAPM

A vast amount of research has been undertaken on empirically testing whether the CAPM is supported by real-world data on stocks and many different regression-based tests have been proposed. Particularly important journal articles on this issue are Lintner (1965a, 1965b), Black, Jensen and Scholes (1972) and Fama and MacBeth (1973). A simple two-step regression-based empirical test of the CAPM can be computed as follows:

Step (i) Collect a sample of time series data on the returns for a sample of stocks (e.g. the monthly returns for N US stocks listed on the NYSE) over a particular time period (e.g. five years), and on a proxy for the market portfolio (e.g. the NYSE Composite index) and the risk-free rate (e.g. a US Treasury bill rate), and estimate the parameters of the security characteristic line (SCL) for each stock using ordinary least squares (OLS),

$$r_{i,t} - r_{f,t} = \alpha_i + \beta_i(r_{m,t} - r_{f,t}) + \varepsilon_{i,t} \tag{5.9}$$

Assume that $\varepsilon_{i,t} \sim NID(0, \sigma_{\varepsilon_i}^2)$. These are referred to as the **first-pass regressions**.

Step (ii) Run a second cross-sectional regression of the sample mean excess return for the stocks $\bar{r}_i - \bar{r}_f$ on the estimated betas from the first-pass regressions,

$$\bar{r}_i - \bar{r}_f = \gamma_0 + \gamma_1 \hat{\beta}_i + u_i \tag{5.10}$$

Assume that $u_i \sim NID(0, \sigma_{u_i}^2)$. This is referred to as the **second-pass regression**. Note that the regressand in (5.10) is an $N \times 1$ vector of sample mean excess returns and the regressor is an $N \times 1$ vector of estimated beta values. Note also that an intercept parameter γ_0 is included in (5.10). The CAPM implies that $H_0 : \gamma_0 = 0$ should not be rejected. The CAPM also implies that $H_0 : \gamma_1 = \bar{r}_m - \bar{r}_f$ should not be rejected. These hypotheses can be tested using t-tests. A rejection implies that the CAPM expected return-beta relationship can be rejected.

An extended version of this approach can be used to test the null hypothesis that non-systematic risk is not priced (as the CAPM predicts). This involves including the estimated error variance from (i), $\hat{\sigma}_{\varepsilon_i}^2$, as a regressor in the second-pass regressions to capture non-systematic risk,

$$\bar{r}_i - \bar{r}_f = \gamma_0 + \gamma_1 \hat{\beta}_i + \gamma_2 \hat{\sigma}_{\varepsilon_i}^2 + u_i \tag{5.11}$$

The relevant null hypothesis is $H_0 : \gamma_2 = 0$, which can be tested using a t-test. If (5.11) is used for testing and $H_0 : \gamma_2 = 0$ is rejected with $\hat{\gamma}_2 > 0$, it suggests that investors earn a risk premium for bearing non-systematic risk. This contradicts the CAPM prediction that only systematic risk matters, measured by an asset's beta.

The early empirical applications of this two-pass testing procedure to US stock market data produced mixed results (e.g. see Lintner, 1965b). These applications tend to find that risk premiums are positively related to beta values, which is supportive of the CAPM. However, the hypotheses discussed above are often rejected and a common finding is that $\hat{\gamma}_1 < \bar{r}_m - \bar{r}_f$, which implies that the actual SML is too flat relative the SML predicted by the CAPM. Thus, firms with a low beta have expected returns that are higher than the CAPM predicts (given their beta), and vice versa. Furthermore if (5.11) is used for testing, a common result is that $H_0 : \gamma_2 = 0$ is rejected with $\hat{\gamma}_2 > 0$, suggesting that non-systematic risk *is* being priced. Although the early empirical work produced somewhat mixed results, the CAPM became extremely popular both in academic research and in practice. It was not until the work of Fama and French (1992, 1993) that alternatives to the CAPM emerged with significantly greater explanatory power. This work is discussed in Section 5.3.

Although the CAPM does not appear to be strongly supported by two-pass empirical tests using stock market data, it is important to recognise that the results from tests of a theory that involve the use of random sample data should always be treated with a degree of caution because there is always a non-zero probability that the test conclusions are incorrect (even if a null hypothesis is rejected – this could be a Type I error). Furthermore, there are several methodological and technical problems with the two-pass testing technique described here, which are discussed in more detail in the next section.

5.2.4 Strengths and Weaknesses

The CAPM model is an attractive theoretical model, yet in empirical studies using stock market data and the basic two-pass tests discussed in Section 5.2.3, the empirical support for the CAPM is often rather weak. However, this empirical failure is not necessarily evidence that the CAPM is fundamentally wrong because there are numerous methodological and technical problems with the two-pass testing procedure.

The main methodological problem that affects regression-based tests of the CAPM is **Roll's critique**, first pointed out by Roll (1977) (see also Roll and Ross, 1994; Kandel and Stambaugh, 1995). This critique is based on the fact that in empirical tests of the CAPM, such as the two-pass test, since the true market portfolio is unobservable a proxy for the market portfolio has to be used. Typically, the proxy employed is a broad value-weighted stock market index: for example, for an empirical test using US data, the NYSE Composite index or the S&P Composite index. Roll (1977) shows that when using historical data to empirically test the CAPM, for any *ex post* efficient portfolio, the CAPM expected return-beta relationship will be satisfied, and that testing this feature of the CAPM using historical data is simply a test of whether the market proxy is efficient (*ex post*). However, the proxy being used might be inefficient leading to a rejection of the CAPM, even if the true market portfolio is efficient and the CAPM actually holds (a spurious rejection). Conversely, the proxy might be efficient even though the true market portfolio is inefficient, leading to erroneous support for the CAPM. A more general methodological criticism of the CAPM is that the assumptions required are unrealistic. Note, however, that Ross (1976) shows how the CAPM expected return-beta relationship can follow from a theoretical model without imposing all of the restrictive assumptions of the CAPM. This contribution is discussed again in Section 5.3.1.

In addition to these methodological problems, there are numerous technical problems with the basic two-pass CAPM tests discussed in Section 5.2.3. For instance, in the second-pass cross-sectional regressions the error terms can be correlated, leading to biased standard errors and unreliable *t*-tests.[4] Another

---

[4]Compared with OLS, generalised least squares (GLS) has superior asymptotic properties for the second-pass regressions: see Shanken and Zhou (2007) for more details.

potentially significant problem is the **errors-in-variables** or **measurement error** problem, which refers to the fact that the regressors in the second-pass of the two-pass testing procedure will contain errors, since they are the OLS betas from the first-pass regressions, which, because they are computed from sample data, will not be exactly equal to the population betas. If the first-pass models are stable over time then the errors will be smaller if longer samples of data are used. However, if the first-pass models are unstable then using long samples of data can lead to biased parameter estimates. The analyst faces a paradox: use short samples in the first-pass and produce noisy but unbiased estimates for the second-pass, or use longer samples in the first-pass to produce tighter parameter estimates for the second-pass, but these could be biased due to model instability. A possible solution is to use shorter samples but group the assets into a smaller number of equally weighted portfolios, which *ceteris parabus* produces tighter parameter estimates from the first-pass regressions because the non-systematic risk of the portfolios is lower than that of the individual assets. Applying the test to portfolios of assets also means that the cross-sectional dependence of the error terms is reduced.[5] Black, Jensen and Scholes (1972) point out that if this approach is used when testing the CAPM, it is important that there is enough variation in the portfolio betas. To help achieve this variation, a popular approach is to estimate first-pass regressions to get initial estimates of the betas and then to form portfolios of assets according to the size of the estimated betas. For example, portfolio 1 has N assets with the N largest betas, portfolio 2 has N assets with the next N largest betas, and so on. Then the first-pass and second-pass regressions can be re-estimated using these portfolios. When forming portfolios to test the CAPM, Black, Jensen and Scholes (1972) propose using different formation and estimation periods to try to avoid selection bias (in this context, "selection bias" means that the measurement error of the portfolios depends on their ranking). For example, the following approach might be used.

Step (i)   Estimate betas using monthly data over the previous n years and form J equally sized and weighted beta-ranked portfolios of excess returns $r_{j,t} - r_{f,t}$ ($j = 1, 2, \ldots, J$) for the next 12 months.

Step (ii)   Move forward 12 months in the sample and estimate betas using monthly sample data over the previous n years and form J equally sized and weighted beta-ranked portfolios of excess returns $r_{j,t} - r_{f,t}$ ($j = 1, 2, \ldots, J$) for the next 12 months.

This process is repeated until the end of the total sample period and the portfolio data $r_{j,t} - r_{f,t}$ can then be used for the usual two-pass testing procedure. Fama and MacBeth (1973) employ an extended version of this approach which reduces the impact of cross-sectionally correlated errors. In first-pass regressions they estimate

---

[5]For example, see Blume (1970), Blume and Friend (1973) and Black, Jensen and Scholes (1972).

beta parameters for portfolios of returns each month using historical data. Then a second-pass cross-sectional model is estimated on a month-by-month basis giving a series of monthly estimated gamma parameters. The statistical significance of the estimated gamma parameters is examined by computing a t-test for testing the statistical significance of the sample mean of the monthly estimated gamma parameters. For the ith parameter the relevant test statistic can be written,

$$t_i = \frac{\bar{\hat{\gamma}}_i}{\hat{s}_i/T^{1/2}} \tag{5.12}$$

where $\bar{\hat{\gamma}}_i$ is the sample mean of the monthly $\hat{\gamma}_i$ values, $\hat{s}_i$ is the sample standard deviation and T is the sample size.

Note that the discussion here has focused on just a small proportion of the literature on the CAPM. As well as numerous different ways of testing the CAPM, there are also numerous different types of CAPM. For example, the basic CAPM discussed here can be extended to allow for a non-linear relationship between expected returns and betas (e.g. see Fama and MacBeth, 1973). The **consumption CAPM** leads to a model where the risk premium for an asset is proportional to the covariance of its return with the growth rate of consumption (e.g. see Breeden, 1979). The **multi-beta CAPM** generalises the basic CAPM to multiple sources of risk (e.g. see Merton, 1973).

5.3 Factor Models

5.3.1 Single-Index Model and APT Model

Factor models are most often applied to stock market data; hence we will tend to refer to "stocks" rather than "assets" in this section. In the CAPM, investors are rewarded for bearing systematic risk, which for an individual stock is measured by its beta. In factor models, expected stock returns are also related to systematic risk, but there are various different sources of systematic risk (there are various **common risk factors**). The common risk factors might include specific macroeconomic risks priced by investors. The beta parameter on the risk factor is referred to as the **factor loading**. Important journal articles on this topic include Sharpe (1963), Rosenberg and Marathe (1976), Ross (1976, 1977), Chen, Ross and Ross (1986) and Fama and French (1992, 1993, 1996).

Sharpe (1963) discusses a model for stocks where the stock market index is used to proxy a single common risk factor. In this **single-index** model the return on a stock can be written as a linear function of the return on the stock market index (which captures systematic risk) plus a random error term (which captures non-systematic risk),

$$r_i = \alpha_i + \beta_i r_m + \varepsilon_i \tag{5.13}$$

where $E(\varepsilon_i) = 0$, $Var(\varepsilon_i) = \sigma_{\varepsilon_i}^2$, $E(\varepsilon_i \varepsilon_j) = 0 \; (i \neq j)$, $Cov(r_m, \varepsilon_i) = 0$. In practice, to estimate the parameters α_i and β_i a regression model can be used with time series data,

$$r_{i,t} = \alpha_i + \beta_i r_{m,t} + \varepsilon_{i,t} \tag{5.14}$$

Assuming the relevant regularity conditions are satisfied and that sufficient data are available, the parameters α_i and β_i can be consistently estimated for each stock using OLS. Thus an estimate of the factor loading for stock i can be obtained, giving an estimate of the sensitivity of the stock return to the factor. The single-index model (5.14) is similar to the model used in the first-pass of the CAPM testing procedure discussed in Section 5.2.1, although in the latter the stock market index is a proxy for the market portfolio while in the single-index model it is a proxy for a common risk factor.

The work of Ross (1976) is particularly important because it provides a link between factor models and the main CAPM results. Ross (1976) defines the following single factor model for stocks,

$$r_i = E(r_i) + \beta_i F + \varepsilon_i \tag{5.15}$$

where F is the common risk factor and ε_i captures non-systematic risk (i.e. firm-specific risk); assume that $E(\varepsilon_i) = 0, Var(\varepsilon_i) = \sigma_{\varepsilon_i}^2, E(\varepsilon_i \varepsilon_j) = 0 \; (i \neq j)$, $E(F) = 0, Var(F) = \sigma_F^2, E(F\varepsilon_i) = 0$. Note that in this case F is an *unanticipated* variable. Ross (1976) shows that for a well-diversified portfolio the return r_P can be written,

$$r_P = E(r_P) + \beta_P F \tag{5.16}$$

The variance of the portfolio return is $\sigma_P^2 = \beta_P^2 \sigma_F^2$. Therefore portfolio risk is affected by the variance of the risk factor but it is unaffected by firm-specific risks. Furthermore, by appealing to the condition that arbitrage opportunities cannot exist, Ross (1976) shows that the expected return for *all* well-diversified portfolios, including the market portfolio, lies on a SML that passes through the risk-free rate, as in Figure 5.1. Therefore Ross (1976) derives the CAPM SML relationship given in (5.5) without the need for the CAPM assumptions.

This approach is called **Arbitrage Pricing Theory** (APT). Although Ross (1976) shows that the CAPM relationship is implied by APT for well-diversified portfolios, for individual assets this relationship does not have to hold under APT. Therefore, although APT is less restrictive than the CAPM, the latter has clear implications for individual assets that can be used to test the underlying theory empirically. Note that APT can be extended to the case of multiple risk factors (see below). Hence factor models are often called **APT models** and they can be justified theoretically by appealing to the arguments made by Ross (1976).

5.3.2 Macroeconomic Factor Models

A macroeconomic factor model is essentially an extension of the single-index model to the case of multiple sources of risk, where the risk factors are unanticipated changes in macroeconomic variables,

$$r_{i,t} = E(r_{i,t}) + \beta_{i1}F_{1,t} + \beta_{i2}F_{2,t} + \cdots + \beta_{ik}F_{k,t} + \varepsilon_{i,t} \tag{5.17}$$

where $r_{i,t}$ is the return for stock i, $F_{1,t}, F_{2,t}, \ldots, F_{k,t}$ are the risk factors, and as before firm-specific risk is captured by the error term $\varepsilon_{i,t}$; assume here that $\varepsilon_{i,t} \sim NID(0, \sigma_{\varepsilon_i}^2)$, $E(F_{l,t}) = 0$, $E(F_{l,t}\varepsilon_{i,t}) = 0$ $(l = 1, 2, \ldots, k)$ and that the factors and the errors are uncorrelated across time. This model says that the difference between the actual return for a stock and the expected return is explained by the risk factors that here capture specific macroeconomic risks, and an error term that captures non-systematic risk.

Assuming that the relevant regularity conditions are satisfied and that sufficient monthly data are available, OLS can be used to obtain consistent estimates of the factor loadings $\beta_{i1}, \beta_{i2}, \ldots, \beta_{ik}$ for each month by regressing returns on the factors in a series of first-pass regressions. To examine the contribution of particular risk factors to the risk premium for a stock, a second-pass cross-sectional model can be estimated for each month,

$$r_i = \gamma_0 + \gamma_1\hat{\beta}_{i1} + \gamma_2\hat{\beta}_{i2} + \cdots + \gamma_k\hat{\beta}_{ik} + u_i \tag{5.18}$$

Again OLS can be used for consistent parameter estimation. The estimated gamma parameters in the second-pass regression model (5.18) can be interpreted as the estimated risk premium for the relevant factor (the **price of risk** for the factor).

Note that in factor models the risk premium for a particular factor can be negative; for example, assume that stocks with a positive loading for a particular factor are seen as more desirable (*ceteris parabus*). Investors will be willing to pay a higher price for these stocks meaning that the expected return will be lower than for stocks with a negative loading. The measurement error problem that exists when testing the CAPM also applies to factor models. Hence, in empirical work, rather than applying factor models to individual stocks, portfolios of stocks are often used.

Macroeconomic factor models can be used to understand how particular macroeconomic risks are priced, which is useful information that might then influence stock selection in the future. For example, a portfolio manager might want to construct a portfolio with a low (or high) sensitivity to a particular source of systematic risk. More generally, factor models can be used to help construct tracking portfolios, by choosing stocks with estimated factor loadings that are similar to the estimated factor loadings for the portfolio being tracked. As will be discussed in more detail in Section 5.3.4, factor models can also be used to estimate the covariance matrix for groups of stock returns which can then be used for portfolio optimisation and for risk management.

As with the CAPM, an enormous amount of empirical research has been undertaken to assess the performance of macroeconomic factor models for explaining the cross-section of expected stock returns. The majority of these studies suggest that they have greater explanatory power than the CAPM for stock market data. In their study of US stocks, Chen, Roll and Ross (1986) examine various combinations of macroeconomic risk factors (*e.g.* growth rate of industrial production, inflation, the spread between corporate and government bond yields). They employ a version of the Fama and MacBeth (1973) technique to analyse the relationship between these factors and the cross-section of expected US stock returns. They find that some but not all of the factors considered are statistically significant. In particular, the growth rate of industrial production (which captures business cycle risk) and the bond-spread variable (which captures changes in the aggregate level of risk) are strongly significant. The model used by Chen, Roll and Ross (1986) is a macroeconomic factor model – the risk factors capture systematic macroeconomic risks. Rosenberg and Marathe (1976) propose that rather than directly employ macroeconomic variables to capture systematic risks, the risks can be captured more precisely using microeconomic characteristics such as information on book value, earnings and sales.[6]

5.3.3 Fama and French Models

Another popular class of factor models are the models proposed by Fama and French (1992, 1993). Fama and French (1992) analyse the extent to which the market index beta, size (measured by market value, MV), E/P, leverage and BV/MV explain the cross-section of expected stock returns for NYSE, AMEX, and NASDAQ stocks. They find that when considered alone the market index beta has only weak explanatory power, and that the other variables have stronger explanatory power. A closer analysis reveals that size and BV/MV together have the greatest explanatory power. This comprehensive piece of empirical work had a profound impact on future academic research in this area and on asset pricing in practice.

---

[6]This type of factor model has become known as a **BARRA model** after Barr Rosenberg, who established the approach.

Building on their 1992 work, Fama and French (1993) estimate factor models using time series data for both the stock and bond markets with five factors – three stock market factors and two bond market factors. The three stock market factors are the excess return for the market index; the difference between the return on a portfolio of large stocks and small stocks (SMB_t); and the difference between the return on a portfolio of stocks with high book-to-market ratios and low book-to-market ratios (HML_t). The first of the three Fama and French (1993) factors is conventional, but the SMB_t and HML_t factors are more unusual; they are variables that proxy for unobserved systematic risks related to size and BV/MV that are constructed from stock returns (hence, they are sometimes referred to as **mimicking** portfolios). Their three-factor model for stocks can thus be written,

$$R_{i,t} = \alpha + \beta_{i1}R_{m,t} + \beta_{i2}SMB_t + \beta_{i3}HML_t + \varepsilon_{i,t} \tag{5.19}$$

where $R_{m,t}$ is the excess return on the stock market index. Note that the regressand in (5.19) is not the excess return on individual stocks, but rather it is the excess return on portfolios formed by ranking stocks according to both their size and their BV/MV (see Fama and French (1993) for details on the ranking technique used).

Fama and French (1993) find that the three-factor model (5.19) appears to have very high explanatory power. The time series variation of the excess returns for ranked portfolios is explained very well by the three factors, with R^2 values of around 0.90 being obtained for some of the portfolios considered. Hence the Fama-French **three-factor model** has become a widely used model in practice. Subsequent studies have found that, in addition to the three Fama and French (1993) factors, an additional factor, **winners minus losers** (WML), computed by subtracting the returns for stocks with good previous performance from those for stocks with poor previous performance, has explanatory power (e.g. see Carhart, 1997).

5.3.4 Covariance Matrix Estimation

The unconditional and conditional covariance matrices for asset returns are important inputs in many different areas of finance. For example, as shown in Chapter 4 an estimate of the covariance matrix for the relevant asset returns is required for portfolio optimisation using MPT. Define the unconditional covariance matrix for N asset returns as,

$$\Sigma = \begin{bmatrix} \sigma_1^2 & \sigma_{12} & \cdots & \sigma_{1N} \\ \sigma_{21} & \sigma_2^2 & \cdots & \sigma_{2N} \\ \vdots & \vdots & \ddots & \vdots \\ \sigma_{N1} & \sigma_{N2} & \cdots & \sigma_N^2 \end{bmatrix} \tag{5.20}$$

In Chapters 3 and 4 we discussed several different methods for estimating and forecasting covariance matrices, such as for example using a sample covariance matrix. Let $\mathbf{R}$ be a $T \times N$ matrix of returns on the N assets over T days in mean-deviation form; the unbiased sample covariance matrix is,

$$\hat{\Sigma} = (T - 1)^{-1}(\mathbf{R}'\mathbf{R}) \tag{5.21}$$

Whilst the simplicity of this estimate is an attractive feature, as discussed in Chapter 4 this approach does have some weaknesses. One weakness is that for large numbers of assets the number of terms in the covariance matrix becomes extremely large, making the sample covariance matrix a computationally expensive estimate. Another weakness is that the sample covariance matrix is not guaranteed to be positive-definite. If the sample covariance matrix is not positive-definite then the ORP weights might not be computable using this estimate.[7] Other approaches to estimating conditional covariance matrices are discussed in Chapter 3 (e.g. the EWMA approach, multivariate GARCH models), and these can have similar problems.

The covariance matrix for a group of asset returns can also be estimated using a factor model. Moreover the computational cost of the estimate can be significantly lower than for orthodox estimates such as the sample covariance matrix. Assume that the return on N stocks can be explained using a single-factor model,

$$r_{i,t} = \alpha_i + \beta_i F_t + \varepsilon_{i,t} \tag{5.22}$$

where $\varepsilon_{i,t} \sim NID(0, \sigma_{\varepsilon_i}^2)$, $E(\varepsilon_{i,t}\varepsilon_{j,t}) = 0$ $(i \neq j)$, $E(F_t) = 0$ and $E(F_t\varepsilon_{i,t}) = 0$. Using (5.22) it can be shown that the unconditional variance of the return for stock i can be written,

$$Var(r_{i,t}) = \beta_i^2 \sigma_F^2 + \sigma_{\varepsilon_i}^2 \tag{5.23}$$

where σ_F^2 is the unconditional variance of the factor, and the unconditional covariance between stock i and stock j can be written,

$$Cov(r_{i,t}, r_{j,t}) = \beta_i\beta_j\sigma_F^2 \tag{5.24}$$

Therefore, to estimate the unconditional covariance matrix for the returns on two stocks,

$$\Sigma = \begin{bmatrix} \sigma_1^2 & \sigma_{12} \\ \sigma_{21} & \sigma_2^2 \end{bmatrix} \tag{5.25}$$

requires two estimated betas, $\hat{\beta}_1$ and $\hat{\beta}_2$, and three estimated variance terms, $\hat{\sigma}_{\varepsilon_1}^2, \hat{\sigma}_{\varepsilon_2}^2$ and $\hat{\sigma}_F^2$. For two assets this is more estimates than if we had used the sample covariance matrix, since in that case we only need three estimates ($\hat{\sigma}_1^2, \hat{\sigma}_2^2, \hat{\sigma}_{12}$). However, more generally, with N assets there are $2N + 1$ parameters to be estimated when the single-factor model is used. In the orthodox case the number of parameters to

---

[7]See Chapter 4 for more details.

be estimated is $(N^2 + N)/2$. Therefore, for large numbers of assets, estimating the covariance matrix using this type of factor model becomes much more efficient compared with using the sample covariance matrix.

When the single-factor model (5.22) is used to estimate the unconditional covariance matrix for N assets, the estimate can be written,

$$\hat{\Sigma} = \begin{bmatrix} \hat{\beta}_1\hat{\beta}_1\hat{\sigma}_F^2 + \hat{\sigma}_{\varepsilon_1}^2 & \hat{\beta}_1\hat{\beta}_2\hat{\sigma}_F^2 & \cdots & \hat{\beta}_1\hat{\beta}_N\hat{\sigma}_F^2 \\ \hat{\beta}_2\hat{\beta}_1\hat{\sigma}_F^2 & \hat{\beta}_2\hat{\beta}_2\hat{\sigma}_F^2 + \hat{\sigma}_{\varepsilon_2}^2 & \cdots & \hat{\beta}_2\hat{\beta}_N\hat{\sigma}_F^2 \\ \vdots & \vdots & \ddots & \vdots \\ \hat{\beta}_N\hat{\beta}_1\hat{\sigma}_F^2 & \hat{\beta}_N\hat{\beta}_2\hat{\sigma}_F^2 & \cdots & \hat{\beta}_N\hat{\beta}_N\hat{\sigma}_F^2 + \hat{\sigma}_{\varepsilon_N}^2 \end{bmatrix} \tag{5.26}$$

which can be written more concisely as,

$$\hat{\Sigma} = \hat{\beta}\hat{\beta}'\hat{\sigma}_F^2 + \hat{\Omega}_{\varepsilon} \tag{5.27}$$

where $\hat{\beta} = [\hat{\beta}_1 \ldots \hat{\beta}_N]'$ and $\hat{\Omega}_{\varepsilon}$ are estimated values ($\hat{\Omega}_{\varepsilon}$ is a diagonal matrix with the firm-specific estimated variances down the main diagonal, and hence this type of factor model is called a **diagonal model**). For models with multiple factors, similar formulas can be easily derived. Estimating and forecasting the *conditional* covariance matrix for returns can also be done using factor models that allow for time-variation. The formulas above can be used, replacing the unconditional terms with the relevant conditional terms: for example,

$$\hat{\Sigma}_t = \hat{\beta}_t\hat{\beta}_t'\hat{\sigma}_{F,t}^2 + \hat{\Omega}_{\varepsilon,t} \tag{5.28}$$

where the time subscripts denote possible time-variation. In practice, statistical models for the betas and the conditional variance terms would have to be specified to capture any time-variation. Then to forecast the conditional covariance matrix using this approach the estimated statistical models for the time-subscript terms would have to be used to compute forecasts of these terms.

Having estimated a returns covariance matrix using a factor model, the estimated matrix might then be employed by portfolio managers for portfolio optimisation using MPT, or for risk-management purposes. Low computational cost is an attractive feature for analysts who might need to estimate many different large covariance matrices to assess the likely impact of different scenarios and stock selections.

5.3.5 Strengths and Weaknesses

In practice it appears that factor models are more successful than the CAPM in explaining variations in expected stock returns: for example, see Chen, Roll and Ross (1986) and Fama and French (1992, 1993). However, the methodological and technical difficulties associated with empirically testing asset pricing models and the issue of **data-snooping** (see below) all need to be kept in mind when making statements regarding the relative performance of the CAPM versus factor models. As we have seen, another attractive feature of factor models is that, for large numbers of assets, they provide a way of estimating and forecasting the covariance matrix of returns at a much lower computational cost than orthodox approaches.

Factor models have a number of potential weaknesses. For example, the relationship between the risk factors and stock returns will in some cases be time-varying. If this time-variation is ignored when estimating the first-pass regression models then the estimated factor loadings will be biased. Also, in most cases there is no strong theoretical guidance as to which variables to use as risk factors, meaning that the decision as to which model is the most appropriate for a particular data set becomes subjective. This means that in practice factor models are susceptible to data-snooping. In this context data-snooping refers to analysts searching over many different factors until they find a set of factors that performs well on the basis of hypothesis tests (e.g. t-tests, F-tests). Since these test statistics are random variables computed using sample data, it follows that if analysts search over a large enough number of regressors then they will always be able to find regressors that perform well on the basis of the test statistics even if the regressors do not have genuine explanatory power. Data-snooping is a subtle statistical problem that affects many different topics in empirical finance and often it is not recognised in empirical studies involving factor models. Correcting for the effects of data-snooping is not straightforward but it can be done using computer simulation methods.

An alternative approach to choosing macroeconomic/microeconomic variables as risk factors is to use statistical techniques to estimate the risk factors. The two main techniques that are popular for doing this are principal components analysis (PCA) and factor analysis (FA). These techniques are outside of the scope of this book, but in short they involve estimating the factors and the factor loadings simultaneously, with the factors being estimated using linear combinations of the original returns data (e.g. see Rao, 1996).

The next section discusses the empirical examples for this chapter. Further details on the MATLAB® programs and the data used are given in Section 5.7. Critical values for the test statistics used can be obtained from the statistical tables in the Appendix. To keep things simple the examples here use a limited data set (100 stocks or fewer). Typically in journal articles on this topic, a much larger sample of stocks is used for a particular stock exchange, sometimes the entire universe of stocks.

5.4 Empirical Examples

> ### Example 5.1: Testing the CAPM
>
> **(a)** Using monthly data on the prices of 100 stocks listed on the NYSE for 2002:12–2007:12 (see Table 5.A1), the NYSE Composite index and the US three-month Treasury bill, test the CAPM using the basic two-pass approach.
> **(b)** Repeat (a) including the estimated error variance from the first-pass regression for each stock as an additional regressor.

The relevant MATLAB® programs are given in the files E51a.m and E51b.m for the two versions of the test. A portion of E51a.m is given in Box 5.1. Note that in this program the regression model parameters and the relevant test statistics are computed explicitly in the program using matrix algebra. These could instead be computed using the Statistics Toolbox in MATLAB®, along with other useful statistical information if required.

Box 5.1 E51a.m

```
%EXAMPLE 5.1(a)
clear;
%Load the data.
D1=xlsread('C5stocks');
D2=xlsread('nyse');
tb=xlsread('TB3MS');
%Define the variables.
P1=flipud(D1);
P2=flipud(D2(:,6));
nr1=size(P1,1);
ret1=(P1(2:nr1,:)-P1(1:nr1-1,:))./P1(1:nr1-1,:);
ret2=(P2(2:nr1,1)-P2(1:nr1-1,1))./P2(1:nr1-1,1);
[nr2 nc2]=size(ret1);
rf=tb(1:nr2,1)/12/100;
%Use a loop to estimate the first-pass regressions.
i=1;
while i<=nc2;
%Estimate the parameters using OLS.
exret1=ret1(:,i)-rf;
exret2=ret2-rf;
```

```
u=ones(nr2,1);
Y=exret1;
X=[u exret2];
params(:,i)=inv(X'*X)*X'*Y;
%Compute the sample mean excess return for the stocks.
mexret1(i,1)=mean(exret1);
%Update the loop.
i=i+1;
end;
%Collect the estimated parameters from the first-pass regressions.
alpha=params(1,:)';
beta=params(2,:)';
%Compute the sample mean excess return for the index.
mexret2=mean(exret2);
%Estimate the second-pass regression using OLS, compute t-tests,
%R-squared and Adjusted-R-squared.
Y=mexret1;
u=ones(nc2,1);
X=[u beta];
gamma=inv(X'*X)*X'*Y;
spe=Y-X*gamma;
spev=sum(spe.^2)/(nc2-2);
gammacv=spev*inv(X'*X);
tstat1=gamma(1,1)/sqrt(gammacv(1,1));
tstat2=gamma(2,1)/sqrt(gammacv(2,2));
tstat3=(gamma(2,1)-mexret2)/sqrt(gammacv(2,2));
ess=sum((X*gamma-mean(Y)).^2);
tss=sum((Y-mean(Y)).^2);
rsquared=ess/tss;
adjrsquared=1-(1-rsquared)*(nc2-1)/(nc2-2);
```

The second-pass regression results for Example 5.1(a) are given in Table 5.1, along with relevant test statistics.

Although the estimated betas have only weak explanatory power in the second-pass regression, the results in Table 5.1 offer some support for the CAPM in the sense that $\hat{\gamma}_1 > 0$ and $\hat{\gamma}_1$ is statistically significant at the 1% level. Furthermore $H_0 : \gamma_1 = \bar{r}_m - \bar{r}_f$ is not rejected by a t-test at conventional significance levels. Note, however, that $H_0 : \gamma_0 = 0$ is rejected by a t-test at the 1% level of significance, which is not supportive of the CAPM.

The second-pass regression results and test statistics for Example 5.1(b) are given in Table 5.2.

Table 5.1   Second-pass regression results and test statistics

$\hat{\gamma}_0$	0.005
$\hat{\gamma}_1$	0.006
R^2	0.131
$\bar{R}^2$	0.123
$H_0 : \gamma_0 = 0$	$t = 2.925$***
$H_0 : \gamma_1 = 0$	$t = 3.851$***
$\bar{r}_m - \bar{r}_f$	0.009
$H_0 : \gamma_1 = \bar{r}_m - \bar{r}_f$	$t = -1.555$

Note: ***denotes statistical significance at the 1% level.

Table 5.2   Second-pass regression results and test statistics

$\hat{\gamma}_0$	0.005
$\hat{\gamma}_1$	0.005
$\hat{\gamma}_2$	0.592
R^2	0.154
$\bar{R}^2$	0.137
$H_0 : \gamma_0 = 0$	$t = 2.606$**
$H_0 : \gamma_1 = 0$	$t = 2.572$**
$H_0 : \gamma_2 = 0$	$t = 1.611$
$\bar{r}_m - \bar{r}_f$	0.009
$H_0 : \gamma_1 = \bar{r}_m - \bar{r}_f$	$t = -2.160$**

Note: **denotes statistical significance at the 5% level.

In this case the R^2 and $\bar{R}^2$ values indicate only slightly stronger explanatory power than in Example 5.1(a); hence the additional regressor – the error variance terms from the first-pass regressions – appears not to be relevant in this case. The t-test of the hypothesis $H_0 : \gamma_2 = 0$ does not lead to a rejection at conventional significance levels, which suggests that investors are not being rewarded for bearing firm-specific risk, supporting the CAPM prediction that only systematic risk is priced. However, the other results are generally not supportive of the CAPM: for example, $H_0 : \gamma_0 = 0$ is rejected by a t-test at the 5% significance level; furthermore, while $H_0 : \gamma_1 = 0$ is rejected by a t-test at the 5% level of significance, $H_0 : \gamma_1 = \bar{r}_m - \bar{r}_f$ is also rejected at the 5% level of significance, which is not supportive of the CAPM.

Example 5.2: Estimating a factor model

Using monthly data on 100 stocks listed on the NYSE for 1997:12–2007:12 (see Table 5.A1), estimate relevant first-pass and second-pass factor model regressions to investigate the price of risk and its statistical significance for the following five risk factors:

(i) The return on the NYSE Composite index.
(ii) The first-difference of the natural logarithm of the industrial production index.
(iii) The spread between the 10-year Treasury bond rate and the three-month Treasury bill rate.
(iv) The spread between the BAA bond rate and the 10-year Treasury bond rate.
(v) The first-difference of the natural logarithm of the consumer price index.

The relevant MATLAB® program is given in the file E52.m. The second-pass regression results and test statistics are given in Table 5.3.

Table 5.3 Second-pass regression results and test statistics

$\overline{\hat{\gamma}}_0$	0.007
$\overline{\hat{\gamma}}_1$	0.007
$\overline{\hat{\gamma}}_2$	7.537e−04
$\overline{\hat{\gamma}}_3$	−2.527e−04
$\overline{\hat{\gamma}}_4$	−1.661e−04
$\overline{\hat{\gamma}}_5$	2.585e−04
$H_0 : \overline{\gamma}_0 = 0$	$t = 2.576^{**}$
$H_0 : \overline{\gamma}_1 = 0$	$t = 2.065^{**}$
$H_0 : \overline{\gamma}_2 = 0$	$t = 0.987$
$H_0 : \overline{\gamma}_3 = 0$	$t = -1.637$
$H_0 : \overline{\gamma}_4 = 0$	$t = -2.975^{***}$
$H_0 : \overline{\gamma}_5 = 0$	$t = 0.986$

Note: *** and ** denote statistical significance at the 1% and 5% levels respectively. $\overline{\hat{\gamma}}_0$ is the sample mean of the monthly estimated intercepts, $\overline{\hat{\gamma}}_1 - \overline{\hat{\gamma}}_5$ are the sample means of the monthly estimated parameters on the five risk factors. The *t*-tests are computed from the monthly second-pass regressions.

It can be seen from the results in Table 5.3 that the price of risk for the NYSE Composite index is positive and statistically significant at the 5% level, but for the other risk factors the prices are extremely small and only the bond-spread price of risk is statistically significant (at the 1% level).

When factor models are used there is no theoretical restriction as to the appropriate signs of the estimated factor loadings from the first-pass regressions or the estimated gamma parameters from the second-pass regressions, although one might expect a particular sign. For example, since the industrial production risk factor captures business cycle risk, one might expect that in the first-pass regressions most stocks would be positively sensitive to this factor, and that in the second-pass regressions the sample mean of the estimated gamma parameters for this factor will be positive. Here it is positive, but statistically insignificant. Here the bond-spread price of risk is negative and statistically significant at the 1% significance level. A statistically significant negative price of risk indicates lower expected returns for stocks with a positive sensitivity to this risk factor than for those with a negative sensitivity, suggesting that, *ceteris parabus*, investors are willing to pay a higher price for those stocks whose returns are positively sensitive to this risk factor.

Note that the results from these simple examples should be treated with a degree of caution both because of the limited data set and also because of the possibility they are detrimentally affected by the problems discussed in Sections 5.2.4 and 5.3.5. Note also that, for simplicity, here we assume that as constructed the variables used capture *unanticipated* risk. A more comprehensive empirical analysis might use econometric techniques to ensure that the regressors only contain unanticipated information, leading to a different set of results and conclusions (see e.g. Chen, Roll and Ross, 1986).

Example 5.3: Covariance matrix estimation using a factor model

Using monthly data on the price of GE, UTX, MMM, DHR and PPG stocks for 1997:12–2007:12 and an annual risk-free rate of 4%, compute the ORP and OFP assuming a one-year investment horizon, a quadratic utility function with $\alpha = 4$, no borrowing and no short sales. Use a diagonal single-factor model to estimate the unconditional covariance matrix of returns, with returns on the NYSE Composite index as the risk factor.

The relevant MATLAB® program is given in the file E53.m and a portion of the program is given in Box 5.2. The results are graphed in Figure 5.2.

Box 5.2   E53.m

```
%EXAMPLE 5.3
clear;
%Load the data.
D1=xlsread('C5stocks3');
D2=xlsread('nyse2');
%Define the variables.
P1=flipud(D1);
P2=flipud(D2(:,6));
nr1=size(P1);
ret1=log(P1(2:nr1,:))-log(P1(1:nr1-1,:));
ret2=log(P2(2:nr1,1))-log(P2(1:nr1-1,1));
[nr2 nc2]=size(ret1);
u=ones(nr2,1);
%Use a loop to estimate the first-pass regressions.
i=1;
while i<=nc2;
%Estimate the parameters using OLS.
Y=ret1(:,i);
X=[u ret2];
params(:,i)=inv(X'*X)*X'*Y;
fpe(:,i)=Y-X*params(:,i);
fpev(i,1)=sum(fpe(:,i).^2)/(nr2-2);
%Update the loop;
i=i+1;
end;
%Compute the covariance matrix.
alpha=params(1,:)';
beta1=params(2,:)';
vret2=var(ret2);
omega=diag(fpev,0);
sigma=beta1*beta1'*vret2+omega;
cvret1=sigma;
```

Running E53.m reveals that in this case the expected return and risk of the ORP are $E(r_{ORP}) = 0.202, \sigma_{ORP} = 0.234$. The asset weights for the ORP are given in Table 5.4.

Table 5.4   Asset weights for ORP

w_{GE}	w_{UTX}	w_{MMM}	w_{DHR}	w_{PPG}
0	0.331	0.252	0.417	0

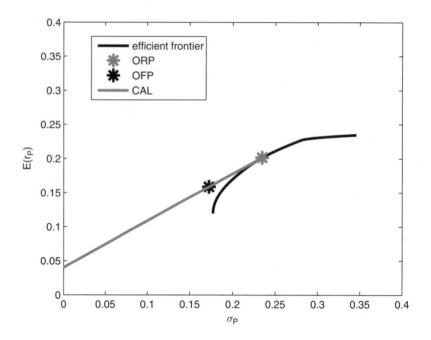

Figure 5.2 Asset allocation: five stocks and a risk-free asset.

The OFP involves investing 73.5% of funds in the ORP and the remainder in the risk-free asset. The expected return and risk of the OFP are $E(r_{OFP}) = 0.159$, $\sigma_{OFP} = 0.172$.

Note that the results obtained here are similar to those obtained if the traditional sample covariance matrix is used. This case is considered in Chapter 4, Example 4.3.

5.5 Summary

This chapter has focused on the empirical analysis and application of asset pricing models and factor models. This topic follows naturally from the main topics discussed in Chapter 4 – MPT and asset allocation. The CAPM is a theoretical model that tells us what the expected returns on risky assets will be under a set of assumptions, one of these assumptions being that all investors employ MPT. Since its development in the mid-1960s, several different empirical tests of the CAPM have been proposed and using these tests an enormous amount of empirical research has been carried out examining the empirical support for the CAPM. Typically, the CAPM is not strongly supported by empirical studies using stock market data. Factor models offer an alternative to the CAPM that typically have greater explanatory power when applied to stock market data and they are widely used by analysts in financial institutions. The empirical examples in this chapter have covered testing the CAPM, estimating and interpreting a factor model and using a factor model to estimate a covariance matrix for stock returns.

5.6 End of Chapter Questions[8]

Q1. Download monthly data for a five-year sample period on the prices of 100 stocks listed on the NYSE. Download monthly data on the NYSE Composite index and the US three-month Treasury bill rate for the same sample period.[9] Using these data, test the CAPM employing the basic two-pass approach.

Q2. Repeat Question 1 including the estimated error variance for each stock from the first-pass regressions as an additional regressor in the second-pass regression. Compare your results with those obtained for Question 1.

Q3. **(a)** Explain what is meant by the "measurement error problem" when testing the CAPM.

(b) Download monthly data on the stocks and stock market index in Question 1 for a 10-year sample period. Repeat Question 1 employing beta-ranked portfolios of stocks with a five-year formation period to reduce the measurement error problem.

Q4. Using the data for Question 3(b) and data on a selection of relevant macro-economic variables for the same sample period, estimate factor model regressions to investigate the price of risk for each of the risk factors and its statistical significance.[10]

Q5. Using the data for Question 1, estimate the covariance matrix for a selection of the stock returns employing a single-factor model. Using this estimated covariance matrix and an appropriate annual risk-free rate, compute the ORP and OFP assuming a one-year investment horizon, a quadratic utility function with α set to 2, 3 or 4, no borrowing and no short sales.

---

[8]A guide to answering these questions and relevant MATLAB® programs are given on the companion website (go to www.wileyeurope.com/college/sollis).

[9]Yahoo! Finance is one possible source of the stock market data (www.finance.yahoo.com). The Federal Reserve Economic Data (FRED) database at the Federal Reserve Bank of St Louis is one possible source of the Treasury bill data (www.research.stlouisfed.org/fred2/).

[10]The Federal Reserve Economic Data (FRED) database at the Federal Reserve Bank of St Louis is one possible source of the macroeconomic data (www.research.stlouisfed.org/fred2/).

5.7 Appendix

5.7.1 Data

Example 5.1

C5stocks.xls

Monthly data on the prices of the stocks in Table 5.A1 for 2002:12 – 2007:12 from Yahoo! Finance (www.finance.yahoo.com).

nyse.xls

Monthly data on the NYSE Composite index for 2002:12 – 2007:12 from Yahoo! Finance (www.finance.yahoo.com).

TB3MS.xls

Monthly data on TB3MS (three-month Treasury Bill: Secondary Market Rate) for 2003:1 – 2007:12, from the Federal Reserve Bank of St Louis FRED database (www.research.stlouisfed.org/fred2/).

Example 5.2

C5stocks2.xls

Monthly data on the prices of the stocks in Table 5.A1 for 1997:12 – 2007:12 from Yahoo! Finance (www.finance.yahoo.com).

nyse2.xls

Monthly data on the NYSE Composite index for 1997:12 – 2007:12 from Yahoo! Finance (www.finance.yahoo.com).

TB3MS2.xls

Monthly data on TB3MS (three-month Treasury Bill: Secondary Market Rate) for 1998:1 – 2007:12, from the Federal Reserve Bank of St Louis FRED database (www.research.stlouisfed.org/fred2/).

BAA.xls, CPIAUCSL.xls, GS10.xls, INDPRO.xls

Table 5.A1   Stock symbols

ABT	BCE	CCE	DD	F	HON	LLY	NLY	PGN	TOT
AEP	BCS	CNH	DE	FMC	HPQ	LMT	NOC	PHG	TXT
AF	BF-B	COP	DEO	GD	IBM	MCD	NVS	PPG	UN
AGCO	BMY	COT	DHR	GE	IPG	MHP	NYB	RDS-B	USB
AKO-A	BP	CPB	DOW	GIS	JNJ	MMM	OCN	SLE	UTX
APD	C	CR	DRI	GMCR	JPM	MRK	OLN	SNE	VZ
ASH	CAG	CTL	DUK	GR	JW-A	MTW	OMC	SO	WBK
AZN	CAT	CVR	EAT	GSK	K	MWW	PC	STD	WFC
BA	CBB	D	EMN	HIT	KO	NC	PEP	TEX	XOM
BAC	CBE	DB	ETR	HMC	KOF	NEE	PFE	TM	YUM

Monthly data on the following macroeconomic and financial variables from the Federal Reserve Bank of St Louis FRED database (www.research.stlouisfed.org/fred2/).

BAA (Moody's Seasoned Baa Corporate Bond Yield) (1998:1 – 2007:12)
CPIAUCSL (Consumer Price Index for All Urban Consumers: All Items)
  (1997:12 – 2007:12)
GS10 (10-Year Treasury Constant Maturity Rate) (1998:1 – 2007:12)
INDPRO (Industrial Production Index) (1998:1 – 2008:1)

Example 5.3

C5stocks3.xls

Monthly data on the price of the stocks GE, UTX, MMM, DHR, PPG for 1997:12 – 2007:12 from Yahoo! Finance (www.finance.yahoo.com).

nyse2.xls

See above.

5.7.2 MATLAB® Programs and Toolboxes[11]

Example 5.1

(a) E51a.m

(b) E51b.m

---

[11]See www.wileyeurope.com/college/sollis for the programs E##.m.

Example 5.2

E52.m

Example 5.3

E53m, MATLAB® Financial Toolbox

5.8 References

Black, F., Jensen, C.J. and M. Scholes (1972) The capital asset pricing model: some empirical tests. In Jensen, M. (ed.) *Studies in the Theory of Capital Markets*. New York: Praeger Publishers, pp 79–121.

Blume, M. (1970) Portfolio theory: a step towards its practical application, *Journal of Business*, 43, 152–174.

Blume, M. and I. Friend (1973) A new look at the capital asset pricing model, *Journal of Finance*, 28, 19–33.

Bodie, Z., Kane, A. and A.J. Marcus (2009) *Investments*, 8th edn. New York: McGraw-Hill.

Breeden, D. (1979) An intertemporal asset pricing model with stochastic consumption and investment opportunities, *Journal of Financial Economics*, 7, 265–296.

Carhart, M.M. (1997) On persistence in mutual fund performance, *Journal of Finance*, 52, 57–82.

Chen, N-Fu, Roll, R. and S. Ross (1986) Economic forces and the stock market, *Journal of Business*, 59, 383–403.

Elton, E.J. and M.J. Gruber (1995) *Modern Portfolio Theory and Investment Analysis*, 5th edn. New York: John Wiley & Sons.

Fabozzi, F.J., Gupta, F. and H.M. Markowitz (2002) The legacy of modern portfolio theory, *The Journal of Investing*, Fall, 7–22.

Fama, E.F. (1970) Efficient capital markets: a review of theory and empirical work, *Journal of Finance*, 25, 383–417.

Fama, E.F. (1991) Efficient capital markets II, *Journal of Finance*, 46, 1575–1617.

Fama, E.F. and K.R. French (1992) The cross-section of expected stock returns, *Journal of Finance*, 47, 427–465.

Fama, E.F. and K.R. French (1993) Common risk factors in the returns on stocks and bonds, *Journal of Financial Economics*, 33, 3–56.

Fama, E.F. and K.R. French (1996) Multifactor explanations of asset pricing anomalies, *Journal of Finance*, 51, 55–84.

Fama, E.F. and J.D. MacBeth (1973) Risk, return and equilibrium: empirical tests, *Journal of Political Economy*, 81, 607–636.

Jensen, M.C. (1968) The performance of mutual funds in the period 1945–1964, *Journal of Finance*, 23, 389–416.

Kandel, S. and R.F. Stambaugh (1995) Portfolio inefficiency and the cross-section of expected returns, *Journal of Finance*, 50, 157–184.

Lintner, J. (1965a) The valuation of risk assets and the selection of risky investments in stock portfolios and capital budgets, *Review of Economics and Statistics*, 47, 13–37.

Lintner, J. (1965b) Security prices, risk and maximal gains from diversification, *Journal of Finance*, 20, 587–615.

Markowitz, H.M. (1952) Portfolio selection, *Journal of Finance*, 7, 77–91.

Markowitz, H.M. (1959) *Portfolio Selection: Efficient Diversification of Investments*. New York: John Wiley & Sons.

Merton, R. (1973) An intertemporal capital asset pricing model, *Econometrica*, 41, 867–888.

Mossin, J. (1966) Equilibrium in a capital asset market, *Econometrica*, 34, 768–783.

Reilly, F.K. and K.C. Brown (2006) *Investment Analysis and Portfolio Management*, 8th edn. Ohio: Thomson South-Western.

Rao, C.R. (1996) Principal component and factor analyses. In Maddala, G.S. and C.R. Rao (eds) *Handbook of Statistics, Vol. 14*. Amsterdam: Elsevier.

Roberts, H. (1967) Statistical versus clinical prediction of the stock market, unpublished manuscript, CRSP, University of Chicago.

Roll, R. (1977) A critique of the asset pricing theory's tests, part I: on past and potential testability of the theory, *Journal of Financial Economics*, 4, 129–176.

Roll, R. and S.A. Ross (1994) On the cross-sectional relation between expected returns and betas, *Journal of Finance*, 49, 101–121.

Rosenberg, B. and V. Marathe (1976) Common factors in security returns: microeconomic determinants and macroeconomic correlates, *Proceedings of the Seminar on the Analysis of Security Prices*, University of Chicago, May, pp. 61–115.

Ross, S. (1976) The arbitrage theory of capital asset pricing, *Journal of Economic Theory*, 13, 341–360.

Ross, S. (1977) Return, risk, and arbitrage. In Friend, I. and J. Bicksler (eds) *Risk and Return in Finance*. Cambridge, MA: Balinger.

Shanken, J. and G. Zhou (2007) Estimating and testing beta pricing models: alternative methods and their performance in simulations, *Journal of Financial Economics*, 84, 40–86.

Sharpe, W.F. (1963) A simplified model for portfolio analysis, *Management Science*, 9, 277–293.

Sharpe, W.F. (1964) Capital asset prices: a theory of market equilibrium under conditions of risk, *Journal of Finance*, 19, 425–442.

Sharpe, W.F. (1966) Mutual fund performance, *Journal of Business*, 39, 119–138.

Sharpe, W.F. (1994) The Sharpe ratio, *Journal of Portfolio Management*, 21, 49–58.

Sharpe, W.F., Alexander, G.J. and J.V. Bailey (1998) *Investments*, 6th edn. New Jersey: Prentice Hall.

Treynor, J.L. (1965) How to rate management of investment funds, *Harvard Business Review*, 43, 63–75.

Chapter 6

Market Efficiency

6.1 Introduction

In finance the label **efficient market** refers to a financial market (e.g. a stock market, the foreign exchange market) that is informationally efficient, in the sense that current asset prices reflect all relevant information. The **efficient market hypothesis** (EMH) states that financial markets are efficient in this way. The EMH is a topic of practical importance for investors. If a market is informationally inefficient then it might be possible to earn **abnormal profits** by exploiting the information that has not been incorporated into prices. In this context, profits (returns) are said to be *abnormal* if they are larger than those from a passive investment strategy, such as a buy-and-hold strategy. In practice, the abnormal return associated with a particular active investment strategy might be assessed by comparing the sample mean return generated from the strategy with the sample mean return for a buy-and-hold strategy.

The journal article by Fama (1970) formalises the EMH and assesses the empirical evidence on the efficiency of the US stock market. There are three forms of the EMH. The **weak form** is that current asset prices reflect all historical market information such as the information from historical prices. The **semi-strong form** is that current asset prices reflect all publicly available information, including all market information. The **strong form** is that current asset prices reflect all relevant information, including historical market information, all publicly available information and all private information.[1] The results from early empirical studies of market efficiency (from the 1950s to the 1970s) support the weak form EMH.[2]

Formal empirical tests of market efficiency typically involve making assumptions about the underlying equilibrium asset pricing model used by investors. This means that such tests are actually joint hypothesis tests; they test the hypothesis of market efficiency and that the assumed asset pricing model is correct. Therefore, any apparent rejections of the EMH from this type of empirical test might be due to the asset pricing model being incorrect in some way. This subtle but important point is highlighted by Fama (1991):

> Ambiguity about information and trading costs is not, however, the main obstacle to inferences about market efficiency. The joint-hypothesis problem is more serious. Thus, market efficiency *per se* is not testable. It must be tested jointly with some model of equilibrium, an asset-pricing model...As a result, when we find anomalous evidence on the behavior of returns, the way it should be split between market inefficiency or a bad model of market equilibrium is ambiguous.[3]

This chapter focuses on some key topics related to the informational efficiency of financial markets where empirical methods play an important role. As well as discussing traditional empirical tests of market efficiency this chapter also discusses forecasting financial markets using econometric models and using **technical analysis**. Technical analysis is an approach to investing based on the belief that asset prices over time will trend. Technical analysts believe that by analysing historical inter- and intra-day price data (and/or data on volume), these trends can be identified and exploited to earn abnormal profits. Whilst many academic economists tend to be sceptical of technical analysis, it remains popular with investors.

When analysts undertake an econometric analysis of financial assets they tend to use data on asset returns rather than asset prices. This is because asset returns

---

[1]Distinguishing between weak and strong forms of EMH is also discussed in an unpublished paper by Roberts (1967).
[2]For example, see Kendall (1953), Fama (1965, 1970), Sharpe (1966) and Jensen (1968).
[3]Fama, E.F. (1991) Efficient capital markets II, *Journal of Finance*, 46, 1575–1617. The quote is from page 1575. Reproduced by permission of Wiley-Blackwell.

have statistical properties (e.g. stationarity) that make them more amenable than asset prices to analysis using conventional econometric methods.[4] Conversely, technical analysts primarily use data on asset prices. Following the work of Fama (1970) and others (see footnote 1), in the 1970s the consensus among academic economists was that most stock markets in developed countries were consistent with the weak form EMH. Therefore it was widely believed that any investment strategy involving the analysis of historical data on asset prices or returns (e.g. using econometric analysis or technical analysis) would not be able to generate abnormal profits. However, from the 1980s onwards empirical studies began to uncover empirical evidence that questioned even the weak form EMH (e.g. see Lo and MacKinlay, 1988). In the early 1990s, several empirical studies found that for some sample periods, some technical analysis trading rules did appear to be able to generate abnormal returns when applied to US stock market data (e.g. see Brock, Lakonishok and LeBaron, 1992). More recently, however, these abnormal returns seem to have disappeared (e.g. see Sullivan, Timmermann and White, 1999). This chapter discusses the empirical techniques used in these journal articles and the empirical results obtained. The penultimate section of the main text presents five empirical examples that demonstrate a selection of the empirical methods covered.

6.2 Market Efficiency Tests

6.2.1 The Efficient Market Hypothesis

There are three forms of the EMH: the weak form, semi-strong form and strong form. Importantly, even the weak form of the EMH implies that analysis of historical data on prices or returns will not help an investor earn abnormal profits. However, under the weak form EMH, fundamental analysis might be able to generate abnormal profits, since current asset prices might not reflect some particular company information that an investor might have access to (e.g. information about dividend growth rates, earnings, sales). If a market is semi-strong form or strong form efficient then the analysis of historical data on prices (using technical analysis), returns (using econometric analysis), or on company fundamentals (using fundamental analysis), will not generate abnormal profits.

Let r_{t+1} denote the simple return for a representative risky asset between time t and time $t + 1$; let Ω_t denote the investor's information about the asset known at time t; and let $r_{f,t}$ denote the one-period rate of return for a risk-free asset known at time t. Formal empirical tests of market efficiency typically involve making assumptions about the underlying equilibrium asset pricing model used by investors. For

---

[4]Financial asset prices are usually non-stationary. See Chapter 2 for a recap on non-stationary variables.

example, we might assume that investors are risk-neutral. In this case, it follows from simple algebra that,

$$E(r_{t+1} - r_{f,t}|\Omega_t) = 0 \tag{6.1}$$

which can be thought of as an equilibrium asset pricing model. Under market efficiency Ω_t contains *all* relevant information and therefore it follows from (6.1) that,

$$r_{t+1} = r_{f,t} + \varepsilon_{t+1} \tag{6.2}$$

where $\varepsilon_t \sim IID(0, \sigma_\varepsilon^2)$.[5] Furthermore, if $r_{f,t}$ is constant, (6.2) implies that $p_t \equiv \ln(P_t)$ approximately follows a random walk,

$$p_t = \mu + p_{t-1} + \varepsilon_t \tag{6.3}$$

where $\varepsilon_t \sim IID(0, \sigma_\varepsilon^2)$. Hence the joint hypothesis of the asset pricing model (6.1) and market efficiency can be empirically tested by testing whether p_t follows a random walk. Note, therefore, that a rejection of this hypothesis does not necessarily imply an inefficient market because (6.1) might not be the correct asset pricing model (this is an example of the joint-hypothesis problem).

Instead of assuming risk-neutrality, we might assume that investors are risk-averse with a constant risk premium,

$$E(r_{t+1} - r_{f,t}|\Omega_t) = x \tag{6.4}$$

where $x > 0$. It can be shown that in this case the joint hypothesis of the asset pricing model and market efficiency can also be empirically tested by testing whether p_t follows a random walk. However, other asset pricing models might be inconsistent with the hypothesis that p_t follows a random walk. If the true asset pricing model is one of these models, then empirically testing whether p_t follows a random walk is not an appropriate test of market efficiency.

A common misconception is that under informational efficiency excess returns cannot be forecast. However, this property also depends on the equilibrium asset pricing model. For example, assume that investors are risk-averse but the risk premium is time-varying so that the asset pricing model can be written,

$$E(r_{t+1} - r_{f,t}|\Omega_t) = x_t \tag{6.5}$$

where $x_t > 0$. If x_t is a known function of observable variables then analysts might be able to forecast excess returns to some extent using these variables, but this does not necessarily mean that the market is informationally inefficient.[6]

---

[5]More specifically we have assumed a rational expectations (RE) version of market efficiency so that $E(r_{t+1}|\Omega_t) = r_{t+1} + \varepsilon_{t+1}$, where ε_{t+1} is a zero mean white noise error term.
[6]See Pesaran (2006) for further technical details.

6.2.2 Random Walk Tests

An enormous amount of research has been undertaken on empirically testing market efficiency, much of which has focused on stock markets, and there are many different tests available. Random walk tests are particularly popular because of their simplicity. In practice the tests are usually applied to data on stock market indices rather than individual stocks. The random walk model is a univariate time series model that we have already discussed in some detail in previous chapters. To recap, a random walk model for the natural logarithm of a stock market index p_t is,

$$p_t = \mu + p_{t-1} + \varepsilon_t \tag{6.6}$$

where $t = 1, 2, \ldots, T$ and assume here that $\varepsilon_t \sim NID(0, \sigma_\varepsilon^2)$. This model implies the following model for log-returns ($r_t \equiv p_t - p_{t-1}$),

$$r_t = \mu + \varepsilon_t \tag{6.7}$$

Therefore, if p_t is generated by (6.6) then returns are independent random variables. Note that in this case the optimal one-step ahead forecast of returns is,

$$E(r_{t+1}|\Omega_t) = \mu \tag{6.8}$$

where Ω_t denotes the relevant information set. It follows from the arguments in Section 6.2.1 that a test of the null hypothesis that p_t is generated by (6.6) provides a simple test of the EMH.

One way of testing whether the natural logarithm of a stock market index p_t is generated by (6.6) is to collect sample data for the relevant index and apply the Dickey–Fuller (DF) test (Dickey and Fuller, 1979), which is discussed in Chapter 3. In this case the DF test involves testing the null hypothesis $H_0 : \phi_1^* = 0$ in the model,

$$\Delta p_t = \mu + \phi_1^* p_{t-1} + \varepsilon_t \tag{6.9}$$

Note that $\phi_1^* = (\phi_1 - 1)$, where ϕ_1 is the slope in a first-order autoregressive (AR(1)) model for p_t. Therefore the null hypothesis $H_0 : \phi_1^* = 0$ is equivalent to the null hypothesis $H_0 : \phi_1 = 1$. The alternative hypothesis is that $H_1 : \phi_1^* < 0$, in which case p_t is stationary. The relevant test statistic is,

$$\tau_\mu = \frac{\hat{\phi}_1^*}{se(\hat{\phi}_1^*)} \tag{6.10}$$

It is important to remember that, in this case, although the DF test statistic (6.10) resembles a t-test, under the null hypothesis it does not have a Student's t-distribution, but rather it has a non-standard distribution which lies to the left of the t-distribution. Therefore bespoke critical values have to be used, as given in Table A.5 in the Appendix.

Another popular group of random walk tests developed by Lo and MacKinlay (1988) are variance ratio (VR) tests. If p_t is a random walk with NID errors and there are $nq + 1$ historical observations on p_t where $q > 1$ (the first observation being p_0), then an unbiased and consistent estimator of the variance of r_t is,

$$\hat{\sigma}^2 = (nq - 1)^{-1} \sum_{t=1}^{nq} (p_t - p_{t-1} - \bar{r})^2 \tag{6.11}$$

An unbiased and consistent estimator of the variance of r_t can also be obtained by computing an unbiased and consistent estimator of the variance of $(p_t - p_{t-q})$ and dividing by q,

$$\hat{\sigma}_q^2 = m^{-1} \sum_{t=q}^{nq} (p_t - p_{t-q} - q\bar{r})^2 \tag{6.12}$$

where

$$m = q(nq - q + 1) \left(1 - \frac{q}{nq} \right) \tag{6.13}$$

Therefore if p_t is generated by (6.6), the following statistic will converge asymptotically to zero,

$$VR(q) = \frac{\hat{\sigma}_q^2}{\hat{\sigma}^2} - 1 \tag{6.14}$$

Lo and MacKinlay (1988) show that under the null hypothesis that p_t is generated by (6.6) the asymptotic distribution of $(nq)^{1/2} VR(q)$ is,

$$(nq)^{1/2} VR(q) \sim N \left(0, \frac{2(2q - 1)(q - 1)}{3q} \right) \tag{6.15}$$

Therefore the test statistic,

$$z(q) = \frac{(nq)^{1/2} VR(q)}{\left(\frac{2(2q-1)(q-1)}{3q} \right)^{1/2}} \tag{6.16}$$

can be compared with the standard normal distribution to decide whether to accept or reject the hypothesis that p_t is generated by (6.6) (Table A.1 in the Appendix can be used to choose a critical value for the test statistic). The test statistic given by (6.16) assumes that returns are homoscedastic. An extended version of the VR test has also been proposed that allows for conditional heteroscedasticity: see Lo and MacKinlay (1988) for more details.

It follows from (6.7) that we can also test if p_t follows a random walk with IID errors by examining the statistical properties of returns; in particular, the sample autocorrelations. Recall from Chapter 2 that the sample autocorrelations of T observations on a white noise process are normally distributed with a mean of zero and standard deviation $T^{-1/2}$. Therefore, the sample autocorrelations for returns can be compared with $\pm 2T^{-1/2}$ confidence bands as a test of the null hypothesis that returns are white noise at the 5% significance level (i.e. that p_t is a random walk with IID errors). Alternatively the Ljung and Box (1978) test might be used,

$$Q = T(T+2) \sum_{\tau=1}^{M} (T-\tau)^{-1} \hat{\rho}_\tau^2 \qquad (6.17)$$

where in this case $\hat{\rho}_\tau^2$ represents the squared autocorrelations for the returns. If p_t is generated by (6.6), Q has a $\chi^2(M)$ distribution. Note that if strong evidence of autocorrelation is found from the sample autocorrelations, this suggests that a time series model for returns might have superior out-of-sample forecasting power compared with the random walk model.

6.2.3 Other Tests

In addition to the random walk tests discussed in Section 6.2.2, there are many other tests of market efficiency that have been employed in empirical studies. A popular test for stock market efficiency involves analysing whether the mean daily (monthly) return from investing in stocks or a stock market index depends on the day of the week (month of the year). This type of anomaly is referred to as **seasonality in returns** (or as evidence of a **calendar effect**).

Empirical studies of seasonality in returns typically employ regressions of returns on deterministic dummy variables. A simple example for monthly returns r_t is given by the following model,

$$r_t = \mu + \sum_{i=1}^{11} \delta_i D_{i,t} + \varepsilon_t \qquad (6.18)$$

where $D_{i,t} = 1$ if returns fall in month i and $D_{i,t} = 0$ otherwise, and ε_t can be a white noise process or a more general process (e.g. a GARCH process). If the null hypothesis $H_0 : \delta_1 = \delta_2 = \ldots = \delta_{11} = 0$ is rejected using a statistical test such as an F-test, then seasonality is present and market efficiency can be rejected.[7]

The results from early empirical studies of market efficiency are generally support-ive of the weak form EMH. However, since the 1980s many empirical studies have reported results that suggest market inefficiency, particularly for stock returns. For example, numerous empirical studies of seasonality in stock returns have uncov-ered statistically significant evidence of its presence. Keim (1983) finds strong and statistically significant evidence of a positive **January effect** in US stock market data, where the mean daily returns in January are significantly higher than in other months. A traditional explanation for this effect is that it reflects **tax-loss sell-ing**, where for tax reasons investors sell in December and buy back in January. Seasonality has also been found using data for countries where the end of the tax

---

[7]Assuming that risk premiums do not vary with the same seasonal pattern.

year occurs at a different point in time (see e.g. Gultekin and Gultekin, 1983; Jaffe and Westerfield, 1989). Ariel (1987) finds evidence of a more general **monthly effect** where mean daily stock returns are higher at the start of each month relative to the rest of the month.

Many empirical studies of other anomalies have also uncovered statistically significant evidence that suggests stock market inefficiency. For example, using the CAPM as a reference asset pricing model, Banz (1981) finds that the risk-adjusted returns for small firms (firms with a small market capitalisation value) tend to be higher than the risk-adjusted returns for large firms. A study by De Bondt and Thaler (1985) finds that stocks that have low historical returns tend to have higher future returns and vice versa. They suggest a "behavioural" explanation for this finding. More specifically they suggest it is consistent with stock market investors overreacting to news, causing stocks with low past returns to be underpriced and vice versa. This overreaction is subsequently corrected. Consequently, stocks that have low past returns have higher future returns when compared to stocks which have high past returns. Jegadeesh and Titman (1993) find that stocks with high past returns over the short and medium term tend to have high future short-term returns. This has become known as evidence of stock market **momentum**. A study by Lakonishok, Shleifler and Vishny (1994) finds that stocks with low market prices compared with their book values, dividends or historical prices (a class of stocks referred to as **value stocks**, with the opposite class being **glamour stocks**) tend to out-perform the market. This finding can be interpreted as evidence that undervalued stocks return to their intrinsic values. An alternative behavioural interpretation is that, in general, investors are naive and tend to overreact to previous performance. This overreaction can lead to value stocks being underpriced, which generates superior returns.

A type of empirical study of market efficiency that we have not yet mentioned is the **event study**. This type of study is somewhat different to the previous ones discussed in the sense that it is based on directly measuring the impact of specific events on market prices, such as mergers and acquisitions or stock-splits. Recall the semi-strong form EMH states that asset prices reflect all publicly available information. Therefore, when an unanticipated event occurs, prices should change rapidly due to the event when the event occurs but not for a long period afterwards. When an anticipated event occurs, prices should change due to the event up to the point in time the event occurs but not for a long period afterwards. Event studies involve measuring the difference in the cumulative abnormal returns (CAR) before and after the event to assess market efficiency. See Fama *et al.* (1969) for an early example of an event study (which supports the EMH) and Binder (1998) for a review of the literature.

It is important to recognise that the efficiency of financial markets might also be affected by the structure of the market, trading costs and certain features of particular trading systems. These issues have been focused on in an area of finance called **market microstructure**. The seminal journal article on market microstructure is Bagehot (1971).[8] This article splits investors into different groups, those that are informed and those that are uninformed, and considers the interaction between these groups and the "dealer". Later papers in this area build up theoretical models to study the interrelationships between informed traders, dealers and uninformed **noise traders**: see e.g. Kyle (1985).[9] More recently market microstructure explanations for financial market anomalies have become increasingly popular (e.g. see Francioni *et al.*, 2008).

In Chapter 5 the issue of **data-snooping** is discussed in the context of factor models. In that case, data-snooping refers to analysts searching over many different regressors (risk factors) until they find a set of regressors that performs well on the basis of hypothesis tests (e.g. *t*-tests, *F*-tests). Since the test statistics are random variables computed using sample data, it follows that if analysts search over a large enough number of regressors then they will always be able to find regressors that perform well on the basis of the test statistics even if the regressors do not have genuine explanatory power. In most empirical studies of market anomalies the effects of data-snooping are not considered. However, it is a relevant issue. For example, Sullivan, Timmermann and White (2001) investigate evidence of seasonality using a technique developed by White (2000) that corrects for the effects of data-snooping. Before applying the correction they find strong statistically significant evidence of seasonality in the Dow Jones Industrial Average (DJIA) index, but on applying the correction the evidence disappears. The issue of data-snooping is discussed in more detail with reference to technical analysis in Section 6.5.

An alternative and increasingly popular type of test of market efficiency is a forecasting-based test. A simple forecasting-based analysis of market efficiency might involve using a time series model to forecast log-returns (e.g. an ARMA model), and then analysing the forecasting accuracy of the model relative to the forecasts computed assuming that log-prices follow a random walk. If the time series model is superior, then this might be considered to be evidence against the EMH. However, this approach assumes that the random walk model holds under market efficiency, and therefore it makes implicit assumptions about the underlying asset pricing model (see e.g. Section 6.2.2). A less restrictive forecasting-based approach to testing market efficiency involves analysing whether forecasts could have been successfully exploited by investors over a historical sample period to generate economically significant abnormal profits (or statistically significant abnormal returns) relative to a buy-and-hold strategy. If significant abnormal profits (or abnormal returns) are identified, this indicates market inefficiency for the

---

[8]Written under a pseudonym by Jack Treynor.
[9]See O'Hara (1995) for a comprehensive review of market microstructure theory.

period considered. Many of the studies that take this approach fall into one of two sub-groups: either they employ econometric models to compute the forecasts, or they employ technical analysis. These two sub-groups are discussed in more detail in Section 6.3 and Section 6.4.

6.3 Econometric Forecasting

We will assume here that a stock market index is the relevant risky asset and that by "return" we mean the simple return. Let excess stock index returns be denoted by $R_t \equiv r_t - r_{f,t}$. Assume that $X_{1,t-1}, X_{2,t-1}, \ldots, X_{k,t-1}$ are a set of lagged variables that have explanatory power for R_t, possibly because of time-varying risk premiums and/or market inefficiency. Consider the multiple linear regression model,

$$R_t = \beta_0 + \beta_1 X_{1,t-1} + \beta_2 X_{2,t-1} + \cdots + \beta_k X_{k,t-1} + \varepsilon_t \qquad (6.19)$$

and assume that $\varepsilon_t \sim NID(0, \sigma_\varepsilon^2)$. Assuming that the relevant regularity conditions are satisfied and that sufficient historical data are available, the parameters of (6.19) can be consistently estimated by ordinary least squares (OLS). It follows straightforwardly that the optimal forecasting model for producing a one-step ahead excess return forecast is,

$$\hat{R}_{t+1} = \hat{\beta}_0 + \hat{\beta}_1 X_{1,t} + \hat{\beta}_2 X_{2,t} + \cdots + \hat{\beta}_k X_{k,t} \qquad (6.20)$$

Many empirical studies have found evidence suggesting that lagged financial and macroeconomic variables have forecasting power when employed as regressors in models like (6.19).[10] It is important to recognise that forecasting power can be assessed using **in-sample** evidence and using **out-of-sample** evidence. In-sample evidence consists of information on the statistical significance of lagged-regressors and R^2 values for a regression model with lagged regressors; out-of-sample evidence consists of information on the accuracy of out-of-sample forecasts obtained from **backtesting** (e.g. the root mean squared forecast error (RMSFE) associated with the forecasts). To distinguish between the two we will use the term **predictability** when referring to in-sample evidence, and **forecasting** when referring to out-of-sample evidence. Several of the earlier journal articles in this area report apparently strong evidence of long-horizon predictability by regressing excess returns on lags of the dividend yield.[11] Note, however, that evidence of in-sample predictability does not always imply out-of-sample forecasting power.

---

[10]See, for example, Balvers, Cosimano and McDonald (1990), Breen, Glosten and Jagannathan (1990), Campbell and Shiller (1988), Fama and French (1988, 1989), Ferson and Harvey (1991), Pesaran and Timmermann (1995).

[11]See, in particular, Fama and French (1988) and Campbell and Shiller (1988). Note, however, that recent research has shown that evidence of apparent long-horizon forecasting power is weaker than first thought and could even be spurious: see for example Ang and Bekaert (2007), Boudoukh, Richardson and Whitelaw (2008).

Therefore, evidence of predictability does not necessarily reject all definitions of market efficiency. For example, it does not necessarily mean that abnormal profits could have been generated by trading on the basis of forecasts from the relevant model.

Since the mid-1990s a considerable amount of research has been undertaken on whether abnormal profits can be generated by trading on the information in out-of-sample forecasts of stock index returns from regression models; a seminal journal article on this issue being Pesaran and Timmermann (1995).

Pesaran and Timmermann (1995) analyse the economic significance of the profits generated by a trading strategy that exploits real-time forecasts of the monthly excess returns for the S&P 500 stock market index computed using a linear regression model with lagged macroeconomic and financial variables as regressors. The sample period in this study is 1954:1–1992:12. Pesaran and Timmermann (1995) allow for econometric learning when computing their forecasts. More specifically, they assume that at each month a representative investor has a base set of candidate regressors consisting of lagged macroeconomic and financial variables, and that they estimate linear regression models with the S&P 500 excess return as the regressand, for all possible combinations of the regressors. When forecasting the next month's excess return, the investor is assumed to choose the combination of regressors that is optimal on the basis of a model selection criterion. If there are k variables in the base set of regressors this approach involves estimating 2^k models each month.

Pesaran and Timmermann (1995) test whether the excess return forecasts obtained using this approach could have been exploited to earn abnormal profits in a trading strategy where an investor switches funds between the stock market index and Treasury bill depending on the sign of the forecasts. They find that, net of transaction costs, economically significant abnormal profits could have been generated over the sample period considered. Relative to a passive investment in the index, this approach was most profitable in the 1970s when an average annual return of between 10% and 15% was generated depending on the measures of fit used and transaction costs level, relative to a buy-and-hold return of around 7.5%. The size of these profits suggests that markets were not informationally efficient over this period. Interestingly, relative to a passive buy-and-hold investment in the relevant index, Pesaran and Timmermann (1995) find that the profitability of their switching investment strategy was weaker or non-existent in the 1980s, suggesting that the stock market became more efficient.

Building on their 1995 work, Pesaran and Timmermann (2000) undertake a similar study using UK data and a generalised version of their recursive modelling approach. As in the US case, they find that such an approach could have been used by investors to earn economically significant abnormal profits relative to a passive investment strategy. Other empirical studies that focus on forecasting UK stock returns using econometric models include Fletcher and Hillier (2002) and McMillan (2003). Fletcher and Hillier (2002) use econometric forecasts of returns to inform an active asset allocation strategy in which optimal portfolios are constructed using the return forecasts as inputs. They find that the econometric forecasts add significant value. McMillan (2003) employs non-linear smooth transition models to forecast UK stock index returns, and finds that allowing for non-linearity improves the accuracy of the forecasts obtained compared with those from a competing linear model.[12] Empirical research on analysing the economic value of econometric forecasts of financial asset returns is not confined to stock index returns. For example, Abhyankar, Sarno and Valente (2005) analyse the economic value of econometric exchange rate return forecasts from a monetary model by using the forecasts to inform asset allocation between countries.[13] They find that, compared with forecasts from a random walk model, the forecasts from a monetary model add value.

6.4 Technical Analysis

6.4.1 Overview

Technical analysis takes many different forms linked by the underlying belief that over time, asset prices trend, and that trends and trend-reversals can be confirmed and even identified before they occur by analysing inter- and intra-day price data (and/or data on volume). This is done either visually by finding patterns in graphs of the price data over time, or by exploiting **technical trading rules** based on simple algebraic formulas. Technical analysts believe that abnormal profits can be generated by trading using the information from charts and technical trading rules. Technical analysis is not concerned with understanding the reasons for asset price trends *ex ante*. Technical analysts typically accept that asset prices might trend for many different reasons (e.g. financial reasons, macroeconomic reasons, changes in market psychology) and that identifying the reason for a trend might not be possible or necessary. Technical analysis focuses on identifying price trends, irrespective of why they might exist. Although academic economists tend to be sceptical of the usefulness of technical analysis, evidence suggests that a substantial proportion of professional investors believe that certain technical trading rules are able to generate abnormal profits.[14] Reasons to be sceptical include the expectation that developed financial markets are highly efficient; the fact that many technical trading

---

[12]See Chapter 2 for a more detailed discussion of smooth transition models.
[13]Exchange rate forecasting using a monetary model is discussed in more detail in Chapter 8.
[14]See Taylor and Allen (1992); Menkhov (1997); Gehrig and Menkhoff (2004); Menkhoff and Taylor (2007). Technical analysis applied to exchange rates is discussed in more detail in Chapter 8.

rules have no formal statistical justification; and the fact that interpreting many of the rules and price patterns can be highly subjective.

An example of a popular technical analysis price pattern is the **head-and-shoulders** pattern. This pattern is thought to signal the impending reversal of an existing price trend. A simplified simulated example is given in Figure 6.1.

In Figure 6.1, LS indicates the left shoulder, H indicates the head, RS indicates the right shoulder and the grey line represents what is known as the **neckline**, which is a line that connects the troughs to the right of LS and the left of RS. The idea is that when an asset's price is trending upwards, then each peak tends to be above the previous peak. When an asset's price is trending downwards, each peak tends to be below the previous peak. Therefore, if price has been trending upwards for a prolonged period and a peak fails to move above a previous peak, this is thought to be evidence of an impending trend reversal and the investor should take a short position in the asset. When this occurs, it generates a visual pattern similar to a head with two shoulders either side. In Figure 6.1, RS is clearly below the previous peak H. Furthermore, after the peak RS, price then moves below the neckline which is thought to represent a point of support for further price increases. Breaking through the neckline from above is thought to confirm the beginning of a downtrend. A downtrend followed by an inverse head-and-shoulders

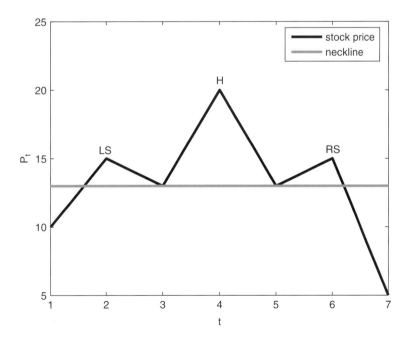

Figure 6.1   Head-and-shoulders pattern.

pattern is thought to indicate the start of an uptrend, meaning the investor should take a long position in the asset.

Figure 6.1 is a simplified simulated example and in practice it is often less clear whether a particular technical analysis price pattern has occurred. The search for price patterns was traditionally done by looking at graphs of the relevant price data (hence technical analysts are sometimes called **chartists**); however, computer pattern recognition algorithms can also be employed (see e.g. Lo, Mamaysky and Wang, 2000; Savin, Weller and Zvingelis, 2007). Note that, in practice, professional traders using technical analysis will tend to employ information from numerous different trading rules rather than relying on a single rule. They might also combine information obtained from technical trading rules with information obtained from fundamental analysis.

A particularly popular family of technical trading rules are **moving average** (MA) rules. A basic MA rule involves calculating two arithmetic moving averages of the asset price series, where one ($\text{MA}_{N_L,t}$), is calculated over N_L periods and the other ($\text{MA}_{N_S,t}$) is calculated over N_S periods, where $N_S < N_L$. Therefore, $\text{MA}_{N_S,t}$ tracks the price series more closely than $\text{MA}_{N_L,t}$. If $\text{MA}_{N_S,t}$ rises above (falls below) $\text{MA}_{N_L,t}$ this is thought to be confirmation of an uptrend (downtrend) and so generates a buy (sell) signal. The short-period and long-period moving average can be written,

$$\text{MA}_{N_S,t} = N_S^{-1} \sum_{i=t-N_S+1}^{t} P_i \tag{6.21}$$

$$\text{MA}_{N_L,t} = N_L^{-1} \sum_{i=t-N_L+1}^{t} P_i \tag{6.22}$$

The rule is therefore to buy (or buy and hold) if $\text{MA}_{N_S,t} > \text{MA}_{N_L,t}$, and sell if $\text{MA}_{N_S,t} \leq \text{MA}_{N_L,t}$. The sample period over which the MAs are computed has to be chosen by the analyst. Let $\text{MA}(N_S, N_L)$ indicate an MA rule with short- and long-period N_S and N_L respectively; in practice, popular MA rules are MA(1,50), MA(1,150), MA(1,200), MA(2,200), MA(5,150), MA(5,200).

As an example, a simulated stock price P_t and an $\text{MA}_{200,t}$ are graphed in Figure 6.2. It certainly appears from a quick visual inspection of Figure 6.2 that the MA(1,200) rule (i.e. with the stock price as the short MA and $\text{MA}_{200,t}$ as the long MA) might be a profitable investment tool. For most of the initial 500 observations price appears to be trending upwards, and around observation 100 the stock price rises above $\text{MA}_{200,t}$, generating a buy signal. Just after observation 500, there appears to be a sharp downtrend and price falls below $\text{MA}_{200,t}$, generating a sell signal. However, this interpretation demonstrates how easy it is to incorrectly conclude that a particular technical trading rule adds value just from looking at a graph, since this simulated series is actually an unpredictable log-normal series (the eagle-eyed reader

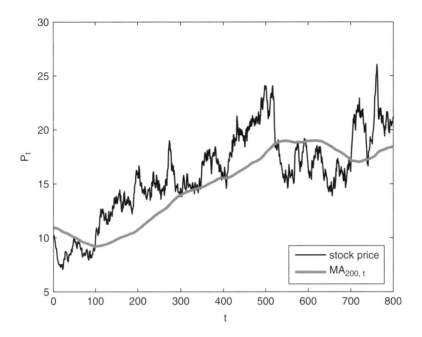

Figure 6.2   Stock price and MA$_{200,t}$.

will recognise it from Chapter 4, Figure 4.2). The price changes are unpredictable by construction and so the MA rule will not generate abnormal profits.

Other popular technical trading rules include **filter rules, support and resistance rules**, and **on-balance volume averages**. Filter rules involve buying (selling) an asset if price moves up (down) by a certain amount. They are an attempt to profit from **momentum**. Support and resistance rules involve trying to identify periods where an asset is **overbought** or **oversold** by looking at particular functions of historical data on its price. A popular function used is the **relative strength index** (RSI) proposed by Wilder (1978). The RSI is defined as the ratio of average upwards and downwards price changes converted to an index between 0 and 100. The RSI can be computed as follows,

$$RS = \frac{\text{MA}(\Delta P_t^+)}{\text{MA}(\Delta P_t^-)} \tag{6.23}$$

$$RSI = 100 - \frac{100}{1 + RS} \tag{6.24}$$

where $\text{MA}(\Delta P_t^+)$ $(\text{MA}(\Delta P_t^-))$ denote a moving average of the positive (negative) price changes, typically computed over a reasonably short time period. An RSI value above 70 is thought to indicate that an asset is overbought, while an RSI below 30 is thought to indicate an asset that is oversold.

Information on volume is also used by technical analysts, often to support the evidence from a price-based trading rule. It can also be used as a primary trading rule. The on-balance volume (OBV) indicator is an indicator introduced by Granville (1963), thought to help show whether volume is supporting a price rise or price fall. OBV involves adding to the previous day's volume the current daily volume when the closing price increases, and subtracting the current day's volume when the closing price decreases. An uptrend in OBV is thought to indicate an uptrend in prices while a downtrend in OBV is thought to indicate a downtrend in prices.[15]

Identifying whether a technical trading rule would have earned abnormal profits when applied to historical data by looking at a graph is not feasible, since it is easy to miss periods where the rule would have generated a loss (and vice versa). A more sensible approach is to test the statistical significance of the sample mean returns from applying the rule to historical data relative to the sample mean returns from a buy-and-hold investment strategy. This approach is discussed in Section 6.4.2.

6.4.2 Testing the Profitability of Technical Trading Rules

The ability of technical trading rules to earn abnormal returns can be empirically tested by applying the rule(s) to historical sample data on a relevant asset and computing the sample mean return associated with the buy and sell signals generated. The statistical significance of these sample means relative to the sample mean return for a buy-and-hold investment strategy, and/or of the difference between them, can be empirically tested using conventional t-tests (e.g. see Sweeney, 1988; Brock, Lakonishok and LeBaron, 1992). The following t-tests can be used,

$$t_b = \frac{\hat{\mu}_b - \hat{\mu}}{se(\hat{\mu}_b - \hat{\mu})} \tag{6.25}$$

$$t_s = \frac{\hat{\mu}_s - \hat{\mu}}{se(\hat{\mu}_s - \hat{\mu})} \tag{6.26}$$

$$t_{bs} = \frac{\hat{\mu}_b - \hat{\mu}_s}{se(\hat{\mu}_b - \hat{\mu}_s)} \tag{6.27}$$

where $\hat{\mu}_b$ is the sample mean return associated with the buy signal, $\hat{\mu}_s$ is the sample mean return associated with the sell signal, $\hat{\mu}$ is the sample mean return associated with the buy-and-hold strategy and the relevant standard errors can be computed as

---

[15]This is just a small sub-set of the available technical trading rules. See Murphy (1999) for further information on the huge number of technical trading rules available.

follows,

$$se(\hat{\mu}_b - \hat{\mu}) = (\hat{\sigma}^2 N^{-1} + \hat{\sigma}^2 N_b^{-1})^{1/2} \tag{6.28}$$

$$se(\hat{\mu}_s - \hat{\mu}) = (\hat{\sigma}^2 N^{-1} + \hat{\sigma}^2 N_s^{-1})^{1/2} \tag{6.29}$$

$$se(\hat{\mu}_b - \hat{\mu}_s) = (\hat{\sigma}^2 N_b^{-1} + \hat{\sigma}^2 N_s^{-1})^{1/2} \tag{6.30}$$

where N denotes the total number of returns, N_b is the number of buy signals, N_s is the number of sell signals and $\hat{\sigma}^2$ is the sample variance of the returns. t_b can be used to test the null hypothesis $H_0 : \mu_b - \mu = 0$; t_s can be used to test the null hypothesis $H_0 : \mu_s - \mu = 0$; t_{bs} can be used to test the null hypothesis $H_0 : \mu_b - \mu_s = 0$. If the weak-form EMH holds then each of these tests should fail to reject the relevant null hypothesis.

As Brock, Lakonishok and LeBaron (1992) discuss, this approach to empirically testing the profitability of technical trading rules has some weaknesses. In particular, the t-tests are only valid if the asset returns are uncorrelated and conditionally homoscedastic, which in practice might not be true. A possible solution to this problem is to use **bootstrapping** to assess the statistical significance of the sample mean buy and sell returns. Bootstrapping is a statistical simulation technique whereby the empirical distributions of estimated parameters and test statistics under a particular null hypothesis (or null model) are simulated using randomly re-sampled data.[16] These empirical distributions can then be used for inference. In this context, bootstrapping can be split into the following steps.

Step (i)   Using a sample of data of size T, estimate the parameters of a null model for returns – e.g. an AR(1) model – to allow for autocorrelation,

$$r_t = \delta + \phi_1 r_{t-1} + \varepsilon_t \tag{6.31}$$

The estimated parameters are $\hat{\delta}$ and $\hat{\phi}_1$ and the fitted errors are $\hat{\varepsilon}_t, t = 2, 3, \ldots, T$.

Step (ii)   Randomly re-sample with replacement from the fitted errors $\hat{\varepsilon}_t$ to simulate B series of returns each of T observations in length using the estimated model as the data generation process (DGP),

$$r_{t,j} = \hat{\delta} + \hat{\phi}_1 r_{t-1,j} + \hat{\varepsilon}_{t,j} \tag{6.32}$$

where $j = 1, 2, \ldots, B$, B is a positive integer usually set to 500 or larger, $r_{1,j}$ (the starting value) is a random draw from the empirical sample and $\hat{\varepsilon}_{t,j}$ is a random draw from $\hat{\varepsilon}_t$. For each bootstrapped return series recover the price series and apply the relevant technical analysis rule to compute the bootstrap sample mean returns $\hat{\mu}_{j,b}$ and $\hat{\mu}_{j,s}$.

---

[16]Seminal statistical journal articles on bootstrapping include Efron (1979, 1981, 1982). For a comprehensive specialist textbook, see Efron and Tibshirani (1993).

Step (iii) The empirical distribution of the $\hat{\mu}_{j,b}$ and $\hat{\mu}_{j,s}$ values can then be used in place of the actual distribution for inference. The p-value for a hypothesis test is the exact statistical significance level of the test statistic. To compute the bootstrapped p-values for testing the statistical significance of $\hat{\mu}_b$ and $\hat{\mu}_s$, find where $\hat{\mu}_b$ and $\hat{\mu}_s$ fall on the empirical distribution of the $\hat{\mu}_{j,b}$ and $\hat{\mu}_{j,s}$ values. For example, if $B = 500$ and there are 100 values of $\hat{\mu}_{j,b}$ at least as large as $\hat{\mu}_b$, then the p-value is 0.20. The p-value obtained in this way can be interpreted as a p-value for testing the null hypothesis that the expected return from applying the trading rule to the relevant asset is no larger than the expected return from applying the rule if the null model is true.

Both the t-test and bootstrapping approaches have been widely employed in empirical studies.[17] The study of technical trading rules by Brock, Lakonishok and LeBaron (1992) uses almost 90 years of daily data on the DJIA index (1897–1986) and analyses the performance of a number of technical trading rules, including MA rules. They find that on the basis of both the t-test and bootstrapping approaches there is statistically significant evidence that a number of the rules generate abnormal returns over this period. They do not examine the impact of transaction costs on their results. Bessembinder and Chan (1998) reconsider the Brock, Lakonishok and LeBaron (1992) example and find that when transaction costs are incorporated there is no statistically significant evidence of abnormal returns.

When bootstrapping is used in this way a functional form for the null DGP needs to be selected. Typically low-order autoregressive AR models for returns are employed (e.g. see Brock, Lakonishok and LeBaron, 1992). It is important to recognise that if the null model used in the bootstrapping procedure is not appropriately specified then this approach can lead to incorrect conclusions regarding the trading rule's profitability.

6.5 Data-Snooping

Whilst Brock, Lakonishok and LeBaron (1992) recognise the importance of allowing for certain statistical features of returns when analysing the performance of technical analysis rules (e.g. autocorrelation, GARCH), there is another subtle but important issue which they acknowledge but do not correct for: data-snooping. We have referred to this problem in Chapter 5 when discussing factor models and in Section 6.2.3 when discussing seasonality in asset returns. Data-snooping is also relevant to empirical studies of the profitability of technical trading rules. Since

---

[17]For example, see Brock, Lakonishok and LeBaron (1992), Levich and Thomas (1993), LeBaron (1999) and Day and Wang (2002).

the technical trading rules typically used are based on random variables, if analysts search over a large enough universe of rules they will always be able to find a rule that appears to have been profitable for a historical sample period even if no rule actually has genuine forecasting power. Sullivan, Timmermann and White (1999) recognise that this could be an important issue when analysing the performance of technical analysis rules. As they point out, data-snooping might not be deliberate and could be due to survivorship bias.

Using the same data as Brock, Lakonishok and LeBaron (1992), Sullivan, Timmermann and White (1999) investigate the impact of data-snooping using a bootstrap technique developed by White (2000), called **White's reality check**. White's reality check is a bootstrap technique that corrects for the effects of data-snooping when testing a particular null hypothesis involving the performance of a statistical rule. Applied to technical analysis the approach works by comparing a measure of the performance of the best performing technical analysis rule from the entire universe of technical analysis rules against a distribution of values for this measure. This distribution is obtained under the null hypothesis that the best performing rule from the entire universe of rules has no forecasting power relative to a benchmark, by bootstrapping. To explain, define the following term,

$$f_{k,t+1} = \ln(1 + r_{t+1}S_k) \tag{6.33}$$

where r_{t+1} is the simple return for the relevant asset, and S_k is an indicator for the kth technical analysis rule ($k = 1, 2, \ldots, l$) that takes the value 1 for a buy signal and -1 for a sell signal. A relevant null hypothesis considered by Sullivan, Timmerman and White (1999) is,

$$H_0 : \max_{k=1,2,\ldots,l} [E(f_k)] \leq 0 \tag{6.34}$$

Thus, the null hypothesis is that the expected return for the best performing rule is negative or zero (the benchmark). If this hypothesis is rejected then the best performing rule adds value relative to the benchmark. The test is computed utilising the $l \times 1$ statistic,

$$\bar{f} \equiv n^{-1} \sum_{t=R}^{T} \hat{f}_{t+1} \tag{6.35}$$

where n is the number of time periods over which the rule is operating, and $T = R + n - 1$. Using this sample statistic the following test statistic is computed,

$$\bar{V}_l = \max_{k=1,2,\ldots,l} [\sqrt{n}(\bar{f}_k)] \tag{6.36}$$

and the following bootstrapped values,

$$\overline{V}_{l,i} = \max_{k=1,2,\dots,l} [\sqrt{n}(\overline{f}_{k,i}^{*} - \overline{f}_{k})], \qquad i = 1, 2, \dots, B \qquad (6.37)$$

where for each $i, \overline{f}_{k,i}^{*}$ denotes the bootstrapped value of $\overline{f}_{k}$ computed using the stationary bootstrap method of Politis and Romano (1994). Sullivan, Timmermann and White (1999) set $B = 500$. It can be shown that the empirical distribution of the $\overline{V}_{l,i}$ values can be used to proxy the asymptotic distribution of (6.36) (see White, 2000, Corollary 2.4, for technical details); hence, p-values can be computed by comparing where $\overline{V}_{l}$ falls on the empirical distribution of the $\overline{V}_{l,i}$ values.

Sullivan, Timmermann and White (1999) employ this approach to re-evaluate the performance of the technical trading rules used by Brock, Lakonishok and LeBaron (1992). Their universe of trading rules consists of 7846 different rules, including filter rules, MA rules, support and resistance rules, channel breakouts and OBV averages. Interestingly, they find that for the same sample of data on the DJIA index used by Brock, Lakonishok and LeBaron (1992) (1897–1986), even after allowing for the effects of data-snooping, the best performing rule out-performs the benchmark. Note, however, that for a more recent sub-sample, 1986–1996, which is outside of the original sample used by Brock, Lakonishok and LeBaron (1992), Sullivan, Timmermann and White (1999) find that none of the trading rules are statistically significant, suggesting that the stock market became more efficient.

The next section discusses the empirical examples for this chapter. Further details on the MATLAB® programs and the data used are given in Section 6.9. Critical values for the test statistics used can be obtained from the tables in the Appendix.

6.6 Empirical Examples

Example 6.1:   Empirical tests of the efficient market hypothesis: Dickey–Fuller test

(a) Using daily data and the DF test τ_{μ}, test the random walk hypothesis for the natural logarithm of the FTSE 100 stock market index (02/01/98–31/12/07).

(b) Repeat (a) for the Hang Seng index (02/01/98–31/12/07).

(c) Repeat (a) for the Nikkei 225 index (05/01/98–28/12/07).

(d) Repeat (a) for the S&P 500 index (02/01/98–31/12/07).

The relevant MATLAB® programs are given in the files E61a.m – E61d.m. E61a.m is given in Box 6.1. The empirical results are given in Table 6.1.

Box 6.1   E61a.m

```
clear;
%Load the data.
D=xlsread('ftse');
%Define the variable.
P=flipud(D(:,6));
p=log(P);
%Apply the adf function.
[beta,t,adft]=adf(p,0);
```

Table 6.1   Dickey–Fuller test results

	τ_μ
FTSE 100	−1.588
Hang Seng	−0.309
Nikkei 225	−1.447
S&P 500	−1.892

Comparing the values in Table 6.1 with the relevant critical values reveals that the null hypothesis of a random walk is not rejected for any of the indices at conventional significance levels. These results are consistent with market efficiency under the assumptions discussed in Section 6.2.1.

Example 6.2:   Empirical tests of market efficiency: Variance ratio test

(a) Using daily data and the variance ratio (VR) test $z(q)$, test the random walk hypothesis for the natural logarithm of the FTSE 100 stock market index (02/01/98–31/12/07).
(b) Repeat (a) for the Hang Seng index (02/01/98–31/12/07).
(c) Repeat (a) for the Nikkei 225 index (05/01/98–28/12/07).
(d) Repeat (a) for the S&P 500 index (02/01/98–31/12/07).

The relevant MATLAB® programs are given in the files E62a.m – E62d.m. E62a.m is given in Box 6.2. The empirical results are given in Table 6.2.

Comparing the results in Table 6.2 with the relevant critical values indicates that for the Hang Seng index the random walk hypothesis can be rejected by the

---

Box 6.2   E62a.m

```
clear;
%Load the data.
D=xlsread('ftse');
%Define the variable.
P=flipud(D(:,6));
p=log(P);
%Apply the vr function.
[vr,vhat]=vr(p,2);
```

Table 6.2   Variance ratio test results

	$z(q)$
FTSE 100	−1.159
Hang Seng	2.493**
Nikkei 225	−0.835
S&P 500	−1.599

Note: **denotes significance at the 5% level.

VR test at the 5% level of significance, but that for the other indices this hypothesis cannot be rejected at conventional significance levels. Under the assumptions discussed in Section 6.2.1, these results support market efficiency for the FTSE 100, Nikkei 225 and S&P 500 indices, but not for the Hang Seng index. Note that the VR test used here is specifically designed for testing the null hypothesis of a random walk with drift and IID errors with a mean of zero and a *constant* variance. In practice, when applying the VR test to financial data the constant variance assumption is likely to be unrealistic: see Lo and MacKinlay (1988) for further technical details on a version of the test that allows for heteroscedasticity.

Example 6.3:   Forecasting stock index returns with time series models

Using daily data on the FTSE 100 stock market index for 02/01/98–31/12/07:

(a) Compute the log-returns and graph the SACF for the returns with 95% confidence bands.
(b) Starting on the last trading day of 1999, recursively estimate ARMA(p,0) models for the returns in percentage form and produce one-step ahead forecasts

through to the end of the sample. Compare the forecasting accuracy of each model with the forecasts computed assuming that the natural logarithm of each index is generated by a random walk model. Use the RMSFE and compute the Diebold and Mariano (1995) (DM) test of equal forecasting accuracy. Produce results for $p = 1, 3, 5$.

(c) Repeat (a) for the Hang Seng index (02/01/98–31/12/07).

(d) Repeat (b) for the Hang Seng index (02/01/98–31/12/07).

(e) Repeat (a) for the Nikkei 225 index (05/01/98–28/12/07).

(f) Repeat (b) for the Nikkei 225 index (05/01/98–28/12/07).

(g) Repeat (a) for the S&P 500 index (02/01/98–31/12/07).

(h) Repeat (b) for the S&P 500 index (02/01/98–31/12/07).

The relevant MATLAB® programs are given in the files E63a.m – E63h.m. E63a.m is given in Box 6.3 and a portion of E63b.m is given in Box 6.4. The SACF for the relevant series with 95% confidence bands (as dashed lines) are given in Figures 6.3 – 6.6. The empirical results are given in Table 6.3.

Box 6.3   E63a.m

```
clear;
%Load the data.
D=xlsread('ftse');
%Define the variables.
P=flipud(D(:,6));
p=log(P);
nr1=size(p,1);
ret=p(2:nr1,1)-p(1:nr1-1,1);
nr2=size(ret,1);
%Compute the SACF.
lag=30;
r=sacf(ret,lag);
%Draw the graph.
index=0:1:lag;
band=ones(lag+1,1)*2/sqrt(nr2);
set(gcf,'color','white','PaperPositionMode','auto');
bar(index,r,'k');
hold on;
plot(index,band,'k--',index,-band,'k--')
hold off;
title('Figure 6.3 SACF for FTSE 100 returns', 'FontSize',14,...
'FontName','Times New Roman');
xlabel('\tau','FontSize',14,'FontName','Times New Roman');
ylabel('Sample Autocorrelation','FontSize',14,'FontName',...
'Times New Roman');
```

Box 6.4   E63b.m

```
%Use a loop to recursively estimate the model and compute a forecast.
nl=nr2-nf;
while nl<=nr2-1;
y=ret(1:nl,1);
%Estimate the ARMA model (subtracting the sample mean
%to be added on later).
my=mean(y);
ny=y-my;
m=armax(ny,[1 0]);
A=get(m,'A');
A=-A;
%Compute a forecast.
yf(nl+1,1)=my+A(1,2)*ny(nl,1);
%Update the loop.
nl=nl+1;
end;
```

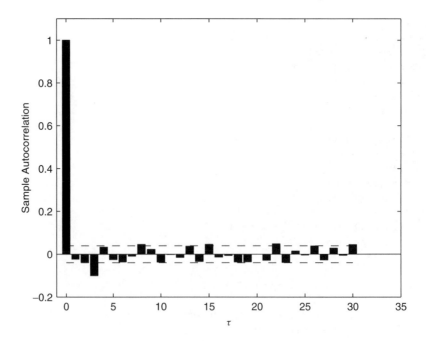

Figure 6.3   SACF for FTSE 100 returns.

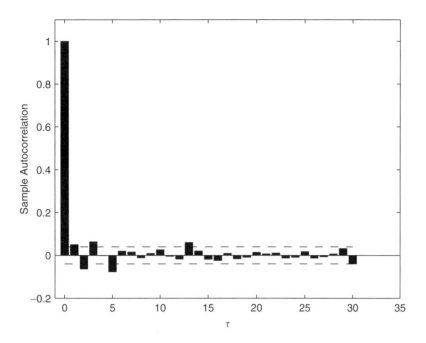

Figure 6.4   SACF for Hang Seng returns.

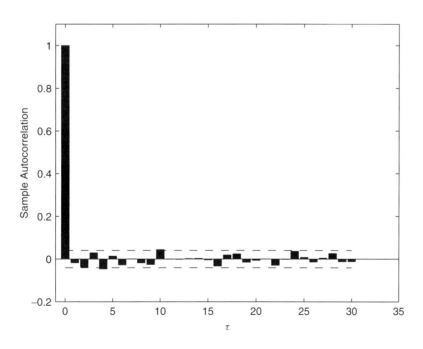

Figure 6.5   SACF for Nikkei 225 returns.

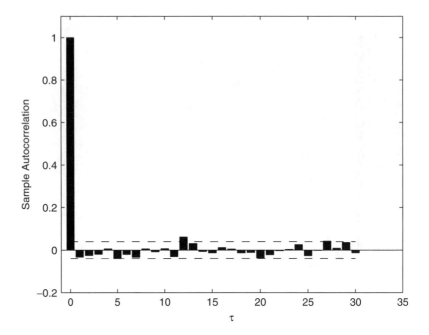

Figure 6.6   SACF for S&P 500 returns.

Table 6.3   Forecasting results

	RMSFE	RMSFE	DM
	ARMA(1,0)	Random walk	
FTSE 100	1.135	1.132	1.572
Hang Seng	1.356	1.354	0.677
Nikkei 225	1.380	1.379	1.260
S&P 500	1.116	1.115	1.522
	ARMA(3,0)		
FTSE 100	1.131		−0.209
Hang Seng	1.352		−0.390
Nikkei 225	1.383		1.717*
S&P 500	1.118		1.351
	ARMA(5,0)		
FTSE 100	1.132		0.019
Hang Seng	1.351		−0.630
Nikkei 225	1.384		1.498
S&P 500	1.119		1.494

Note: *denotes statistical significance at the 10% level.

The SACFs in Figures 6.3–6.6 show that in the majority of cases the SACF values are within the relevant confidence bands indicating white noise returns. However, in some instances (e.g. the FTSE 100 index with $\tau = 3$, the Hang Seng index with $\tau = 1, 2, 3, 5$) the sample autocorrelations are outside of the bands indicating a rejection of white noise returns at the 5% significance level. Note that although some of the sample autocorrelations for these indices are statistically significant and the VR test in Example 6.2 rejects the random walk hypothesis for the Hang Seng index, this does not necessarily mean that ARMA model forecasts of these indices will be significantly more accurate than random walk model forecasts on the basis of the DM test.

It is clear from Table 6.3 that on the basis of the DM test the difference in the forecasting accuracy of the ARMA models and random walk model is in general not statistically significant at conventional significance levels. In one case (the Nikkei 225 index) the null hypothesis of equal forecasting accuracy is rejected at the 10% significance level in favour of the random walk model. Hence, these results are supportive of the EMH.

Example 6.4: Forecasting stock index excess returns with a regression model

Using monthly data on the NYSE Composite index and the US three-month Treasury bill rate for 1998:1–2007:12, compute the simple excess stock index returns. Using the data up to 1999:12, estimate a regression model for the excess returns in percentage form and produce a one-month ahead forecast of the excess return. Repeat through to the end of the sample. At each month use the Pesaran and Timmermann (1995) methodology to select the optimal forecasting model employing the Akaike Information Criterion (AIC) with lags of the following variables as the base set of candidate regressors (a one period lag of all the variables is included and a two period lag of variable (iii)):

  (i) The excess return on the NYSE Composite index.
 (ii) The first-difference of the natural logarithm of the industrial production index.
(iii) The three-month Treasury bill rate.
 (iv) The spread between the 10-year Treasury bond rate and the three-month Treasury bill rate.
  (v) The spread between the BAA bond rate and the 10-year Treasury bond rate.
 (vi) The first-difference of the natural logarithm of the consumer price index.

> Run a switching investment strategy which involves investing in the stock market index if the excess return forecast from the regression model is positive and investing in the Treasury bill if the excess return forecast is negative. Report the sample mean monthly return associated with this strategy, with a buy-and-hold strategy and with the Treasury bill ($\hat{\mu}_S, \hat{\mu}_{BH}, \hat{\mu}_{TB}$). Compute the monthly Sharpe ratio for the switching and buy-and-hold strategies (SR_S, SR_{BH}) and the final wealth for each of the investment strategies assuming an initial investment of $100 and that transaction costs are zero ($\hat{W}_S, \hat{W}_{BH}, \hat{W}_{TB}$).

The relevant MATLAB® program is given in the file E64.m. The results are given in Table 6.4.

The results in Table 6.4 show that on the basis of the final wealth criterion the switching investment strategy performs slightly better than the buy-and-hold strategy, while both perform better than an investment in the Treasury bill. The Sharpe ratio for the switching strategy is higher than for the buy-and-hold strategy. Note, however, that we have assumed here that transaction costs are zero; therefore, in practice, the switching strategy would have been less profitable than the results here suggest. Therefore, these results are consistent with a high degree of market efficiency. Of course, using a different set of candidate regressors and a different evaluation criterion will lead to different results; hence the results here do not rule out the possibility that a regression-based investment strategy would have generated economically significant profits over this period.

Table 6.4 Forecasting results

Treasury bill	
$\hat{\mu}_{TB}$	0.265
$\hat{W}_{TB}$	$128.885
Buy-and-hold	
$\hat{\mu}_{BH}$	0.429
SR_{BH}	0.045
$\hat{W}_{BH}$	$141.655
Switching	
$\hat{\mu}_S$	0.416
SR_S	0.068
$\hat{W}_S$	$145.490

Example 6.5:   Technical analysis

(a) Apply the MA(1,50) and MA(1,200) rules to daily data on the FTSE 100 stock market index for 02/01/98–31/12/07. Graph the data and the MAs. Compute the sample mean daily return associated with the buy and sell signals ($\hat{\mu}_b$ and $\hat{\mu}_s$) and with a buy-and-hold strategy ($\hat{\mu}$) assuming that transaction costs are zero. Test for the statistical significance of $\hat{\mu}_b$ and $\hat{\mu}_s$ relative to $\hat{\mu}$, and the statistical significance of $\hat{\mu}_b - \hat{\mu}_s$ using the t-tests employed by Brock, Lakonishok and LeBaron (1992).

(b) Repeat (a) for the Hang Seng index (02/01/98–31/12/07).

(c) Repeat (a) for the Nikkei 225 index (05/01/98–28/12/07).

(d) Repeat (a) for the S&P 500 index (02/01/98–31/12/07).

The relevant MATLAB® programs are given in the files E65a.m – E65d.m. The relevant indices and MAs are graphed in Figures 6.7–6.10. The sample mean buy and sell returns and t-tests are given in Table 6.5.

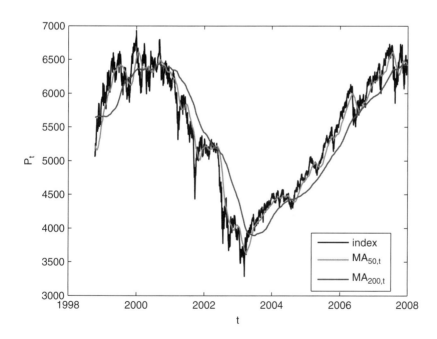

Figure 6.7   FTSE 100, MA$_{50,t}$, MA$_{200,t}$.

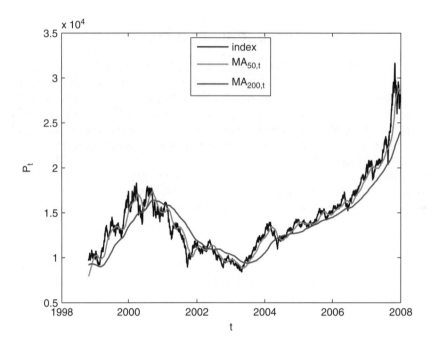

Figure 6.8   Hang Seng, MA$_{50,t}$, MA$_{200,t}$.

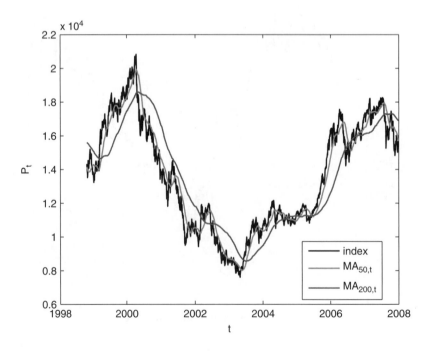

Figure 6.9   Nikkei 225, MA$_{50,t}$, MA$_{200,t}$.

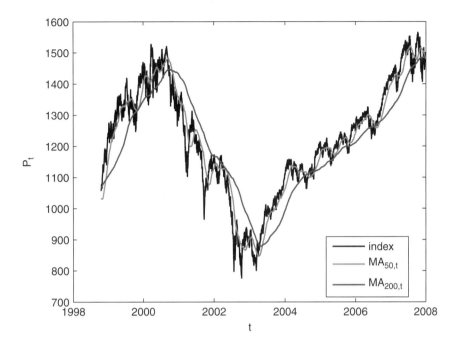

Figure 6.10   S&P 500, $MA_{50,t}$, $MA_{200,t}$.

Table 6.5   Technical analysis results

	FTSE 100	Hang Seng	Nikkei 225	S&P 500
$\hat{\mu}$	1.052e−04	4.639e−04	3.276e−05	1.423e−04
		MA(1,50)		
$\hat{\mu}_b$	−1.151e−04	4.493e−04	3.336e−05	1.998e−05
$\hat{\mu}_s$	2.207e−04	1.679e−05	−4.227e−08	1.223e−04
t_b	−0.575	−0.031	0.001	−0.323
t_s	0.259	−0.785	−0.064	−0.046
t_{bs}	−0.694	0.707	0.058	−0.216
		MA(1,200)		
$\hat{\mu}_b$	−4.251e−05	5.373e−04	1.869e−04	6.335e−05
$\hat{\mu}_s$	1.480e−04	−7.652e−05	−1.499e−04	7.900e−05
t_b	−0.388	0.159	0.315	−0.214
t_s	0.095	−0.890	−0.355	−0.139
t_{bs}	−0.391	0.962	0.581	−0.032

The sample mean buy and sell returns from the MA rules are not statistically significant on the basis of the *t*-tests computed for any of the indices. In several cases the sample mean returns have the incorrect sign, in the sense that negative mean buy returns are obtained and positive mean sell returns. Clearly, therefore, when evaluated in this way the technical analysis rules considered do not appear to generate abnormal returns relative to the returns from a buy-and-hold strategy, which is consistent with market efficiency. Note also that in the results presented here we have assumed that transaction costs are zero. Therefore, in practice these technical trading rules would have been even less profitable than the results here suggest.

6.7 Summary

This chapter has focused on several important topics related to the informational efficiency of financial markets where empirical methods play an important role. We have discussed the EMH, empirical tests of market efficiency and techniques to exploit market inefficiencies when they exist. There has been an enormous amount of empirical research on whether financial markets are informationally efficient, much of it focusing on stock markets. This research has uncovered convincing empirical evidence against the random walk model for the natural logarithm of asset prices and other evidence of market inefficiencies. However, empirical evidence on whether abnormal returns can be generated by trading stocks or stock market indices on the basis of forecasts, either from econometric models or from technical trading rules, is mixed. Several empirical studies have found evidence that statistically significant abnormal returns could have been generated by trading US stock market indices using information from econometric forecasts. This evidence is strongest for the 1970s and seems to be weaker or non-existent for the 1980s and 1990s. A similar result is found in studies of technical trading rules applied to US stock market indices. As Sullivan, Timmermann and White (1999) point out, these results suggest that in the US, stock markets have become more efficient over time. This is consistent with the perpetual increase in computer power available to investors (particularly large investors like investment banks and hedge funds), the increased resources that such large investors allocate to exploiting market inefficiencies and the reduction in transaction costs that followed the full computerisation of stock exchanges in the 1980s.

6.8 End of Chapter Questions[18]

Q1. Download daily data on the level of the DJIA stock market index for the period 02/01/98 – 31/12/07.[19]

   (a) Test the random walk hypothesis for the natural logarithm of the index using the DF test.

   (b) Test the random walk hypothesis for the natural logarithm of the index using the VR test.

   (c) Critically discuss what your empirical results in parts (a) and (b) suggest about the informational efficiency of the US stock market.

Q2. **(a)** Using the data for Question 1, compute the DJIA log-returns and graph the SACF for the log-returns.

   (b) Comment on what the SACF implies about the optimal time series model for forecasting the log-returns.

Q3. Using the data for Question 1, compute one-month ahead forecasts of the DJIA log-returns for a five-year period from a small selection of ARMA(p,0) models and from a random walk model. Evaluate and compare the forecasting accuracy of the various models.

Q4. Download monthly data on the level of the DJIA stock market index for 1998:1 – 2007:12 and the three-month US Treasury bill rate for the same sample period. Using the data for 1998:1 – 1999:12, estimate a regression model for the excess returns and produce a one-month ahead forecast of the excess return. Repeat through to the end of the sample. At each month use the Pesaran and Timmermann (1995) methodology to select the optimal forecasting model employing the Schwarz Information Criterion (SIC) to choose from all possible combinations of at least three relevant regressors lagged one period.[20] Run a switching investment strategy that involves investing in the stock market index if the excess return forecast from the regression model is positive and investing in the Treasury bill if the excess return forecast is negative.

   (a) Compute the monthly sample mean return associated with this strategy, with a buy-and-hold strategy and with investing in the Treasury bill.

   (b) Compute the monthly Sharpe ratio for the switching and buy-and-hold strategies.

---

[18]A guide to answering these questions and relevant MATLAB® programs are given on the companion website (www.wileyeurope.com/college/sollis).

[19]Yahoo! Finance is one possible source of these data (www.finance.yahoo.com).

[20]The Federal Reserve Economic Data (FRED) database at the Federal Reserve Bank of St Louis is one possible source of these data (www.research.stlouisfed.org/fred2/).

(c) For each investment strategy, assume that the same monetary amount is invested and compute the final wealth at the end of the investment period.

(d) Critically discuss what your empirical results suggest about the informational efficiency of the US stock market.

Q5. Download daily data on the level of the FTSE 100 stock market index for the period 02/01/98–31/12/07 and apply the MA(1,50) and MA(5,150) rules over this period.[21]

(a) Compute the sample mean return associated with the buy and sell signals ($\hat{\mu}_b$ and $\hat{\mu}_s$) and with a buy-and-hold strategy ($\hat{\mu}$).

(b) Test for the statistical significance of $\hat{\mu}_b$ and $\hat{\mu}_s$ relative to $\hat{\mu}$, and the statistical significance of $\hat{\mu}_b - \hat{\mu}_s$ using t-tests.

(c) Critically discuss what your empirical results suggest about the informational efficiency of the UK stock market.

6.9 Appendix

6.9.1 Data

Example 6.1

ftse.xls, hang.xls, nikkei.xls, sp.xls

Daily data on the following stock market indices taken from Yahoo! Finance (www.finance.yahoo.com).

FTSE 100 index (02/01/98–31/12/07)
Hang Seng index (02/01/98–31/12/07)
Nikkei 225 index (05/01/98–28/12/07)
S&P 500 index (02/01/98–31/12/07)

Example 6.2

ftse.xls, hang.xls, nikkei.xls, sp.xls

See above.

---

[21]Yahoo! Finance is one possible source of these data (www.finance.yahoo.com).

Example 6.3

ftse.xls, hang.xls, nikkei.xls, sp.xls

See above.

Example 6.4

nyse.xls

Monthly data on the NYSE Composite index for 1998:1 – 2007:12 from Yahoo! Finance (www.finance.yahoo.com).

BAA.xls, CPIAUCSL.xls, GS10.xls, INDPRO.xls, TB3MS.xls

Monthly data on the following macroeconomic and financial variables for 1998:1 – 2007:12 from the Federal Reserve Bank of St Louis FRED database (www.research.stlouisfed.org/fred2/).

BAA (Moody's Seasoned Baa Corporate Bond Yield)
CPIAUCSL (Consumer Price Index for All Urban Consumers: All Items)
GS10 (10-Year Treasury Constant Maturity Rate)
INDPRO (Industrial Production Index)
TB3MS (three-month Treasury Bill: Secondary Market Rate)

Example 6.5

ftse.xls, hang.xls, nikkei.xls, sp.xls

See above.

6.9.2 MATLAB® Programs and Toolboxes[22]

Example 6.1

(a) E61a.m

(b) E61b.m

---

[22]See www.wileyeurope.com/college/sollis for the programs E##.m.

(c) E61c.m

(d) E61d.m

Example 6.2

(a) E62a.m

(b) E62b.m

(c) E62c.m

(d) E62d.m

Example 6.3

(a) E63a.m

(b) E63b.m, MATLAB® System Identification Toolbox

(c) E63c.m

(d) E63d.m, MATLAB® System Identification Toolbox

(e) E63e.m

(f) E63f.m, MATLAB® System Identification Toolbox

(g) E63g.m

(h) E63h.m, MATLAB® System Identification Toolbox

Example 6.4

E64.m

Example 6.5

(a) E65a.m, MATLAB® Financial Toolbox

(b) E65b.m, MATLAB® Financial Toolbox

(c) E65c.m, MATLAB® Financial Toolbox

(d) E65d.m, MATLAB® Financial Toolbox

6.10 References

Abhyankar, A., Sarno, L. and G. Valente (2005) Exchange rates and fundamentals: evidence on the economic value of predictability, *Journal of International Economics*, 66, 325-348.

Ang, A. and G. Bekaert (2007) Stock return predictability: Is it there?, *Review of Financial Studies*, 20, 651-707.

Ariel, R. (1987) A monthly effect in stock returns, *Journal of Financial Economics*, 18, 161-174.

Bagehot, W. (1971) The only game in town, *Financial Analysts Journal*, 27, 12-17.

Balvers, R.J., Cosimano, T.F. and B. McDonald (1990) Predicting stock returns in an efficient market, *Journal of Finance*, 45, 1109-1128.

Banz, R.W. (1981) The relationship between return and market value of common stocks, *Journal of Financial Economics*, 9, 3-18.

Bessembinder, H. and K. Chan (1998) Market efficiency and the returns to technical analysis, *Financial Management*, 27, 5-13.

Binder, J.J. (1998) The event study methodology since 1969, *Review of Quantitative Finance and Accounting*, 11, 111-137.

Boudoukh J, Richardson, M.P. and R.F. Whitelaw (2008) The myth of long-horizon predictability, *Review of Financial Studies*, 21, 577-1605.

Breen, W., Glosten, L.R. and R. Jagannathan (1990) Predictable variations in stock index returns, *Journal of Finance*, 44, 1177-1189.

Brock, W., Lakonishok, J. and B. LeBaron (1992) Simple technical trading rules and the stochastic properties of stock returns, *Journal of Finance*, 47, 1731-1764.

Campbell, J.Y. and R. Shiller (1988) The dividend-price ratio and expectations of future dividends and discount factors, *Review of Financial Studies*, 1, 195-228.

Chen, N., Roll, R. and S. Ross (1986) Economic forces and the stock market, *Journal of Business*, 59, 383-403.

Day, T.E. and P. Wang (2002) Dividends, nonsynchronous prices, and the returns from trading the Dow Jones Industrial Average, *Journal of Empirical Finance*, 9, 431-454.

De Bondt, W. and R. Thaler (1985) Does the stock market overreact? *Journal of Finance*, 40, 793-805.

Dickey, D.A. and W.A. Fuller (1979) Distribution of the estimators for autoregressive time series with a unit root, *Journal of the American Statistical Association*, 74, 427-431.

Diebold, F.X. and R. Mariano (1995) Comparing predictive accuracy, *Journal of Business and Economic Statistics*, 13, 253–262.

Efron, B. (1979) Computer and the theory of statistics: thinking the unthinkable, *SIAM Review*, 21, 460–480.

Efron, B. (1981) Nonparametric estimates of standard error: the jackknife, the bootstrap and other methods, *Biometrika*, 68, 589–599.

Efron, B. (1982) The jackknife, the bootstrap, and other resampling plans, *Society of Industrial and Applied Mathematics CBMS-NSF Monographs*, 38.

Efron, B. and R.J. Tibshirani (1993) *An Introduction to the Bootstrap*. New York: Chapman & Hall.

Fama, E.F. (1965) The behavior of stock-market prices, *Journal of Business*, 38, 34–105.

Fama, E.F. (1970) Efficient capital markets: a review of theory and empirical work, *Journal of Finance*, 25, 383–417.

Fama, E.F. (1991) Efficient capital markets II, *Journal of Finance*, 46, 1575–1617.

Fama, E.F. and K.R. French (1988) Dividend yields and expected stock returns, *Journal of Financial Economics*, 22, 3–25.

Fama, E.F. and K.R. French (1989) Business conditions and expected returns on stocks and bonds, *Journal of Financial Economics*, 25, 23–48.

Fama, E.F., Fisher, L., Jensen, M. and R. Roll (1969) The adjustment of stock prices to new information, *International Economic Review*, 10, 1–21.

Ferson, W.E. and C.R. Harvey (1991) The variation of economic risk premiums, *Journal of Political Economy*, 99, 385–413.

Fletcher, J. and J. Hillier (2002) An examination of the economic significance of stock return predictability in UK stock returns, *International Review of Economics and Finance*, 11, 373–392.

Francioni, R., Hazarika, S., Reck, M. and R.A. Schwartz (2008) Equity market microstructure: taking stock of what we know, *Journal of Portfolio Management*, 35, 52–56.

Gehrig, T. and L. Menkhoff (2004) The use of flow analysis in foreign exchange: exploratory evidence, *Journal of International Money and Finance*, 23, 573–594.

Granville, J. (1963) *Granville's New Key to Stock Market Profits*. New Jersey: Prentice Hall.

Gultekin, M.N. and B. Gultekin (1983) Stock market seasonality: international evidence, *Journal of Financial Economics*, 12, 469–482.

Jaffe, J. and R. Westerfield (1989) Is there a monthly effect in stock market returns? Evidence from foreign countries, *Journal of Banking and Finance*, 13, 237–244.

Jegadeesh, N. and S. Titman (1993) Returns to buying winners and selling losers: implications for stock market efficiency, *Journal of Finance*, 48, 65–91.

Jensen, M. (1968) The performance of mutual funds in the period 1945–1964, *Journal of Finance*, 23, 389–416.

Keim, D.B. (1983) Size related anomalies and stock return seasonality: further empirical evidence, *Journal of Financial Economics*, 12, 13–32.

Kendall, M. (1953) The analysis of economic time-series, part I: prices, *Journal of the Royal Statistical Society*, Series A, 96, 11–25.

Kyle, A. (1985) Continuous auctions and insider trading, *Econometrica*, 53, 1315–1335.

Lakonishok, J., Shleifler, A. and R. Vishny (1994) Contrarian investment, extrapolation, and risk, *Journal of Finance*, 49, 1541–1578.

LeBaron, B. (1999) Technical trading rule profitability and foreign exchange intervention, *Journal of International Economics*, 49, 125–143.

Levich, R. and L. Thomas, III (1993) The significance of technical trading-rule profits in the foreign exchange market: a bootstrap approach, *Journal of International Money and Finance*, 12, 451–474.

Ljung, G.M. and G.E.P. Box (1978) On a measure of a lack of fit in time series models, *Biometrika*, 65, 297–303.

Lo, A.W. and C. MacKinlay (1988) Stock market prices do not follow random walks: evidence from a simple specification test, *Review of Financial Studies*, 1, 41–66.

Lo, A.W., Mamaysky, H. and J. Wang (2000) Foundations of technical analysis: computational algorithms, statistical inference and empirical implementations, *Journal of Finance*, 55, 1705–1765.

McMillan, D. (2003) Non-linear predictability of UK stock market returns, *Oxford Bulletin of Economics and Statistics*, 65, 557–573.

Menkhoff, L. (1997) Examining the use of technical currency analysis, *International Journal of Finance and Economics*, 2, 307–318.

Menkhoff, L. and M.P. Taylor (2007) The obstinate passion of foreign exchange professionals: technical analysis, *Journal of Economic Literature*, 45, 936–972.

Murphy, J.J. (1999) *Technical Analysis of the Financial Markets*. New York: New York Institute of Finance.

O'Hara, M. (1995) *Market Microstructure Theory*. Oxford: Blackwell Publishers.

Pesaran, M.H. (2006) Market efficiency today, *Medium for Econometric Applications*, 14, 47–54.

Pesaran, M.H. and A. Timmermann (1995) The robustness and economic significance of the predictability of stock returns, *Journal of Finance*, 50, 1201–1228.

Pesaran, M.H. and A. Timmermann (2000) A recursive modelling approach to predicting UK stock returns, *The Economic Journal*, 110, 159–191.

Politis, D.N. and J.P. Romano (1994) The stationary bootstrap, *Journal of the American Statistical Association*, 89, 1303–1313.

Roberts, H. (1967) Statistical versus clinical prediction of the stock market, unpublished manuscript, CRSP, University of Chicago.

Savin, G., Weller, P. and J. Zvingelis (2007) The predictive power of "head-and-shoulders" price patterns in the US stock market, *Journal of Financial Econometrics*, 5, 243–265.

Sharpe, W. (1966) Mutual fund performance, *Journal of Business*, 39, 119–138.

Sweeney, R.J. (1988) Some new filter rule tests: methods and results, *Journal of Financial and Quantitative Analysis*, 23, 285–300.

Sullivan, R., Timmermann, A. and H. White (1999) Data-snooping, technical trading rule performance, and the bootstrap, *Journal of Finance*, 54, 1647–1691.

Sullivan, R., Timmermann, A. and H. White (2001) Dangers of data mining: the case of calendar effects in stock returns, *Journal of Econometrics*, 105, 249–286.

Taylor, M.P. and H. Allen (1992) The use of technical analysis in the foreign exchange market, *Journal of International Money and Finance*, 11, 304–314.

White, H. (2000) A reality check for data-snooping, *Econometrica*, 68, 1097–1126.

Wilder, J.W. (1978) *New Concepts in Technical Trading Systems*. Greensboro, NC: Trend Research.

Chapter 7
Modelling and Forecasting Exchange Rates

7.1 Introduction

This chapter focuses on modelling and forecasting exchange rates. An exchange rate can be defined as the number of units of one currency that can be exchanged for a single unit of another. For example, if the GBP/USD exchange rate is 2, this tells us that $2 can be exchanged for £1. Other major exchange rates against the US dollar with high trading volumes include the EUR/USD (the euro–US dollar rate) and USD/JPY (the US dollar–Japanese yen rate). The exchange rate for immediate delivery is called the **spot** exchange rate. The **forward** exchange rate refers to the rate agreed now for delivery at a future date. When two parties agree on a forward exchange rate, a **forward contract** is written. The most popular forward contracts are for standard time periods (e.g. one-week, one-month contracts). **Futures contracts** are a type of standardised forward contract that are exchange traded.

An important feature of exchange rates is that efficiency of the foreign exchange market suggests that certain relationships between current exchange rates, interest rates, forward exchange rates and actual future exchange rates will hold (where the forward exchange rate is an exchange rate agreed now for delivery at a future time period). Therefore, empirically testing for whether these relationships do hold can provide useful empirical evidence on the efficiency of the foreign exchange market. This chapter discusses these relationships and how they can be empirically tested. This chapter also focuses on the relationship between exchange rates and domestic and foreign price levels. In the absence of tariffs, non-tariff barriers and transaction costs, the law of one price (LOOP) states that when converted into a common currency the price of a good in different countries should be equal. When applied to the price of a basket of goods (measured using a price index) this concept is referred to as the **purchasing power parity** (PPP) hypothesis. The main empirical tests of the PPP hypothesis are discussed here.

There are many different techniques that analysts might use to forecast exchange rates. Two approaches are discussed here: the first approach considered involves using an econometric model (a regression model where the exchange rate is determined by economic **fundamentals**, or a time series model); the second approach involves **technical analysis**. Technical analysis is also discussed in Chapter 6, and we noted that whilst academic economists tend to be sceptical of technical analysis it remains popular with investors. This is particularly true for exchange rates. There is a substantial amount of survey evidence suggesting that technical analysis is widely used by professional currency traders. The penultimate section of the main text presents seven empirical examples that demonstrate a selection of the empirical methods covered.

7.2 Exchange Rates

In this chapter we will use "exchange rate" to mean "spot exchange rate". The notation that will be used is S_t for the exchange rate and F_t^k for the k-period ahead forward exchange rate. To distinguish between domestic country and foreign country variables a superscript $*$ will be used. For example, i_t denotes the domestic interest rate and i_t^* the foreign interest rate; P_t denotes the domestic price index (e.g. consumer price index (CPI)) and P_t^* a foreign price index. The interest rates referred to in this chapter can be assumed to be risk-free nominal interest rates. In much of this chapter we will actually work with the natural logarithm

of variables (apart from interest rates where the raw value is used). Natural logarithms are denoted using lower case letters. Hence s_t is the natural logarithm of
the exchange rate. Consider the following graphs of monthly data on the GBP/USD
(1973:1 – 2009:12), USD/JPY (1973:1 – 2009:12) and EUR/USD (1999:1 – 2009:12)
exchange rates.

Prior to 1973 the Bretton Woods system of fixed exchange rates was in operation.
After the eventual collapse of Bretton Woods in March 1973 the major exchange
rates were floating. It can be seen in Figure 7.1 that for the initial post-Bretton
Woods period the GBP/USD exchange rate is extremely volatile with some large
swings in value, particularly in the first 10 – 15 years of the sample. In Figure 7.2
it can be seen that the USD/JPY exchange rate is also highly volatile for the initial
post-Bretton Woods period, and that by the mid-1980s the US dollar had depreci-
ated against the yen by a substantial amount relative to its Bretton Woods value.
In Figure 7.3 it can be seen that over the first two years of the relevant sample the
euro depreciates against the US dollar. This is followed by a long period of appreciation peaking in the second half of 2008, after which there is a sharp depreciation
followed by a recovery in 2009. A common feature of all three exchange rates is
that visually they appear to be non-stationary in a similar way to asset prices in an
informationally efficient market. Recall from Chapter 6 that in an informationally
efficient market (subject to certain simplifying assumptions), the natural logarithm

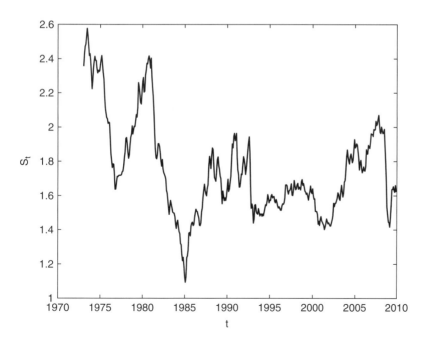

Figure 7.1   GBP/USD exchange rate, 1973:1 – 2009:12.

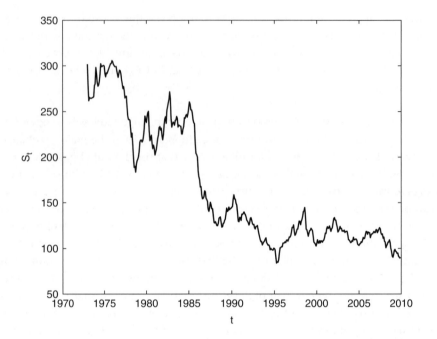

Figure 7.2   USD/JPY exchange rate, 1973:1–2009:12.

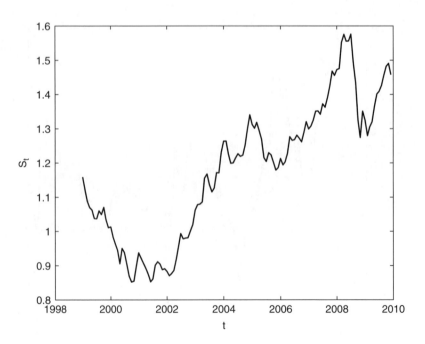

Figure 7.3   EUR/USD exchange rate, 1999:1–2009:12.

of the asset price will follow a random walk with white noise error terms. If this is the case for exchange rates, then it will be impossible to generate **abnormal profits** from trading using the information from forecasts computed using historical information.[1] Clearly, therefore, the extent to which the natural logarithm of exchange rates are random walks is an important point for investors.[2]

Section 7.1 introduced the concept of PPP. This is an important concept not just because if it does not hold this suggests that profitable goods arbitrage opportunities might exist but also because long-run PPP is commonly assumed in macroeconomic models. This chapter discusses how to empirically test the PPP hypothesis using time series data on the **real exchange rate** defined as,

$$Y_t \equiv S_t P_t^* / P_t \tag{7.1}$$

where the exchange rate S_t is the domestic price of foreign currency and P_t and P_t^* are the domestic and foreign price indices. Typically the logarithmic form is used,

$$y_t \equiv s_t + p_t^* - p_t \tag{7.2}$$

An enormous amount of empirical research has been undertaken on testing the PPP hypothesis. This research, discussed in more detail in Section 7.5, utilises many of the econometric and statistical techniques covered here in Chapters 2 and 3.

7.3 Market Efficiency and Exchange Rate Parity Conditions

7.3.1 Uncovered Interest Rate Parity

Uncovered interest rate parity (UIP) is an equality involving exchange rates and domestic and foreign interest rates that should hold if investors are risk-neutral and the foreign exchange market is efficient.[3] Therefore, empirically testing for UIP is often interpreted as a test of a version of the efficient market hypothesis (EMH) for the foreign exchange market.[4] It is important to recognise, however, that a rejection of UIP does not necessarily imply that the foreign exchange market is inefficient, because the assumption of risk-neutrality might be incorrect. This is an example of the joint-hypothesis problem highlighted by Fama (1991) and discussed here in more detail in Chapter 6.

---

[1] In this context abnormal profits are profits that are larger than those from a passive investment strategy, such as a buy-and-hold strategy.
[2] See Chapter 6 for more details on market efficiency and the random walk model for asset prices.
[3] Assume that **market efficiency** refers to informational efficiency, where investors have rational expectations. Assume also in this section that transaction costs are insignificant.
[4] See Chapter 6 for more details on market efficiency and the EMH.

UIP can be defined as follows,

$$E(s_{t+k}|\Omega_t) - s_t = i_t - i_t^* \tag{7.3}$$

where $E(s_{t+k}|\Omega_t)$ denotes the market's expected value of s_{t+k} conditional on an information set available at time t, Ω_t, which contains all relevant information, and the interest rates are for a k-period investment. UIP states that the expected exchange rate return must be equal to the difference between the nominal interest rates.[5] Define the following terms:

$$s_t \equiv \text{natural logarithm of the GBP/USD exchange rate}$$
$$i_t \equiv \text{US interest rate}$$
$$i_t^* \equiv \text{UK interest rate}$$

Therefore, if $i_t < i_t^*$, in this case UIP tells us that the US dollar is expected to appreciate against sterling. Equivalently, if sterling is expected to depreciate against the US dollar, UIP tells us that to invest in sterling requires a higher interest rate. Market efficiency and risk neutrality imply that UIP must hold. If it does not hold then an arbitrage opportunity exists that will be exploited, leading to changes in s_t, i_t and i_t^* until UIP is restored. Note in this case that the arbitrage is said to be **uncovered** since the actual exchange rate return might not be equal to the expected return, and so the actual profit is not riskless.

7.3.2 Covered Interest Rate Parity

A second important parity condition implied by market efficiency is **covered interest rate parity** (CIP). Define,

$$f_t^k \equiv \text{natural logarithm of the } k\text{-period forward rate}$$

The CIP condition can be written,

$$f_t^k - s_t = i_t - i_t^* \tag{7.4}$$

If this condition does not hold then a **covered** arbitrage opportunity exists, meaning that a riskless profit can be made. For example, let s_t, i_t, and i_t^* be defined as before and,

$$i_t < f_t^k - s_t + i_t^* \tag{7.5}$$

Assume that US investors borrow dollars at i_t, exchange for sterling and then invest at i_t^* for k-periods. If at time t they purchase a forward contract on GBP/USD, at period $t + k$ they can convert back to dollars and the entire transaction will generate a riskless profit. Hence if CIP does not hold, market forces will operate to eliminate the arbitrage opportunity until CIP is restored.

---

[5]Note that in this chapter "return" refers to log-return.

7.3.3 Forward Rate Unbiasedness

A third parity condition implied by market efficiency is the **forward rate unbiasedness** (FRU) hypothesis, which states that the forward rate is an unbiased forecast of the future exchange rate. The FRU hypothesis can be linked to CIP and UIP. It follows straightforwardly from (7.3) and (7.4) that if CIP holds, UIP implies that,

$$f_t^k - s_t = E(s_{t+k}|\Omega_t) - s_t \qquad (7.6)$$

and therefore that the FRU hypothesis holds,

$$f_t^k = E(s_{t+k}|\Omega_t) \qquad (7.7)$$

Note that under UIP we assume that investors have rational expectations (RE), therefore,

$$E(s_{t+k}|\Omega_t) = s_{t+k} + \varepsilon_{t+k} \qquad (7.8)$$

where $\varepsilon_{t+k} \sim IID(0, \sigma_\varepsilon^2)$, and thus,

$$f_t^k - s_{t+k} = \varepsilon_{t+k} \qquad (7.9)$$

Therefore the difference between the relevant forward rate and the actual future exchange rate (which is unknown at time t) is an IID error with a mean of zero.

7.4 Market Efficiency Tests

7.4.1 Random Walk Tests

A vast amount of research has been undertaken on empirically testing the exchange rate parity conditions discussed in Section 7.3. If we assume for simplicity that the interest rate differential is constant then it follows straightforwardly from (7.3) that UIP can be empirically tested by testing whether s_t follows a random walk,

$$s_t = \mu + s_{t-1} + \varepsilon_t \qquad (7.10)$$

where $\varepsilon_t \sim IID(0, \sigma_\varepsilon^2)$. Recall from Chapter 6 that two popular tests of the random walk hypothesis in finance are the Dickey–Fuller (DF) test (Dickey and Fuller, 1979) and the variance ratio (VR) test (Lo and MacKinlay, 1988). In this case the DF test involves estimating the following time series model,

$$\Delta s_t = \mu + \phi_1^* s_{t-1} + \varepsilon_t \qquad (7.11)$$

where $\varepsilon_t \sim IID(0, \sigma_\varepsilon^2)$ and $\phi_1^* = (\phi_1 - 1)$, where ϕ_1 is the slope in a first-order autoregressive model (AR(1)) for s_t. The null hypothesis $H_0 : \phi_1^* = 0$ is equivalent to the null hypothesis $H_0 : \phi_1 = 1$, and therefore under this null hypothesis s_t

follows a random walk (it is non-stationary, I(1)). The alternative hypothesis that s_t is stationary, I(0), is $H_0 : \phi_1^* < 0$. The relevant test statistic is,

$$\tau_\mu = \frac{\hat{\phi}_1^*}{se(\hat{\phi}_1^*)} \tag{7.12}$$

where ordinary least squares (OLS) can be used for parameter estimation. Under the null hypothesis τ_μ has a non-standard distribution and therefore to decide whether to accept or reject the null hypothesis it is compared with bespoke DF critical values given in Table A.5 in the Appendix.

The VR test involves comparing the variance of the one-period return for an asset with the q-period return, where $q > 1$. Under the null hypothesis that s_t is a random walk the ratio of these variances is equal to q. This null hypothesis can be tested using the test statistic,

$$z(q) = \frac{(nq)^{1/2} VR(q)}{\left(\dfrac{2\,(2q-1)\,(q-1)}{3q} \right)^{1/2}} \tag{7.13}$$

where there are $nq + 1$ historical observations on s_t (the first observation is s_0), and where,

$$VR(q) = \frac{\hat{\sigma}_q^2}{\hat{\sigma}^2} - 1 \tag{7.14}$$

$$\hat{\sigma}^2 = (nq - 1)^{-1} \sum_{t=1}^{nq} (s_t - s_{t-1} - \bar{s})^2 \tag{7.15}$$

$$\hat{\sigma}_q^2 = m^{-1} \sum_{t=q}^{nq} (s_t - s_{t-q} - q\bar{s})^2 \tag{7.16}$$

$$m = q(nq - q + 1)\left(1 - \frac{q}{nq}\right) \tag{7.17}$$

$z(q)$ can be compared with the critical values for a standard normal distribution to decide whether to accept or reject the null hypothesis of a random walk (Table A.1 can be used to choose a critical value for the test statistic).[6] As discussed in Chapter 6 another way of assessing the empirical support for the random walk hypothesis is to test for the presence of autocorrelation in returns. This might be done by computing the SACF and comparing with appropriate confidence bands or using a hypothesis test based on the sample autocorrelations such as the Ljung and Box (1978) test.[7]

The early literature on testing for foreign exchange market efficiency focuses on testing for whether the natural logarithm of the exchange rate follows a random

---

[6]More details on the VR test are given in Chapter 6.
[7]See Chapter 6 for more details on these methods.

walk by examining the degree of serial correlation in exchange rate returns.[8] The evidence from these tests is mixed. Later work on testing for foreign exchange market efficiency tends to focus on the UIP and CIP conditions and the FRU hypothesis.

7.4.2 Regression Model Tests

There are several different regression-based tests of UIP, CIP and the FRU hypothesis that have been employed in empirical research. A simple empirical test of CIP involves collecting an appropriate sample of data on the relevant variables and estimating the parameters of the regression model,

$$f_t^k - s_t = \alpha + \beta(i_t - i_t^*) + \varepsilon_t \tag{7.18}$$

Assume that $\varepsilon_t \sim NID(0, \sigma_\varepsilon^2)$ and that OLS provides consistent parameter estimates. The estimated α and β parameters obtained using OLS can be used to test the hypotheses $H_0 : \alpha = 0$ and $H_0 : \beta = 1$ using t-tests, or the joint hypothesis $H_0 : \alpha = 0, \beta = 1$ can be tested using an F-test.[9] If CIP holds, these hypotheses should not be rejected. Note however that the model (7.18) is strictly only a valid representation of CIP in the presence of zero transaction costs. If transaction costs are not zero then arbitrage opportunities will only be exploited when the profits from arbitrage are likely to be greater than the transaction costs involved; therefore, small deviations will persist for longer than large deviations (in the terminology of time series modelling – small deviations from CIP will have slower **mean reversion** than large deviations). Studies to have considered CIP allowing for the impact of transaction costs include Frenkel and Levich (1975), Balke and Wohar (1998), Peel and Taylor (2002).

The work of Balke and Wohar (1998) and Peel and Taylor (2002) is particularly novel, as they utilise non-linear time series models to investigate the empirical support for CIP allowing for the effects of transaction costs on arbitrage. More specifically they model the deviations from CIP using a threshold autoregressive (TAR) model – a type of **regime-switching** model that allows the deviations to mean revert at a different rate depending on their size. To clarify, define the deviation from CIP as,

$$\delta_t \equiv f_t^k - s_t - i_t + i_t^* \tag{7.19}$$

and consider the following three-regime TAR(1) model for δ_t,

$$\delta_t = \phi_{1,1}\delta_{t-1}I_{1,t} + [-\tau(1 - \phi_{1,2}) + \phi_{1,2}\delta_{t-1}]I_{2,t}$$
$$+ [\tau(1 - \phi_{1,3}) + \phi_{1,3}\delta_{t-1}]I_{3,t} + \varepsilon_t \tag{7.20}$$

---

[8]For example, see Poole (1967), Giddy and Dufey (1975) and Cornell and Dietrich (1978).
[9]See Chapter 3 for a recap on regression modelling.

where $\varepsilon_t \sim IID(0, \sigma_\varepsilon^2)$, and $I_{1,t} = 1$ if $|\delta_{t-1}| < \tau$ and 0 otherwise, $I_{2,t} = 1$ if $\delta_{t-1} \leq -\tau$ and 0 otherwise, $I_{3,t} = 1$ if $\delta_{t-1} \geq \tau$ and 0 otherwise. The threshold parameter τ defines a band around the unconditional mean of δ_t. The parameter $\phi_{1,1}$ determines the mean reversion of δ_t inside this band; the parameters $\phi_{1,2}$ and $\phi_{1,3}$ determine the reversion of δ_t below and above the band. Restricting the intercept to be $-\tau(1 - \phi_{1,2})$ below the band and $\tau(1 - \phi_{1,3})$ above the band means that in both cases deviations from CIP revert to the edge of the band. The transaction costs argument suggests that $|\phi_{1,2}| < 1$ and $|\phi_{1,3}| < 1$ and that $\phi_{1,1}$ is closer to unity than $\phi_{1,2}$ or $\phi_{1,3}$, so that small deviations from CIP are eliminated more slowly than large deviations. If there is no arbitrage at all for deviations inside the band then $\phi_{1,1} = 1$ and δ_t is a non-stationary, I(1), process within the band. The TAR(1) model can be easily extended to deal with higher order dynamics. Subject to weak assumptions the parameters of TAR models can be consistently estimated using conditional least squares (CLS), including the threshold parameter τ.

In their empirical application of this type of model to daily data on the USD/GBP exchange rate and forward exchange rates Balke and Wohar (1998) find that deviations from CIP are less persistent outside of the band than inside the band, which is consistent with the impact of transaction costs on arbitrage. Peel and Taylor (2002) analyse weekly data on GBP/USD exchange rates during the 1920s. They find that only deviations from CIP that generate an annual return equal to or greater than 0.5% are arbitraged away.

It is also possible to empirically test the FRU hypothesis using a regression-based test. As discussed in Section 7.3.3, we know that under both UIP and CIP the FRU hypothesis is true,

$$f_t^k = E(s_{t+k}|\Omega_t) \tag{7.21}$$

Therefore, empirically testing whether the FRU hypothesis is true is a test of UIP conditional on CIP. This can be done by rewriting (7.21) in the form of a regression model (subtract s_t from both sides and rearrange),

$$\Delta_k s_{t+k} = \alpha + \beta(f_t^k - s_t) + \varepsilon_{t+k} \tag{7.22}$$

where $\varepsilon_{t+k} \sim IID(0, \sigma_\varepsilon^2)$. Assuming risk-neutrality, if CIP and UIP both hold, $\alpha = 0$ and $\beta = 1$. If CIP and UIP both hold and the market risk-premium is non-zero but constant then $\alpha \neq 0$ and $\beta = 1$. Using an appropriate sample of data on the relevant variables and employing OLS for parameter estimation, $H_0 : \alpha = 0$ and $H_0 : \beta = 1$ can be tested with t-tests, or the joint hypothesis $H_0 : \alpha = 0, \beta = 1$ can be tested with an F-test.

The empirical evidence from tests involving (7.22) is puzzling. Typically the null hypothesis $H_0 : \beta = 1$ is strongly rejected and often $\hat{\beta} < 0$. Therefore, not only is the FRU hypothesis rejected, but the empirical results suggest that currencies at a forward discount are expected to appreciate. This contradictory result has become known as the **forward discount bias**. For example, Fama (1984) uses monthly data on US dollar exchange rates against seven currencies over 1973–1982 and finds $\hat{\beta}$ estimates ranging from -0.51 to -1.58. For the GBP/USD exchange rate over the sub-period May 1978 to December 1981, Fama (1984) finds that $\hat{\beta} = -2.83$ and that on the basis of a t-test this is significantly different from zero at conventional significance levels. Several explanations for the forward discount bias have been proposed. A population explanation is that it is due to time-variation in the market risk premium. It can be shown that this can cause the OLS estimator of the slope parameter in (7.22) to be downward biased, $E(\hat{\beta}) - \beta < 0$.[10]

7.5 Purchasing Power Parity

7.5.1 The Law of One Price and the Purchasing Power Parity Hypothesis

The **law of one price** (LOOP) states that in the absence of tariffs, non-tariff barriers and transaction costs, for any good,

$$P_t = S_t P_t^* \tag{7.23}$$

where P_t is the domestic currency price of the good, P_t^* is the foreign currency price, and S_t is the exchange rate (the domestic currency price of foreign currency). Therefore, the LOOP tells us that prices of the same goods in different countries should be the same when converted to a common currency. Since, in practice, tariffs, non-tariff barriers and transaction costs are not zero, the LOOP does not generally hold.

The purchasing power parity (PPP) hypothesis refers to (7.23) where P_t is an index of domestic prices and P_t^* is an index of foreign prices.[11] Strictly, when involving price indices, (7.23) defines **absolute PPP**. **Relative PPP** refers to the relationship between the exchange rate and inflation rates in two countries; specifically, if relative PPP holds then the percentage change in the exchange rate is equal to the

---

[10]For example, see Fama (1984). There are many other possible explanations for empirical rejections of foreign exchange market efficiency, including the presence of **rational bubbles** (see e.g. Meese, 1986), the **peso problem** (see e.g. Lewis, 1988) and **rational learning** (see e.g. Lewis, 1989; Evans and Lewis, 1995). An interesting alternative explanation for the forward discount bias is that it is simply an artefact of the small sample bias of the OLS estimator. Note, however, that Tauchen (2001) argues that under market efficiency the OLS estimator of the slope parameter in (7.22) will actually be an upward-biased estimator. Thus it appears that rejections of the FRU hypothesis from regressions involving (7.22) with $\hat{\beta} < 0$ cannot be explained by small sample bias.

[11]For early discussions of PPP, see Cassel (1921, 1922); Terborgh (1926).

difference in the inflation rates between the two countries. Here we will assume PPP refers to absolute PPP.

Tariffs, non-tariff barriers, and transaction costs can all prevent the LOOP from holding for individual products and will thus prevent PPP from holding in the short-run. However, in the long-run one would expect to see some empirical support for PPP from data on the real exchange rate. Indeed Rogoff (1996) notes,

> While few empirically literate economists take PPP seriously as a short-term proposition, most instinctively believe in some variant of purchasing power parity as an anchor for long-run real exchange rates. Warm, fuzzy feelings about PPP are not, of course, a substitute for hard evidence.[12]

"Hard evidence" on long-run PPP comes in the form of empirical tests utilising time series data.

7.5.2 Testing the Purchasing Power Parity Hypothesis: Linear Tests

The real exchange rate in logarithmic form can be written,

$$y_t \equiv s_t + p_t^* - p_t \tag{7.24}$$

where s_t is the natural logarithm of the exchange rate (domestic price of foreign currency) and p_t and p_t^* are the natural logarithms of the domestic and foreign price indices respectively. Of course, in practice the presence of tariffs, non-tariff barriers and transaction costs means that PPP will not hold at all times. However, if PPP holds in the long-run then in practice y_t should not deviate persistently from zero; therefore, statistically, y_t should be a stationary, I(0) variable (i.e. mean reverting). Thus a simple test of the **long-run PPP hypothesis** involves collecting sample data on the relevant variables, computing the real exchange rate y_t and testing the hypothesis that y_t is stationary, I(0), against the hypothesis it is non-stationary, I(1). This can be done using a unit root test such as the DF test already discussed in Section 7.4.1. The relevant model is,

$$\Delta y_t = \mu + \phi_1^* y_{t-1} + \varepsilon_t \tag{7.25}$$

and the null and alternative hypotheses are $H_0 : \phi_1^* = 0$ (y_t is non-stationary, I(1), and therefore reject long-run PPP), $H_0 : \phi_1^* < 0$ (y_t is stationary, I(0), and therefore accept long-run PPP). The test statistic is given here in (7.12), and the computed value should be compared with the DF critical values (given here in the

---

[12]Rogoff (1996), p. 647.

Appendix, Table A.5). In practice it might be more appropriate to use an augmented Dickey–Fuller (ADF) test to allow for higher order real exchange rate dynamics,

$$\Delta y_t = \mu + \phi_1^* y_{t-1} + \sum_{i=1}^{k} \beta_i \Delta y_{t-i} + \varepsilon_t \qquad (7.26)$$

Again, the null and alternative hypotheses are $H_0 : \phi_1^* = 0$ (reject long-run PPP), $H_0 : \phi_1^* < 0$ (accept long-run PPP).

An alternative test of the long-run PPP hypothesis is provided by writing the real exchange rate relationship in the form of a regression model. For example,

$$s_t = \alpha + \beta_1 p_t + \beta_2 p_t^* + \varepsilon_t \qquad (7.27)$$

Under long-run PPP, $\beta_1 = 1, \beta_2 = -1$ and ε_t is a stationary error term with $E(\varepsilon_t) = 0$; α captures the impact of permanent barriers to PPP. Therefore the long-run PPP hypothesis can be tested by estimating the parameters of (7.27) using OLS and employing t-tests of these relevant null hypotheses, $H_0 : \beta_1 = 1$ and $H_0 : \beta_2 = -1$. A test of the joint hypothesis $H_0 : \beta_1 = 1, \beta_2 = -1$ might also be done using an F-test.

As discussed in Chapter 3, when estimating the parameters of regression models using time series data, analysts need to allow for the possibility that the relevant variables might be non-stationary. Recall from Chapter 3 that if the variables in a regression model are statistically unrelated but non-stationary, there is a high probability that OLS and conventional hypothesis tests will lead to the conclusion that the variables are statistically related (see e.g. Granger and Newbold, 1974). Therefore, it is important when using a regression model to test for long-run PPP that one first tests for whether s_t, p_t and p_t^* are stationary, I(0), or non-stationary, I(1). If they are found to be I(0) then conventional hypothesis tests can be used to evaluate the relevant hypotheses. However, if they are found to be I(1), the cointegration methodology should be employed, such as the two-step approach proposed by Engle and Granger (1987). Step (i) of this approach involves estimating the parameters of the static regression model (7.27) using OLS. Step (ii) of the approach involves using the fitted errors $\hat{\varepsilon}_t$ to test for cointegration.[13] If the null hypothesis is not rejected, then PPP is not supported and the estimated parameters from (7.27) are uninformative. If the null hypothesis is rejected this supports the PPP hypothesis and the estimated parameters from (7.27) are valid. In fact the OLS estimator of these parameters is **superconsistent**, in the sense that it converges asymptotically to the unknown population parameter at a faster rate than in OLS regressions involving I(0) variables.

Although the OLS estimator of the parameters in a static single equation cointegrating regression model is a superconsistent estimator, in practice testing the relevant

---

[13]See Chapter 3 for more details on testing for cointegration using the Engle and Granger (1987) two-step approach.

hypotheses required for long-run PPP ($\beta_1 = 1$, $\beta_2 = -1$) is typically a non-standard problem because of bias due to autocorrelation and because the regressors are endogenous variables. A solution is to use a modified version of OLS for parameter estimation (see e.g. the fully modified OLS (FM-OLS) estimator of Phillips and Hansen, 1990). The t-tests computed in the usual way employing the FM-OLS estimator are asymptotically normal. An alternative solution is to employ the vector error correction model (VECM) framework of Johansen (1988). In this framework maximum likelihood (ML) can be used for parameter estimation and the PPP hypothesis can be tested using a likelihood ratio (LR) test.[14]

Empirical applications of unit root tests to data on real exchange rates tend to find that the unit root null hypothesis cannot be rejected, implying that the long-run PPP hypothesis is not supported by the data (e.g. see Meese and Rogoff, 1988; Mark, 1990). Similarly in empirical applications of cointegration-based tests the hypothesis of no cointegration between the exchange rate and domestic and foreign price indices tends not be rejected (e.g. see Enders, 1988; Taylor, 1988). Hence there is very little empirical support for long-run PPP from these studies. As Rogoff (1996) discusses, these empirical results are puzzling because deviations from PPP are thought to be driven by financial and monetary shocks which have low persistence. It is thought that these shocks affect the exchange rate which then translates through to the real exchange rate because prices are sticky. Since these shocks will have low persistence it is puzzling why real exchange deviations have such high persistence.

A convenient measure for comparing the persistence of real exchange rates is the **half-life** measure,

$$\hat{b} = \frac{\ln(0.5)}{\ln(\hat{\phi}_1)} \qquad (7.28)$$

where $\hat{\phi}_1$ is the OLS estimated slope parameter from an AR(1) model for the real exchange rate (or its natural logarithm). This amount is a measure of the time that it takes for a shock to the real exchange rate to decay by 50% (e.g. if $\hat{b} = 6$ and the data are monthly then the half-life is six months). If the model is an AR(p) model then the half-life estimate (7.28) can still be used to measure the persistence of the real exchange rate but it does not have the same interpretation as in the AR(1) case.[15] Rogoff (1996) notes that the empirical work undertaken on real exchange rates suggests a half-life of between three and five years, which is much higher than the persistence of financial and monetary exchange rate shocks. One might argue therefore that significant movements in the real exchange rate are not due to financial and monetary exchange rate shocks, but that they are due to ''real''

---

[14]See Chapter 3 for more details and Johansen and Juselius (1992) for an application of this approach to testing the long-run PPP hypothesis.

[15]See Rossi (2005) for more details on this issue.

shocks – such as shocks to tastes and technology. The problem with this argument is that real shocks cannot explain the high volatility of the real exchange rate. Rogoff (1996) calls this conundrum the **PPP puzzle**.

The lack of strong empirical support for long-run PPP from conventional unit root and cointegration tests has led to a vast amount of research on this topic using newly developed econometric techniques. Many of the more recent empirical studies of the PPP hypothesis have focused on using tests with greater power, including, for example, panel data-based tests (in this context ''power'' refers to the probability of correctly rejecting a false null hypothesis). We have not yet discussed panel data but the basic idea is that rather than focus only on a single bilateral real exchange rate relationship over time (e.g. UK–US), multiple bilateral real exchange rate relationships over time are studied assuming the same base currency (i.e. a panel of data is used). The advantage of employing a panel of data is that it gives more sample observations for computing the relevant parameter estimators and tests. This means that *ceteris parabus* the tests will tend to have greater power. Both the unit root and cointegration approaches to testing the long-run PPP hypothesis can be extended to the panel data setting. Panel versions of the DF unit root tests were initially developed by Levin and Lin (1992, 1993), and since their development large numbers of different panel unit root tests have been proposed.[16] Similarly, tests for cointegration using panel data have also been proposed.[17]

The evidence from the early empirical studies of long-run PPP employing panel unit root and cointegration tests is generally more supportive than the evidence from studies that employ single-equation techniques.[18] This is consistent with the panel unit root and cointegration tests having greater power. However, it has also been argued that panel data unit root and cointegration tests have some significant weaknesses that might be responsible for generating spurious rejections. For example, many of the earlier panel unit root studies of PPP do not explicitly allow for cross-sectional correlations. O'Connell (1998) shows that in the presence of cross-sectional correlations, panel unit root tests employing the critical values of Levin and Lin (1992) will be over-sized, the extent of this problem increasing with the numbers of variables in the panel (in this context **size** refers to the probability of making a spurious rejection of a true null hypothesis – a Type I error). The size distortion of panel unit root tests that do not correct for cross-sectional correlations might explain why the studies that apply these tests to real exchange rates find strong rejections of the unit root null hypothesis, whereas the evidence against this

---

[16]For example, see Maddala and Wu (1999), Breitung (2000), Levin, Lin and Chu (2002) and Im, Pesaran and Shin (2003).
[17]For example, see Kao (1999), Pedroni (1999) and Breitung (2002).
[18]See: Abuaf and Jorion (1990); Frankel and Rose (1996); Jorion and Sweeney (1996); Oh (1996); Wu (1996); Papell (1997).

hypothesis from univariate tests is weak or non-existent. More recently, modified panel unit root tests have been proposed that correct for cross-sectional correlations: see, for example, the journal articles by Harris, Leybourne and McCabe (2005) and Pesaran (2007). In empirical applications of these modified tests the results are not supportive of the PPP hypothesis, thus demonstrating the importance of allowing for cross-sectional correlations when using panel unit root tests.

7.5.3 Testing the Purchasing Power Parity Hypothesis: Non-linear Tests

The tests discussed in Section 7.5.2 assume that the real exchange rate is a linear random process. Note, however, that the presence of transaction costs can cause deviations from the law of one price to be non-linear in nature (see e.g. Dumas, 1992; Sercu, Uppal and Van Hulle, 1995). The underlying logic is simple: when deviations from the LOOP are small relative to the transaction costs of goods arbitrage, then arbitrage will not be profitable and so it will not be undertaken and the deviations will persist. Conversely, for large deviations from the LOOP relative to transaction costs, arbitrage will be profitable and so the deviations will be arbitraged away. Michael, Nobay and Peel (1997) and Taylor, Sarno and Peel (2001) argue that even if long-run PPP does hold, the presence of transaction costs means that real exchange rates over time might be some kind of non-linear mean reverting process, where the degree of mean reversion depends on the distance that the real exchange rate is from its unconditional mean (the mean of the real exchange can be thought of as the PPP equilibrium level). If this is the case, the linear tests discussed in Section 7.5.2 are computed from misspecified models and this could be why such puzzling results are obtained from these tests.

This section explains how non-linear time series models can be used to assess the empirical evidence on long-run PPP allowing for the effects of transaction costs. As before, let y_t denote the natural logarithm of the real exchange rate. In this section it is convenient to work with deviations of y_t from its unconditional mean. If y_t is thought to have a constant non-zero unconditional mean, then we work with $z_t = y_t - \hat{\mu}$ where $\hat{\mu}$ is a consistent estimate of the unconditional mean (e.g. the sample mean). If y_t is thought to contain a deterministic trend we work with $z_t = y_t - \hat{\theta}_1 - \hat{\theta}_2 t$, where the relevant parameters can be estimated in a pre-regression using OLS. Note, therefore, that z_t can be interpreted as a measure of the deviation of the real exchange rate from its PPP level.

Threshold autoregressive (TAR) models already discussed in Section 7.4.2 might also be useful for modelling the deviation of the real exchange rate from its PPP level, since they allow for non-linear mean reversion consistent with the effects of transaction costs on arbitrage. Consider the following three-regime TAR(1) model for z_t,

$$z_t = \phi_{1,1}z_{t-1}I_{1,t} + \phi_{1,2}z_{t-1}I_{2,t} + \phi_{1,3}z_{t-1}I_{3,t} + \varepsilon_t \qquad (7.29)$$

where $\varepsilon_t \sim IID(0, \sigma_\varepsilon^2)$; $I_{1,t} = 1$ if $|z_{t-1}| < \tau$ and 0 otherwise; $I_{2,t} = 1$ if $z_{t-1} \leq -\tau$ and 0 otherwise; $I_{3,t} = 1$ if $z_{t-1} \geq \tau$ and 0 otherwise. The threshold parameter τ defines a band around the unconditional mean of z_t. The parameter $\phi_{1,1}$ determines the speed with which deviations from PPP mean revert inside the band; the parameters $\phi_{1,2}$ and $\phi_{1,3}$ determine how fast deviations from PPP mean revert below and above the band. The existence of transaction costs suggests that $|\phi_{1,2}| < 1$ and $|\phi_{1,3}| < 1$ and that $\phi_{1,1}$ should be closer to unity than either of the other slope parameters, since because of transaction costs small deviations from PPP should be corrected more slowly than large deviations. If there is no arbitrage at all for deviations inside the band it follows that $\phi_{1,1} = 1$, and therefore z_t will be a non-stationary, I(1), process inside the band. The TAR(1) model can be easily extended to deal with higher order dynamics. Subject to weak assumptions the parameters of TAR models can be consistently estimated using CLS, including the threshold parameter τ.

To help clarify the difference between AR and TAR variables, in Figure 7.4 a stationary AR(1) variable is graphed simulated using the following data generation

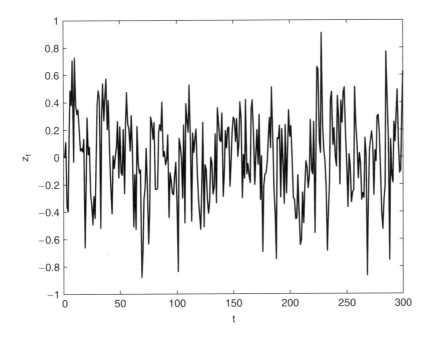

Figure 7.4   AR(1) variable.

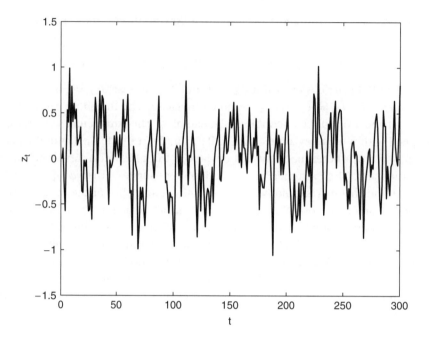

Figure 7.5 TAR(1) variable: narrow band.

process (DGP),

$$z_t = 0.30z_{t-1} + \varepsilon_t \tag{7.30}$$

$$\varepsilon_t \sim NID(0, 0.10) \tag{7.31}$$

In Figure 7.5 a three-regime TAR(1) model is graphed simulated using the DGP,

$$z_t = z_{t-1}I_{1,t} + 0.30z_{t-1}I_{2,t} + 0.30z_{t-1}I_{3,t} + \varepsilon_t \tag{7.32}$$

where $I_{1,t} = 1$ if $|z_{t-1}| < 0.50$ and 0 otherwise, $I_{2,t} = 0.50$ if $z_{t-1} \leq -0.50$ and 0 otherwise, $I_{3,t} = 1$ if $z_{t-1} \geq 0.50$ and 0 otherwise, and the same ε_t values are used as in Figure 7.4. Thus the inner regime is non-stationary, I(1), but the outer regimes are stationary, I(0). In Figure 7.6 a variable is graphed, simulated using the TAR(1) DGP (7.32) but with $I_{1,t} = 1$ if $|z_{t-1}| < 1.50$ and 0 otherwise, $I_{2,t} = 1$ if $z_{t-1} \leq -1.50$ and 0 otherwise, $I_{3,t} = 1$ if $z_{t-1} \geq 1.50$ and 0 otherwise, and again the same ε_t values are used as in Figure 7.4. Therefore the DGP used for Figure 7.5 has a wider band than the DGP used for Figure 7.4. Note how the persistence of small shocks to the variables in Figures 7.4 and 7.5 differs from the persistence of large shocks (the "shocks" are the ε_t values, which are the same for each variable).

If the TAR(1) model given by (7.29) is assumed to be an appropriate model for the real exchange rate then long-run PPP can be tested formally, allowing for a **no-arbitrage** band, by testing the null hypothesis $H_0 : \phi_{1,1} = \phi_{1,2} = \phi_{1,3} = 1$ (reject

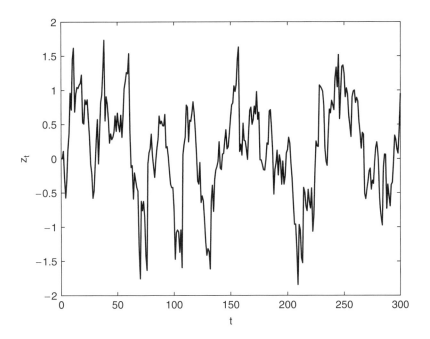

Figure 7.6   TAR(1) variable: wide band.

long-run PPP) against the alternative hypothesis $H_1 : \phi_{1,1} = 1, |\phi_{1,2}| < 1, |\phi_{1,3}| < 1$ (accept long-run PPP) using an F-test and employing CLS for parameter estimation. This is effectively a unit root test, where under the null hypothesis z_t is a non-stationary, I(1), process and under the alternative hypothesis the variable is I(0) outside of the band and I(1) inside the band. Under the alternative hypothesis the variable is not a linear stationary variable, but it can be thought of as a **globally stationary** variable. Since under the null hypothesis $H_0 : \phi_{1,1} = \phi_{1,2} = \phi_{1,3} = 1$ the variable z_t is non-stationary, the asymptotic distribution for this test statistic is not the conventional F-distribution. In practice, bespoke critical values for the test can be computed using Monte Carlo simulation techniques (e.g. see Kapetanios and Shin, 2006).

In TAR models a regime change occurs when the level of the series reaches a particular threshold value. A limitation with TAR models is that any regime changes that do occur do so in a single time period. Both Michael, Nobay and Peel (1997) and Taylor, Sarno and Peel (2001) point out that since the real exchange rate is a highly aggregated variable, it is more likely that any non-linearity that occurs due to the effects of transaction costs is gradual. A family of non-linear autoregressive models that allow for gradual regime changes is the smooth transition autoregressive (STAR) family, which is discussed briefly in Chapter 2.[19]

---

[19]See also Granger and Teräsvirta (1993) and Teräsvirta (1994) for more details.

Consider the following first-order exponential STAR (ESTAR) model for the deviation of the real exchange rate from its unconditional mean (z_t),

$$z_t = \phi_{1,1}z_{t-1}F(z_{t-1}) + \phi_{1,2}z_{t-1}[1 - F(z_{t-1})] + \varepsilon_t \qquad (7.33)$$

$$F(z_{t-1}) = 1 - \exp(-\gamma z_{t-1}^2), \quad \gamma \geq 0 \qquad (7.34)$$

where $\varepsilon_t \sim NID(0, \sigma_\varepsilon^2)$. In a STAR model non-linearity is captured using a cumulative distribution function (CDF). Here the exponential CDF is used. This particular ESTAR model has first-order dynamics; hence it is an ESTAR(1) model. First-order STAR models can be easily extended to deal with higher order dynamics. Subject to weak assumptions non-linear least squares (NLS) and ML are consistent estimators of the parameters of STAR models.

The ESTAR(1) model given by (7.33) allows the degree of autoregression to be different depending on whether the lagged real exchange rate is large (positive or negative) or small relative to its unconditional mean (which can be thought of as the long-run equilibrium value). For example, assuming $\gamma > 0$, $z_{t-1}^2 \to 0$ implies that $F(z_{t-1}) \to 0$, and the AR parameter $\phi_{1,2}$ dominates. As $z_{t-1}^2 \to \infty$, then since $F(z_{t-1}) \to 1$, $\phi_{1,1}$ is the dominant parameter. For small values of γ the transition from one AR parameter to another is gradual, whilst for large values it takes place rapidly. Therefore, the ESTAR(1) model (7.33) allows small deviations of the real exchange rate from its PPP level to be more persistent than large deviations. Note that if $\phi_{1,2} = 1$, then for small deviations of the real exchange rate from its PPP level, z_t is a highly persistent process. z_t is said to be a **globally stationary** variable if $\phi_{1,1} < 1$ and $\phi_{1,1} + \phi_{1,2} < 1$.

To help clarify, in Figure 7.7 an ESTAR(1) variable z_t is graphed simulated using the DGP,

$$z_t = 0.30z_{t-1}F(z_{t-1}) + z_{t-1}[1 - F(z_{t-1})] + \varepsilon_t \qquad (7.35)$$

$$F(z_{t-1}) = 1 - \exp(-z_{t-1}^2) \qquad (7.36)$$

$$\varepsilon_t \sim NID(0, 0.10) \qquad (7.37)$$

In this model small deviations of the variable from its unconditional mean are highly persistent and large deviations mean revert rapidly. In Figure 7.8 the exponential function $F(z_{t-1})$ is graphed against the amount z_{t-1}.

The exponential function used by Michael, Nobay and Peel (1997) and Taylor, Sarno and Peel (2001) is symmetric. Therefore, positive deviations of the real exchange rate from its PPP level have the same persistence as negative deviations of the same absolute value. This is a reasonable assumption to make since one would expect that goods arbitrageurs would operate in the same way when a currency is over-valued in real terms as when it is undervalued by the same absolute amount. Since the seminal work of Michael, Nobay and Peel (1997) and Taylor, Sarno and Peel

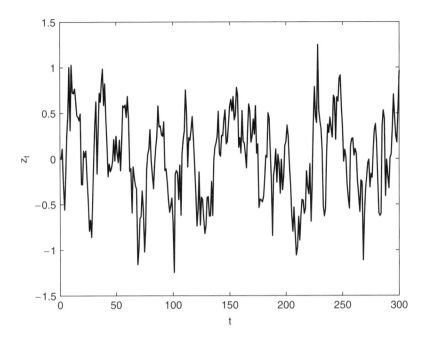

Figure 7.7   ESTAR(1) variable.

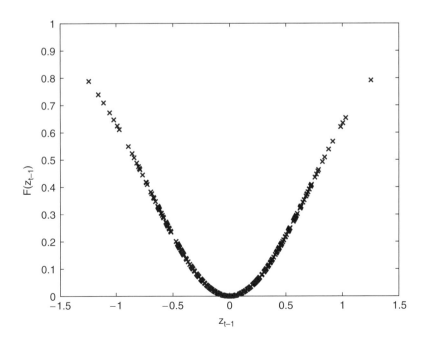

Figure 7.8   Exponential function.

(2001), there have been numerous extensions and developments of non-linear PPP tests, including extensions to allow for asymmetric mean reversion of the real exchange rate towards its PPP level. These studies have found evidence suggesting that for some countries, reversion of the real exchange rate to PPP levels is asymmetric.[20]

Kapetanios, Shin and Snell (2003) develop a formal test of the null hypothesis that a variable is I(1) allowing for globally stationary ESTAR non-linearity under the alternative hypothesis, which can be used to test the long-run PPP hypothesis allowing for the effects of transaction costs on arbitrage. As before let z_t denote the deviation of the real exchange rate y_t from its unconditional mean.[21] The Kapetanios, Shin and Snell (2003) ESTAR model for z_t can be written,

$$\Delta z_t = \phi_1 z_{t-1} F(z_{t-1}) + \varepsilon_t \tag{7.38}$$

$$F(z_{t-1}) = 1 - \exp(-\gamma z_{t-1}^2), \quad \gamma \geq 0 \tag{7.39}$$

where $\varepsilon_t \sim IID(0, \sigma_\varepsilon^2)$. If $\gamma = 0$ then, since $F(z_{t-1}) = 0$, z_t is a non-stationary, I(1), variable. Therefore, under the null hypothesis $H_0 : \gamma = 0$, long-run PPP does not hold. The relevant alternative hypothesis is $H_1 : \gamma > 0$, $\phi_1 < 0$, which is consistent with long-run PPP. Therefore, applied to real exchange rates the Kapetanios, Shin and Snell (2003) test can be used to test the long-run PPP hypothesis allowing for the effects of transaction costs.

In practice, testing the null hypothesis $H_0 : \gamma = 0$ is a non-standard problem not only because under this null hypothesis z_t is non-stationary but also because under this null hypothesis the parameter ϕ_1 in (7.38) is **unidentified**, meaning that it can take any value. Consequently, deriving the asymptotic distribution of a test of $H_0 : \gamma = 0$ theoretically using conventional methods is not feasible. However, following Luukkonen, Saikkonen and Teräsvirta (1988), Kapetanios, Shin and Snell (2003) simplify this problem by replacing $F(z_{t-1})$ with a first-order **Taylor series approximation** around $\gamma = 0$.[22] On rearranging, this gives an auxiliary model,

$$\Delta z_t = \delta z_{t-1}^3 + \eta_t \tag{7.40}$$

The null hypothesis of $H_0 : \gamma = 0$ in (7.38) becomes $H_0 : \delta = 0$ in (7.40). Kapetanios, Shin and Snell (2003) propose testing the unit root hypothesis using the

---

[20]For example, see Sollis, Leybourne and Newbold (2002) and Cerrato, Kim and MacDonald (2010).

[21]Note, therefore, that if y_t is thought to have a constant non-zero unconditional mean, we work with $z_t = y_t - \hat{\mu}$ where $\hat{\mu}$ is a consistent estimate of the unconditional mean (e.g. the sample mean). If y_t is thought to contain a deterministic trend, we work with $z_t = y_t - \hat{\theta}_1 - \hat{\theta}_2 t$, where the relevant parameters can be estimated in a pre-regression using OLS.

[22]A Taylor series approximation is a mathematical technique for approximating a function at a particular point using the derivatives of the function. See Luukkonen, Saikkonen and Teräsvirta (1988) for more details.

t-statistic,

$$t_{NL} = \frac{\hat{\delta}}{se(\hat{\delta})} \tag{7.41}$$

where $\hat{\delta}$ is the OLS estimate of δ and $se(\hat{\delta})$ is the OLS standard error. Since under the null hypothesis z_t is a non-stationary variable, t_{NL} will have a non-standard asymptotic distribution. The distribution depends on whether $z_t = y_t$ (Case 1), $z_t = y_t - \hat{\mu}$ (Case 2) or $z_t = y_t - \hat{\theta}_1 - \hat{\theta}_2 t$ (Case 3) is used when computing the test. For these three cases Kapetanios, Shin and Snell (2003) are able to derive the theoretical form of the asymptotic distribution for t_{NL} and they provide the bespoke critical values. Higher order dynamics can be dealt with in the same way as in the ADF test, by including additional lags of Δy_t. The underlying ESTAR model becomes,

$$\Delta z_t = \phi_1 z_{t-1} F(z_{t-1}) + \sum_{i=1}^{k} \beta_i \Delta z_{t-i} + \varepsilon_t \tag{7.42}$$

The relevant auxiliary model for testing becomes,

$$\Delta z_t = \delta z_{t-1}^3 + \sum_{i=1}^{k} \beta_i \Delta z_{t-i} + \eta_t \tag{7.43}$$

and the null hypothesis is $H_0 : \delta = 0$ which can be tested using the relevant t-statistic. Using Monte Carlo simulations Kapetanios, Shin and Snell (2003) show that the test statistic t_{NL} has good small sample properties. They demonstrate the usefulness of this test with empirical applications to real exchange rates and real interest rates.

If the Kapetanios, Shin and Snell (2003) test rejects the unit root hypothesis, the parameters of the underlying ESTAR model can then be consistently estimated by NLS (or by ML). When estimating the parameters of STAR models it can be helpful to simplify the model as much as possible to avoid identification problems. For example, when estimating (7.42) the estimated parameter $\hat{\phi}_1$ is often poorly identified, meaning that it can take a large range of values without the fit of the model being affected. This can lead to convergence problems with the NLS or ML algorithm employed and can make interpretation more difficult. A solution in this case is to set $\phi_1 = -1$: see, for example, Taylor, Sarno and Peel (2001) and Kapetanios, Shin and Snell (2003). Typically, this does not significantly affect the fit of the underlying model since the estimated γ parameter compensates.

The evidence from non-linear tests of the long-run PPP hypothesis is considerably more supportive than the evidence from linear tests. For example, Michael, Nobay and Peel (1997) examine monthly and annual data on several major real exchange rates using ESTAR models and find clear evidence that large deviations of the real exchange rate from PPP levels mean revert more quickly than small deviations, consistent with the transaction costs argument and supporting long-run PPP. Similarly, using monthly data since 1973 on real exchange rates against the US dollar Taylor, Sarno and Peel (2001) find evidence supporting the non-linear adjustment of real exchange rates to long-run PPP levels. They find that only small shocks to the real exchange rate have a half-life of between three and five years, but for larger shocks the half-life is much shorter, in some cases being less than 12 months.

7.6 Forecasting Exchange Rates

7.6.1 Econometric Models

The forecastability of exchange rates is obviously an important issue for professional currency traders, but it is also relevant to any investor contemplating investing in a foreign asset. This section discusses two approaches to forecasting exchange rates. The first approach considered involves using an econometric model. Two different types of econometric model might be employed – an econometric version of an economic model where the exchange rate is determined by economic **fundamentals**, or a time series model. The second approach to forecasting considered here involves using technical analysis.[23] Technical analysis applied to exchange rates does not strictly generate point forecasts of exchange rates, but it generates forecasts of the sign of exchange rate changes and is widely employed by professional currency traders.

There are many different economic exchange rate models. Recent developments in this area have been termed the "new" open-economy macroeconomics (e.g. see Lane, 2001). Explaining the full range of economic exchange rate models is beyond the scope of this book and readers are encouraged to refer to a specialist exchange rate book if more details are required.[24] Monetary exchange rate models, developed in the 1970s, offer a simple introduction to this area, and it is easy to translate theoretical monetary models to empirical versions that can be used for forecasting exchange rates.

A traditional monetary model of the exchange rate is the sticky-price monetary model (SPMM) proposed by Dornbusch (1976) (see also Frankel, 1979, 1982). Note that in the SPMM, UIP holds and PPP holds in the long-run. The basic logic of the SPMM is that prices take time to adjust, and that, because of this, when there is a change in monetary policy the exchange rate **overshoots** its long-run equilibrium value. For example, assume that the money market is initially in equilibrium and

---

[23]See Chapter 2 for more details on time series models and Chapter 6 for more details on technical analysis.

[24]For example, see MacDonald and Marsh (1999) and Sarno and Taylor (2002).

consider the impact of an increase in the domestic money supply. In the long-run this will lead to an increase in domestic prices and a depreciation of the exchange rate (because prices are a positive function of the money supply and long-run PPP holds). However, if prices are sticky then domestic interest rates will fall. This occurs because the increase in money supply (and no increase in prices) means that there has been an increase in the real money supply. For the money market to clear (i.e. real money demand = real money supply) macroeconomic theory tells us that there must be a fall in the domestic interest rate. UIP tells us that the expected appreciation of the domestic currency is equal to the interest rate differential. Therefore, prior to the new long-run equilibrium being reached the domestic currency must depreciate beyond its long-run equilibrium value to generate an expected appreciation consistent with the interest rate differential under sticky prices. In the medium-run, prices and consequently interest rates adjust (as real money supply falls) and the exchange rate appreciates towards its long-run equilibrium value. A natural alternative to the SPMM is the flexible price monetary model (FPMM), which has its origins in the work of Frenkel (1976). The FPMM model can be summarised using the same equations as the SPMM, with the assumption that prices are perfectly flexible, meaning that adjustment to the long-run equilibrium values takes place instantaneously.

Theoretical monetary models are usually written assuming **continuous time**. For empirical analysis the models are usually translated to discrete time. For example, translating a general monetary model that nests the SPMM and FRMM to discrete time means that for the two countries we can write,

$$m_t = p_t + \phi y_t - \theta i_t \tag{7.44}$$
$$m_t^* = p_t^* + \phi^* y_t^* - \theta^* i_t^* \tag{7.45}$$

The variables are as follows: m_t is the natural logarithm of the domestic money supply; p_t is the natural logarithm of the domestic price level; y_t is the natural logarithm of domestic real income; i_t is the domestic interest rate. A superscript * denotes the equivalent foreign variable. Typically, the domestic interest rate is treated as an exogenous variable and PPP is assumed to hold in the short-, medium- and long-run,

$$s_t = p_t - p_t^* \tag{7.46}$$

If we substitute (7.46) into (7.45) and rearrange using (7.44), and simplify by assuming that $\phi = \phi^*$ and $\theta = \theta^*$, an equation for the exchange rate can be written,

$$s_t = (m_t - m_t^*) - \phi(y_t - y_t^*) + \theta(i_t - i_t^*) \tag{7.47}$$

Assuming that a large enough sample of data on the variables in (7.47) is available, the parameters of this equation can then be estimated, for example by OLS. The relevant regression model can be written,

$$s_t = \alpha_0 + \alpha_1(m_t - m_t^*) + \alpha_2(y_t - y_t^*) + \alpha_3(i_t - i_t^*) + \varepsilon_t \tag{7.48}$$

where for simplicity assume that $\varepsilon_t \sim NID(0, \sigma_\varepsilon^2)$. The estimated version of (7.48) can then be used for forecasting. It is important to note that, as discussed in Chapter 3, when the regression model is static like (7.48), to compute forecasts involves forecasting the explanatory variables. In practice this might be done using a time series model, such as an AR model, or a vector autoregressive (VAR) model.

The forecasting ability of monetary models is studied by Meese and Rogoff (1983). Their empirical analysis investigates the forecasting accuracy of a number of different exchange rate models, including the SPMM and FPMM discussed above, compared with some time series models, including AR models, VAR models, and a random walk model. Meese and Rogoff (1983) find that none of the monetary models produce more accurate point forecasts than the random walk model, where forecasting accuracy is assessed using the root mean squared forecast error (RMSFE). This result raised serious questions as to the usefulness of the monetary model for investors and policymakers.

Since the journal article by Meese and Rogoff (1983) many authors have replicated their general finding. One of the more significant econometric problems with early empirical studies of this issue that employ regression models is that they do not deal with the econometric implications of the possible non-stationarity of the variables used. The regressand in these studies, which is the natural logarithm of the exchange rate, is likely to be non-stationary, I(1). This means that unless the regressors are non-stationary and there is cointegration, the estimated parameters will be uninformative. If the regressors are non-stationary, I(1), and there is no cointegration then the estimated parameters in (7.48) do not converge to zero even though there is no long-run relationship between the regressand and regressors.

The journal article by Mark (1995) investigates the forecasting ability of a monetary model using a simplified version in error correction model (ECM) form,

$$s_{t+k} - s_t = \alpha + \beta(f_t - s_t) + \varepsilon_{t+k} \tag{7.49}$$

where the monetary fundamentals are captured in a single term,

$$f_t = [(m_t - m_t^*) - (y_t - y_t^*)] \tag{7.50}$$

If s_t and f_t are both non-stationary, I(1), and cointegrated with the cointegrating vector $[1 \quad -1]$, the regressor $(f_t - s_t)$ represents the long-run disequilibrium between f_t and s_t. Mark (1995) uses quarterly data on four exchange rates against the US dollar for the period 1973:2 – 1991:4 and computes forecasts of each exchange rate for the period 1984:1 – 1991:4. He considers forecasts for several different horizons (specifically, $k = 1, 4, 8, 12, 16$). Mark (1995) evaluates out-of-sample forecasting accuracy using the RMSFE and the Diebold and Mariano (1995) test of equal forecasting accuracy. At short horizons Mark (1995) confirms the results of Meese and Rogoff (1983); however, he also finds that at longer forecasting horizons the monetary model generates more accurate forecasts than a random walk model.

When estimating the model (7.49) with small samples it can be shown that the OLS estimator will be biased if $(f_t - s_t)$ is highly autocorrelated. Furthermore, it can be shown that irrespective of the sample size, the forecast errors associated with the model will be autocorrelated which makes forecast evaluation more difficult. The empirical analysis by Mark (1995) uses **bootstrapping** to deal with these problems. However, this aspect of his analysis has since been the subject of criticism: for example, see Killian (1999), who finds that when an alternative bootstrap method is used there is no evidence of long-horizon predictability.

Berkowitz and Giorgianni (2001) note that, in his bootstrapping procedure, Mark (1995) implicitly assumes that f_t and s_t are cointegrated with a cointegrating vector of $[1 \quad -1]$. Berkowitz and Giorgianni (2001) use a test for cointegration developed by Horvath and Watson (1995) and find that out of the four countries analysed by Mark (1995), for only one of the countries (Switzerland) is the exchange rate cointegrated with the monetary fundamentals term. Berkovitz and Giorgianni (2001) find no evidence of increased predictability at longer horizons apart from for the Swiss franc series.[25]

The majority of the empirical studies undertaken on forecasting exchange rates using monetary models suggest that these models do not generate more accurate forecasts than a random walk model. This could simply be due to market efficiency and/or that the monetary models are fundamentally wrong. However it is also possible that the forecasting ability of monetary models is "masked" by other features of the data and the econometric techniques used, such as, for example, structural change due to oil price shocks; misspecification of the monetary model; sampling error (i.e. that estimated parameters are being used rather than unknown population parameters); and ignored non-linearity due to the presence of transaction costs.[26]

Both linear and non-linear time series models can also be employed for directly forecasting exchange rates. We will not dwell here on the application of time series models to forecasting exchange rates as the relevant forecasting theory has been discussed in Chapter 2. Although Meese and Rogoff (1983) find that traditional linear time series models (AR and VAR) do not yield any statistically significant improvement in forecasting accuracy for nominal exchange rates relative to the random walk model, more recently non-linear time series models have been shown to yield some forecasting advantages compared with linear time series models.[27]

---

[25]See Neely and Sarno (2002) for a more detailed review of these journal articles.
[26]See Killian (1999) and Killian and Taylor (2003) for more details.
[27]For example, see Boero and Marrocu (2002) and Gradojevic and Yang (2006).

7.6.2 Technical Analysis

As discussed in Chapter 6, technical analysis takes many different forms linked by the underlying belief that asset prices trend (here the "price" is the exchange rate), and that trends and trend-reversals can be confirmed and even identified before they occur by analysing inter- and intra-day price data (and/or data on volume). This is done either visually by finding indicative patterns in graphs of the price data over time, or by exploiting **technical trading rules** based on simple algebraic formulas. Technical analysts believe that abnormal profits can be generated by trading using the information from graphs and from technical trading rules. Although academic economists tend to be sceptical of the usefulness of technical analysis, survey evidence suggests that a substantial proportion of professional investors employ technical analysis. This is particularly true of professional currency traders. Menkhoff and Taylor (2007) summarise the evidence and conclude that,

> Almost all foreign exchange professionals use technical analysis as a tool in decision making at least to some degree.[28]

There are many different technical trading rules available and in practice professional currency traders using technical analysis might employ several different rules. A particularly popular family of trading rules, discussed in more detail in Chapter 6, are **moving average** (MA) rules. A basic MA rule involves calculating two arithmetic moving averages of the asset price series, where one ($MA_{N_L,t}$) is calculated over N_L periods and the other ($MA_{N_S,t}$) is calculated over N_S periods, where $N_S < N_L$. Therefore, $MA_{N_S,t}$ tracks the price series more closely than $MA_{N_L,t}$. If $MA_{N_S,t}$ rises above (falls below) $MA_{N_L,t}$ this is thought to be confirmation of an uptrend (downtrend) and so generates a buy (sell) signal. Other popular technical analysis rules discussed in more detail in Chapter 6 include the head-and-shoulders price pattern, the relative strength indicator (RSI), and filter rules.

Assume the exchange rate is defined as the domestic price of foreign currency and that a buy signal from the technical trading rule refers to taking a long position in the foreign currency, whilst a sell signal refers to taking a short position in the foreign currency (a long position in the domestic currency). The return associated with these positions will depend not only on the actual exchange rate return for the relevant time period, but also on the difference in the domestic and foreign interest rates for when the positions are held. So, for example, in the case of a US investor applying a technical trading rule to the daily GBP/USD exchange rate, the

---

[28]Menkhoff and Taylor (2007), p. 940. See also Taylor and Allen (1992), Menkhoff (1997) and Gehrig and Menkhoff (2004).

daily excess return before transaction costs can be written,

$$r_{t+1} = (\Delta s_{t+1} + i_t^* - i_t)I_t \tag{7.51}$$

where $I_t = 1$ for a long position, $I_t = -1$ for a short position, and $I_t = 0$ for a neutral position. Note that if UIP holds (see Section 7.3.1. and equation (7.3)) then the expected excess return will be zero, $E(r_{t+1}) = 0$. Hence the ability of a technical trading rule to earn abnormal profits when applied to exchange rates can be studied by computing the sample excess returns from applying the rule over a historical period. This information might then be used to statistically test the hypothesis that the expected excess return is zero. The performance of Sharpe ratios and simulated trading strategies might also be analysed, as in the studies of econometric forecasting and technical analysis applied to stock market indices discussed in Chapter 6.

Numerous empirical studies have been undertaken that analyse the ability of technical analysis applied to exchange rates to generate abnormal profits and/or abnormal returns.[29] Many studies of this issue find evidence of abnormal profits, particularly for volatile currencies. Qi and Wu (2006) is an important study because they employ the reality check bootstrap methodology developed by White (2000) to allow for the impact of **data-snooping** (see Chapter 6 and White, 2000). Using daily data on seven US dollar exchange rates over the period 1973–1998, Qi and Wu (2006) find evidence suggesting that technical analysis was profitable over this period even after correcting for the effects of data-snooping and taking account of transaction costs. However, for more recent periods, other studies find weaker evidence and some studies find no evidence of abnormal returns (e.g. see Neely, Weller and Ulrich, 2009).

Menkhoff and Taylor (2007) undertake a comprehensive analysis of the empirical evidence on technical analysis and the use of technical analysis by professional currency traders. They argue,

> There remains a need for further explanation of the continued and passionate obsession of foreign exchange professionals with technical analysis, however, as profitability studies have not to date arrived at a clear verdict.[30]

Menkhoff and Taylor (2007) present a useful set of **stylised facts** regarding the use of technical analysis by currency traders and they discuss four broad possible arguments for why technical analysis continues to be so widely used:

(i) Technical analysis reflects irrational behaviour.
(ii) Technical analysis exploits the impact of central bank interventions.

---

[29]See Menkhoff and Taylor (2007) and Park and Irwin (2007) for extensive references.
[30]Menkhoff and Taylor (2007), p. 954.

(iii) Technical analysis allows less-informed investors to process information contained in exchange rates.

(iv) Technical analysis provides information about non-fundamental exchange rate determinants.

All four of these arguments and combinations of them could explain the continued use of technical analysis by currency traders and so it may not be possible to distinguish which is the more important. Menkhoff and Taylor (2007) point out that argument (iv) is perhaps the most attractive explanation since non-fundamental elements are likely to be more important determinants of exchange rates in the short-run than in the long-run and survey findings suggest that technical analysis is more widely used by professional currency traders for short-run forecasting than for long-run forecasting.

The next section discusses the empirical examples for this chapter. Further details on the MATLAB® programs and the data used are given in Section 7.10. Critical values for the test statistics used can be obtained from the statistical tables in the Appendix.

7.7 Empirical Examples

Example 7.1: Random walk tests

Using monthly data on the GBP/USD exchange rate (1973:1–2009:12) test the null hypothesis that the natural logarithm of the exchange rate is a random walk:

(a) Using the DF test, τ_μ.

(b) Using the VR test, $z(q)$.

The relevant MATLAB® programs are given in the files E71a.m, E71b.m. The results are given in Table 7.1.

The results in Table 7.1 show that in this case the null hypothesis of a random walk cannot be rejected by the DF test at conventional significance levels, which is supportive of market efficiency with risk-neutrality. However, a strong rejection of this hypothesis is obtained from the VR test. Therefore, the result from the DF test supports UIP (assuming a constant interest rate differential) while the result from

Table 7.1   Random walk tests

τ_μ	−2.230
$z(q)$	7.800***

Note: *** denotes statistical significance at the 1% level.

the VR test suggests market inefficiency. Since these two tests lead to contrasting conclusions, further empirical analysis of the data is recommended before drawing firm conclusions. In this particular case further analysis of the data reveals that the GBP/USD exchange rate returns contain higher order autocorrelation, which explains the VR test rejection and indicates a degree of market inefficiency.

Example 7.2:   Regression test of the FRU hypothesis

Using monthly data on the GBP/USD exchange rate (1979:1–2009:12) and the GBP/USD one-month forward rate, test the FRU hypothesis using a regression model test. Compute robust t-tests (Newey and West, 1987) of the null hypothesis that the constant and slope parameters are equal to zero and the null hypothesis that the slope parameter is equal to one, and an F-test of the joint null hypothesis that the constant is equal to zero and the slope parameter is equal to one.

The relevant MATLAB® program is given in the file E72.m and in Box 7.1. The results are given in Table 7.2.

Table 7.2   Regression results

$\hat{\alpha}$	−0.004
$\hat{\beta}$	−2.233
$H_0 : \alpha = 0$	$t = -1.881^*$
$H_0 : \beta = 0$	$t = -2.123^{**}$
$H_0 : \beta = 1$	$t = -3.074^{***}$
$H_0 : \alpha = 0, \beta = 1$	$F = 9.162^{***}$

Note: ***,** and * denote statistical significance at the 1%, 5% and 10% levels respectively.

Box 7.1   E72.m

```
clear;
%Load the data.
S=xlsread('GBPUSDM_short_end');
F=xlsread('GBPUSDFM_short_end');
%Define the variables.
y=log(S);
x=log(F)-log(S);
nr1=size(y,1);
dy=y(2:nr1,1)-y(1:nr1-1,1);
lx=x(1:nr1-1,1);
nr2=size(dy,1);
%Use the olsnw function from the Oxford MFE Toolbox to
%estimate the parameters by OLS and compute t-tests.
[b,tstat,s2,vcvnw,R2,Rbar,yhat]=olsnw(dy,lx,1);
%Compute a t-test and F-test.
tbeta=(b(2,1)-1)/sqrt(vcvnw(2,2));
rssu=sum((dy-yhat).^2);
rssr=sum((dy-lx).^2);
ftest=((rssr-rssu)/2)/(rssu/(nr2-2));
```

The results in Table 7.2 indicate that the FRU hypothesis is convincingly rejected. As in much of the empirical research on this issue a negative slope parameter is estimated (under the FRU hypothesis it should be unity), illustrating the forward discount bias.

Example 7.3:   Linear test of the PPP hypothesis and half-life estimation

Using monthly data on the GBP/USD exchange rate (1973:1–2009:12) and relevant consumer price indices for the same period:

(a) Test the PPP hypothesis using an ADF test with a constant and three lagged differences.
(b) Use the estimated model to compute the approximate half-life of shocks to the real exchange rate.

The relevant MATLAB® program is given in the file E73.m. The results are given in Table 7.3.

Table 7.3   Linear test of the PPP hypothesis and half-life estimation

τ_μ	−2.766*
h	30.267

Note: * denotes statistical significance at the 10% level.

The results in Table 7.3 show that the null hypothesis that the real exchange rate contains a unit root cannot be rejected at the 5% significance level, but can be rejected at the 10% significance level. Hence there is only weak evidence supporting the long-run PPP hypothesis for the US and UK over this period. The estimated half-life computed from this model is approximately 30 months, consistent with the real exchange rate being a highly persistent process.

Example 7.4:   Non-linear test of the PPP hypothesis and half-life estimation

Using monthly data on the GBP/USD exchange rate (1973:1–2009:12) and relevant consumer price indices for the same period:

(a) Graph the natural logarithm of the real exchange rate series and using this data test the PPP hypothesis employing the Kapetanios, Shin and Snell (2003) test with a constant and no trend ($t_{NL,\mu}$), and one lagged difference.

(b) Estimate the underlying ESTAR model including one lagged difference and setting the slope ϕ_1 to − 1 to simplify estimation. Compute the fastest half-life of shocks to the real exchange rate. Graph the fitted non-linear AR(1) parameter $1 - F(z_{t-1})$ against z_{t-1}.

The relevant MATLAB® programs are given in the files E74a.m and E74b.m. A portion of E74a.m is given in Box 7.2. The graphs are given in Figures 7.9 and 7.10. The results are given in Table 7.4.

The results in Table 7.4 show that the unit root hypothesis is rejected at the 10% significance level, and the fastest half-life speed is 10 months, which is significantly lower than the half-life speed when a linear AR model is employed. Figure 7.10 illustrates that large deviations from PPP are less persistent than small deviations. The non-linear AR(1) parameter is as low as 0.934 for the largest negative deviation from PPP.

Box 7.2   E74a.m

```
clear;
%Load the data.
S=xlsread('GBPUSDM_long');
CPID=xlsread('USCPIM_long');
CPIF=xlsread('UKCPIM_long');
%Define the variables.
y=log(S)+log(CPIF)-log(CPID);
nr1=size(y,1);
y=y-mean(y);
dy=y(3:nr1,1)-y(2:nr1-1,1);
ldy=y(2:nr1-1,1)-y(1:nr1-2,1);
ly=y(2:nr1-1,1);
nr2=size(dy,1);
x=[ly.^3 ldy];
%Estimate the parameters using OLS and compute the test statistic.
beta=inv(x'*x)*x'*dy;
e=dy-x*beta;
ev=sum(e.^2)/(nr2-2);
se=sqrt(diag(ev*inv(x'*x)));
t=beta./se;
tnl=t(1,1);
```

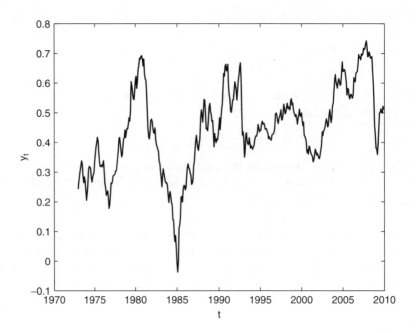

Figure 7.9   GBP/USD real exchange rate, 1973:1–2009:12.

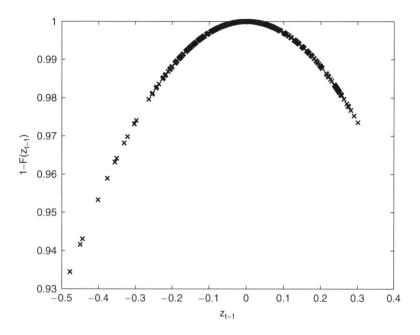

Figure 7.10 Non-linear AR(1) parameter.

Table 7.4 Non-linear test of the PPP hypothesis and half-life estimation

$t_{NL,\mu}$	-2.910^*
h	10.220

Note: * denotes statistical significance at the 10% level using the critical values in Kapetanios, Shin and Snell (2003).

Example 7.5: Exchange rate forecasts from a monetary model

Using monthly data on the GBP/USD exchange rate (1983:1–2009:12), consumer price indices, industrial production indices and money supply for the UK and US, compute one-step ahead forecasts of the exchange rate for the period 1997:1–2009:12 from a simple monetary model in ECM form (MM), and from a random walk (RW) model. Evaluate the exchange rate forecasts using the root mean squared forecast error (RMSFE) and the Diebold and Mariano (1995) (DM) test of equal forecasting accuracy.

Table 7.5 Forecasting results

RMSFE (MM)	0.0219
RMSFE (RW)	0.0219
DM	0.816

The relevant MATLAB® program is given in the file E75.m. The results are given in Table 7.5.

The results in Table 7.5 indicate that, when evaluated using the RMSFE, the forecasting accuracy of the random walk model is virtually identical to that of the monetary model. The DM test does not reject the null hypothesis of equal forecasting accuracy at conventional significance levels. These results are consistent with the extant empirical evidence discussed in Section 7.6.1.

Example 7.6:   Exchange rate forecasts from a time series model

Using monthly data on the GBP/USD exchange rate (1983:1–2009:12), compute one-step ahead forecasts of the exchange rate for the period 1997:1–2009:12 from an ARIMA(1,1,0) model and a random walk (RW) model. Evaluate the exchange rate forecasts using the RMSFE and the Diebold and Mariano (1995) (DM) test of equal forecasting accuracy.

The relevant MATLAB® program is given in the file E76.m. The results are given in Table 7.6.

The results in Table 7.6 indicate that, when evaluated using the RMSFE, the random walk model provides less accurate forecasts than the ARIMA(1,1,0) model. However, the null hypothesis of equal forecasting accuracy cannot be rejected by the DM test at conventional significance levels.

Table 7.6 Forecasting results

RMSFE (ARIMA)	0.0209
RMSFE (RW)	0.0219
DM	−1.236

Example 7.7: Technical analysis

Using daily data on the GBP/USD exchange rate for the period 02/01/96–31/12/09 and assuming for simplicity that US and UK interest rates are equal and transaction costs are zero, apply the MA(1,20), MA(1,50) and MA(5,20) rules. Report the sample mean daily return for a buy-and-hold strategy, $\hat{\mu}$; for each rule, report the number of buy and sell signals generated, compute the sample mean daily return, $\hat{\mu}_{N_S,N_L}$, and test the null hypothesis that the expected return is zero using a t-test $H_0 : \mu_{N_S,N_L} = 0$.

The relevant MATLAB® program is given in the file E77.m. The results are given in Table 7.7.

The results in Table 7.7 suggest that, over this sample period, the MA rules considered would not have generated abnormal profits. Only the MA(1,50) rule generates a higher sample mean return than a buy-and-hold strategy, and for all of the rules the null hypothesis $H_0 : \mu_{N_S,N_L} = 0$ cannot be rejected at conventional significance levels. Hence, these results are supportive of market efficiency. Note also that here we have assumed that transaction costs are zero and therefore in practice these technical trading rules would have been even less profitable than the results here suggest.

Table 7.7 Technical analysis results

$\hat{\mu}$	1.658e−05
MA(1,20)	
Buy	1835
Sell	1655
$\hat{\mu}_{1,20}$	−6.224e−05
$H_0:\mu_{1,20} = 0$	$t = -0.633$
MA(1,50)	
Buy	1800
Sell	1690
$\hat{\mu}_{1,50}$	4.071e−05
$H_0:\mu_{1,50} = 0$	$t = 0.414$
MA(5,20)	
Buy	1823
Sell	1667
$\hat{\mu}_{5,20}$	−3.235e−06
$H_0:\mu_{5,20} = 0$	$t = -0.033$

7.8 Summary

This chapter has focused on several key topics associated with modelling and forecasting exchange rates. Important parity conditions implied by market efficiency have been discussed, and how to empirically test whether these conditions hold. The linkage between exchange rates, domestic price levels and foreign price levels implied by the PPP hypothesis has also been discussed. A vast amount of empirical research has been undertaken on testing the PPP hypothesis. This chapter has explained the main empirical tests available and discussed some of the research on this topic. This chapter has also focused on two approaches to forecasting exchange rates: econometric forecasting and technical analysis. Technical analysis remains popular with professional currency traders despite scepticism from academic economists and recent empirical evidence suggesting that its profitability has diminished. The empirical examples in this chapter demonstrate testing the exchange rate parity conditions, testing the long-run PPP hypothesis and forecasting the GBP/USD exchange rate using econometric models and technical trading rules.

7.9 End of Chapter Questions[31]

> **Q1. (a)** Download monthly data on the GBP/USD exchange rate, the GBP/USD one-month forward rate and relevant US and UK interest rates for the period 1979:1 – 2009:12.[32] Using these data, test the CIP hypothesis employing a regression-based test.
>
> **(b)** Critically discuss what your empirical results from part (a) suggest about the informational efficiency of the foreign exchange market.
>
> **Q2.** Download monthly data on an exchange rate of your own choice for the period 1973:1 – 2009:12.[33] Using monthly data on the relevant consumer price indices for the domestic and foreign country test the long-run PPP hypothesis employing an ADF test.[34]

---

[31] A guide to answering these questions and relevant MATLAB® programs are given on the companion website (www.wileyeurope.com/college/sollis).

[32] The Bank of England Statistics database is one possible source of these data (www.bankofengland.co.uk/statistics).

[33] The Bank of England Statistics database is one possible source of sterling exchange rates (www.bankofengland.co.uk/statistics). The Federal Reserve Economic Data (FRED) database at the Federal Reserve Bank of St Louis is one possible source for US dollar exchange rates (www.research.stlouisfed.org/fred2/).

[34] One possible source for consumer price index data is the IMF database on international financial statistics (IFS). Another possible source is a relevant national statistics database, such as, for the UK, the Office for National Statistics (www.statistics.gov.uk/default.asp).

Q3. **(a)** For the exchange rate in Question 2, compute one-month ahead forecasts for the period 2000:1 – 2009:12 from a simple monetary model in ECM form and a random walk model.[35]

(b) Evaluate and compare the forecasting accuracy of the models in part (a).

Q4. **(a)** For the exchange rate in Question 2, compute one-month ahead forecasts for the period 2000:1 – 2009:12 from an appropriate ARIMA model and a random walk model.

(b) Evaluate and compare the forecasting accuracy of the models in part (a).

Q5. Download daily data on an exchange rate of your own choice for the period 02/01/96 – 31/12/09 and apply the MA(1,5), MA(1,10) and MA(1,500) rules to these data.[36]

(a) Report the number of buy and sell signals generated.

(b) Test the null hypothesis that the expected return associated with each rule is zero using a t-test.

(c) Critically discuss what your empirical results suggest about the informational efficiency of the foreign exchange market.

7.10 Appendix

7.10.1 Data

Figure 7.1

GBPUSDM_long.xls

Monthly data on the GBP/USD exchange rate for 1973:1 – 2009:12 from the Federal Reserve Bank of St Louis FRED database (www.research.stlouisfed.org/fred2/).

Figure 7.2

USDJPYM_long.xls

Monthly data on the USD/JPY exchange rate for 1973:1 – 2009:12 from the Federal Reserve Bank of St Louis FRED database (www.research.stlouisfed.org/fred2/).

---

[35] Money supply data can often be obtained from the relevant central bank. Industrial production data can often be obtained from a relevant national statistics database.

[36] The Bank of England Statistics database is one possible source of sterling exchange rates (www.bankofengland.co.uk/statistics). The Federal Reserve Economic Data (FRED) database at the Federal Reserve Bank of St Louis is one possible source of US dollar exchange rates (www.research.stlouisfed.org/fred2/).

Figure 7.3

EURUSDM_long.xls

Monthly data on the EUR/USD exchange rate for 1999:1 – 2009:12 from the Federal Reserve Bank of St Louis FRED database (www.research.stlouisfed.org/fred2/).

Example 7.1

GBPUSDM_long.xls

See above.

Example 7.2

GBPUSDM_short_end.xls

Monthly data on the end-of-month GBP/USD exchange rate for 1979:1 – 2009:12 from the Bank of England Statistics database (www.bankofengland.co.uk/statistics/index.htm).

GBPUSDFM_short_end.xls

Monthly data on the end-of-month GBP/USD one-month forward exchange rate for 1979:1 – 2009:12 from the Bank of England Statistics database (www.bankofengland.co.uk/statistics/index.htm).

Example 7.3

GBPUSDM_long.xls

See above.

UKCPIM_long.xls

USCPIM_long.xls

Monthly data on the UK and US consumer price index (CPI) for 1973:1 – 2009:12 from the IMF database on international financial statistics (IFS) (www.imf.org/external/data.htm) accessed using Thomson Reuters Datastream.

Example 7.4

GBPUSDM_long.xls

UKCPIM_long.xls

USCPIM_long.xls

See above.

Example 7.5

GBPUSDM_short.xls

Monthly data on the GBP/USD exchange rate for 1983:1 – 2009:12 from the Federal Reserve Bank of St Louis FRED database (www.research.stlouisfed.org/fred2/).

UKCPIM_short.xls

USCPIM_short.xls

Monthly data on the UK and US consumer price index (CPI) for 1983:1 – 2009:12 from the IMF database on international financial statistics (IFS) (www.imf.org/external/data.htm) accessed using Thomson Reuters Datastream.

UKIPM_short.xls

Monthly data on the UK industrial production index for 1983:1 – 2009:12 from the Office for National Statistics (www.statistics.gov.uk/default.asp).

USIPM_short.xls

Monthly data on the US industrial production index for 1983:1 – 2009:12 from the Federal Reserve Bank of St Louis FRED database (www.research.stlouisfed.org/fred2/).

UKM4M_short.xls

Monthly data on UK M4 for 1983:1 – 2009:12 from the Bank of England Statistics database (www.bankofengland.co.uk/statistics/index.htm).

USM2M_short.xls

Monthly data on US M2 for 1983:1–2009:12 from the Federal Reserve Bank of St Louis FRED database (www.research.stlouisfed.org/fred2/).

Example 7.6

GBPUSDM_short.xls

See above.

Example 7.7

GBPUSDD.xls

Daily data on the GBP/USD exchange rate for 02/01/96–31/12/09 from the Bank of England Statistics database (www.bankofengland.co.uk/statistics/index.htm).

7.10.2 MATLAB® Programs and Toolboxes[37]

Example 7.1

(a) E71a.m

(b) E71b.m

Example 7.2

E72.m, Oxford MFE Toolbox

Example 7.3

E73.m

---

[37]See www.wileyeurope.com/college/sollis for the programs E##.m.

Example 7.4

(a) E74a.m

(b) E74b.m, MATLAB® Statistics Toolbox

Example 7.5

E75.m

Example 7.6

E76.m, MATLAB® System Identification Toolbox

Example 7.7

E77.m, MATLAB® Financial Toolbox

7.11 References

Abuaf, N. and P. Jorion (1990) Purchasing power parity in the long-run, *Journal of Finance*, 45, 157–174.

Balke, N.S and M.E. Wohar (1998) Nonlinear dynamics and covered interest rate parity, *Empirical Economics*, 23, 535–559.

Berkowitz, J. and L. Giorgiannio (2001) Long-horizon exchange rate predictability? *Review of Economics and Statistics*, 83, 81–91.

Boero, G. and E. Marrocu (2002) The performance of non-linear exchange rate models: a forecasting comparison, *Journal of Forecasting*, 21, 513–542.

Breitung, J. (2000) The local power of some unit root tests for panel data. In Baltagi, B. (ed.) *Nonstationary Panels, Panel Cointegration, and Dynamic Panels*, Advances in Econometrics, 15. Amsterdam: JAI Press, pp. 161–178.

Breitung, J. (2002) Nonparametric tests for unit roots and cointegration, *Journal of Econometrics*, 108, 343–363.

Cassel, G. (1921) *The World's Money Problems*. New York: E.P. Dutton and Co.

Cassel, G. (1922) *Money and Foreign Exchange After 1914*. New York: MacMillan.

Cerrato, M., Kim, H. and R. MacDonald (2010) Three-regime asymmetric STAR modeling and exchange rate reversion, *Journal of Money, Credit and Banking*, 42, 1447–1467.

Cornell, B.W. and J.K. Dietrich (1978) The efficiency of the market for foreign exchange under floating exchange rates, *The Review of Economics and Statistics*, 60, 111–120.

Dickey, D.A. and W.A. Fuller (1979) Distribution of the estimators for autoregressive time series with a unit root, *Journal of the American Statistical Association*, 74, 427–431.

Diebold, F.X. and R. Mariano (1995) Comparing predictive accuracy, *Journal of Business and Economic Statistics*, 13, 253–262.

Dornbusch, R. (1976) Expectations and exchange rate dynamics, *Journal of Political Economy*, 84, 1161–1176.

Dumas, B. (1992) Dynamic equilibrium and the real exchange rate in a spatially separated world, *The Review of Financial Studies*, 5, 153–180.

Enders, W. (1988) ARIMA and cointegration tests of PPP under fixed and flexible exchange rate regimes, *Review of Economics and Statistics*, 70, 504–508.

Engle, R. and C.W.J. Granger (1987) Co-integration and error correction: representation, estimation and testing, *Econometrica*, 55, 251–276.

Evans, M.D.D. and K.K. Lewis (1995) Do long-term swings in the dollar affect estimates of the risk premia? *Review of Financial Studies*, 8, 709–742.

Fama, E.F. (1984) Forward and spot exchange rates, *Journal of Monetary Economics*, 14, 319–338.

Fama, E.F. (1991) Efficient Capital Markets II, *Journal of Finance*, 46, 1575–1617.

Frankel, J. (1979) On the mark: a theory of floating exchange rates based on real interest rate differentials, *American Economic Review*, 69, 610–622.

Frankel, J (1982) The mystery of the multiplying marks: a modification of the monetary model, *Review of Economics and Statistics*, 64, 515–519.

Frankel, J.A. and A.K. Rose (1996) Exchange rate economics: what's wrong with the conventional macro approach? In Frankel, J.A., Galli, G. and A. Giovanni (eds) *The Microstructure of Foreign Exchange Markets*. Chicago: Chicago University Press, pp. 261–301.

Frenkel, J. (1976) A monetary approach to the exchange rate: doctrinal aspects and empirical evidence, *Scandinavian Journal of Economics*, 78, 200–224.

Frenkel, J.A. and R.M. Levich (1975) Covered interest arbitrage: unexploited profits? *Journal of Political Economy*, 83, 325–338.

Gehrig, T. and L. Menkhoff (2004) The use of flow analysis in foreign exchange: exploratory evidence, *Journal of International Money and Finance*, 23, 573–594.

Giddy, D.H. and G. Dufey (1975) The random behavior of flexible exchange rates, *Journal of International Business Studies*, 6, 1–32.

Gradojevic, N. and J. Yang (2006) Non-linear, non-parametric, non-fundamental exchange rate forecasting, *Journal of Forecasting*, 25, 227–245.

Granger, C.W.J. and P. Newbold (1974) Spurious regressions in econometrics, *Journal of Econometrics*, 2, 111–120.

Granger, C.W.J. and T. Teräsvirta (1993) *Modelling Nonlinear Economic Relationships*. Oxford: Oxford University Press.

Harris, D., Leybourne S.J. and B.P.M. McCabe (2005) Panel stationarity tests for purchasing power parity with cross-sectional dependence, *Journal of Business and Economic Statistics*, 23, 395–409.

Horvath, M.T.K. and M.W. Watson (1995) Testing for cointegration when some of the cointegrating vectors are prespecified, *Econometric Theory*, 11, 984–1014.

Im, K., Pesaran, M.H. and Y. Shin (2003) Testing for unit roots in heterogeneous panels, *Journal of Econometrics*, 115, 53–74.

Johansen, S. (1988) Statistical analysis of cointegrating vectors, *Journal of Economic Dynamics and Control*, 12, 231–254.

Johansen, S. and K. Juselius (1994) Testing structural hypotheses in a multivariate cointegration analysis of PPP and the UIP for UK, *Journal of Econometrics*, 53, 211–244.

Jorion, P. and R.J. Sweeney (1996) Mean reversion in real exchange rates: evidence and implications for forecasting, *Journal of Money and Finance*, 15, 535–550.

Kao, C. (1999) Spurious regression and residual-based tests for cointegration in panel data, *Journal of Econometrics*, 90, 1–44.

Kapetanios, G., and Y. Shin (2006) Unit root tests in three-regime SETAR models, *Econometrics Journal*, 9, 252–278.

Kapetanios, G., Shin, Y. and A. Snell (2003) Testing for a unit root in the nonlinear STAR framework, *Journal of Econometrics*, 112, 359–379.

Killian, L. (1999) Exchange rates and monetary fundamentals: what do we learn from long-horizon regressions? *Journal of Applied Econometrics*, 14, 491–510.

Killian, L. and M.P. Taylor (2003) Why is it so difficult to beat the random walk forecast of exchange rates? *Journal of International Economics*, 60, 85–107.

Lane, P. (2001) The new open economy macroeconomics: a survey, *Journal of International Economics*, 54, 518–538.

Levin, A. and C.-F. Lin (1992) Unit root tests in panel data: asymptotic and finite-sample properties, Discussion Paper No. 92-23, Department of Economics, University of California at San Diego.

Levin, A., and C.-F. Lin (1993) Unit root tests in panel data: new results. Discussion Paper No. 93-56, Department of Economics, University of California at San Diego.

Levin, A., Lin, C.-F. and C. Chu (2002) Unit root tests in panel data: asymptotic and finite sample properties, *Journal of Econometrics*, 108, 1–24.

Lewis, K.K. (1988) The persistence of the 'peso problem' when policy is noisy, *Journal of International Money and Finance*, 7, 5–21.

Lewis, K.K. (1989) Can learning affect exchange rate behavior? The case of the dollar in the early 1980s, *Journal of Monetary Economics*, 23, 79-100.

Ljung, G.M. and G.E.P. Box (1978) On a measure of a lack of fit in time series models, *Biometrika*, 65, 297-303.

Lo, A.W. and C. MacKinlay (1988) Stock market prices do not follow random walks: evidence from a simple specification test, *Review of Financial Studies*, 1, 41-66.

Luukkonen, R., Saikkonen, P. and T. Teräsvirta (1988) Testing linearity against smooth transition autoregressive models, *Biometrika*, 75, 491-499.

MacDonald, R. and I.W. Marsh (1999) *Exchange Rate Modelling*. Boston: Kluwer Academic Publishers.

Maddala, G.S. and S. Wu (1999) A comparative study of unit root tests with panel data and new simple test, *Oxford Bulletin of Economics and Statistics*, 61, 631-652.

Mark, N. (1990) Real and nominal exchange rates in the long-run: an empirical investigation, *Journal of International Economics*, 28, 115-136.

Mark, N.C. (1995) Exchange rates and fundamentals: evidence on long-horizon predictability, *American Economic Review*, 85, 201-218.

Meese, R. (1986) Testing for bubbles in exchange rates: a case of sparkling rates? *Journal of Political Economy*, 94, 345-373.

Meese, R. and K. Rogoff (1983) Empirical exchange rate models of the seventies: do they fit out of sample? *Journal of International Economics*, 14, 3-24.

Meese, R.A. and K. Rogoff (1988) Was it real? The exchange rate-interest differential relation over the modern floating-rate period, *Journal of Finance*, 43, 933-948.

Menkhoff, L. (1997) Examining the use of technical currency analysis, *International Journal of Finance and Economics*, 2, 307-318.

Menkhoff, L. and M.P. Taylor (2007) The obstinate passion of foreign exchange professionals: technical analysis, *Journal of Economic Literature*, 45, 936-972.

Michael, P., Nobay A.R. and D.A. Peel (1997) Transactions costs and nonlinear adjustment in real exchange rates: an empirical investigation, *Journal of Political Economy*, 105, 862-879.

Neely, C.J. and L. Sarno (2002) How well do monetary fundamentals forecast exchange rates? *The Federal Reserve Bank of St Louis Review*, 84, 51-74.

Neely, C.J., Weller P.A. and J.M. Ulrich (2009) The adaptive markets hypothesis: evidence from the foreign exchange market, *Journal of Financial and Quantitative Analysis*, 44, 467-488.

Newey, W.K. and K.D. West (1987) A simple, positive-definite, heteroskedasticity and autocorrelation consistent covariance matrix, *Econometrica*, 55, 703-708.

O'Connell, P.G.J. (1998) The overvaluation of purchasing power parity, *Journal of International Economics*, 44, 1-19.

Oh, K.-Y. (1996) Purchasing power parity and unit root tests using panel data, *Journal of International Money and Finance*, 15, 405-418.

Papell, D.H. (1997) Searching for stationarity: purchasing power parity under the current float, *Journal of International Economics*, 43, 313–332.

Park, C. and S.H. Irwin (2007) What do we know about the profitability of technical analysis? *Journal of Economic Surveys*, 21, 786–826.

Pedroni, P. (1999) Critical values for cointegration tests in heterogeneous panels with multiple regressors, *Oxford Bulletin of Economics and Statistics*, 61, 653–669.

Peel, D.A. and M.P. Taylor (2002) Covered interest arbitrage in the interwar period and the Keynes-Einzig Conjecture, *Journal of Money, Credit and Banking*, 34, 51–75.

Pesaran, M.H. (2007) A Simple panel unit root test in the presence of cross-section dependence, *Journal of Applied Econometrics*, 22, 265–312.

Phillips, P.C.B. and Hansen, B. (1990) Statistical inference in instrumental variables regressions with I(1) processes, *Review of Economic Studies*, 57, 99–125.

Poole, W. (1967) Speculative prices as random walks: an analysis of ten time series of flexible exchange rates, *Southern Economic Journal*, 33, 468–478.

Qi, M. and Y. Wu (2006) Technical trading-rule profitability, data snooping, and reality check: evidence from the foreign exchange market, *Journal of Money, Credit and Banking*, 30, 2135–2158.

Rogoff, K.S. (1996) The purchasing power parity puzzle, *Journal of Economic Literature*, 34, 647–668.

Rossi, B. (2005) Confidence intervals for half-life deviations from purchasing power parity, *Journal of Business and Economic Statistics*, 23, 432–442.

Sarno, L. and M.P. Taylor (2002) *The Economics of Exchange Rates*. Cambridge: Cambridge University Press.

Sercu, P., Uppal R., and C. Van Hulle (1995) The exchange rate in the presence of transactions costs: implications for tests of purchasing power parity, *Journal of Finance*, 50, 1309–1319.

Sollis, R., Leybourne, S.J. and P. Newbold (2002) Tests for symmetric and asymmetric nonlinear mean reversion in real exchange rates, *Journal of Money, Credit and Banking*, 34, 686–700.

Tauchen, G. (2001) The bias of tests for a risk premium in forward exchange rates, *Journal of Empirical Finance*, 8, 695–704.

Taylor, M.P. (1988) An empirical examination of long-run purchasing power parity using cointegration techniques, *Journal of Economic Literature*, 33, 13–47.

Taylor, M.P. and H. Allen (1992) The use of technical analysis in the foreign exchange market, *Journal of International Money and Finance*, 11, 304–314.

Taylor, M.P., Sarno, L. and D. Peel (2001) Nonlinear mean reversion in real exchange rates: towards a solution to the purchasing power parity puzzles, *International Economic Review*, 42, 1015–1042.

Teräsvirta, T. (1994) Specification, estimation and evaluation of smooth transition autoregressive models, *Journal of the American Statistical Association*, 89, 208–218.

Terborgh, G.W. (1926) The purchasing-power parity theory, *Journal of Political Economy*, 34, 197–208.

White, H. (2000) A reality check for data snooping, *Econometrica*, 68, 1097–1126.

Wu, Y. (1996) Are real exchange rates nonstationary? Evidence from a panel data test, *Journal of Money, Credit and Banking*, 28, 54–63.

Chapter 8
Modelling and Forecasting Interest Rates

8.1 Introduction

This chapter focuses on modelling and forecasting interest rates, beginning with a discussion of the main types of bonds and the traditional formulas for computing bond yields and bond prices. The relationship between bond yields and the time-to-maturity of bonds, referred to as the **term structure of interest rates**, is then considered. This chapter also introduces an important family of **continuous time** interest rate models. These models assume that interest rates are time-varying random processes that can be represented using **stochastic differential equations**. A continuous time model can be thought of as a discrete time model (e.g. a first-order autoregressive (AR(1)) model), where the time interval is infinitesimally small. Continuous time interest rate models can be used to obtain analytical formulas for pricing bonds, bond derivatives, and for describing the term structure of interest rates. These models and formulas arc widely employed in practice.

The expectations hypothesis of the term structure of interest rates states that long-term interest rates depend on investors' expectations of future short-term interest rates, where these expectations are formed rationally. In this context "expectations" can be interpreted as meaning **rational forecasts**, where the rational forecast of a future interest rate is the expected value of the future interest rate computed using all the relevant information currently available.[1] If the expectations hypothesis of the term structure of interest rates is correct, the yield curve (a graph of bond yields against time to maturity) contains information on market forecasts of future short-term interest rates, which is valuable information for investors, macroeconomists and policymakers, and hence a significant amount of academic research has been undertaken on empirically testing the expectations hypothesis. The final topic covered in this chapter is empirically testing the expectations hypothesis using econometric tests developed by Campbell and Shiller (1987, 1991). The penultimate section of the main text presents five empirical examples that demonstrate a selection of the empirical methods covered, including computing bond yields and bond prices, estimating the parameters of a continuous time interest rate model, forecasting interest rates and testing the expectations hypothesis.

8.2 Bonds

8.2.1 Yields and Prices

Bonds are issued by companies and governments as a way of borrowing money. Investors in bonds will expect to receive a yield that is competitive with the yield from alternative investments with a similar level of risk. On average, bonds are typically less risky investments than stocks, and are expected to offer higher yields than conventional savings accounts with banks.[2] There are many different types of bonds. Some bonds pay a series of regular cash flows over their life called **coupons**. Others do not. The **maturity** date of a bond is the point in time when the bond investor receives the bond's **principal** amount, also called the bond's **par value** (or **face value**), and possibly a final coupon payment.

A Treasury bill is a popular type of government bond with a relatively short maturity that does not pay any coupons over its life. US government Treasury bills have a par

---

[1]In this chapter the terms **expectations** and **forecasts** are used interchangeably.
[2]The terms **yield** and **interest rate** are often used interchangeably when discussing bonds. The phrase **market interest rates** refers to the interest rates currently available to investors on other investments. It is helpful to think of market interest rates as referring to some broad average of the interest rates currently available to investors.

value of $1000.[3] The issue price of a Treasury bill is less than its par value, and this generates a positive yield. There are four different maturities for US and UK Treasury bills: four weeks, 13 weeks, 26 weeks and 52 weeks (corresponding to approximately one month, three months, six months and one year).

There are various different types of yield that can be computed for a bond. For US Treasury bills the discount yield (DY) is traditionally reported by the US Treasury and in the financial press,

$$DY = \left(\frac{par - P}{par}\right)\left(\frac{360}{n}\right) \tag{8.1}$$

where P denotes the current price, par denotes the par value, and n is the number of days until maturity. For example, the DY for a 13-week Treasury bill issued at $985 is,

$$DY = \left(\frac{15}{1000}\right)\left(\frac{360}{91}\right) = 0.0593 \tag{8.2}$$

or 5.93%. An alternative to the DY is the **bond equivalent yield** (BEY),

$$BEY = \left(\frac{par - P}{P}\right)\left(\frac{365}{n}\right) \tag{8.3}$$

For the example used above, the BEY is,

$$BEY = \left(\frac{15}{985}\right)\left(\frac{365}{91}\right) = 0.0611 \tag{8.4}$$

Note, therefore, that since the BEY annualises using 365 days and divides by P rather than par, DY < BEY. The BEY is useful when comparing Treasury bills with other coupon paying bonds. The DY is also called the **discount rate** and the BEY is also called the **investment rate**. The **money market yield** (MMY) is similar to the BEY, although a 360-day year is assumed,

$$MMY = \left(\frac{par - P}{P}\right)\left(\frac{360}{n}\right) \tag{8.5}$$

Treasury notes and Treasury bonds are US government bonds that offer longer maturities than Treasury bills. Treasury notes have a maturity of between one year and 10 years. Treasury notes are coupon paying bonds and the coupon is paid every six months. Treasury bonds also pay coupons and have long maturities ranging from 10 to 30 years. In the UK, longer term coupon paying government bonds (with maturities ranging from five to 50 years) are called **Gilts**.

Many corporations issue coupon paying bonds as a means of raising funds. Typically, corporate bonds have maturities greater than one year. For coupon paying

---

[3]With the introduction of TreasuryDirect (a website run by the US Treasury), domestic investors can invest a minimum amount of $100 directly in Treasury bills. In the UK, the minimum par value for UK government Treasury bills is £25 000.

bonds such as corporate bonds, investors focus on the yield to maturity (YTM), which will be discussed in more detail below. In the US, corporate bonds usually have a par value of $1000. Since corporate bonds are usually issued at par value, the coupon rate (CR) needs to be set so that the bond is a competitive investment relative to market interest rates. If a bond's CR is lower than market interest rates then rational investors will only be prepared to pay a price for the bond that is below its par value.

A bond's price can be computed from its yield by rearranging the relevant yield formula. For example we can rearrange the DY formula (8.1) to give,

$$P = par\left[1 - DY\left(\frac{n}{360}\right)\right]$$

(8.6)

The MMY formula (8.5) can be rearranged to give,

$$P = \frac{par}{1 + \left(\dfrac{MMY \times n}{360}\right)}$$

(8.7)

Computing the price of coupon paying bonds is more involved since the value of the bond depends on the present value of the coupon payments associated with the bond and its par value. Assume that coupons are paid semi-annually. A traditional formula for computing the current price of a coupon paying bond is,

$$P = \sum_{t=1}^{2T}\left[\frac{C/2}{(1 + YTM/2)^t}\right] + \frac{par}{(1 + YTM/2)^{2T}}$$

(8.8)

where $T \equiv$ years to maturity, $C \equiv$ annual coupon and $YTM \equiv$ yield to maturity.

The YTM is a measure of the annual rate of return the investor will receive if they purchase a bond and hold the bond until maturity. Note that here the annual coupon is assumed to be constant and both the annual coupon and YTM are divided by two, because the coupon payments are assumed to occur semi-annually. The CR is the coupon as a percentage of par. So, for example, with $par = \$1000$ and $CR = 5\%, C = \$50$. Consider the following simple example,

$$par = \$1000$$
$$CR = 5\%$$
$$YTM = 6\%$$
$$T = 2$$

It follows that the bond price is,

$$P = \sum_{t=1}^{4}\left[\frac{50/2}{(1 + 0.06/2)^t}\right] + \frac{1000}{(1 + 0.06/2)^4} = \$981.41$$

(8.9)

After a bond has been issued, it can typically be traded in the secondary bond market. Therefore, its price and the YTM for new investors are not constant, but they depend on investors' demand for the bond in the light of several factors including market interest rates, the bond's maturity, the CR, the risk of default by the issuer, the general macroeconomic and financial conditions at the time of the investment and expectations regarding these conditions.

For coupon paying bonds traded in secondary markets, the reported price is called the **clean price**. The **dirty price** is the full price that must be paid, which depends on the **accrued interest** – the interest owed to the seller of the bond if the bond is sold between coupon payments. For example, if the CR is 5% and *par* is $1000 then the semi-annual coupon is $25. If the bond is sold three-months after the last coupon payment (say 91 days) and the semi-annual period in days is 182, then the seller is owed 91/182 of the semi-annual coupon from the buyer. If the clean price is $980, the dirty price is $980 + 25(91/182) = $992.50. Note also that it is also important to distinguish between the **bid** price (the price that the bond dealer is willing to pay) and the **ask** price (the price paid to buy from a bond dealer). Naturally the ask price is higher than the bid price. The prices and yields for many different bonds are reported on a daily basis in the financial press.

8.2.2 The Term Structure of Interest Rates

The **term structure of interest rates** refers to the relationship between bond yields and time to maturity. Intuitively one would expect that the annual YTM for two bonds with similar features apart from their different maturities should not stray too far from each other because they are competing assets. If bond markets are informationally efficient then *ceteris paribus* any bond that gives a significantly higher annual yield than any other bond will quickly become popular, causing its price to rise and yield to fall. The opposite is true for bonds that have a significantly lower yield. In practice, yields for similar bonds do tend to vary depending on their time to maturity and we might argue that this is due to investors' expectations of future short-term interest rates.

The **expectations hypothesis** (EH) of the term structure of interest rates states that long-term interest rates depend on investors' expectations of future short-term interest rates, where these expectations are formed rationally. If we assume that the EH is correct and plot a graph of YTM against time to maturity for zero-coupon bonds (the yield curve) and it slopes upwards, it suggests that short-term interest rates are forecast to increase. Conversely a downward sloping graph suggests that short-term interest rates are forecast to decrease. In practice, in developed bond markets the observed yield curve is usually upwards sloping, and other shapes are rarer. To illustrate the type of shape often observed, Figures 8.1 and 8.2 graph the yield curves for UK and US government bonds in March 2011.

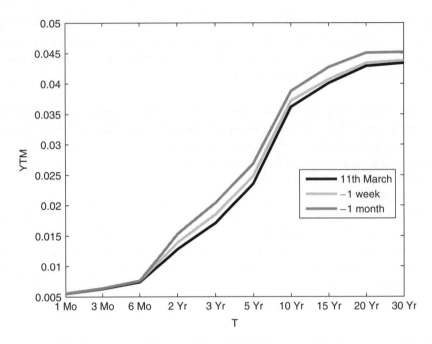

Figure 8.1   UK yield curve, February/March 2011. *Source*: **UK yield curve data for 11 March 2011 from The Financial Times website http://markets.ft.com/ markets/bonds.asp.**

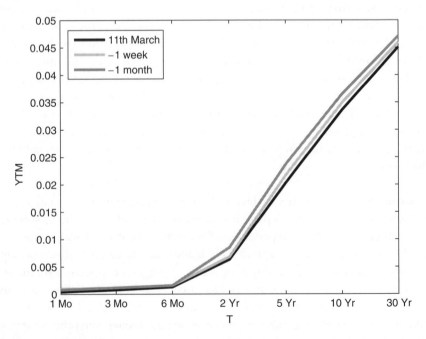

Figure 8.2   US yield curve, February/March 2011. *Source*: **US yield curve data for 11 March 2011 from The Financial Times website http://markets.ft.com/ markets/bonds.asp.**

Occasionally the yield curve will **invert**, meaning that short-term rates are higher than long-term rates. In the US this occurred in the early 1980s and it had important consequences for many financial institutions, particularly those that were attempting to profit from the difference in interest rates charged on deposits and loans. Since the average maturity of deposits is typically shorter than the average maturity of loans, when the yield curve inverted many of these institutions suffered significant losses as a result.

The main theories of the term structure of interest rates can be formalised using the concept of the **forward interest rate**. The forward interest rate is the interest rate for a future time period that is implied by the current YTM on bonds with different maturities. Consider a simple example involving one-year (short-term) and two-year (long-term) zero-coupon bonds with yields, YTM_1 and YTM_2. Let YTM_{2f} denote the YTM for a one-year bond in year two, and assume this amount is known at the start of year one. It follows that,

$$(1 + YTM_2)^2 = (1 + YTM_1)(1 + YTM_{2f}) \qquad (8.10)$$

If this were not the case and, for example,

$$(1 + YTM_2)^2 > (1 + YTM_1)(1 + YTM_{2f}) \qquad (8.11)$$

then the relative demand for the two-year bond will rise causing its price to rise and YTM_2 to fall. Conversely, if,

$$(1 + YTM_2)^2 < (1 + YTM_1)(1 + YTM_{2f}) \qquad (8.12)$$

then the relative demand for the two-year bond will fall, causing its price to fall and YTM_2 to rise. The rational behaviour of investors ensures that (8.10) holds. Of course, this is a highly unrealistic example since YTM_{2f} is unknown in year one. Note, however, since YTM_1 and YTM_2 are known in year one, if we assume that (8.10) holds, we can then calculate YTM_{2f} using the known YTM values. This future short-term interest rate calculated using information that is currently available is called a **forward interest rate**. The one-year forward interest rate is given by,

$$(1 + YTM_{2f}) = \frac{(1 + YTM_2)^2}{(1 + YTM_1)} \qquad (8.13)$$

More generally, we can calculate forward interest rates from all YTM values that are one period apart,

$$(1 + YTM_{nf}) = \frac{(1 + YTM_n)^n}{(1 + YTM_{n-1})^{n-1}} \qquad (8.14)$$

where n denotes maturity in years. We can formalise the EH by stating that under the EH the forward interest rate is equal to the expected value of the relevant future short-term interest rate; thus, assuming rational expectations (RE), forward rates are unbiased forecasts of future short-term rates. Hence it follows from (8.14) that if investors forecast a rise in short-term interest rates, the yield curve will slope upwards.

The **liquidity premium theory** (or **liquidity preference theory**) (LPT) is an alternative view of the term structure of interest rates based on the argument that *ceteris paribus* risk-averse investors prefer short-term bonds to long-term bonds because of the greater risk associated with long-term bonds. For example, long-term bonds have a higher degree of interest rate risk than short-term bonds, since for the same change in interest rates their price will change by a greater amount (this point is discussed in more detail in Section 8.2.3). Consequently, if investors are to hold long-term bonds, they require a **liquidity premium** (or **risk premium**) relative to the yield on short-term bonds. Therefore, bonds will be priced so that forward rates are higher than expected future short-term rates. Thus, under the LPT, forward rates are positively biased forecasts of future short-term interest rates.

There has been much debate and empirical research on whether the EH or the LPT provides a better theory of the term structure of interest rates. The EH is particularly attractive to economists because of its simplicity and assumption of RE. However, in practice, for developed bond markets we typically observe upwards sloping yield curves and, therefore, if the EH is correct this suggests that investors consistently forecast higher interest rates, which is typically not supported by forecasting evidence from econometric models, or survey evidence on interest rate forecasts. This contradiction suggests that some combination of the EH and LPT could be a more realistic description of how bond market investors actually behave.

8.2.3 Duration and Convexity

Assume that an investor holds a long position in a portfolio of bonds where the bond prices are such that their yields are competitive with market interest rates. If market interest rates rise, then *ceteris paribus* the value of the bond portfolio will fall. This must occur because as market interest rates rise, for bond yields to remain competitive, bond prices must fall. Hence, when market interest rates change, bond yields change. For obvious reasons bond investors will be concerned with the interest rate sensitivity of their bond portfolios; that is, the sensitivity of the value of their portfolio to changes in interest rates, which depends on the relationship between changes in bond yields and changes in bond prices. It can be shown that this relationship depends on several factors:[4]

  (i) The sign of the yield change (positive yield changes are consistent with larger price changes than negative yield changes).
 (ii) Maturity (long-term bonds are more sensitive than short-term bonds).
(iii) The CR (bonds with a high CR are less sensitive than those with a low CR).

---

[4]A seminal journal article on the relationship between bond yields and bond prices is Malkiel (1962). See also Homer and Liebowitz (1972).

(iv) The initial yield (bonds with a low initial YTM are more sensitive than those with a high initial YTM).

Since the interest rate sensitivity of a bond is known to depend on several observable factors bond portfolio managers might attempt to exploit this information to improve returns. For example, if a bond portfolio manager with a long position in bonds forecasts that market interest rates will rise and they believe that this has not been incorporated into the current yield curve, then they might consider a strategy of rebalancing their portfolio towards less interest-sensitive bonds. This might be done by investing in short-term bonds with a high CR. Conversely if they forecast that market interest rates will fall, they might consider rebalancing towards more interest-sensitive bonds. When deciding whether to rebalance, the associated transaction costs need to be considered.

For zero-coupon bonds the **maturity** of the bond is a simple concept: it is the amount of time until the par value is paid. For coupon paying bonds, however, the concept of maturity is more complex since the presence of coupon payments creates a type of gradual maturity. Since the CR and time to maturity are both important in determining the interest rate sensitivity of bonds, a measure of maturity that takes into account coupon payments would be helpful for comparing bonds. The concept of **duration**, proposed by Macaulay (1938), provides such a measure. Duration can be defined mathematically as,

$$D = \frac{\sum_{t=1}^{T} \left[\dfrac{C_t \times t}{(1 + YTM)^t} \right]}{P} \tag{8.15}$$

where C_t denotes a cash flow for period t and we simplify notation by assuming that YTM is the period YTM, and there are T periods. Therefore, duration is just the weighted time to maturity where the weight in each time period depends on the present value of the cash flow, all as a proportion of the bond price. It is a measure that can be used to compare the maturity of bonds, which recognises the fact that over the life of the bond there are regular cash flows to the investor.

It can be shown that the sensitivity of the relationship between changes in bond yield and changes in bond price is a positive function of a bond's duration – the higher the duration, the bigger the price change for a given change in yield. Therefore, if a portfolio manager with a long position in bonds forecasts a fall in market interest rates and they believe that this has not been incorporated into the current yield curve, they might choose to rebalance their portfolio to increase its duration. If they forecast a rise in market interest rates, they might choose to rebalance their portfolio to reduce its duration. In practice, the costs of rebalancing relative to the size of the forecast change in interest rates would be considered in deciding whether to undertake this type of strategy.

Duration can be formally linked to price changes by defining the modified duration (*MD*),

$$MD = \frac{D}{(1 + YTM)} \tag{8.16}$$

It can be shown that,

$$\frac{\Delta P}{P} = -MD \times \Delta YTM \tag{8.17}$$

where $\Delta P \equiv$ the price change, $P \equiv$ the initial price and $\Delta YTM \equiv$ the change in *YTM*.

The formula given by (8.17) is a simple and useful way of modelling the impact of interest rate changes on the value of a bond portfolio. However, whilst (8.17) is accurate when interest rate changes are small, it can be much less accurate for larger changes. This is because the true relationship between the YTM and bond prices is non-linear and (8.17) is only a linear approximation.[5] A simple illustration is given in Figure 8.3. In this example the bond has a par value of $1000, a CR of 5% and starts with a YTM of 6%.

It can be seen from Figure 8.3 that for small changes in YTM the actual price change is closely estimated by the linear approximation (8.17), but this is not the case

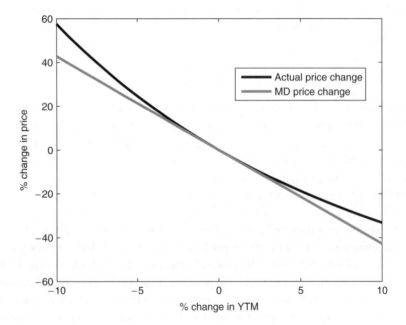

Figure 8.3   Bond price sensitivity.

---

[5]More specifically it is a first-order **Taylor series approximation**, which is a mathematical technique for approximating a function at a particular point using the derivatives of the function.

for larger price changes. The actual relationship between changes in yield and changes in price is convex. Mathematically this convexity can be quantified using the measure,

$$CVX = \frac{\left(\dfrac{\partial^2 P}{\partial YTM^2} \right)}{P} \tag{8.18}$$

Thus the convexity of a bond is measured by the second partial derivative of the bond price with respect to YTM, standardised by the price. The relevant partial derivative is,

$$\frac{\partial^2 P}{\partial YTM^2} = \frac{1}{(1 + YTM)^2} \sum_{t=1}^{T} \left[t(t+1) \frac{C_t}{(1 + YTM)^t} \right] \tag{8.19}$$

A more accurate alternative to (8.17) involves adding an additional term involving CVX to capture the convexity of the relationship,

$$\frac{\Delta P}{P} = -MD \times \Delta YTM + \frac{1}{2} CVX \times (\Delta YTM)^2 \tag{8.20}$$

The simple portfolio management strategies described above are active strategies in the sense that they seek to profit from forecasts of interest rate changes. In contrast, a more passive approach to bond portfolio management is to focus on minimising the impact of interest rate fluctuations on the value of the bond portfolio. There are many different techniques that a portfolio manager might use to try to **immunise** a bond portfolio against interest rate changes. One technique, referred to as **duration matching** or **duration gap management**, is particularly appropriate if a portfolio consists of both assests and liabilities. Assume that such a portfolio exists where the assests and liabilities are linked to the value of bonds and are approximately equal in size. Recall from (8.17) that the impact of interest rate changes on bond prices depends on the duration of the bonds. Hence, in this case, if interest rates fall (rise), the value of the assests and liabilities will rise (fall) by a similar amount if they have a similar duration. If, for example, the duration of the liabilities is higher than the duration of the assests, a fall in interest rates will cause the value of the liabilities to rise by more than the value of the assests, reducing the overall value of the portfolio. Hence, matching the duration of the assests and liabilities will help to reduce the impact of interest rate changes on overall value. Duration matching is a popular technique with banks, whose balance sheets can be thought of as a portfolio consisting of assets (loans) and liabilities (deposits).

For financial institutions that invest in portfolios of assets in order to meet obligations to pay cash-flows in the future (e.g. pension funds), a different type of immunisation technique is popular, called **target date immunisation**. Portfolio managers need to ensure that the value of the portfolio at the relevant date in the future (the target date) will match the future liabilities. Assume the portfolio consists of coupon paying bonds chosen so that its value increases to the required amount. Changes in interest rates will have a converse effect on the value of the assets and the return on coupon payments that are reinvested. For example, if interest rates rise then the final value of the portfolio falls (there is a price risk associated with the possibility that interest rates can change), but the final value of the reinvested bond coupon payments rises (there is a reinvestment risk associated with the possibility that interest rates can change). It can be shown in this example that when the duration of the portfolio is set equal to the investment horizon, the price risk and reinvestment risk are such that the overall impact of interest rate changes on the future value of the portfolio is neutralised.[6] Immunisation strategies focus on reducing the impact of interest rate changes on the value of a portfolio, and might involve regular rebalancing to ensure the portfolio has the correct duration. Therefore, although not an active strategy immunisation is not a completely "passive" investment strategy.

8.3 Interest Rate Models

8.3.1 Vasicek Model

In practice, interest rates vary over time and they can be interpreted as **random processes**.[7] It is important to take this into account when modelling and forecasting interest rates and bond prices. In a seminal journal article on this topic, Vasicek (1977) shows how from a simple model for the **spot rate** it is possible to derive analytical formulas for zero-coupon bond prices at all maturities, and for the term structure that incorporates features of how the spot rate evolves over time. The spot rate is defined as the instantaneous interest rate on a zero-coupon bond (the interest rate as the time to maturity approaches zero),

$$r(t) = R(t, 0) = \lim_{T \to 0} R(t, T) \tag{8.21}$$

where $R(t, T)$ denotes the interest rate at period t for a zero-coupon bond with maturity $s = t + T$. Therefore, $R(t, T)$ as a function of T is the term structure of interest rates.

Vasicek (1977) makes the following general assumptions:

(i) The spot rate follows a continuous Markov process.[8]
(ii) The price of a zero-coupon bond at time t with maturity s, $P(t, s)$, is determined by the spot rate over the relevant term of the bond.

---

[6]For further technical details on immunisation and bond portfolio management, see the seminal academic journal articles by Reddington (1952) and Fisher and Weil (1971), the collection of specialist work on fixed-income securities by Fabozzi (2005) and the textbook by Johnson (2010).
[7]See Chapter 2 for more details on random processes.
[8]These are summaries of the assumptions in Vasicek (1977).

(iii) The bond market is efficient (there are no transaction costs, the same information is available to all investors, investors are rational).

The particular spot rate model considered by Vasicek (1977) (the **Vasicek
model**) is,

$$dr = \alpha(\gamma - r)\,dt + \sigma\,dz \tag{8.22}$$

where α, γ and σ are three parameters; dr denotes the instantaneous change in r;
and dz is the instantaneous change in a Wiener process. dz captures the random
element of the spot rate change. Clearly the spot rate model (8.22) is fundamentally
different to the econometric models that we have seen in previous chapters since
it assumes continuous time (rather than discrete time). Formally it is a stochastic
differential equation (SDE) – a type of mathematical model widely used in physics
and other sciences for modelling random processes, also used for pricing derivatives
(see e.g. Black and Scholes, 1973). This particular type of SDE is also called an
Ornstein–Uhlenbeck model and the parameters can be interpreted in a similar
way to the parameters of the AR(1) model introduced in Chapter 2. The parameter α
determines the persistence of the spot rate in the sense that as α gets closer to zero
the impact of a random shock on r decays more slowly. Vasicek (1977) assumes
that $\alpha > 0$, which means that r is a stationary variable (it is **mean reverting**). The
parameter γ is the unconditional mean of the spot rate. The parameter σ is the
unconditional standard deviation of the spot rate.

Vasicek (1977) shows that if the spot rate evolves according to (8.22), and the
market price of risk is assumed to be a constant, an equation giving the price of *any*
zero-coupon bond can be derived as a function of the spot rate and its parameters.[9]
It can be shown that the relevant pricing formula is,

$$P(t,s) = \exp\left[\frac{1}{\alpha}(1 - e^{-\alpha(s-t)})(R(\infty) - r(t)) - (s-t)R(\infty) - \frac{\sigma^2}{4\alpha^3}(1 - e^{-\alpha(s-t)})^2\right] \tag{8.23}$$

$$R(\infty) = \gamma + \sigma q/\alpha - \sigma^2/2\alpha^2 \tag{8.24}$$

where $R(\infty)$ denotes the yield on a zero-coupon bond as $T \to \infty$ and q is the market
price of risk. An alternative representation under risk-neutrality ($q = 0$) is,

$$P(t,s) = A(t,s)\exp[-B(t,s)r(t)] \tag{8.25}$$

$$A(t,s) = \exp\left[(B(t,s) - (s-t))\left(\gamma - \frac{\sigma^2}{2\alpha^2}\right) - \frac{\sigma^2 B(t,s)^2}{4\alpha}\right] \tag{8.26}$$

$$B(t,s) = \frac{1 - \exp(-\alpha(s-t))}{\alpha} \tag{8.27}$$

---

[9]Note that **market price of risk** refers to the increase in expected return for taking on an additional
unit of risk.

Therefore the Vasicek (1977) approach leads to a pricing formula for zero-coupon bonds that incorporates certain features of how the spot rate is thought to evolve randomly over time. This approach is particularly attractive since the entire term structure of interest rates can be described using the parameters of the spot rate model and the market price of risk, and a formula for the term-structure can be derived,

$$R(t, T) = R(\infty) + [r(t) - R(\infty)] \frac{1}{\alpha T}(1 - e^{-\alpha T}) + \frac{\sigma^2}{4\alpha^3 T}(1 - e^{-\alpha T})^2 \qquad (8.28)$$

Note that the formulas above allow bond prices and the term structure to be calculated both for the current period and for future periods (set $t = 0$ for a current period value and $t > 0$ for a future value). Hence these formulas can be used for forecasting. When forecasting using these formulas a forecast of the spot rate at the relevant future period is required. The forecasting theory discussed in Chapter 2 could be utilised to compute this forecast; however, in practice it is popular to employ Monte Carlo simulation on a computer to simulate multiple paths for the spot rate over the required forecasting horizon and then to average over the simulations.

Importantly, the Vasicek (1977) approach can also be used to derive a pricing formula for options on zero-coupon bonds.[10] Jamshidian (1989) shows that assuming the option is a European call option on a zero-coupon bond, if the spot rate evolves according to the Vasicek model the relevant option price is,

$$c[P(t, s), T] = P(t, s)N(b) - KP(t, T)N(b - \sigma_P) \qquad (8.29)$$

where

$$b = \frac{1}{\sigma_P} \ln \left[\frac{P(t, s)}{P(t, T)K} \right] + \frac{\sigma_P}{2} \qquad (8.30)$$

$$\sigma_P = v(t, T)B(T, s) \qquad (8.31)$$

$$v(t, T)^2 = \frac{\sigma^2 [1 - \exp(-2\alpha(T - t))]}{2\alpha} \qquad (8.32)$$

and where T denotes the expiration period, K is the strike price, $N(b)$ is the cumulative distribution function (CDF) for a standard normal random variable evaluated at b, and the other terms are defined above. Similarly, formulas can be derived for the price of a put option on a zero-coupon bond. European options on coupon paying bonds are also straightforward to price using the Vasicek (1977) approach because the option can be decomposed into a series of zero-coupon bonds (for further details, see Jamshidian, 1989). Pricing American options on coupon paying

---

[10]Although we will briefly discuss options again in Chapter 9, this book does not provide comprehensive details on the theoretical properties of options and other derivatives and how they are priced. It is envisaged that many readers will either be currently taking a specialist derivatives module, or will have had some exposure to such a module. Readers are encouraged to refer to the specialist textbook by Hull (2005) if further technical details on derivatives are required.

bonds using the Vasicek (1977) approach requires the application of more advanced numerical techniques (see e.g. Hull and White, 1990).

In order to use the Vasicek (1977) approach to price bonds and bond derivatives, estimates of α, γ, σ and q are required. In practice these parameters are unknown. If risk-neutrality is assumed, $q = 0$. However, it is also possible to estimate q from data on bond prices, conditional on the estimated parameters for the spot rate model (for more details, see Vasicek, 1977). The parameters of the spot rate model can be estimated using sample data on an appropriate short-term interest rate.

Although the Vasicek model is written in continuous time, to estimate its parameters the standard approach involves using a discrete time approximation,

$$\Delta r_t = a + b r_{t-1} + c \varepsilon_t \tag{8.33}$$

where $\varepsilon_t \sim NID(0, 1)$ and where r_t is an observed short-term interest rate for a zero-coupon bond. It can be shown that b determines the persistence of the spot rate, c determines the unconditional variance, and the unconditional mean depends on both a and b. Assuming that a large enough sample of data is available on r_t, estimates of the parameters a, b and c can be obtained using ordinary least squares (OLS), or by maximum likelihood (ML), or using a generalised method of moments (GMM) estimator. We have not yet discussed GMM estimation but will do so later in this chapter. It is important to recognise that when estimating the parameters of a discrete time version of the Vasicek model some additional computation is required to recover estimates of the original parameters of the Vasicek model. It can be shown that the relevant formulas are,

$$\hat{\alpha} = -\frac{\ln(\hat{b}^*)}{\Delta t} \tag{8.34}$$

$$\hat{\gamma} = \frac{\hat{a}}{1 - \hat{b}^*} \tag{8.35}$$

$$\hat{\sigma} = \hat{c} \left[\frac{\Delta t (\hat{b}^{*2} - 1)}{2 \ln(\hat{b}^*)} \right]^{-1/2} \tag{8.36}$$

where $\hat{b}^* = 1 + \hat{b}$ and where Δt is the time increment in fraction of a year (e.g. for monthly data, 1/12).[11]

Assuming that the same sample of data is used, all three estimation methods (OLS, ML, GMM) will produce similar estimates, but there can be small differences, particularly if the sample size is small. Note that although this approach to parameter estimation is widely used in practice, the estimated parameters obtained will be biased because the estimated model is a discrete time approximation of the true

---

[11]See Brigo *et al.* (2010) for advanced technical details on estimating the Vasicek spot rate model and other mean reverting spot rate models.

model. Note, however, that the bias is likely to be reasonably small if the data frequency is monthly or higher. More accurate ML estimation using a discrete time approximation is possible for continuous time interest rate models using an extension developed by Nowman (1997) (see also Yu and Phillips, 2001).

Despite the simplicity of the spot rate model used, the Vasicek (1977) approach is reasonably flexible and can generate a number of different yield curve shapes. For example, the following three inequalities give an upward sloping (monotonically increasing), hump-shaped and downward sloping (monotonically decreasing) yield curve respectively,

$$r(t) \leq R(\infty) - \frac{\sigma^2}{4\alpha^2} \tag{8.37}$$

$$R(\infty) - \frac{\sigma^2}{4\alpha^2} \leq r(t) \leq R(\infty) + \frac{\sigma^2}{4\alpha^2} \tag{8.38}$$

$$r(t) \geq R(\infty) + \frac{\sigma^2}{4\alpha^2} \tag{8.39}$$

and in each case the yield curve asymptotically approaches $R(\infty)$. To illustrate, three different simulated yield curves obtained using the Vasicek (1977) term structure model are graphed in Figures 8.4–8.6.

The Vasicek (1977) approach does have a number of weaknesses. For example, the number of different yield curve shapes is limited by the simplicity of the spot rate

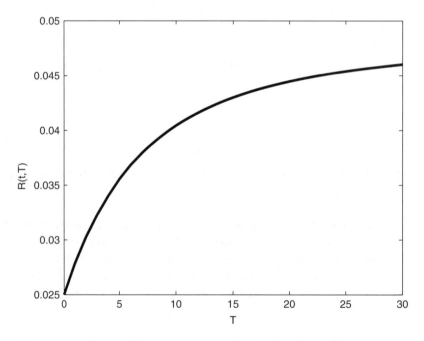

Figure 8.4 Vasicek yield curve: upward sloping.

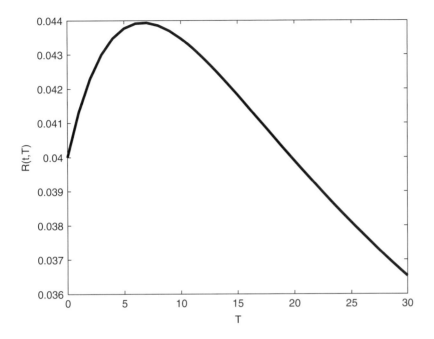

Figure 8.5   Vasicek yield curve: hump-shaped.

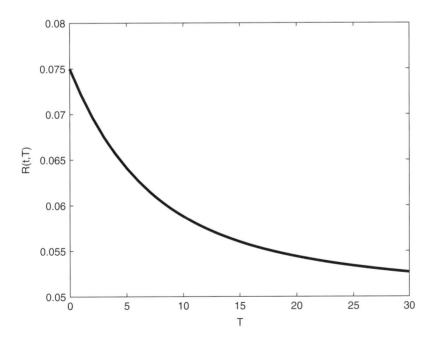

Figure 8.6   Vasicek yield curve: downward sloping.

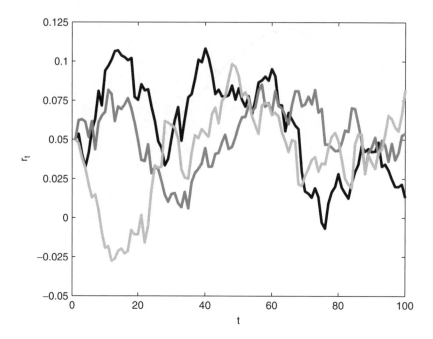

Figure 8.7   Simulated Vasicek spot rates.

model. Furthermore, the Vasicek spot rate model allows for negative spot rates, which in practice is not feasible and can lead to problems if an analyst employs the Vasicek model for simulating the spot rate. To illustrate this final point, a graph of three simulated spot rates using a discretised version of (8.22) is given in Figure 8.7. Clearly two of the simulated spot rates take negative values. Note also that under the Vasicek (1977) approach it can be shown that the bond yields across the yield curve are perfectly correlated, which is unrealistic in practice.

The approach proposed by Vasicek (1977) can be thought of as a **single-factor** approach in the sense that a single factor – the spot rate – drives the entire term structure. However, multi-factor approaches have also been proposed (see e.g. Cox, Ingersoll and Ross, 1985). Using more than one factor allows for more complex yield curve shapes. A two-factor Vasicek model assumes that the spot rate is a linear function of two factors,

$$r = x_1 + x_2 \tag{8.40}$$

which are both generated by Ornstein–Uhlenbeck models,

$$dx_1 = \alpha_1(\gamma_1 - x_1)\,dt + \sigma_1 dz_1 \tag{8.41}$$
$$dx_2 = \alpha_2(\gamma_2 - x_2)\,dt + \sigma_2 dz_2 \tag{8.42}$$

The relevant bond pricing formula becomes,

$$P(t,s) = A_1(t,s)A_2(t,s)\exp[-B_1(t,s)x_{1t}]\exp[-B_2(t,s)x_{2t}] \tag{8.43}$$

$$A_i(t,s) = \exp\left[(B_i(t,s) - (s-t))\left(\gamma_i - \frac{\sigma_i^2}{2\alpha_i^2}\right) - \frac{\sigma_i^2 B_i(t,s)^2}{4\alpha_i}\right] \tag{8.44}$$

$$B_i(t,s) = \frac{1 - \exp(-\alpha_i(s-t))}{\alpha_i} \tag{8.45}$$

for $i = 1, 2$. A multi-factor Vasicek model with more than two factors follows straightforwardly. The general bond-pricing formula is,

$$P(t,s) = \prod_{i=1}^{k} A_i(t,s) \exp[-B_i(t,s)x_{it}] \tag{8.46}$$

If the factors are known then the relevant parameters for a multi-factor Vasicek model can be estimated from a sample of data on the factors using conventional techniques (see e.g. Nowman, 2001).[12]

8.3.2 CIR Model

There have been several extensions of the Vasicek (1977) approach to allow for more general spot rate models. For example Cox, Ingersoll and Ross (1985) (CIR) employ the following spot rate model,

$$dr = \alpha(\gamma - r)\,dt + \sigma r^{1/2}\,dz \tag{8.47}$$

The presence of $r^{1/2}$ is an important feature of the CIR model because it guarantees that interest rates will be positive. Bond pricing formulas and bond derivative pricing formulas can be obtained assuming the spot rate is generated by (8.47). The parameters of the CIR spot rate model which are required to implement the relevant pricing formulas can be estimated using conventional ML applied to a discretised version of the model. GMM can also be used for parameter estimation.

The CIR spot rate model improves on the Vasicek model because it only allows for positive values. To illustrate this, a graph of three spot rates simulated using a discretised version of (8.47) is given in Figure 8.8 The same set of pseudo-random numbers and the same starting values are used as in Figure 8.7.

Clearly, in contrast to Figure 8.7, none of the simulated spot rates in Figure 8.8 is negative at any point over the sample. Note also it can be shown that the conditional variance of the CIR spot rate is given by,

$$Var[r(s)|r(t)] = r(t)\left(\frac{\sigma^2}{\alpha}\right)[\exp(-\alpha(s-t)) - \exp(-2\alpha(s-t))]$$

$$+ \gamma\left(\frac{\sigma^2}{2\alpha}\right)[1 - \exp(-\alpha(s-t))]^2 \tag{8.48}$$

---

[12]If the factors are assumed to be unknown then by treating them as state variables the Kalman filter algorithm (Kalman, 1960) can be combined with ML to estimate both the factors and the relevant parameters from data on a short-term interest rate.

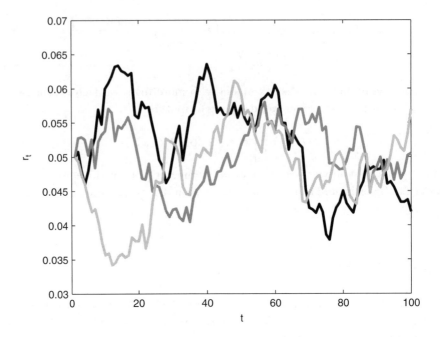

Figure 8.8 Simulated CIR spot rates.

Therefore, the CIR spot rate is conditionally heteroscedastic where the conditional variance is a positive function of the level of the spot rate. The Vasicek (1977) spot rate does not have this property. The level-dependent nature of the conditional heteroscedasticity is both intuitively attractive and it is something empirically observed in data on interest rates. For example, the three-month UK Treasury bill rate (1975:1 – 2009:12) and the three-month US Treasury bill rate (1960:1 – 2009:12) are graphed in Figures 8.9 and 8.10. In both cases the conditional variance of higher rates appears to be larger than the conditional variance of lower rates, which the CIR spot rate model is able to capture.

8.3.3 CKLS Model

The two spot rate models discussed so far can be nested within a single model,

$$dr = \alpha(\gamma - r)\,dt + \sigma r^{\theta}\,dz \tag{8.49}$$

where θ is a free parameter. For the Vasicek model $\theta = 0$, for the CIR model $\theta = 1/2$. This particular spot rate model was proposed by Chan, Karolyi, Longstaff and Sanders (1992) (CKLS). It is traditional to write the CKLS model as follows,

$$dr = \alpha + \beta r\,dt + \sigma r^{\gamma}\,dz \tag{8.50}$$

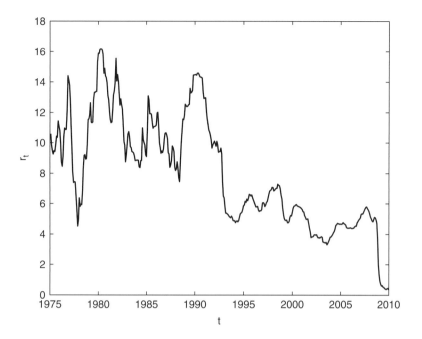

Figure 8.9   Three-month UK Treasury bill rate, 1975:1–2009:12.

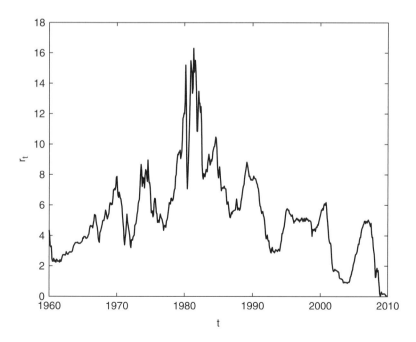

Figure 8.10   Three-month US Treasury bill rate, 1960:1–2009:12.

Therefore, the unconditional mean is $\alpha/-\beta$, the persistence of the spot rate is governed by β, and γ refers to the parameter determining the power to which the spot rate is raised when scaling the variance. As with the Vasicek and CIR approaches, formulas for bond prices, the term structure and the price of bond derivatives can be derived assuming the spot rate is generated by (8.50). Importantly the γ parameter in (8.50) can be estimated along with the other parameters in the model. Therefore, rather than have to choose *a priori* from between the Vasicek or CIR model, the CKLS model is more flexible and allows the data to determine the appropriate scaling term on dz.

The parameters of the CKLS spot rate model can be estimated from a sample of data on a short-term interest rate for a zero-coupon bond using ML, or using GMM applied to a discretised version of the model,

$$\Delta r_{t+1} = \alpha + \beta r_t + \varepsilon_{t+1} \tag{8.51}$$

where $E(\varepsilon_{t+1}) = 0$, $E(\varepsilon_{t+1}^2) = \sigma^2 r_t^{2\gamma}$. The GMM technique is used by CKLS. In this case GMM involves defining the following vector function,

$$f_t(\theta) = \begin{bmatrix} \varepsilon_{t+1} \\ \varepsilon_{t+1} r_t \\ \varepsilon_{t+1}^2 - \sigma^2 r_t^{2\gamma} \\ (\varepsilon_{t+1}^2 - \sigma^2 r_t^{2\gamma}) r_t \end{bmatrix} \tag{8.52}$$

where ε_{t+1} refers to the error term in (8.51). It can be shown that under the CKLS spot rate model,

$$E[f_t(\theta)] = 0 \tag{8.53}$$

Therefore, the population moments of the function $f_t(\theta)$ are zero, giving a series of **moment restrictions**. The GMM estimation technique involves approximating the population moments with the relevant sample moments,

$$g(\theta) = T^{-1} \sum_{t=1}^{T} f_t(\theta) \tag{8.54}$$

and then finding the parameters such that these moment restrictions are satisfied. It can be shown that this is equivalent to choosing the parameters that minimise,

$$J(\theta) = g'(\theta) W(\theta) g(\theta) \tag{8.55}$$

where $W(\theta)$ is a positive-definite symmetric weighting matrix. Following Hansen (1982), the weighting matrix used is,

$$W(\theta) = S(\theta)^{-1} \tag{8.56}$$

where

$$S(\theta) = E[f_t(\theta) f_t(\theta)'] \tag{8.57}$$

This weighting matrix minimises the asymptotic covariance matrix of the estimated parameters. Let $D_0(\theta)$ be the Jacobian matrix for $g(\theta)$ computed using the estimated parameters.[13] It follows that the asymptotic covariance matrix for the estimated parameters can be written,

$$Cov(\hat{\theta}) = \frac{1}{T}[D_0(\theta)'S_0(\theta)^{-1}D_0(\theta)]^{-1} \tag{8.58}$$

When minimised, (8.58) is a χ^2 random variable under the null hypothesis of a correct specification, where the degrees of freedom is given by number of moment restrictions minus the number of estimated parameters. Therefore, this amount can be reported as a general specification test. Note also that a convenient test of parameter restrictions is given by,

$$R = T[J(\tilde{\theta}) - J(\hat{\theta})] \tag{8.59}$$

where $J(\tilde{\theta})$ denotes the restricted value of (8.55) and $J(\hat{\theta})$ is the unrestricted value. R is asymptotically distributed as χ^2 with degrees of freedom equal to the number of restrictions.[14] GMM has some advantages relative to ML; in particular, as CKLS point out, GMM does not require interest rate changes to be normally distributed, and the estimates and standard errors are unaffected by conditional heteroscedasticity.

A potential weakness with all of the interest rate models discussed so far is that the current prices they produce might not be consistent with the actual current term structure. Note however that by extending the models it is possible to generate prices that are consistent with the current term structure. For example, Hull and White (1990) develop an extended version of the Vasicek model that can be calibrated so that the prices generated are consistent with the current term structure. This type of interest rate model is referred to as a **no-arbitrage** model. In their model, the spot rate is given by,

$$dr = (\theta_t - \alpha r)dt + \sigma\,dz \tag{8.60}$$

where θ_t is a time-varying parameter that can be computed using the current yield curve so as to make the model consistent with the current term structure and eliminate arbitrage opportunities.

8.3.4 Forecasting Interest Rates

Econometric forecasts of short-term interest rates might be computed using a discrete time version of one of the continuous time spot rate models discussed, such

---

[13]In this case the Jacobian matrix is a matrix consisting of all the first-order partial derivatives of the function $g(\theta)$ with respect to the relevant parameters.
[14]For further technical details on GMM estimation, see the comprehensive textbook by Hall (2005).

as the Vasicek model, replacing the unknown parameters with the estimated parameters. If a discrete time Vasicek model is used the relevant forecasting function for the optimal h-step ahead forecast follows from the forecasting theory discussed in Chapter 2,

$$\hat{r}_{t+h} = (\hat{b}^{*h-1} + \hat{b}^{*h-2} + \cdots + \hat{b}^* + 1)\hat{a} + \hat{b}^{*h}r_t \tag{8.61}$$

where $\hat{b}^* = 1 + \hat{b}$ and $\hat{b}$ is the estimated slope parameter in (8.33). Forecasts of the entire yield curve (and hence interest rates at various maturities) can be computed using the relevant mathematical formulas for the term structure associated with a particular spot rate model (e.g. (8.28) for the Vasicek model) by setting t in the formula to the relevant period being forecast and replacing the unknown parameter values with the estimated parameters (see Section 8.3.1 for more details).

A potential weakness with forecasting short-term rates using a discrete time version of one of the spot rate models considered here is that in all cases the spot rate models discussed are first-order differential equations. Consequently, when discrete time approximations are used, the autoregressive dynamics are first-order. In practice, however, sample data on short-term interest rates might contain higher order autocorrelations, meaning that in practice a first-order model might not be the statistically optimal forecasting model. Furthermore, there might be other features of the data (e.g. particular types of non-linearity) that the traditional spot rate models do not capture, but which might be important for forecasting. Therefore, rather than employ a discrete time version of one of the continuous time spot rate models discussed, a less restrictive econometric model might be preferred, such as one of the more general time series models discussed in Chapter 2.

8.4 Empirically Testing the Expectations Hypothesis

8.4.1 Introduction

The term structure of interest rates is important to investors, macroeconomists and policymakers. This is particularly true of the expectations hypothesis (EH) of the term structure of interest rates since, if the EH holds, the yield curve contains information on expected future interest rates. Furthermore, if the EH holds then certain relationships between short-term and long-term interest rates hold, which can be exploited for macroeconomic modelling and interest rate forecasting. It is not surprising therefore that a vast amount of research has focused on empirically testing the EH. Here we will consider three types of econometric test that use discrete data on interest rates: a cointegration-based test developed by Campbell and Shiller

(1987) and regression model and vector autoregressive (VAR) tests developed by Campbell and Shiller (1991).

8.4.2 Testing the Expectations Hypothesis

Let $r_{n,t}$ be the interest rate for a zero-coupon bond with n periods to maturity and $r_{m,t}$ the interest rate for a zero-coupon bond with m periods to maturity. Assume that $n > m$; therefore, $r_{n,t}$ is the long-term rate and $r_{m,t}$ is the short-term rate. Campbell and Shiller (1987) note that under the EH the relationship between long-term and short-term rates (with $m = 1$) can be written,

$$r_{n,t} = (1 - \delta) \sum_{i=0}^{\infty} \delta^i E_t(r_{m,t+i}) + c \tag{8.62}$$

where δ (a discount factor) and c (a constant) are parameters and $E_t r_{m,t+i}$ denotes the expected value of $r_{m,t+i}$ calculated at time t (a conditional expectation). Define the spread between long-term and short-term rates as,

$$S_t \equiv r_{n,t} - r_{m,t} \tag{8.63}$$

which can also be written,

$$S_t = [1/(1 - \delta)]\Delta r_{n,t} - \theta \Delta r_{m,t} - [\delta/(1 - \delta)]\xi_t \tag{8.64}$$

where, under the EH,

$$\xi_t = r_{n,t} - E_{t-1}r_{n,t} + c(1 - 1/\delta) \tag{8.65}$$

If investors have rational expectations (RE), it can be shown that,

$$S_t = E_t S_t^* + c \tag{8.66}$$

$$S_t^* = \theta \sum_{i=0}^{\infty} \delta^i \Delta r_{m,t+i} \tag{8.67}$$

$$S_t = \left(\frac{\delta}{1 - \delta} \right) E_t \Delta r_{n,t+1} + c \tag{8.68}$$

Consequently, if $\Delta r_{m,t}$ is a stationary variable, (8.67) and (8.66) imply that S_t is a stationary variable and (8.68) implies that $\Delta r_{n,t}$ is a stationary variable.[15,16] Therefore, the EH implies something interesting about the statistical properties of these variables that can be exploited for the purposes of hypothesis testing. In particular, if $r_{n,t}$ and $r_{m,t}$ can be shown to be non-stationary in levels but stationary in first-differences (they are I(1)), then the EH implies that $r_{n,t}$ and $r_{m,t}$ should be cointegrated, with a cointegrating vector of $[1 \quad -1]$. The cointegrating vector is said to

---

[15]See Chapter 2 and Chapter 3 for more details on stationary and non-stationary variables.
[16]Recall from Chapter 6 that if investors have RE, then the difference between the expected value and the actual value is an IID random variable with a mean of zero.

be [1 −1] since we can write the spread as,

$$S_t = \beta_1 r_{n,t} + \beta_2 r_{m,t} \tag{8.69}$$

where $\beta_1 = 1, \beta_2 = -1$.[17] It follows that the Engle and Granger (1987) two-step approach to testing for cointegration can be used to empirically test the EH. In this case the two steps are:

Step (i) Assuming that an appropriate test applied to relevant sample data on $r_{n,t}$ and $r_{m,t}$ determines they are I(1), compute the spread using (8.63).

Step (ii) Test for whether the spread is I(1) or I(0). If the spread is found to be I(1) then the EH is not supported by the data. If the spread is found to be I(0) then this is supportive of the EH.

This is equivalent to testing for cointegrating between $r_{n,t}$ and $r_{m,t}$ where the cointegrating vector is assumed to be [1 −1]. Note that this test assumes just two variables (the long-term rate and short-term rate) and so can be carried out using the single-equation cointegration framework; however, the EH implies that if all interest rates are I(1) variables then spreads between interest rates for all different maturities should be stationary variables. Therefore, multivariate cointegration techniques can also be used to test the EH.

As discussed in previous chapters, there are numerous different tests for whether a variable is I(1) or I(0), with the most popular being the Dickey–Fuller (DF) (Dickey and Fuller, 1979) and augmented Dickey–Fuller (ADF) test (Said and Dickey, 1984). For a short-term interest rate $r_{m,t}$ the relevant model for computing the ADF test is,

$$\Delta r_{m,t} = \mu + \phi_1^* r_{m,t-1} + \sum_{i=1}^{k} \beta_i \Delta r_{m,t-i} + \varepsilon_t \tag{8.70}$$

where $\varepsilon_t \sim IID(0, \sigma_\varepsilon^2)$ and the ADF test statistic is,

$$\tau_\mu = \frac{\hat{\phi}_1^*}{se(\hat{\phi}_1^*)} \tag{8.71}$$

The null hypothesis that r_t is I(1) is $H_0 : \phi_1^* = 0$ and the alternative hypothesis of I(0) is $H_1 : \phi_1^* < 0$. To decide whether to accept or reject H_0, the test statistic τ_μ should be compared with the appropriate DF critical values, given here in Table A.5 in the Appendix.

Testing for cointegration using the single-equation framework involves testing whether the fitted errors from a static regression of the dependent variable on independent variable(s) are I(0) (there is cointegration) or I(1) (no cointegration)

---

[17]See Chapter 3 for more details on cointegration.

using a unit root test (e.g. the ADF test). In this case, bespoke critical values can be computed using information provided by MacKinnon (1991) (given in Table A.6). However, if the cointegrating vector of $[1 \quad -1]$ is imposed, the relevant test is simply a test for the presence of a unit root in a single variable (the spread), and the usual ADF critical values can be used (given in Table A.5). When testing for cointegration using the multivariate framework the tests of Johansen (1988) and Johansen and Juselius (1992) can be used. Campbell and Shiller (1987) also propose a vector autoregressive (VAR)-based test of the EH. This test is developed further in Campbell and Shiller (1991).

Campbell and Shiller (1991) discuss several different tests of the EH, including the VAR-based test mentioned above, and some simple bivariate regression-based tests. These latter tests involve regressing functions of changes in interest rates on the spread and a constant. The estimated slope parameters in the relevant regression models can then be used to test the EH. Under the null hypothesis that the EH holds, the errors in the relevant regression models are functions of expectations errors, which in theory are uncorrelated with the spread if investors have RE. Thus, if RE are assumed, the regression parameters can be consistently estimated by OLS. The regression test with a function of changes in the short-term rate as regressand will be referred to as the **ST test** and the test with a function of changes in the long-term rate as regressand will be referred to as the **LT test**.

In the case of zero-coupon bonds the EH implies that the n-period interest rate will equal the average of the current m-period interest rate plus the expected value of the m-period interest rate for the next $k - 1$ periods, where $k = n/m$,

$$r_{n,t} = \frac{1}{k} \sum_{i=0}^{k-1} E_t r_{m,t+mi} + \pi_{n,m} \tag{8.72}$$

where $r_{n,t}$ is the n-period rate, $r_{m,t}$ is the m-period rate, and $\pi_{n,m}$ is a constant risk premium.[18] It is straightforward to show by rearranging (8.72) that under the EH,

$$k^{-1} \sum_{i=0}^{k-1} r_{m,t+mi} - r_{m,t} = -\pi_{n,m} + (r_{n,t} - r_{m,t}) + v_t \tag{8.73}$$

and

$$r_{n-m,t+m} - r_{n,t} = n(n-m)^{-1}\pi_{n,m} + m(n-m)^{-1}(r_{n,t} - r_{m,t}) + w_t \tag{8.74}$$

where v_t and w_t are random errors. The ST and LT tests of the EH involve estimating the regression models,

$$k^{-1} \sum_{i=0}^{k-1} r_{m,t+mi} - r_{m,t} = \delta_1 + \phi_1(r_{n,t} - r_{m,t}) + v_t \tag{8.75}$$

---

[18]Note therefore that Campbell and Shiller (1991) allow for a non-zero but constant risk premium in their investigation of the EH.

and

$$r_{n-m,t+m} - r_{n,t} = \delta_2 + \phi_2 m(n-m)^{-1}(r_{n,t} - r_{m,t}) + w_t \qquad (8.76)$$

and testing the restrictions $H_0 : \phi_1 = 1$ and $H_0 : \phi_2 = 1$ respectively, which can be done using a t-test. Note that it is important to employ robust standard errors when computing t-tests for these models because of overlapping regression errors (e.g. Newey and West, 1987; Hansen and Hodrick, 1980).

The VAR-based tests developed by Campbell and Shiller (1991) involve computing the theoretical spread between long-term and short-term rates under the EH (the **theoretical spread** is the spread when the EH holds) using the empirical forecasts from a VAR model for the actual spread and the change in the spot rate. Statistical properties of the theoretical spread can then be compared with the same properties of the actual spread as tests of the EH. Let $S_{n,t}$ denote the actual spread. The VAR model involves both $S_{n,t}$ and the change in the short-term rate $\Delta r_{m,t}$. The relevant VAR(p) model can be written using the **companion form** as,

$$\mathbf{Z}_t = \mathbf{A}\mathbf{Z}_{t-1} + \boldsymbol{\varepsilon}_t \qquad (8.77)$$

where $\mathbf{Z}_t$ is a $(2p \times 1)$ vector consisting of the current value and $p-1$ lags of $\Delta r_{m,t}$ and the current value and $p-1$ lags of $S_{n,t}$, $\mathbf{A}$ is a $(2p \times 2p)$ matrix of parameters and $\boldsymbol{\varepsilon}_t$ is a $(2p \times 1)$ vector of errors. It follows from (8.77) that optimal forecasts of the spread are given by $\hat{\mathbf{Z}}_{t+i} = \mathbf{A}^i \mathbf{Z}_t$. In the light of this, under the EH it can be shown that the theoretical spread can be computed using the following formula,

$$\tilde{S}_{n,t} = \mathbf{e}'\mathbf{A}[\mathbf{I} - (m/n)(\mathbf{I} - \mathbf{A}^n)(\mathbf{I} - \mathbf{A}^m)^{-1}](\mathbf{I} - \mathbf{A})^{-1}\mathbf{Z}_t \qquad (8.78)$$

where $\mathbf{e}$ is a $(2p \times 1)$ vector such that $\mathbf{e}'\mathbf{Z}_t = \Delta r_{m,t}$ and $\mathbf{I}$ is a $(2p \times 2p)$ identity matrix. Therefore, an estimate of the theoretical spread can be obtained using (8.78) with the estimated VAR parameters replacing $\mathbf{A}$. If the EH holds then the actual spread should be equal to the theoretical spread. Therefore by comparing the statistical properties of the actual spread with the estimated theoretical spread obtained using (8.78) one has a test of the null hypothesis that the EH holds. Campbell and Shiller (1991) recommend computing the correlation coefficient for the estimated theoretical spread and the actual spread, $\hat{\rho}_{ts,as}$ (the CC test), and the ratio of standard deviations for the estimated theoretical spread and the actual spread, $\hat{\sigma}_{ts}/\hat{\sigma}_{as}$ (the SD test). Both of these measures should be unity under the null hypothesis that the EH holds.

8.4.3 Results and the Expectations Hypothesis Paradox

In empirical applications of the Campbell and Shiller (1987) cointegration-based approach to testing the EH, typically the results are supportive of the hypothesis that in a bivariate model, long-term and short-term interest rates are cointegrated

with a cointegrating vector of [1   −1].[19] Hence the results are supportive of the
EH. However, in empirical applications of the Campbell and Shiller (1991) ST and LT
tests, typically no support is found for the EH from the LT test and in many applications the OLS slope estimate is negative. Therefore, Campbell and Shiller (1991) find
that the EH is contradicted by the empirical results obtained from estimating the LT
model. Empirical applications of the ST test tend to be more supportive of the EH,
although the degree of support depends on the term to maturity of the long-term
rate. Positive slope estimates are obtained at the short end of the term structure,
albeit substantially below unity, but as the term to maturity of the long-term rate
increases the slope estimates fall, rising again at the long end of the term structure.

In empirical applications typically the SD test leads to rejections of the EH for all
maturities, while the CC test leads to rejections of the EH apart from when longer
maturity bonds are used. This pattern of results seems to hold irrespective of the
time-period considered. A selection of some of the ST, LT, SD and CC test results
obtained by Campbell and Shiller (1991) using the McCulloch (1990) data on US
Government bond yields are reproduced in Table 8.1 as an example. The results
reported are for a one-month short-term rate and n-month long-term rate.

**Table 8.1   ST, LT, SD and CC tests
applied to US Treasury bonds.[20]**

n	$\hat{\phi}_1$	$\hat{\phi}_2$	$\hat{\rho}_{ts,as}$	$\hat{\sigma}_{ts}/\hat{\sigma}_{as}$
2	0.501	0.002	0.736	0.681
	(0.119)	(0.238)	(0.148)	(0.136)
3	0.446	−0.176	0.761	0.586
	(0.190)	(0.362)	(0.190)	(0.145)
6	0.237	−1.029	0.486	0.501
	(0.167)	(−0.537)	(0.373)	(0.145)
12	0.161	−1.381	0.391	0.382
	(0.228)	(0.683)	(0.486)	(0.119)
24	0.302	−1.815	0.543	0.303
	(0.212)	(1.151)	(0.764)	(0.135)
60	1.232	−3.099	0.912	0.357
	(0.182)	(1.749)	(0.218)	(0.291)
120	1.157	−5.024	0.979	0.474
	(0.094)	(2.316)	(0.045)	(0.285)

Note: The numbers in parentheses are the estimated standard errors for the relevant test statistics. Hansen–Hodrick standard errors are used for
the ST and LT tests.

[19] For example, see Campbell and Shiller (1987) for an application to US data and Cuthbertson (1996)
for an application to UK data.
[20] This table summarises selected results from Campbell and Shiller (1991), Table 1(a), Table 2, Table
3(a) and Table 4(a).

As highlighted by Campbell and Shiller (1991), the results are paradoxical in the sense that the slope of the term structure gives a forecast in the wrong direction for the short-term change in the interest rate on the long-term bonds (the LT model forecast), but gives a forecast in the right direction for long-term changes in short-term rates (the ST model forecast).

The contrasting statistical support for the EH from the ST and LT models and the paradoxical nature of the empirical results obtained has led to a huge amount of further research on this topic. Much of this research has focused on one of two main explanations for these puzzling results. One explanation is simply that RE does not hold and that long-term rates might overreact or underreact to current spot rates or to expected future spot rates. Mankiw and Summers (1984) show that overreaction is consistent with term spread regression models having slopes above unity, and therefore this explanation can be rejected. Campbell and Shiller (1991) show that underreaction can cause the OLS estimator of the ST and LT model slopes to be negatively biased. The other main explanation for the puzzling results is that the risk premium is time-varying, which again can cause the OLS estimator of the slopes to be negatively biased if the risk premium is correlated with the term spread. More recently this latter explanation has come to dominate in the literature.[21]

An interesting alternative to these two main explanations for the puzzling results, investigated by Bekaert, Hodrick and Marshall (1997), is that the EH actually holds but that applications of the ST and LT models fail to uncover evidence of this because the OLS estimator of the slopes is biased when the sample size is small. In the ST and LT models under RE, the regression errors are orthogonal to the term spread, and consequently OLS will be a consistent estimator. However, if the data generation process (DGP) for the spot rate is an AR model, then under RE and assuming that the EH holds, the errors in the ST and LT models will be functions of the errors from the spot rate DGP. As a consequence of non-contemporaneous correlation between these errors and the current spot rate, which is present in the current term spread (the regressor), the OLS estimator of the ST and LT model slopes will be biased. Furthermore, the bias will increase with the persistence of the spot rate.

Interestingly, however, Bekaert, Hodrick and Marshall (1997) show that this type of finite-sample bias does not explain the rejections of the EH obtained from applications of the ST and LT regression models; in fact, it makes the results even more puzzling. Bekaert, Hodrick and Marshall (1997) show that under the null hypothesis that the EH holds, the finite-sample bias of the relevant OLS slope estimate is *positive* (it would need to be negative to explain the rejections). They also show that

---

[21] For example, see Tzavalis and Wickens (1997), Dai and Singleton (2002) and Cochrane and Piazzesi (2005).

the CC test does not suffer from significant bias and that the SD test is positively biased. Thus, it does not appear that rejections of the EH obtained in empirical work using these methods can be blamed on small-sample bias.

The next section discusses the empirical examples for this chapter. Further details on the MATLAB® programs and the data used are given in Section 8.8. Critical values for the test statistics used can be obtained from the statistical tables in the Appendix.

8.5 Empirical Examples

Example 8.1:   Bond prices and bond yields

(a) Compute the DY for a hypothetical four-week US Treasury bill issued on 13 January 2011 that matures on 10 February 2011, assuming a price of $999.50 and a par value of $1000.
(b) Compute the BEY for the Treasury bill in (a).
(c) Compute the YTM for a hypothetical five-year US Treasury note issued on 30 September 2010 that matures on 30 September 2015, with a CR of 1.25%, a price of $999 and a par value of $1000.
(d) Compute the clean and dirty price of the bond in (c) on 29 October 2010, assuming a YTM of 1.5%.

The relevant MATLAB® program for parts (a) and (b) is given in the file E81ab.m. The relevant programs for parts (c) and (d) are given in E81c.m and E81d.m. E81ab.m is given in Box 8.1. E81c.m and E81d.m are given in Box 8.2 and Box 8.3. The results for E81ab.m are given in Table 8.2; the results for E81c.m and E81d.m are given in Table 8.3.

Box 8.1   E81ab.m

```
clear;
%Set the data up.
Par=1000;
Price=999.5;
Settlement='01/13/2011';
Maturity='02/10/2011';
%Compute the yields.
DY=yldtbill(Settlement,Maturity,Par,Price);
BEY=beytbill(Settlement,Maturity,DY);
```

Box 8.2　E81c.m

```
clear;
%Set the data up.
Par=1000;
Price=999;
CouponRate=0.0125;
Settle='09/30/2010';
Maturity='09/30/2015';
Period=2;
Basis=0;
%Compute the yield.
YTM=bndyield(Price,CouponRate,Settle,Maturity,Period,Basis,...
[],[],[],[],[],Par);
```

Box 8.3　E81d.m

```
clear;
%Set the data up.
Par=1000;
CouponRate=0.0125;
Settlement='10/29/2010';
Maturity='09/30/2015';
Period=2;
Basis=0;
YTM=0.015;
%Compute the prices.
[Price,AccruedInt]=bndprice(YTM,CouponRate,Settlement,...
Maturity,Period,Basis,[],[],[],[],[],Par);
Clean=Price;
Dirty=Price+AccruedInt;
```

As expected, the DY at 0.64% (the discount as a proportion of par value, annualised assuming a 360-day year) is less than the BEY at 0.65% (the discount as a proportion of price, annualised assuming a 365-day year).

Table 8.2　Bond yields

DY	0.0064
BEY	0.0065

Table 8.3   Bond prices and yields

YTM	0.0127
Clean price	988.18
Dirty price	989.18

Note: YTM is computed using E81c.m; the clean price and dirty price are computed using E81d.m.

Since the bond price is lower than the par value, the YTM computed using E81c.m is higher than the CR. The prices computed using E81d.m are in both cases lower than the price in E81c.m (consistent with the higher YTM). As expected, the clean price is less than the dirty price since the latter incorporates a proportion of a coupon payment.

Example 8.2:   The Vasicek model

(a) Using monthly data on the three-month UK Treasury bill rate (1975:1–2009:12), estimate the parameters of the Vasicek spot rate model using a discrete time version of the model and OLS.
(b) Repeat (a) for the three-month US Treasury bill rate (1960:1–2009:12).

The relevant MATLAB® programs are given in the files E82a.m and E82b.m. E82a.m is given in Box 8.4. The results are given in Table 8.4.

Box 8.4   E82a.m.

```
clear;
%Load the data.
D=xlsread('UKTB3');
%Define the variables.
y=D/100;
nr1=size(y,1);
ly=y(1:nr1-1,1);
y=y(2:nr1,1);
dy=y-ly;
nr2=size(y,1);
u=ones(nr2,1);
x=[u ly];
%Estimate the parameters of the discretized Vasicek model using
%OLS.
beta=inv(x'*x)*x'*dy;
```

```
e=dy-x*beta;
ev=sum(e.^2)/(nr2-2);
a=beta(1,1);
b=beta(2,1);
bs=1+b;
%Compute the original Vasicek parameters from the OLS estimates.
freq=1/12;
c=sqrt(ev);
alpha=-log(bs)/freq;
gamma=a/(1-bs);
sigma=c/((freq*((bs^2)-1))/(2*log(bs)))^.5;
```

Table 8.4 Estimated parameters, Vasicek model

	UK Treasury bill	US Treasury bill
$\hat{\gamma}$	0.035	0.047
$\hat{\alpha}$	0.065	0.127
$\hat{\sigma}$	0.018	0.016

For the UK Treasury bill $\hat{\alpha}$ is very small, meaning the interest rate is a highly persistent variable. For the US Treasury bill $\hat{\alpha}$ is almost twice as large, indicating a stronger degree of mean reversion. The estimated unconditional mean of the UK rate is slightly lower than that of the US rate. The estimated volatility of the UK rate is slightly higher than that of the US rate. These estimated parameters can then be used for computing and forecasting bond prices, the term structure and bond option prices (e.g. using the formulas (8.25), (8.28) and (8.29).

Example 8.3: Forecasting the short-term interest rate

Using monthly data on the three-month US Treasury bill rate (1960:1–2009:12), compute one-step ahead forecasts over 1990:1–2009:12 from a discretised Vasicek model, a random walk model, and an AR(3) model. Evaluate the forecasts using the root mean squared forecast error (RMSFE). Compare the forecasting accuracy of the Vasicek and AR(3) models with the random walk model using the Diebold and Mariano (1995) (DM) test of equal forecasting accuracy.

Table 8.5   Forecasting results

Vasicek	0.0022 (2.074**)
Random walk	0.0021
AR(3)	0.0020 (−1.473)

Note: The first number is the RMSFE;
the computed DM test is in brackets;
** denotes statistical significance at
the 5% level.

The relevant MATLAB® program is given in the file E83.m. The results are given in Table 8.5.

The results in Table 8.6 show that on the basis of the RMSFE, the random walk model is preferred to the Vasicek model for forecasting the three-month US Treasury bill rate over this period, and the AR(3) model is preferred to the random walk model (but here the difference is not statistically significant). Therefore relative to the Vasicek model, allowing for higher order autocorrelation is beneficial when forecasting the three-month US Treasury bill rate.

Example 8.4:   Testing the expectations hypothesis: cointegration-based test

Using monthly data on the three-month US Treasury bill rate and the six-month US Treasury bill rate for the period 1960:1–2009:12, test the EH using the cointegration-based test of Campbell and Shiller (1987).

The relevant MATLAB® program is given in the file E84.m and in Box 8.5. The results are given in Table 8.6.

Box 8.5   E84.m

```
clear;
%Load the data.
D1=xlsread('TB6MS');
D2=xlsread('TB3MS');
%Define the variables.
r6=D1/100;
r3=D2/100;
y=r6;
x=r3;
```

```
z=y-x;
%Test for a unit root in r6 using the ADF test setting k=2.
[r6_beta,r6_t,r6_adft]=adf(y,2);
%Test for a unit root in r3 using the ADF test setting k=2.
[r3_beta,r3_t,r3_adft]=adf(x,2);
%Test for cointegration using the ADF test setting k=2 and
%imposing a cointegrating vector of [1 -1].
[ce_beta,ce_t,cadft]=adf(z,2);
```

Table 8.6 Unit root and cointegration results

Unit root, $r_{6,t}$	−1.863
Unit root, $r_{3,t}$	−1.961
Cointegration, $r_{6,t} - r_{3,t}$	−7.563***

Note: *** denotes statistical significance at the 1% level.

The results in Table 8.6 show that the null hypothesis of a unit root is not rejected for either of the interest rate series, and the null hypothesis of no cointegration is rejected at the 1% significance level. This evidence is supportive of the EH.

Example 8.5: Testing the expectations hypothesis: regression-based tests

(a) Using monthly data on the three-month US Treasury bill rate and the six-month US Treasury bill rate for the period 1960:1–2009:12, test the EH using the ST regression-based test of Campbell and Shiller (1991). Compute robust standard errors (Newey and West, 1987) for the estimated parameters and a robust t-test of the null hypothesis that the slope parameter is equal to unity.

(b) Repeat (a) using the LT regression-based test.

The relevant MATLAB® program is given in the files E85a.m and E85b.m for the ST test and LT test respectively. The results are given in Table 8.7.

The results in Table 8.7 show that, consistent with the previous evidence (e.g. Campbell and Shiller, 1991), these tests convincingly reject the relevant null hypotheses, suggesting that the EH should be rejected. Note that here the estimated slope parameter in the LT model is negative, contradicting the EH.

Table 8.7   ST and LT test results

	ST test
$\hat{\delta}_1$	−7.221e−04
	(3.671e−04)
$\hat{\phi}_1$	0.420
	(0.172)
$H_0 : \phi_1 = 1$	$t = -3.372^{***}$
	LT test
$\hat{\delta}_2$	−0.001
	(7.343e−04)
$\hat{\phi}_2$	−0.160
	(0.344)
$H_0 : \phi_2 = 1$	$t = -3.372^{***}$

Note: Newey–West standard errors are in parentheses; *** denotes statistical significance at the 1% level.

8.6 Summary

This chapter has focused on modelling and forecasting interest rates. Traditional bond pricing and the concepts of duration and convexity have been discussed. An important family of continuous time interest rate models has been introduced that lead to analytical formulas for pricing bonds, bond derivatives and for describing the term structure of interest rates. These formulas incorporate certain features of how the spot rate randomly evolves over time.

The expectations hypothesis of the term structure of interest rates states that long-term interest rates depend on investors' expectations of future short-term interest rates, where these expectations are formed rationally. The expectations hypothesis has important implications for investors, macroeconomists and policy-makers, hence an enormous amount of research has been undertaken to test the EH empirically. Popular tests of this hypothesis, proposed by Campbell and Shiller (1987, 1991), have been discussed in this chapter. These tests utilise several econometric techniques discussed in Chapter 3. The empirical examples in this chapter demonstrate computing bond yields and bond prices, estimating the parameters of a continuous time interest rate model using data on UK and US Treasury bills, forecasting interest rates and testing the expectations hypothesis using data on UK and US Treasury bills.

8.7 End of Chapter Questions[22]

Q1. **(a)** Explain how to compute the DY for a US Treasury bill using an appropriate numerical example.
   (b) Explain which of the available yields is the most appropriate for comparing Treasury bill yields with other bond yields.
   (c) Explain the difference between the clean and dirty price for a coupon-paying bond using an appropriate numerical example.

Q2. Critically discuss the main theories of the term structure of interest rates and the empirical support for these theories from academic research.

Q3. Using relevant equations and diagrams, explain the importance of duration and convexity to bond portfolio managers.

Q4. **(a)** Discuss the strengths and weaknesses of the Vasicek spot rate model and compare with the CKLS spot rate model.
   (b) Critically discuss the alternative econometric techniques available for forecasting short-term interest rates.

Q5. Download monthly data on the yields of two UK government zero-coupon bonds with different maturities for a sample period of 10 years or longer.[23]
   (a) Test the EH using the ST regression-based test.
   (b) Test the EH using the LT regression-based test.
   (c) Explain what is meant by the Campbell–Shiller paradox and critically discuss some of the solutions to this paradox proposed in the academic literature on this topic.

8.8 Appendix

8.8.1 Data

Figure 8.1

UK yield curve data for 11 March 2011 from the *Financial Times* website.[24]

Figure 8.2

US yield curve data for 11 March 2011 from the *Financial Times* website.

---

[22]A guide to answering these questions and relevant MATLAB® programs are given on the companion website (www.wileyeurope.com/college/sollis).

[23]The Bank of England Statistics database is one possible source of these data (www.bankofengland. co.uk/statistics).

[24]http://markets.ft.com/markets/bonds.asp.

Figure 8.9

UKTB3.xls

Monthly data on the three-month UK Treasury bill rate for 1975:1 – 2009:12 from the Bank of England Statistics database (www.bankofengland.co.uk/statistics/index.htm).

Figure 8.10

TB3MS.xls

Monthly data on the three-month US Treasury bill rate for 1960:1 – 2009:12 from the Federal Reserve Bank of St Louis FRED database (www.research.stlouisfed.org/fred2/).

Example 8.2

UKTB3.xls

See above.

TB3MS.xls

See above.

Example 8.3

TB3MS.xls

See above.

Example 8.4

TB3MS.xls

See above.

TB6MS.xls

Monthly data on the six-month US Treasury bill rate for 1960:1 – 2009:12 from the Federal Reserve Bank of St Louis FRED database (www.research.stlouisfed.org/fred2/).

Example 8.5

TB3MS.xls

TB6MS.xls

See above.

8.8.2 MATLAB® Programs and Toolboxes[25]

Example 8.1

(a) and (b) E81ab.m, MATLAB® Financial Toolbox

(c) E81c.m, MATLAB® Financial Toolbox

(d) E81d.m, MATLAB® Financial Toolbox

Example 8.2

(a) E82a.m

(b) E82b.m

Example 8.3

E83.m, MATLAB® System Identification Toolbox

Example 8.4

E84.m

---

[25]See www.wileyeurope.com/college/sollis for the programs E##.m.

> *Example 8.5*
>
> (a) E85a.m, Oxford MFE Toolbox
>
> (b) E85b.m, Oxford MFE Toolbox

8.9 References

Bekaert, G., Hodrick, R.J. and D.A. Marshall (1997) On biases in tests of the expectations hypothesis of the term structure of interest rates, *Journal of Financial Economics*, 44, 309–348.

Black, F. and M. Scholes (1973) The pricing of options and corporate liabilities, *Journal of Political Economy*, 81, 637–654.

Brigo, D., Neugebauer, M., Triki, F. and A. Dalessandro (2009) A stochastic process toolkit for risk management: geometric brownian motion, jumps, GARCH and variance gamma models, *Journal of Risk Management in Financial Institutions*, 2, 365–393.

Campbell, J.Y. and R.J. Shiller (1987) Cointegration and tests of present value models, *Journal of Political Economy*, 95, 1062–1088.

Campbell, J.Y. and R.J. Shiller (1991) Interest rate spreads and interest rate movements: a bird's eye view, *Review of Economic Studies*, 58, 495–514.

Chan, K.C., Karolyi, G.A., Longstaff, F.A. and A.B. Sanders (1992) An empirical comparison of alternative models of the short-term interest rate, *Journal of Finance*, 47, 1209–1227.

Cochrane, J.H. and M. Piazzesi (2005) Bond risk premia, *American Economic Review*, 95, 138–160.

Cox, J.C., Ingersoll, J.E. and S.A. Ross (1985) A theory of the term structure of interest rates, *Econometrica*, 53, 385–407.

Cuthbertson, K. (1996) The expectations hypothesis of the term structure: the UK interbank market, *Economic Journal*, 106, 578–592.

Dai, Q. and K.J. Singleton (2002) Expectation puzzles, time-varying risk premia, and affine models of the term structure, *Journal of Financial Economics*, 63, 415–441.

Dickey, D.A. and W.A. Fuller (1979) Distribution of the estimators for autoregressive time series with a unit root, *Journal of the American Statistical Association*, 74, 427–431.

Diebold, F.X. and R. Mariano (1995) Comparing predictive accuracy, *Journal of Business and Economic Statistics*, 13, 253–262.

Fabozzi, F. (ed.) (2005) *The Handbook of Fixed Income Securities*, 7th edn. New York: McGraw-Hill.

Fisher L. and R.L. Weil (1971) Coping with the risk of interest-rate fluctuations: returns to bondholders from naive and optimal strategies, *Journal of Business*, 44, 408–431.

Hall, A.R. (2005) *Generalized Method of Moments*. Oxford: Oxford University Press.

Hansen, L.P. (1982) Large sample properties of Generalized Method of Moments estimators, *Econometrica* 50, 1029–1054.

Hansen, L.P. and R.J. Hodrick (1980) Forward exchange rates as optimal predictors of future spot rates: an econometric analysis, *Journal of Political Economy*, 88, 829–853.

Homer, S. and M.L. Liebowitz (1972) *Inside the Yield Book: New Tools for Bond Market Strategy*. Englewood Cliffs, NJ: Prentice Hall.

Hull, J. (2005) *Options, Futures and Other Derivatives*, 6th edn. New York: Prentice Hall.

Hull, J. and A. White (1990) Pricing interest-rate derivative securities, *Review of Financial Studies*, 3, 573–592.

Jamshidian, F. (1989) An exact bond option formula, *Journal of Finance*, 44, 205–209.

Johansen, S. (1988) Statistical analysis of cointegrating vectors, *Journal of Economic Dynamics and Control*, 12, 231–254.

Johansen, S. and K. Juselius (1992) Testing structural hypotheses in a multivariate cointegration analysis of PPP and the UIP for UK, *Journal of Econometrics*, 53, 211–244.

Johnson, R.S. (2010) *Bond Evaluation, Selection and Management*, 2nd edn. New Jersey: John Wiley & Sons.

Kalman, R.E. (1960) A new approach to linear filtering and prediction problems, *Journal of Basic Engineering*, 82, 35–45.

Macaulay, F.R. (1938) *Some Theoretical Problems Suggested by the Movements of Interest Rates, Bond Yields and Stock Prices in the US Since 1856*. New York: National Bureau of Economic Research.

MacKinnon, J.G. (1991) Critical values for cointegration tests. In Engle, R.F. and C.W.J. Granger (eds) *Long-Run Economic Relationships: Readings in Cointegration*. Oxford: Oxford University Press.

Malkiel, B. (1962) Expectations, bond prices, and the term structure of interest rates, *Quarterly Journal of Economics*, 76, 197–218.

Mankiw, G.N. and L. Summers (1984) Do long-term interest rates overreact to short-term interest rates? *Brookings Papers on Economic Activity*, 1, 223–242.

McCulloch, J.H. (1990) US government term structure data. In Friedman, B. and F. Hahn (eds) *The Handbook of Monetary Economics*. Amsterdam: North Holland.

Newey, W.K. and K.D. West (1987) A simple, positive-definite, heteroskedasticity and autocorrelation consistent covariance matrix, *Econometrica*, 55, 703–708.

Nowman, K.B. (1997) Gaussian estimation of single-factor continuous time models of the term structure of interest rates, *Journal of Finance*, 52, 1695–1706.

Nowman, K.B. (2001) Gaussian estimation and forecasting of multi-factor term structure models with an application to Japan and the United Kingdom, *Asia-Pacific
Financial Markets*, 8, 23–34.

Redington, F.M. (1952). Review of the principles of life office valuations, *Journal of
the Institute of Actuaries*, 78, 286–340.

Said E. and D.A. Dickey (1984) Testing for unit roots in autoregressive moving average models of unknown order, *Biometrika*, 71, 599–607.

Tzavalis, E. and M.R. Wickens (1997) Explaining the failure of the term spread models
of the rational expectations hypothesis of the term structure, *Journal of Money,
Credit and Banking*, 29, 364–380.

Vasicek, O. (1977) An equilibrium characterization of the term structure, *Journal of
Financial Economics*, 5, 177–188.

Yu, J. and P.C.B. Phillips (2001) A Gaussian approach for estimating continuous time
models of short term interest rates, *Econometrics Journal*, 4, 210–224.

Chapter 9

Market Risk Management

9.1 Introduction

This chapter discusses statistical techniques to evaluate **market risk** – the risk associated with changes in market prices. In particular, this chapter focuses on **Value at Risk** (VaR), which for some time has been the most popular statistical technique used by banks for managing market risk. VaR is a forecast of a lower quantile of the probability distribution for the change in the value of a portfolio over a particular time horizon. Hence VaR is a monetary measure of downside financial risk. It is traditional to report VaR as a positive number even though it is typically a negative amount. For example, "the one-day VaR for a portfolio is $1 million with a 99% confidence level" should be interpreted as "there is a 99% probability that the actual change in the value of the portfolio over the next day will not be worse than −$1 million (but a 1% probability that it will be worse than −$1 million)''. It is important to recognise that VaR does not say what the change in the portfolio value will be should it exceed the VaR. An alternative measure of downside risk, Expected Shortfall (ES), is a measure of the average loss when VaR is exceeded. [1]

The VaR technique is popular with banks as it provides a single monetary amount that quantifies the degree of market risk associated with a portfolio. VaR can be computed for the total portfolio of financial instruments held by the bank (their **trading book**) to give a single measure of the market risk associated with all of the bank's positions. Moreover, VaR plays an important role in international financial regulation. Under the Basel II Capital Accord, banks can use VaR to help determine the minimum capital they must hold to cope with potential losses. [2] In response to the 2007–2009 global financial crisis, a new Capital Accord, Basel III, has been proposed and it appears that VaR will continue to play an important role. VaR is also increasingly popular for risk management in the insurance and reinsurance industries.

This chapter explains the main approaches to computing VaR and discusses their strengths and weaknesses. This chapter also discusses evaluation of the performance of VaR models using backtesting and the role of VaR and backtesting in international financial regulation. The penultimate section of the main text presents seven empirical examples that demonstrate a selection of the empirical methods covered, including computing VaR for stocks and options and backtesting a VaR model.

9.2 VaR by the Delta-Normal Approach

9.2.1 VaR for a Single Asset

Assume that r_{t+1} is the log-return for a financial asset over a single day. The delta-normal (DN) approach to computing VaR assumes that the returns for assets are conditionally normally independently distributed,

$$r_{t+1} = \mu_{t+1} + \sigma_{t+1}z_{t+1} \tag{9.1}$$

where μ_{t+1} is the conditional mean return, σ_{t+1}^2 is the conditional variance (σ_{t+1} is the conditional volatility) and z_{t+1} denotes an independent standard normal random

---

[1]This chapter focuses only on VaR. For more details on ES and its links with VaR, see Acerbi and Tasche (2002), Tasche (2002), Christoffersen (2003) Chapter 4, and Yamai and Yoshiba (2005).
[2]See Basel Committee on Banking Supervision (2006) for an updated version of Basel II and the website www.bis.org/bcbs/for further details.

variable ($z_{t+1} \sim NID(0, 1)$). [3] It follows from (9.1) that standardised returns are independent standard normal random variables,

$$z_{t+1} = \frac{r_{t+1} - \mu_{t+1}}{\sigma_{t+1}} \tag{9.2}$$

Computing VaR using the DN approach is straightforward since we know from statistical theory the probability of observing values of standard normal random variables within particular intervals (these probabilities are given in Table A.1 in the Appendix). For example, the probability of observing a standard normal random variable less than -1.645 is 5% and the probability of observing a standard normal random variable less than -2.326 is 1%. Consider the following simple example where this information is used to compute one-day VaR at the 99% confidence level:

(i) Just prior to the close of today's stock market a trader working for an investment bank in the US invests \$1 million in the stock of a single US company. Assume that the conditional volatility of the return for the stock over the next day is known to be 1%, $\sigma_{t+1} = 0.01$. Assume for simplicity that the conditional mean return is zero, $\mu_{t+1} = 0$.

(ii) It follows from the assumption of conditional normality that the standardised return $r_{t+1}/0.01$ will not be below -2.326 with a probability of 99% and the raw return r_{t+1} will not be below $-2.326 \times 0.01 = -0.02326$ with a probability of 99%.

(iii) It follows straightforwardly that the one-day VaR at the 99% confidence level is the mark-to-market value of the investment (\$1 million) multiplied by the relevant return quantile -0.02326. This is not quite the VaR since it is traditional to report negative VaR amounts as positive values. So for this example the one-day VaR at the 99% confidence level is,

$$VaR_{t+1} = -1 \times (-2.326 \times 0.01 \times \$1\,000\,000) = \$23\,260 \tag{9.3}$$

The one-day VaR at the confidence level $(1 - p) \times 100\%$, $0 < p < 1$, can be formally written,

$$VaR^p_{t+1} = -F^{-1}(p)\sigma_{t+1}V_t \tag{9.4}$$

where $F^{-1}(p)$ denotes the inverse of the cumulative distribution function (CDF) for the standard normal distribution at the relevant p, also called the **quantile function** (QF). σ_{t+1} is the conditional volatility for the next day's return and V_t is the mark-to-market value of the investment. The amount,

$$r^p_{t+1} = F^{-1}(p)\sigma_{t+1} \tag{9.5}$$

---

[3] Note that with certain restrictions imposed, (9.1) is consistent with the traditional random walk model for the log-price; see Chapters 2, 3, and 4 for more details on the random walk model.

can be thought of as the **return-VaR** – the return quantile at the $(1 - p) \times 100\%$ confidence level.

The assumption that asset returns have a conditional mean of zero, $\mu_{t+1} = 0$, is usually acceptable when computing VaR for short investment periods such as one day, since the conditional mean return over such short horizons is typically extremely small and will not significantly affect the final VaR. In the rest of this chapter $\mu_{t+1} = 0$ is assumed. A convenient consequence of using log-returns to compute VaR in this way is that if the conditional volatility of future one-day returns is constant, the VaR for a horizon of k-days, $k > 1$, can be computed by multiplying the one-day VaR by $\sqrt{k}$.

In the simple example used above, the conditional volatility of the return over the next day σ_{t+1} is assumed to be known at time t (that is, tomorrow's conditional volatility is assumed to be known today). In practice it is usually unknown at time t and therefore a forecast is required. As discussed in Chapter 3, there are several techniques available for forecasting conditional volatility. We will briefly recap the main techniques here.

A simple forecast of the conditional volatility of returns is given by the sample standard deviation,

$$\hat{\sigma}_{t+1} = \sqrt{\frac{\sum_{i=0}^{T-1} r_{t-i}^2}{T}} \tag{9.6}$$

where T is the sample size, which over time can be a fixed value or can expand with each additional observation (note here that since the conditional mean return is assumed to be zero the sample mean does not enter into the formula). The conditional volatility forecast computed in this way using a fixed T is called a **moving average** (MA) forecast of the conditional volatility. If the true volatility σ_{t+1} (i.e. the population volatility) is time-varying then the MA forecast with a large T will be slow to react to changes in the value of σ_{t+1}. In this case using a smaller T will often help improve forecasting accuracy.

An exponentially weighted moving average (EWMA) forecast and an autoregressive conditional heteroscedasticity (ARCH) and generalised ARCH (GARCH) forecast are usually superior to an MA forecast if the true conditional volatility is time-varying. An EWMA forecast is similar to the sample standard deviation but it involves weighting the sample observations so that more recent observations have a greater impact than older observations. The relevant formula is,

$$\hat{\sigma}_{t+1} = \sqrt{(1 - \lambda) \sum_{i=0}^{T-1} \lambda^i r_{t-i}^2} \tag{9.7}$$

In (9.7), historical observations are weighted with an exponentially decaying weight determined by λ ($0 < \lambda < 1$). The lower λ is, the less weight will be given to older observations relative to recent observations, which helps to capture changes in σ_{t+1}. Usually in finance, λ is set to a number in the range 0.940–0.999. In practice, $\lambda = 0.94$ is a popular choice when computing daily VaR and $\lambda = 0.97$ when computing monthly VaR. It can be shown that recursive one-step ahead EWMA forecasts of the conditional variance can be computed using the formula,

$$\hat{\sigma}^2_{t+1|t} = \lambda \hat{\sigma}^2_{t|t-1} + (1 - \lambda) r^2_t \tag{9.8}$$

where $\hat{\sigma}^2_{t|t-1}$ denotes the EWMA conditional variance computed using the data up to time $t - 1$.

We have previously discussed (in Chapter 3) how ARCH and GARCH models offer a more flexible approach to computing conditional volatility forecasts than the EWMA approach. An optimal forecasting function for the conditional volatility can be derived by applying a conditional expectations rule. The optimal one-step ahead forecast of the conditional volatility from a GARCH(1,1) model can be written,

$$\hat{\sigma}_{t+1} = (\hat{\alpha}_0 + \hat{\alpha}_1 r^2_t + \hat{\beta}_1 \hat{\sigma}^2_t)^{1/2} \tag{9.9}$$

where $\hat{\alpha}_0, \hat{\alpha}_1$ and $\hat{\beta}_1$ are consistent parameter estimates. [4]

9.2.2 VaR for a Portfolio

If individual asset returns are assumed to be generated by (9.1) then it can be shown that the return for a portfolio of those assets will be conditionally normally distributed. Therefore, to compute VaR for a portfolio using the DN approach, the procedure is the same as for a single asset, but using a forecast of the conditional volatility of the portfolio returns. For example, assuming a portfolio of two stocks, the conditional variance of the portfolio return can be written,

$$\hat{\sigma}^2_{P,t+1} = w^2_1 \hat{\sigma}^2_{1,t+1} + w^2_2 \hat{\sigma}^2_{2,t+1} + 2w_1 w_2 \hat{\sigma}_{12,t+1} \tag{9.10}$$

where $\hat{\sigma}^2_{1,t+1}, \hat{\sigma}^2_{2,t+1}$ and $\hat{\sigma}_{12,t+1}$ are forecasts of the conditional variance for the individual stocks and the conditional covariance, and w_1, w_2 are the asset weights ($w_1 + w_2 = 1$). The conditional volatility forecast is $\hat{\sigma}_{P,t+1} = \sqrt{\hat{\sigma}^2_{P,t+1}}$.

Consider extending the one-day VaR example in Section 9.2.1 to two stocks:

(i) Assume the trader invests \$500 000 in stock one and \$500 000 in stock two. Assume the conditional volatility of the daily returns for both stocks is 0.01

---

[4] See Chapter 3 for more details on GARCH models and forecasting conditional volatility.

(1%), and the conditional covariance is -0.00005. Using (9.10) the portfolio conditional volatility forecast is,

$$\hat{\sigma}_{P,t+1} = \sqrt{0.5^2 \times 0.01^2 + 0.5^2 \times 0.01^2 + 2 \times 0.5^2 \times -0.00005} = 0.005$$
(9.11)

(ii) It follows from (9.4) that the one-day VaR at the 99% confidence level is,

$$VaR_{t+1}^{0.01} = 2.326 \times 0.005 \times \$1\,000\,000 = \$11\,630 \qquad (9.12)$$

The VaR in this portfolio example is less than the VaR in the single asset example ($23 260), despite the same overall amount being invested and despite the fact that the conditional volatility forecast is the same for both stocks. This is because of the effects of diversification with negatively correlated stocks; the risk of the portfolio is reduced relative to an investment in just one or other of the stocks, hence the VaR is lower.

For larger portfolios it is more efficient to use matrix algebra when discussing conditional volatility forecasts. Let $\mathbf{R}$ be a $T \times N$ matrix of the returns on N assets over T days. Therefore $\mathbf{R}$ can be written,

$$\mathbf{R} = \begin{bmatrix} r_{1,t} & r_{2,t} & \cdots & r_{N,t} \\ r_{1,t-1} & r_{2,t-1} & \cdots & r_{N,t-1} \\ \vdots & \vdots & \ddots & \vdots \\ r_{1,t-T+1} & r_{2,t-T+1} & \cdots & r_{N,t-T+1} \end{bmatrix} \qquad (9.13)$$

An MA forecast of the conditional covariance matrix can be computed using,

$$\hat{\mathbf{\Sigma}}_{t+1} = T^{-1}(\mathbf{R}'\mathbf{R}) \qquad (9.14)$$

Define a $N \times 1$ vector of asset weights,

$$\mathbf{w} = \begin{bmatrix} w_1 & w_2 & \cdots & w_N \end{bmatrix}' \qquad (9.15)$$

An MA forecast of the portfolio conditional volatility is given by,

$$\hat{\sigma}_{P,t+1} = \sqrt{\mathbf{w}'\hat{\mathbf{\Sigma}}_{t+1}\mathbf{w}} \qquad (9.16)$$

To derive an EWMA forecast of the portfolio conditional volatility, use (9.16) with $\hat{\mathbf{\Sigma}}_{t+1} = \tilde{\mathbf{R}}'\tilde{\mathbf{R}}$, where,

$$\tilde{\mathbf{R}} = \sqrt{\frac{1-\lambda}{1-\lambda^T}} \begin{bmatrix} r_{1,t} & r_{2,t} & \cdots & r_{N,t} \\ \sqrt{\lambda}r_{1,t-1} & \sqrt{\lambda}r_{2,t-1} & \cdots & \sqrt{\lambda}r_{N,t-1} \\ \vdots & \vdots & \ddots & \vdots \\ \sqrt{\lambda^{T-1}}r_{1,t-T+1} & \sqrt{\lambda^{T-1}}r_{2,t-T+1} & \cdots & \sqrt{\lambda^{T-1}}r_{N,t-T+1} \end{bmatrix} \qquad (9.17)$$

and $0 < \lambda < 1$.

In theory a portfolio conditional volatility forecast can also be computed using a multivariate GARCH model to forecast the individual variance and covariance terms in the portfolio variance formula.[5] However, in practice, estimating multivariate GARCH models for even moderately sized portfolios is not feasible because of the large number of parameters that would need to be estimated (e.g. the VEC multivariate GARCH model for a portfolio of two assets involves estimating 21 parameters). An alternative approach is to estimate a univariate GARCH model using sample data on the portfolio returns and then use the fitted univariate GARCH model to directly forecast the conditional volatility of the portfolio return.

9.2.3 RiskMetrics and the Delta-Normal Approach

The DN approach to computing VaR has its origins in research carried out at the investment bank JP Morgan. This work evolved into the RiskMetrics approach to VaR. [6] The approach is set out in the RiskMetrics Technical Documents (see Risk-Metrics, 1996, 2001, 2006). The DN approach is one of the cornerstones of the original RiskMetrics approach to VaR. The name **delta-normal** refers to two specific features of the approach. The first of these features is that under the DN approach the change in value of the relevant portfolio is linked via a first-order Taylor series approximation to an underlying risk factor. [7] The first-order approximation involves the partial derivative of the value of the portfolio with respect to the price of the underlying risk factor. This partial derivative is called the portfolio's **delta**.

$$\delta = \frac{\partial V}{\partial P} \qquad (9.18)$$

where V denotes the value of the portfolio and P the price of the risk factor. It follows approximately that the change in the value of the portfolio can be written,

$$\Delta V_{t+1} \approx \delta P_t r_{t+1} \qquad (9.19)$$

where r_{t+1} is the return on the underlying risk factor. The second feature is that the return on the underlying risk factor is assumed to be conditionally normally independently distributed as discussed in Section 9.2.1. When the portfolio only involves a position in a single asset then effectively the underlying risk factor is just the price of the asset, and so VaR is computed as in Section 9.2.1. However, if the portfolio contains many financial instruments then the RiskMetrics approach recommends mapping their associated cash flows to a smaller number of risk factors to reduce the computational cost of computing VaR. For example, in the case of a portfolio of stocks the risk factor would usually be a national stock market index (e.g. for the US, the S&P 500 index might be used). The return for an individual stock can be mapped to the return for the index using a single-index model. Let $r_{i,t}$ denote the return for stock i and $r_{m,t}$ the return for the stock market

---

[5]See Chapter 3 for more details on multivariate GARCH.
[6]RiskMetrics Group became a separate company and in 2008 was listed on the NYSE. In 2010 the Risk-Metrics Group was acquired by Morgan Stanley Capital International (MSCI).
[7]A **Taylor series approximation** is a mathematical technique for approximating a function at a particular point using the derivatives of the function.

index. The relevant single-index model is,

$$r_{i,t} = \alpha_i + \beta_i r_{m,t} + \varepsilon_{i,t} \tag{9.20}$$

where $\varepsilon_{i,t}$ is a random error term that captures non-systematic risk, with $E(\varepsilon_{i,t}) = 0$, $Var(\varepsilon_{i,t}) = \sigma_{\varepsilon_i}^2$, $E(\varepsilon_{i,t}\varepsilon_{j,t}) = 0$ $(i \neq j)$, $Cov(r_{m,t}, \varepsilon_{i,t}) = 0$. Using a sample of data on the stock and the index, and assuming the relevant regularity conditions are satisfied, the stock's beta can be consistently estimated by ordinary least squares (OLS). For a well-diversified portfolio of N stocks it can be shown that as $N \to \infty$ the optimal conditional volatility forecast is,

$$\hat{\sigma}_{P,t+1} = \sqrt{\hat{\beta}_P^2 \hat{\sigma}_{m,t+1}^2} \tag{9.21}$$

where $\hat{\sigma}_{m,t+1}^2$ is a conditional volatility forecast for the stock market index return. For large portfolios, using this approach to forecast the conditional volatility of portfolio returns is more efficient than the traditional approaches discussed in Section 9.2.2, since in (9.21) only the estimated beta for the portfolio and a single conditional volatility forecast are required. It follows that the VaR for the portfolio can be computed in the usual way,

$$VaR_{t+1}^p = -F^{-1}(p)\hat{\sigma}_{P,t+1}V_t \tag{9.22}$$

To further simplify computing VaR in this way, RiskMetrics provides a daily forecast of the conditional volatility of most national stock market indices and the correlations of this index with other asset classes. RiskMetrics also uses cash flow mapping to simplify computing VaR for bond portfolios. This is discussed in more detail in Section 9.5.

VaR is straightforward to compute using the DN approach and the computational cost is reasonably low even for large portfolios, particularly if the RiskMetrics mapping approach is used. Low computational cost is an attractive feature since many investment banks have trading portfolios consisting of thousands of assets and derivatives, for which VaR has to be computed on a daily basis. However, a significant weakness of the DN approach is the restrictive assumption that returns are conditionally normally distributed. For many financial assets a common feature of sample data on their standardised returns is that the empirical distribution has fatter tails than the standard normal distribution, suggesting that the true conditional distribution (i.e. the **population** conditional distribution) is non-normal. Assuming conditional normality if in fact the true conditional distribution is non-normal could lead to the computed VaR underestimating or overestimating the true VaR by a non-trivial amount. Another weakness of the DN approach is that the computed VaR can vary quite significantly depending on the approach used to compute the conditional volatility forecast. Although the original RiskMetrics approach is underpinned theoretically by the assumption that daily asset returns are conditionally normally distributed random variables, more recently, extensions to allow for fat-tailed conditional distributions have been incorporated (see e.g. RiskMetrics, 2006).

9.3 VaR by Historical Simulation

The historical simulation (HS) approach to computing VaR is particularly straight-forward to apply. For example, to compute one-day VaR for a portfolio of assets at the confidence level $(1 - p) \times 100\%$:

(i) Reorder a sample of daily portfolio returns from minimum to maximum (these reordered returns are the **order statistics**, $r_{(t)}$) and then pick the relevant per-centile value of the order statistics (e.g. for VaR at the 99% confidence level, pick the first percentile value).
(ii) Multiply by the mark-to-market value of the portfolio (and -1) to give the VaR.

The VaR can be formally written,

$$VaR_{t+1}^{p} = -r_{(t+1)}^{p} V_t \qquad (9.23)$$

where $r_{(t+1)}^{p}$ denotes the relevant percentile of the order statistics and V_t is the mark-to-market value of the portfolio. The k-day VaR, $k > 1$, can be computed using the same approach applied to the k-day returns. Note that, in practice, when computing VaR repeatedly using this approach, a fixed sample size is typically used, of between one year and five years of data.

As well as having low computational cost, an attractive feature of the HS approach is that it makes no assumption about the conditional or the unconditional distribu-tion for returns. Another attractive feature of the HS approach is that the computed VaR tends to be much smoother over time than the VaR computed using the DN approach, which can vary quite significantly with changes in the conditional volatil-ity forecast.

The main weakness of the HS approach is that it can be highly sensitive to the sample size employed. By changing the sample size to include or exclude certain events (e.g. previous stock market crashes) the VaR for a portfolio can change by a significant amount. Furthermore, if markets become increasingly bullish (due to the presence of asset price **bubbles**), then the VaR computed using the HS approach will tend to continuously fall if small samples are being used, leading analysts, regulators and investors using this approach to conclude that risk is falling, whereas in fact this conclusion might be incorrect. If a crash then occurs, the banks' VaR amounts will be too low, leading to a large number of VaR exceptions (an "exception" is when the actual portfolio loss is greater than the VaR). Most banks that employ the HS approach to compute VaR tend to use between one year and five-years of historical data, hence they are susceptible to this type of problem. The 2007–2009 financial crisis is a good example of the consequences of using the HS approach with historical sample periods that are too small to truly capture the risks being faced. When the crisis occurred the majority of large banks employing the

HS approach were using data from the previous one to five years when many asset markets were bullish, and therefore these VaR amounts were not representative of the true market risks at the start of crisis. Consequently, over the initial period of the crisis many banks using the HS approach experienced large numbers of VaR exceptions. [8]

9.4 VaR by Monte Carlo Simulation

The Monte Carlo simulation (MCS) approach to computing VaR involves the computer simulation of asset returns assuming a particular probability distribution for the returns. The simulated returns are referred to as **pseudo-returns** and the VaR is computed by taking the relevant percentile value of the empirical distribution of these pseudo-returns. Therefore, by using the MCS approach assuming a fat-tailed non-normal distribution, the analyst can compute VaR allowing extreme returns to have a higher probability of occurring than if the DN approach is used.

To compute the one-day VaR for a single asset using the MCS approach, a model for daily returns needs to be specified by the analyst. For example, it might be assumed that the conditional distribution for returns is a Student's t-distribution with v degrees of freedom. Thus we can write,

$$r_{t+1} = \sigma_{t+1}\varepsilon_{t+1} \tag{9.24}$$

where $\varepsilon_{t+1} \sim t(v)$ is a Student's t random variable with v degrees of freedom. In practice, ε_{t+1} would typically be standardised to have a variance of unity so that σ_{t+1} is the conditional volatility of returns (this can be done by dividing a raw Student's t random variable by its standard deviation, which is $\sqrt{v/(v-2)}$). Using this model the analyst simulates pseudo-returns. For example, if a future value for the conditional volatility is specified by the analyst, σ_{t+1}, and $\varepsilon_{j,t+1}$ is the jth simulated value of $\varepsilon_{t+1}(j = 1, 2, \ldots, N)$, then the jth pseudo-return for period $t+1$ is,

$$r_{j,t+1} = \sigma_{t+1}\varepsilon_{j,t+1} \tag{9.25}$$

The relevant VaR can then be computed from the simulated data as follows,

$$VaR_{t+1}^{p} = -r_{(t+1)}^{p}V_t \tag{9.26}$$

where, $r_{(t+1)}^{p}$ is the relevant percentile value of the order statistics for the simulated pseudo-returns and V_t is the mark-to-market value of the investment. Note that

---

[8]For example, in 2007 and 2008 the investment bank UBS experienced 29 and 50 exceptions of its one-day VaR at the 99% confidence level. If the VaR approach being used were perfect then approximately three exceptions should have occurred in each year. We say more about VaR exceptions and backtesting VaR in Section 9.7. http://www.ubs.com/1/e/investors/annual_reporting2008/rtm2008/0003.html

the analyst is not restricted to using any particular distribution for simulating the pseudo-returns $r_{j,t+1}$ and some other distribution could be used instead of Student's t-distribution.

Simulating multiple-day VaR for this asset (k-day VaR, $k > 1$) is straightforward using the MCS approach. The analyst simply has to specify values for the volatility into the future, $\sigma_{t+2}, \sigma_{t+3}, \ldots, \sigma_{t+k}$, and then employ (9.25), replacing σ_{t+1} with the relevant future value and simulating values for each of $\varepsilon_{j,t+2}, \varepsilon_{j,t+3}, \ldots, \varepsilon_{j,t+k}$. For each j, the k pseudo-returns can be summed to give the jth k-day pseudo-return: $r_{j,t+1:t+k} = \sum_{i=1}^{k} r_{j,t+i}$. The relevant percentile of the order statistics for the simulated k-day pseudo-returns, $r_{(t+1:t+k)}^{p}$, can then be used to compute the k-day VaR,

$$VaR_{t+1:t+k}^{p} = -r_{(t+1:t+k)}^{p} V_t \tag{9.27}$$

Computing VaR for portfolios of assets using the MCS approach is more involved. For example, assume that an analyst wants to compute the one-day VaR for a portfolio of two stocks using the MCS approach and they would like the pseudo-returns to be conditionally normally distributed with the following conditional covariance matrix,

$$\boldsymbol{\Sigma}_{t+1} = \begin{bmatrix} \sigma_{1,t+1}^{2} & \sigma_{12,t+1} \\ \sigma_{21,t+1} & \sigma_{2,t+1}^{2} \end{bmatrix} \tag{9.28}$$

One way of doing this is to utilise a mathematical technique called a **Cholesky decomposition** to decompose the conditional covariance matrix into the product of another matrix and its transpose,

$$\boldsymbol{\Sigma}_{t+1} = \mathbf{C}_{t+1}' \mathbf{C}_{t+1} \tag{9.29}$$

$\mathbf{C}_{t+1}$ is an upper-triangular matrix. The transpose of $\mathbf{C}_{t+1}$ multiplied by a conformable vector of simulated standard normal random variables $\mathbf{z}_{t+1}$ gives a vector of correlated conditionally multivariate-normal pseudo-returns with covariance matrix $\boldsymbol{\Sigma}_{t+1}$,

$$\mathbf{r}_{j,t+1} = \mathbf{C}_{t+1}' \mathbf{z}_{j,t+1} \tag{9.30}$$

As in the single asset case the analyst is not restricted to the assumption of normality. For example, a vector of correlated conditionally multivariate-Student's t pseudo-returns can be simulated using the same general approach with some minor alterations.

An attractive feature of the MCS approach relative to the DN and HS approaches is that it allows analysts to compute VaR under *any* chosen probability distribution for asset returns. However, relative to both of these approaches the MCS approach is computationally more expensive, particularly so for large portfolios. Furthermore, the success of the MCS approach depends on the ability of the analyst to identify an appropriate probability distribution to use for the simulations. If an analyst mistakenly assumes a distributional form that is a poor approximation of the unknown true form, then the computed VaR could be seriously misleading. If the assumed distribution has a thinner left tail than the true distribution, then *ceteris parabus* the computed VaR will underestimate the true VaR. If the assumed distribution has a fatter left tail than the true distribution then *ceteris parabus* the computed VaR will overestimate the true VaR.

9.5 VaR for Bonds

Computing the VaR for bonds using the DN approach can be done employing the yield data and the modified duration (MD) for the bond. The MD is a measure of the sensitivity of the bond price to changes in its yield to maturity (YTM) and it can be computed from the bond's duration (D), which for zero-coupon bonds is just the time to maturity. The MD for a bond is given by,

$$MD = D/(1 + YTM) \tag{9.31}$$

The percentage change in the bond price associated with a change in the YTM is given by, [9]

$$\frac{\Delta P}{P} = -MD \times \Delta YTM \tag{9.32}$$

Assume that an analyst wants to compute the one-day VaR for a one-year zero-coupon government bond at the 99% confidence level using the DN approach. The MD relationship can be exploited as follows:

(i) First, let $\hat{\sigma}_{1,t+1}$ denote the one-day ahead forecast of the conditional volatility of the YTM returns for a one-year zero-coupon bond. Multiplying $\hat{\sigma}_{1,t+1}$ by the relevant quantile of the standard normal distribution and the current YTM gives a forecast of the relevant quantile for ΔYTM. This amount can be called the **yield-VaR** and the formula in this case is,

$$YVaR^{0.01}_{t+1} = 2.326 \times \hat{\sigma}_{1,t+1} \times YTM_t \tag{9.33}$$

(ii) Multiplying by $-MD_t$ converts this to the relevant quantile for the % change in prices (the return-VaR):

$$r^{0.01}_{t+1} = -MD_t \times YVaR^{0.01}_{t+1} \tag{9.34}$$

(iii) Multiplying by the current price and -1 converts this to the final VaR for the bond. Therefore, the one-day VaR for this bond at the 99% confidence level is,

$$VaR^{0.01}_{t+1} = -r^{0.01}_{t+1} \times P_t \tag{9.35}$$

---

[9]To be consistent with Chapter 8 we have omitted time subscripts from (9.31) and (9.32), but employ time subscripts when explaining how to use MD to compute VaR. See Jorion (2006) Chapter 8 for more details on using modified duration to compute VaR for bonds.

For zero-coupon bonds the extension to portfolio VaR follows straightforwardly from the portfolio VaR techniques already discussed. In bond portfolio risk management it is common practice to report both the **undiversified VaR** and the **diversified VaR**. For example, if there are N zero-coupon bonds then for each bond the individual VaR can be computed as above. These individual VaR values can then summed to give the undiversified VaR,

$$VaR^p_{P,t+1} = \sum_{i=1}^{N} VaR^p_{i,t+1} \tag{9.36}$$

The diversified VaR takes into account the actual correlation between the bonds' yield changes,

$$VaR^p_{P,t+1} = \sqrt{\sum_{i=1}^{N}\sum_{j=1}^{N} VaR^p_{i,t+1} VaR^p_{j,t+1} \rho_{ij}} \tag{9.37}$$

where ρ_{ij} denotes the correlation coefficient for the change in yield on the ith bond with the change in yield on the jth bond. Note that the DN approach can also be used to compute VaR for bond portfolios using a return-VaR computed directly from sample data on historical prices, employing the techniques discussed in previous sections.

Many bonds involve coupon payments that need to be taken into consideration when computing VaR; the VaR of the bond is affected by the size, number and location of the coupon payments. To compute VaR on coupon paying bonds, Risk-Metrics proposes splitting the bond into a number of separate zero-coupon bonds. For example, consider a seven-year government bond with a par value of $1000, a coupon rate of 5% and annual coupon payments. [10] Such a bond could be split into six zero-coupon bonds each with a cash flow of $50 with one to six years to maturity, respectively, and one zero-coupon bond with a cash flow of $1050 and seven years to maturity. To compute the VaR for the original bond the analyst can simply compute the VaR for a portfolio consisting of the seven zero-coupon bonds using the approach described above, taking care to discount the relevant cash flows when computing the seven individual VaR amounts using an appropriate discount rate. This requires a discount rate (i.e. a YTM) for each individual cash flow. In some cases, this information might be available, but in others it might not. In this situation RiskMetrics uses a cash flow mapping approach that involves the following steps:

Step (i)   Use linear interpolation to interpolate the relevant YTM from known adjacent YTM values. For example, if a cash flow occurs in year six, the relevant yield can be interpolated from the yields in years five and seven,

$$YTM_6 = \hat{a}YTM_5 + (1 - \hat{a})YTM_7 \tag{9.38}$$

---

[10]This example is based on the example in RiskMetrics (1996), Chapter 6, Section 6.2.2.

The weight $\hat{a}$ is chosen by the analyst. In this case the appropriate value is $\hat{a} = 0.50$, because the cash flow is equidistant between the five-year and seven-year vertices.[11]

Step (ii)   Use YTM_6 to compute the present value of the cash flow, PV_6.

Step (iii)   Interpolate the relevant volatility for the price returns using,

$$\hat{\sigma}_{6,t+1} = \hat{a}\hat{\sigma}_{5,t+1} + (1 - \hat{a})\hat{\sigma}_{7,t+1} \qquad (9.39)$$

where $\hat{\sigma}_{5,t+1}$ and $\hat{\sigma}_{7,t+1}$ are provided by RiskMetrics.

Step (iv)   Using $\hat{\sigma}_{6,t+1}, \hat{\sigma}_{5,t+1}$ and $\hat{\sigma}_{7,t+1}$, and employing a formula given in RiskMetrics (e.g. see RiskMetrics, 1996, Chapter 6, equation (6.12)) derive a weight $\hat{\alpha}$.

Step (v)   Use this weight to split PV_6 between the five-year and seven-year vertices. Allocate $\hat{\alpha}PV_6$ to year five and $(1 - \hat{\alpha})PV_6$ to year seven.

Step (vi)   The VaR for the present value cash flow allocated to the five-year and seven-year vertices can then be computed in the usual way using a return-VaR value for each vertex provided by RiskMetrics.[12]

9.6 VaR for Derivatives

9.6.1 VaR by Delta-Gamma

The VaR approaches discussed so far have assumed the portfolio contains assets. This section focuses on the main approaches that can be used to compute VaR for portfolios that contain derivatives. Derivatives are contracts where the value of the contract is linked to the value of an underlying asset, and therefore as one might expect the approaches used to compute VaR for derivatives are similar to the approaches used for assets, albeit with some added complexity.

As we have seen in previous sections of this chapter, when computing VaR for assets there is more than one approach that can be used. The same is true when computing VaR for derivatives. The most popular approaches are a DN-type approach, referred to as the **delta-gamma** approach (DG), and two Monte Carlo simulation (MCS) approaches. For clarity, we will concentrate here on explaining how to compute VaR for plain vanilla options. The techniques discussed can be extended to compute VaR for the many different types of derivatives that exist. [13]

---

[11]The **vertices** are just the points in time when the cash flows occur.
[12]For more details on this approach, see RiskMetrics (1996) Chapter 6.
[13]We will not present comprehensive details on the theoretical properties of derivatives and how they are priced. It is envisaged that many readers will either be currently taking a specialist derivatives module, or will have had some exposure to such a module. For more details on derivatives, readers are encouraged to refer to the comprehensive textbook by Hull (2005).

It is helpful to review very briefly some basic information on derivatives before explaining how to compute VaR. Vanilla options come in two forms: call options and put options. A call option gives the holder the right to buy an asset by a particular date at a particular price. A put option gives the holder the right to sell an asset by a particular date at a particular price. The particular date is referred to as the **expiration** date and the particular buying or selling price is referred to as the **strike** price (or strike rate for exchange rate options). A call (put) option where the underlying asset price is above (below) the strike price is said to be **in-the-money**; a call (put) option where the underlying asset price is below (above) the strike price is said to be **out-of-the-money**; and a call (put) option where the underlying asset price is equal to the strike price is said to be **at-the-money**. There are two general styles of options: American style and European style. The former can be exercised at any time up to the expiration date and the latter can be exercised only on the expiration date. [14]

The price of a stock option over time depends on several factors:

(i) The current stock price, P.
(ii) The strike price, K.
(iii) The time to expiration, T (measured in trading-day years).
(iv) The volatility of the underlying stock price, σ (on an annual basis).
(v) The risk-free interest rate, r.
(vi) The dividends expected during the life of the option.

Consider a European call option on a non-dividend paying stock. Subject to regularity assumptions, one of which is that the stock price has a log-normal distribution, the factors (i)–(v) can be linked to the current option price (denoted by c) through the relevant Black–Scholes formula (Black and Scholes, 1973),

$$c = PN(d_1) - Ke^{-rT}N(d_2) \tag{9.40}$$

where

$$d_1 = \frac{\ln(P/K) + (r + \sigma^2/2)T}{\sigma\sqrt{T}} \tag{9.41}$$

$$d_2 = d_1 - \sigma\sqrt{T} \tag{9.42}$$

$N(x)$ is the CDF for a standard normal distribution and the other terms are defined above. Under the assumptions set out in Black and Scholes (1973), the

---

[14]The biggest options and derivatives exchanges include the International Securities Exchange (ISE) (www.ise.com), the Chicago Board Options Exchange (CBOE) (www.cboe.com), the European exchanges in Amsterdam, Brussels, Lisbon, London and Paris, which are run by NYSE Liffe (www.euronext.com), the Tokyo Stock Exchange Derivatives (TDEX) market (http://www.tse.or.jp/english/index.html) and the Osaka Securities Exchange (OSE) (www.ose.or.jp/e/).

current price of a European put option on a non-dividend paying stock is given by the formula,

$$p = Ke^{-rT}N(-d_2) - PN(d_1) \tag{9.43}$$

Note that the price of European call and put options on non-dividend paying stock are related in the following way,

$$p + P = c + Ke^{-rT} \tag{9.44}$$

This relationship is called the **put–call parity relationship** and a similar relationship holds for dividend paying stock. If this equality is not satisfied then an arbitrage opportunity exists where a riskless profit can be made through buying/selling a call option and simultaneously buying/selling a put option and the stock.[15]

An important feature of derivatives is that the relationship between the price of the underlying asset and the price of the derivative is typically non-linear. This non-linearity makes computing VaR for derivatives more involved than computing VaR for assets. The delta-gamma (DG) approach relies on a second-order Taylor series approximation of this non-linear relationship, which provides a workable formula for option returns as a function of the underlying asset return, the asset return squared, the price of the underlying asset and the **Greeks**, δ, Γ and θ (delta, gamma and theta). We will progress straight to the relevant formula for the one-day returns for a call stock option,

$$r_{c,t+1} = \alpha \delta r_{s,t+1} + 0.5\alpha \Gamma P_{s,t} r_{s,t+1}^2 + \theta c_t^{-1} \tag{9.45}$$

where $r_{c,t+1}$ denotes the return on the call option, $P_{s,t}$ the current stock price, $r_{s,t+1}$ the return on the underlying stock c_t the current option price and $\alpha = P_{s,t}/c_t$.[16] The Greeks δ and Γ are the first and second partial derivatives of the option price with respect to the price of the underlying asset. They describe how the option price changes with changes in the price of the underlying asset,

$$\delta = \frac{\partial c}{\partial P} \tag{9.46}$$

$$\Gamma = \frac{\partial^2 c}{\partial P^2} \tag{9.47}$$

θ describes how the option price changes with changes in time,

$$\theta = \frac{\partial c}{\partial t} \tag{9.48}$$

Note that in practice, for short horizons, θ is usually ignored because it is extremely small. In the rest of this chapter for simplicity we will set $\theta = 0$. An approximation of the conditional variance of the option return can be obtained by taking the

---

[15]See Hull (2005) Chapter. 9, 13 and 14 for further details on option pricing, including how to incorporate dividends in the Black–Scholes framework.
[16]For more details on the relevant Taylor series approximation and a full derivation of this formula, see RiskMetrics (1996) Appendix D.

variance of both sides of (9.45), which after simplification gives,

$$\sigma_{c,t+1}^2 = \alpha^2 \delta^2 \sigma_{s,t+1}^2 + 0.5\alpha^2 \Gamma^2 P_{s,t}^2 \sigma_{s,t+1}^4 \tag{9.49}$$

It is important to be aware that in the Black–Scholes formula σ is the annual conditional volatility for the underlying stock, but when computing $\sigma_{c,t+1}^2, \sigma_{s,t+1}$ refers to the one-trading-day conditional volatility.

When computing VaR for an option, it is convenient to model changes in the *value* of the option rather than the option returns. As shown in RiskMetrics (1996) Appendix D, (9.45) and (9.49) imply that the change in the value of the option is given by,

$$\Delta V_{c,t+1} = \delta P_{s,t} r_{s,t+1} + 0.5\Gamma P_{s,t}^2 r_{s,t+1}^2 \tag{9.50}$$

and the conditional variance of this change is given by,

$$\sigma_{\Delta V_c,t+1}^2 = \delta^2 P_{s,t}^2 \sigma_{s,t+1}^2 + 0.5\Gamma^2 P_{s,t}^4 \sigma_{s,t+1}^4 \tag{9.51}$$

If we assume that $r_{s,t+1}$ and $r_{s,t+1}^2$ are both conditionally normally distributed random variables then $\Delta V_{c,t+1}$ is conditionally normally distributed. Hence the DG VaR can be computed employing the square root of (9.51) as the relevant conditional volatility forecast with the unknown parameters replaced by estimated values. Thus, assuming a mean option return of zero, the one-day VaR for a portfolio containing a single call stock option is,

$$VaR_{t+1}^p = -F^{-1}(p)\sigma_{\Delta V_c,t+1} \tag{9.52}$$

If a portfolio contains multiple numbers of the same option or multiple numbers of different options on the same underlying asset then the relevant δ and Γ for each contract can be aggregated. Consequently, the change in the value of a portfolio consisting of different options on the same underlying stock can be written,

$$\Delta V_{c,t+1} = \sum_{i=1}^{N} n_i \delta_i P_{s,t} r_{s,t+1} + \sum_{i=1}^{N} n_i 0.5\Gamma_i P_{s,t}^2 r_{s,t+1}^2 \tag{9.53}$$

where n_i denotes the number of each of the N options in the portfolio. The portfolio variance is then obtained from (9.53) and the VaR can be computed as in (9.52). More generally for a portfolio consisting of options where each option is dependent on a different underlying market variable, we can write,

$$\Delta V_{p,t+1} = \sum_{i=1}^{N} n_i \delta_i P_{i,t} r_{i,s,t+1} + \sum_{i=1}^{N} n_i 0.5\Gamma_i P_{i,t}^2 r_{i,s,t+1}^2 \tag{9.54}$$

In practice the Greeks δ and Γ and the conditional volatility of the underlying stock returns $\sigma_{s,t+1}$ are unknown. However, the relevant Greeks can be estimated using formulas derived from the Black–Scholes model,

$$\hat{\delta} = N(d_1) \tag{9.55}$$

$$\hat{\Gamma} = \frac{N'(d_1)}{P\hat{\sigma}\sqrt{T}} \tag{9.56}$$

A forecast of the conditional volatility for the underlying asset, $\sigma_{s,t+1}$, can be computed using one of the approaches previously discussed: for example, the MA, EWMA or GARCH approach.[17]

The VaR computed using the DG approach should be treated with a degree of caution because the assumption that option returns are conditionally normally distributed is statistically invalid if the underlying asset returns are conditional normally distributed. Statistical theory tells us that if $r_{s,t+1}$ is conditionally normally distributed then $r_{s,t+1}^2$ will have a χ^2 distribution, and therefore $r_{c,t+1}$ and $\Delta V_{c,t+1}$ also cannot be conditionally normally distributed. More specifically, it can be shown that for a long position in a call option, then since the gamma will be positive, $\Gamma > 0$, the conditional distribution of the change in value will be positively skewed. Conversely, for a short position in a call option the gamma will be negative and the conditional distribution will be negatively skewed. Therefore, for a long position in a call option the basic DG approach will tend to overestimate the true VaR because it assumes that the conditional distribution of the change in value has a fatter left tail than it actually does. For a short position in a call option the basic DG approach will tend to underestimate the true VaR because it assumes that the conditional distribution has a thinner left tail than it actually does. Note also that in practice the conditional mean change in value could be some way from zero, even if the underlying asset has a zero conditional mean return. Assuming a zero conditional mean, as in (9.52), can lead to further non-trivial errors in the computed VaR for the option.

Recall from Section 9.4 that when computing VaR for portfolios of assets using the MCS approach an analyst can assume that the conditional distribution for returns is non-normal. MCS can also be used to compute the VaR for portfolios containing derivatives allowing for non-normality (this is discussed in more detail in Section 9.6.2). An alternative to using MCS to allow for non-normality is to apply an analytical correction to the standard normal QF used when computing VaR using the DN or the basic DG approach. This can be done employing a statistical technique developed by Cornish and Fisher (1937) which involves mathematically expanding the relevant QF. The expanded QF (the **Cornish–Fisher expansion**) allows for the effects of skewness and excess kurtosis to be explicitly incorporated. In this

---

[17]An alternative to forecasting the conditional volatility using the MA, EWMA or GARCH approach is to use the Black–Scholes pricing formula along with existing data on the relevant option contract to **back-out** an estimate of the conditional volatility for the underlying asset and to utilise this estimate to compute the relevant forecast. This estimate is called the **implied volatility**.

case the expanded QF is,

$$F_{CF}^{-1}(p) = F^{-1}(p) + \frac{\tilde{\varsigma}}{6}\left[F^{-1}(p)^2 - 1\right] + \frac{\tilde{\kappa}}{24}\left[F^{-1}(p)^3 - 3F^{-1}(p)\right]$$

$$- \frac{\tilde{\varsigma}^2}{36}\left[2F^{-1}(p)^3 - 5F^{-1}(p)\right] \tag{9.57}$$

where $\tilde{\varsigma}$ and $\tilde{\kappa}$ are the skewness and excess kurtosis coefficients for the standardised returns (or changes in portfolio value). Note, therefore, that if there is no skewness or excess kurtosis, $\tilde{\varsigma} = \tilde{\kappa} = 0$ and the Cornish–Fisher QF is equivalent to the QF for a standard normal distribution. However, if significant skewness and excess kurtosis are present then it will be beneficial to use $F_{CF}^{-1}(p)$ instead of $F^{-1}(p)$ when computing the relevant VaR.

Important strengths of the DG approach are that as with the DN approach it is straightforward to compute and the computational cost is low. However, a significant weakness is that in its most basic form the DG approach assumes that option returns (and so changes in the option value) are conditionally normally distributed and have a conditional mean of zero, which can lead to a non-trivial approximation error. Another assumption that could lead to a non-trivial approximation error is the assumption that the relevant Greeks are constant as the price of the underlying asset changes (this weakness is highlighted in RiskMetrics (1996) Appendix D). In practice this will not always hold, which generates another approximation error. This error gets larger as the underlying asset price approaches the strike price. To illustrate this final point, graphs of the Greeks δ and Γ are given against the price of the underlying stock and the time to expiration in Figures 9.1 and 9.2 for the hypothetical example of a single call option on a non-dividend paying stock with the parameters: (i) $K = \$100$ (ii) $T = 1$ (iii) $\sigma = 25\%$ (iv) $r = 5\%$.

Clearly, as the underlying stock price approaches the strike price (which here is 100), changes in P can generate large changes in both δ and Γ. There is also a spike in Γ as the time to expiration approaches zero and the option price approaches the strike price.[18]

9.6.2 VaR by Monte Carlo Simulation

When computing VaR for portfolios containing derivatives there are two general types of MCS approach used: partial MCS and full MCS. Computing VaR can be done more quickly using partial MCS than full MCS, although both approaches

---

[18]Figures 9.1 and 9.2 are based on Chart D.1 and Chart D.2 in RiskMetrics (1996) Appendix D. See RiskMetrics (1996) Appendix D also for further technical details on the accuracy of the delta-gamma approach.

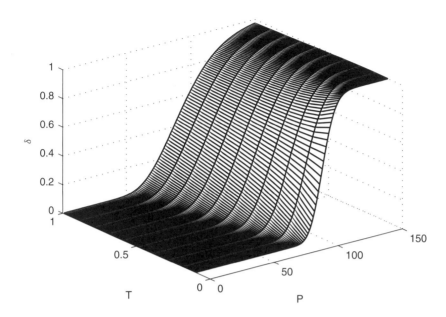

Figure 9.1   Delta vs. time to expiration and underlying price for European call option.

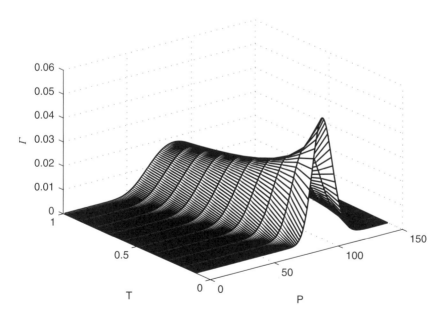

Figure 9.2   Gamma vs. time to expiration and underlying price for European call option.

are computationally more expensive than the DG approach, particularly for large portfolios.

The partial MCS approach involves using the DG formula for the option return and then simulating option pseudo-returns using this formula by simulating values of the underlying asset return. In the case of a call stock option it follows from the DG approach that the one-day return can be simulated using,

$$r_{j,c,t+1} = \alpha \hat{\delta} r_{j,s,t+1} + 0.5 \alpha \hat{\Gamma} P_{s,t} r_{j,s,t+1}^2 \tag{9.58}$$

where $r_{j,s,t+1}$ is the jth simulated value of the underlying stock return ($j = 1, 2, \ldots, N$, where N is the number of replications used), and $\hat{\delta}$ and $\hat{\Gamma}$ are estimated values. It follows that the change in the option value can be simulated using,

$$\Delta V_{j,c,t+1} = \hat{\delta} P_{s,t} r_{j,s,t+1} + 0.5 \hat{\Gamma} P_{s,t}^2 r_{j,s,t+1}^2 \tag{9.59}$$

The one-day VaR for a single option is,

$$VaR_{t+1}^p = -\Delta V_{j,c,(t+1)}^p \tag{9.60}$$

where $\Delta V_{j,c,(t+1)}^p$ denotes the relevant percentile of the order statistics for the simulated changes in the option value.

Full Monte Carlo simulation uses the Black–Scholes formula to directly simulate the option price from which changes in value can be obtained. For example, in the case of a European call option on non-dividend paying stock with T days until maturity the jth simulated Black–Scholes price at time $t + 1$ is,

$$c_{j,t+1} = P_{j,s,t+1} N(d_{1,t+1}) - Ke^{-r(T-0.0040)} N(d_{2,t+1}) \tag{9.61}$$

where $P_{j,s,t+1}$ is the jth simulated value of the underlying stock price. Typically a random walk model is assumed for the natural logarithm of the price of the underlying stock and non-normality can be incorporated into the errors (i.e. the asset returns can be assumed to be conditionally non-normal). $N(d_{1,t+1})$ and $N(d_{2,t+1})$ are draws from the standard normal CDF. Recall that T denotes time to expiration in trading-day years. Therefore, in one day, and assuming 252 trading days in a year, the time to expiration is $T - (1/252) = T - 0.0040$. From the simulated value of the option price, $c_{j,t+1}$, we can then compute changes in the option value directly, $\Delta V_{j,c,t+1} = c_{j,t+1} - c_t$. The relevant VaR is obtained by computing the order statistics for these simulated changes and obtaining the relevant percentile value. Mathematically the formula is the same as (9.60) where $\Delta V_{j,c,(t+1)}^p$ denotes the relevant percentile of the order statistics for the directly simulated value changes. Aggregation can be used to extend the MCS approaches to portfolios containing multiple options.

The main strength of the partial and full MCS approaches relative to the basic DG approach is that they do not assume that the asset returns or the changes in the value of the portfolio are conditionally normally distributed. In the partial MCS approach the non-normality generated by squaring the asset returns in the DG approximation is explicitly incorporated. In both partial and full MCS approaches the analyst can also explicitly incorporate non-normality in the conditional distribution of the asset returns. Note, however, that relative to the DG approach both the partial and full MCS approaches are computationally more expensive, particularly for large portfolios. Furthermore, the success of these approaches will depend on the accuracy of the assumed distributions as proxies for the unknown population distributions when simulating the underlying asset prices/returns. [19]

9.7 Backtesting

Backtesting refers to testing the accuracy of a forecasting technique over a historical sample period – where the true outcomes are known. VaR is a forecast in the sense that it is a measure of potential loss over a future period. The general approach to backtesting VaR for a portfolio is to record the number of occasions over a historical sample period when the actual loss over the VaR horizon exceeds the computed VaR (the number of **exceptions**), and to compare it with the number of exceptions expected from theory if the VaR approach is correct. For example, if one-day VaR is computed at the 99% confidence level then on each day the actual loss associated with the portfolio should be greater than the VaR with a probability of 1%. Therefore, if one-day VaR has been computed over a historical sample period of 250 days, approximately three exceptions should be observed. If the analyst finds that over the sample period the number of exceptions is larger than 1% of the sample size by a statistically significant amount (or smaller), this suggests that for this portfolio the VaR approach used underestimates (or overestimates) the true VaR.

It is possible to statistically test whether the backtesting results for a particular VaR approach display certain desirable features, including the feature that the proportion of VaR exceptions generated by the approach is equal to the desired number for a particular VaR confidence level. The most popular tests are those proposed by Kupiec (1995) and Christoffersen (1998). [20] Let r_{t+1}^p denote the relevant one-day

---

[19]Note that, with minor modifications of the formulas used, the VaR approaches discussed in this and previous sections can be also employed to compute VaR for options on dividend-paying stocks and for other derivatives. The relevant Black–Scholes pricing formulas for options on dividend-paying stocks are given in Hull (2005) Chapter 14. See Artzner *et al.* (1997, 1999), Danielsson *et al.* (2005) and Jorion (2006) Chapter 10 for more details on the strengths and weaknesses of the different approaches to computing VaR and Pritsker (1997) for a comprehensive evaluation of the different simulation approaches.

[20]See also Christoffersen (2003) Chapter 8 for a detailed discussion of these tests applied to VaR, and Jorion (2006) Chapter 6.

return-VaR computed at time t. A key tool when backtesting the different VaR approaches is an indicator of the VaR exceptions,

$$Y_{t+1} = \begin{cases} 1, & \text{if } r_{t+1} < r^p_{t+1} \\ 0, & \text{if } r_{t+1} \geq r^p_{t+1} \end{cases} \tag{9.62}$$

Y_{t+1} indicates when the actual return is more negative than the return-VaR (and thus the actual loss is greater than the VaR). If the VaR approach is perfect then Y_{t+1} should be an independently distributed Bernoulli random variable that takes the value one with probability p and zero with probability $1 - p$.

Let p_x denote the proportion of exceptions associated with the VaR model when calibrated to produce p, and $\hat{p}_x$ the estimated value of p_x from a backtesting exercise (the sample proportion of exceptions). If the VaR approach is correct then,

$$\hat{p}_x \approx p \tag{9.63}$$

where

$$\hat{p}_x = N_1/N \tag{9.64}$$

$$N_1 = \sum_{t=1}^{N} Y_t \tag{9.65}$$

and N is the sample size of the backtesting period. Kupiec (1995) shows that we can statistically test the null hypothesis that the VaR approach generates the correct proportion of exceptions, $H_0 : p_x = p$, using a likelihood ratio (LR) test. The test statistic is,

$$LR_x = -2\ln[L(p)/L(\hat{p}_x)] \tag{9.66}$$

where

$$L(p) = (1-p)^{(N-N_1)} p^{N_1} \tag{9.67}$$

$$L(\hat{p}_x) = (1-\hat{p}_x)^{(N-N_1)} \hat{p}_x^{N_1} \tag{9.68}$$

are the restricted and unrestricted likelihood functions for the indicator of VaR exceptions (the restriction is $p_x = p$). LR_x has a $\chi^2(1)$ asymptotic distribution. Having computed LR_x for our particular sample of data we compare with the relevant critical value $\chi^2(1)$ for a chosen significance level and accept ($LR_x \leq \chi^2(1)$) or reject ($LR_x > \chi^2(1)$) accordingly. The relevant critical values are given in Table A.4.

For a particular VaR approach the null hypothesis that Y_{t+1} is statistically independent can also be tested using an LR test. First define the following conditional probabilities,

$$p_{x,01} = P(Y_{t+1} = 1 | Y_t = 0) \tag{9.69}$$

$$p_{x,11} = P(Y_{t+1} = 1 | Y_t = 1) \tag{9.70}$$

$$p_{x,10} = 1 - p_{x,01} \tag{9.71}$$

$$p_{x,00} = 1 - p_{x,11} \tag{9.72}$$

If we assume that the indicator of exceptions is a first-order Markov process with sample size N then (9.69)-(9.72) are called the **transition probabilities**. It follows that the relevant likelihood function for the indicator is,

$$L(p_{x,ij}) = (1 - p_{x,01})^{N_{00}} p_{x,01}^{N_{01}} (1 - p_{x,11})^{N_{10}} p_{x,11}^{N_{11}} \tag{9.73}$$

where N_{ij} is the number of times that $Y_t = i$ is followed by $Y_{t+1} = j$ where $i = 0, 1, j = 0, 1$. The maximum likelihood estimates of the transition probabilities $p_{x,01}$ and $p_{x,11}$ can be obtained by maximising (9.73), which gives,

$$\hat{p}_{x,01} = N_{01}/(N_{00} + N_{01}) \tag{9.74}$$

$$\hat{p}_{x,11} = N_{11}/(N_{10} + N_{11}) \tag{9.75}$$

$$\hat{p}_{x,10} = 1 - \hat{p}_{x,01} \tag{9.76}$$

$$\hat{p}_{x,00} = 1 - \hat{p}_{x,11} \tag{9.77}$$

Note that the exceptions are independent if $p_{x,01} = p_{x,11}$. This can be tested by computing the following LR test,

$$LR_{ix} = -2 \ln[L(\hat{p}_x)/L(\hat{p}_{x,ij})] \tag{9.78}$$

where $L(\hat{p}_x)$ is the maximised likelihood function in (9.68) and $L(\hat{p}_{x,ij})$ is the maximised version of (9.73). LR_{ix} has a $\chi^2(1)$ asymptotic distribution under the null hypothesis.

In addition to individually testing the hypotheses that the proportion of exceptions is correct and that the exceptions are independent, Christoffersen (1998) shows that the joint hypothesis that both of these are true can be tested using,

$$LR_{cc} = -2 \ln[L(p)/L(\hat{p}_{x,ij})] \tag{9.79}$$

where $L(p)$ and $L(\hat{p}_{x,ij})$ are defined above and subscript cc denotes **conditional coverage**. [21] It can be shown that this test can be computed simply by adding the LR_x and LR_{ix} test statistics together,

$$LR_{cc} = LR_x + LR_{ix} \tag{9.80}$$

---

[21] The LR_x test proposed by Kupiec (1995) is a test of correct *unconditional* coverage.

Backtesting is meant to identify the problems with predictive statistical methods such as VaR. For an analyst intending to compute the VaR for a portfolio it is sensible to undertake backtesting of the different VaR approaches available. It is possible to envisage scenarios where one approach will significantly dominate the others; for example, if the conditional distribution for portfolio returns is strongly non-normal then the HS approach might well dominate the DN approach. Through backtesting the analyst can try and determine which of the VaR approaches is the most appropriate for the relevant portfolio.

It is important to remember that in practice the performance of statistical tests like LR_x and LR_{ix} depends on the **power** of the tests, and the **size** of the tests. Recall that in this context power means the probability of correctly rejecting a false null hypothesis (one minus the probability of making a Type II error), such as the null hypothesis that the VaR approach has correct unconditional coverage; and size means the probability of an incorrect rejection of a true null hypothesis (the probability of making a Type I error). It can be shown that when the sample size used for backtesting is small, both the power and size of backtesting tests like LR_x and LR_{ix} can be quite poor (e.g. see Kupiec, 1995).

Publicly disclosing the number of VaR exceptions has become increasingly popular with banks as a way of trying to increase public confidence in the quality of their risk management procedures, even though for most banks there is no legal requirement to do so. The journal article by Perignon and Smith (2010) investigates samples of large US and Canadian banks over 1995–2006 and finds an increase in the quantity of information on market risk VaR disclosed to the public. However, they find that the *quality* of the computed VaR amounts has not increased. To evaluate this issue they investigate the proportion of the one-day VaR exceptions for a sample of banks in 2005, including US, Canadian and international banks, using the Kupiec (1995) LR_x test discussed above. They also investigate the relationship between banks' one-day VaR amounts and their trading revenues. Their analysis of the proportion of exceptions finds that in the majority of cases the banks consistently overestimate the true VaR, in the sense that there are too few exceptions. Furthermore, the LR_x test rejects the null hypothesis that the proportion of exceptions is correct at conventional significance levels. Their analysis of the relationship between VaR and future trading revenues shows that there is very little information about the volatility of future trading revenues in the VaR amounts computed, suggesting that the VaR amounts are not informative about future risk. Note that the most popular VaR approach used by the sample of banks considered is the HS approach. Perignon and Smith (2010) point out that the HS approach is popular because of its simplicity relative to the main competing approaches when there are large numbers of risk factors, and because the VaR computed using the HS approach evolves smoothly. However, their analysis suggests that for this period it was not an informative approach.

9.8 Financial Regulation and VaR

The Basel Committee on Banking Supervision (BCBS) is a committee set up in 1974 by the Central Bank Governors of the G10 countries. The BCBS's Secretariat is based at the Bank for International Settlements (BIS) in Basel, Switzerland. In the early 1980s following a worsening of capital ratios in member countries' banks, the BCBS agreed to introduce an international Capital Accord to raise capital ratios and help increase confidence in the banking sector. Hence, in 1988, the first Accord, "International Convergence of Capital Measurement and Capital Standards", was proposed (Basel I for short). It is important to recognise that the BCBS does not have formal regulatory powers. Rather it issues guidelines on regulatory issues and expects that the relevant national regulatory authorities will help to implement those guidelines.

Basel I is essentially a set of guidelines devised to ensure that banks maintain a certain amount of capital to be able to absorb losses due to defaults (i.e. losses due to **credit risk**): see BCBS (1988). By late 1993 most large banks in the G10 countries were meeting the minimum requirements proposed in Basel I. The minimum capital requirement under Basel I is 8% of **risk weighted assets** (RWA),

$$\text{Capital ratio} = \frac{\text{Capital}}{\text{RWA}} \geq 8\% \tag{9.81}$$

where RWA is the value of the bank's assets multiplied by weights that depend on their credit risk. The weights are specified in BCBS (1988). Note that RWA incorporates off-balance-sheet activities. Note also that Tier 1 capital must cover 4% of a bank's RWA. [22]

Basel I helped to improve banks' capital ratios; however, it has been criticised on numerous grounds. [23] Four common criticisms of Basel I are:

(i) The way that credit risks are dealt with in Basel I is too general. For example, all OECD bank debt has a 20% weight, and all private sector debt has a 100% weight. Large differences in risk exist within these different categories and this is ignored.

(ii) Since Basel I focuses only on credit risk, it ignores important risks associated with asset price volatility and currency fluctuations (market risk).

---

[22]**Tier 1** capital, also called **core capital** consists of equity capital (i.e. the amount invested by shareholders) plus disclosed reserves and retained earnings. **Tier 2** capital, also called **supplementary capital**, consists mainly of general provisions, hybrid instruments, subordinated term debt, undisclosed reserves and revaluation reserves.

[23]For example, see Altman and Saunders (2001), Rodriguez (2003).

(iii) Short-term debt has a lower weighting than long-term debt in Basel I and this can be exploited by banks. They can reduce their perceived riskiness by converting long-term debt to short-term debt.

(iv) Basel I encourages the use of off-balance-sheet structured investment vehicles (SIVs) to *artificially* reduce risk. For example, banks can move assets with a low credit rating into SIVs, which can be manipulated so that they are given a higher credit rating by a credit ratings agency (CRA) with no change in the assets' risk.

In the light of various banking crises and the criticisms of Basel I, in January 2001 the BCBS proposed a new accord, "A Revised Framework on International Convergence of Capital Measurement and Capital Standards", or Basel II for short (see BCBS, 2006, for an updated version). [24] Basel II improves on Basel I in a number of different areas and is significantly more comprehensive. As with Basel I, Basel II has a clear pillar-based structure: Pillar I Minimum Capital Requirements; Pillar II The Regulatory Process; Pillar III Enhancing Public Disclosure. An important change from Basel I to Basel II is that Basel II links capital requirements not only to credit risk but also to operational risk and market risk.

As we have previously discussed, market risk refers to the risk associated with changes in market prices. Operational risk refers to other risks that do not fall into either the credit risk or market risk categories (e.g. risk due to fraud; risk due to the failure of internal procedures). Like Basel I, the minimum capital ratio under Basel II is 8% of RWA. However, in Basel II the total RWA must specifically allow for operational risk and market risk, as well as for credit risk. Under Basel II, banks must hold half of their total regulatory capital as Tier 1 capital. Furthermore, half of the Tier 1 capital must be common equity.

Basel II allows banks to choose between three approaches for computing credit risk RWA: (i) Standardised Approach; (ii) Foundation Internal Ratings Based (IRB) Approach; (iii) Advanced IRB Approach. [25] The first of these approaches requires banks to use information from authorised external credit ratings agencies to help assess the default risk which they face (e.g. Moody's, S&P, Fitch). The national regulator is responsible for ensuring the CRAs used satisfy certain eligibility criteria. The rating assigned by the authorised CRA determines the capital weighting. So, for example, obligors rated AAA to AAA– by the CRA are assigned a 0% weight while those rated A+ to A– are assigned a 20% weight; BBB+ to BBB– rated obligors are assigned a 50% weight; and those rated BB+ to BB– are assigned a 100% weight. An obligor rated worse than B– is assigned a 150% weight. The second approach allows banks to develop and utilise internal credit risk models under the regulator's

---

[24]In the 1990s there were a number of significant banking and financial crises, including banking crises in Finland and Sweden in the early 1990s, the Asian financial crisis in 1997 and the collapse of the US-based hedge-fund Long Term Capital Management in 1998.

[25]See BCBS (2006) Part 2, Sections II, III and IV.

guidance. The third approach is similar to the IRB approach but requires banks to compute many of the relevant underlying parameters themselves, rather than using those provided by the regulator.

Basel II allows banks to choose between three different approaches for computing their operational risk capital requirement: (i) Basic Indicator Approach; (ii) Standardised Approach; (iii) Advanced Measurement Approach. [26] The first approach involves a single weight: banks must hold capital equivalent to 15% of their average gross income in the past three years to cover operational risk. The second approach is more specific, as it splits a bank into its individual business operations and then assesses the operational risk associated with each of these. The operational risk capital requirement associated with each operation is defined as a proportion of profits. For example, **Corporate Finance** has an 18% weighting, while **Retail Banking** has only a 12% weighting. The third approach is more flexible. It allows banks to develop and employ their own methods to compute operational risk capital requirements subject to the approval of the regulator.

Formally linking capital requirements to the market risk associated with a bank's trading book is perhaps the most significant development in risk management and financial regulation experienced since the introduction of Basel I, and it is at this point that VaR becomes most relevant. [27] Banks are allowed to use their own VaR-based approach to determine market risk regulatory capital for fixed income assets (subject to being ratified by the regulator), or they can use a specified series of weights that depend on the time to maturity of the asset and external credit ratings. In the case of all other market-based assets, there are three broad types of approach that banks can choose between for determining market risk regulatory capital: (i) Simplified Approach; (ii) Scenario Analysis; (iii) Internal Models Approach. The first approach involves a set of weights that the bank must use which depend on certain features of the assets: for example, maturity and volatility. The second approach involves the use of specified risk weights linked to the possible scenarios associated with the relevant assets in each country, which the bank's risk management unit will simulate. The third approach allows banks to use their own VaR models for quantifying market risk and then links the capital requirement directly to this VaR, and to the performance of the bank's VaR models in backtesting.

The Internal Models Approach to market risk has been the most popular approach with large banks. As we have seen, VaR can be computed using a number of different approaches and the main approaches are in theory all applicable under the Internal Models Approach, subject to regulatory

---

[26]See BCBS (2006), Part 2, Section V.
[27]See BCBS (2006) Part 2, Section VI.

agreement. Basel II has a set of detailed **Qualitative Standards** and **Quantitative Standards** which banks must adhere to. The first two Qualitative Standards are: [28]

(a) The bank is required to have a risk management unit which is responsible for daily analysis and reports on the bank's VaR models.
(b) This unit, which should be independent from the trading units in the bank, is required to conduct a comprehensive backtesting programme.

Specific details on the VaR computations required and the associated capital requirement are given in the Quantitative Standards. Some of the key Quantitative Standards are: [29]

(a) VaR must be computed every day.
(b) The 99% confidence level should be used.
(c) A 10-day horizon should be used (banks are allowed to use time-scaling to transform VaR for a shorter horizon to the 10-day VaR).
(d) A minimum sample size of one year should be used when computing VaR.
  . . .

(i) The daily capital requirement is the higher of the previous day's VaR, or an average of the VaR for each of the previous 60 days, multiplied by a multiplication factor, m.
(j) The multiplication factor will have a minimum of $m = 3$. This factor will increase depending on the performance of the bank's VaR model in backtesting.

It follows that the bank's daily market risk regulatory capital can be written,

$$Capital_t = \text{Max}\left[VaR_t^{0.01}, \sum_{i=t-59}^{t} VaR_i^{0.01}/60 \right] \times m \tag{9.82}$$

where $VaR_t^{0.01}$ denotes the previous day's VaR at the 99% confidence level for a 10-day horizon. Note, therefore, that under Basel II, for banks taking the Internal Models Approach, backtesting directly affects their minimum capital requirement, since it determines the bank's **multiplication factor**, m. Specific details on the backtesting procedure under Basel II are set out in one of the Annexes of the Basel II document. [30] The basic philosophy is detailed in the section titled ''Description of the backtesting framework'' as follows,

---

[28]This is a summary of standards (a) and (b). For the full list of the standards, see Basel II (BCBS, 2006) p. 192.
[29]This is a summary of standards (a)–(d), (i) and (j). For the full list of the standards, see Basel II (BCBS, 2006) pp. 195–196.
[30]Basel II (BCBS, 2006) Annex 10a.

> The backtesting framework developed by the Committee is based on that adopted by many of the banks that use internal market risk measurement models. These backtesting programs typically consist of a periodic comparison of the bank's daily value-at-risk measures with the subsequent daily profit or loss ("trading outcome")...[31]

Therefore the backtesting framework involves the concepts we have introduced in the previous sections of this chapter. More specifically, banks are required to compute the number of VaR exceptions over a historical sample period, and the regulator will use this number relative to the number expected from statistical theory as a guide to the performance of the particular VaR approach being employed.

Recall that while we can backtest VaR at different confidence levels (e.g. 99% or 95%), under Basel II banks are required to backtest at the 99% confidence level. Note from Quantitative Standard (c) that for computing regulatory capital under Basel II the bank must use VaR over a 10-day period. This is problematic for backtesting because over such a long period the composition of a bank's trading book is likely to change with a high probability. It is argued, therefore, that comparing the 10-day 99% VaR with actual 10-day returns is not a useful exercise. Hence, backtesting is undertaken using only the one-day VaR.

Under Basel II banks are typically required to report their backtesting results to the regulator on a quarterly basis. The backtesting results reported are the number of one-day VaR exceptions over the previous 12-month period. This number is used to determine the bank's multiplication factor. Unusual results might also lead the regulator to investigate in more detail whether there is a fundamental problem with the bank's VaR models. In cases where serious problems are identified, the regulator may impose an increase in a bank's capital requirement or even reject the model entirely.

It is important to recognise that like any statistical test, when backtesting, Type I and Type II errors can occur. A Type I error refers to incorrectly rejecting a true null hypothesis and a Type II error refers to incorrectly accepting a false null hypothesis. The size of a backtesting procedure refers to the probability of incorrectly rejecting a correct VaR model (i.e. the probability of making a Type I error). The power of a backtesting procedure refers to the probability of correctly identifying an incorrect VaR model (i.e. one minus the probability of a Type II error; with the null hypothesis being that the VaR model is correct). If a backtesting procedure suffers from low power, or is over-sized, then incorrect VaR models might be accepted by the regulator and, conversely, correct VaR models might be rejected. Basel II does recognise that these statistical difficulties exist and a set of simulation experiments are reported in Basel II to illustrate the difficulties. Consequently, rather than

---

[31]Basel II (BCBS, 2006) p. 311.

Table 9.1 Basel II traffic light approach to backtesting[32]

Zone	Exceptions	m
Green	0	3.00
	1	3.00
	2	3.00
	3	3.00
	4	3.00
Yellow	5	3.40
	6	3.50
	7	3.65
	8	3.75
	9	3.85
Red	$\geqslant$10	4.00

use a single cut-off point to determine the acceptance or rejection of a bank's VaR model and the associated multiplication factor, m, Basel II employs a green, yellow, red "traffic light" approach which defines zones of exceptions and an associated multiplication factor. These zones are defined in Table 9.1.

The 2007–2009 global financial crisis has had a significant impact on quantitative risk management. Indeed a popular view is that the crisis occurred because of the impact of long-standing macroeconomic imbalances combined with financial innovation and the procyclicality of the capital requirements under the Basel Capital Accords and the procyclicality of VaR. This is, for example, a view that has been expressed by the UK Financial Services Authority (FSA).[33] Whilst it would be naive to blame the 2007–2009 financial crisis entirely on the Basel Capital Accords, it has highlighted some significant weaknesses and has led to the proposed replacement of Basel II with Basel III (e.g. see BCBS, 2010a, 2010b, 2010c). Initial discussions on Basel III have focused on improving on Basel II in three ways: (i) Improving the quality of capital; (ii) Improving the quantity of capital; (iii) Improving how systematic risk is managed and reducing procyclicality. To help achieve (i), it is proposed that Basel III will increase the common equity component of a bank's capital ratio to 4.5%, from 2% in Basel II. Furthermore, the definition of "common equity" will be stricter in Basel III. To help achieve (ii), it is proposed that the Tier 1 component of a bank's capital ratio is increased to 6% compared to 4% under Basel II. In addition, a **capital conservation buffer** of 2.5% of common equity capital must be held in normal times to be used in times of stress. This means that the standard common

---

[32]This table is based on BCBS (2006) Annex 10a, Table 9.2, p. 320.
[33]For example, see Turner (2009) Chapter 1: What went wrong?

equity ratio will be 7% (with 4.5% minimum) and the Tier 1 ratio will be 8.5% (with 6% minimum). As banks reach these minimum ratios, it is proposed that Basel III will recommend imposing constraints until the required capital ratios are re-established. To help achieve (iii), a **macroprudential overlay** has been proposed. This refers to regulation designed to reduce the risk of financial crises significantly destabilising the macroeconomy by implementing **countercyclical regulation**. For example, in addition to the 2.5% common equity capital conservation buffer, a **countercyclical capital buffer** ratio of between 0% and 2.5% is recommended. It is proposed that this buffer is increased from 0% if the national regulatory authority believes that aggregate credit growth during an economic boom is increasing systematic risk (as it undoubtedly did prior to the 2007 – 2009 financial crisis). This capital can then be used by banks for lending during a recession, which will help to stabilise economic growth. Note that a gradual implementation of Basel III is proposed. The new minimum capital ratios discussed here are scheduled to be introduced gradually over five years, starting in 2013. It is proposed that the new common equity and Tier 1 ratios are implemented from the start of 2015. It is proposed that the capital conservation buffer will be introduced gradually from 2016.

In most developed countries a single national regulatory authority is responsible for regulating banks and other financial services industries such as insurance (e.g. in the UK, the Financial Services Authority (FSA)). In the European Union the national regulator has to ensure that banks and securities issuers implement Basel II under European Law, specifically the Capital Requirements Directives. [34] In the US, financial regulation is more complex, with both federal and state regulatory authorities and separate regulation for different financial services industries. Furthermore, in the US, while large internationally active banks have to implement some aspects of Basel II, smaller banks do not. Financial regulation in the US is set to change in a significant way with the Dodd – Frank Act which was signed into law by US President Barack Obama on 21 July 2010. This is a hugely comprehensive proposal to restructure financial regulation in the US in response to the 2007 – 2009 financial crisis and subsequent recession.

The next section discusses the empirical examples for this chapter. For simplicity, these empirical examples involve individual stocks, a simple portfolio of stocks, and an individual stock option. Note, however, that the MATLAB® programs used can be easily modified to compute VaR for other assets and derivatives and for larger portfolios. Further details on the MATLAB® programs and the data used are given in Section 9.12. Critical values for the test statistics used can be obtained from the statistical tables in the Appendix. Note that for simplicity we actually report the

---

[34]In the EU there are two relevant directives: Directive 2006/49 EC on the capital adequacy of investment firms and institutions, and Directive 2006/48/EC, which relates to the taking up and pursuit of the business of credit institutions. See www.federalreserve.gov/newsevents/press/bcreg/20080626b.htm for further information on the level of implementation in the US.

return-VaR r_{t+1}^p (converted to positive) for Examples 9.1–9.4 rather than a monetary value (and for brevity we refer to this amount as the VaR).

9.9 Empirical Examples

Example 9.1:   Single asset VaR, delta-normal

(a) Using daily data on the price of Exxon Mobil Corporation (XOM) stock for 31/12/97–31/12/08, compute the returns and graph the returns over the period 02/01/08–31/12/08. Using the DN approach compute the one-day VaR for XOM at the 99% confidence level over the period 02/01/08–31/12/08 employing an MA conditional volatility forecast computed using a five-year rolling window of data.

(b) Repeat (a) using an EWMA conditional volatility forecast with $\lambda = 0.94$.

(c) Repeat (a) using a GARCH(1,1) conditional volatility forecast.

The relevant MATLAB® programs are given in the files E91a.m, E91b.m and E91c.m respectively. A portion of E91c.m is given in Box 9.1. The returns are graphed in Figure 9.3. The VaR is graphed in Figures 9.4, 9.5 and 9.6.

Box 9.1   E91c.m

```
clear;
%Load the data.
D=xlsread('xom');
%Define the variables.
P=flipud(D);
date=P(:,1);
P=P(:,7);
nr1=size(P,1);
ret=log(P(2:nr1,1))-log(P(1:nr1-1,1));
date=date(2:nr1,1);
MATLABDate=x2mdate(date);
nr2=size(ret,1);
%Use a loop to compute the VaR.
ind=1;
nl=nr2-253;
while nl<=nr2-1;
%Redefine returns for the loop.
nret=ret(1:nl,1);
%Estimate a GARCH(1,1) model using the
```

```
%Oxford MFE Toolbox.
[parameters,LL,ht]=tarch(nret,1,0,1,'NORMAL',2);
%Compute the conditional volatility forecast.
vfor=sqrt(parameters(1,1)+parameters(2,1)*nret(nl,1)^2+...
parameters(3,1)*ht(nl,1));
%Compute the z quantile.
zq=norminv(0.01,0,1);
%Compute the VaR.
rq=zq*vfor;
%Convert to >0 and collect in fvar.
fvar(ind,1)=-rq;
ind=ind+1;
%Update the loop.
nl=nl+1;
end;
```

It can be seen in Figure 9.3 that clearly the volatility of the Exxon returns is time-varying with a huge rise in volatility in the last three months of 2008, corresponding to the peak of the 2007 – 2009 financial crisis. The results using the EWMA and the GARCH conditional volatility forecast are very similar. Note from Figures 9.5 and 9.6 that at the start of 2008 the VaR is approximately 3%, but it rises dramatically to over 16% towards the end of 2008 before falling again. This is explained by the huge rise

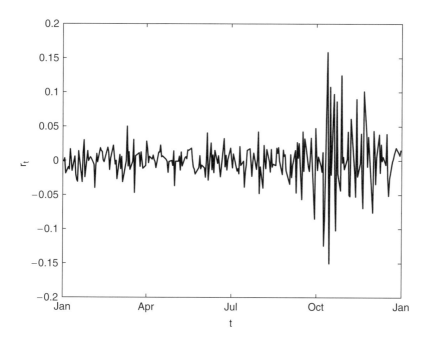

Figure 9.3   Exxon returns, 02/01/08-31/12/08.

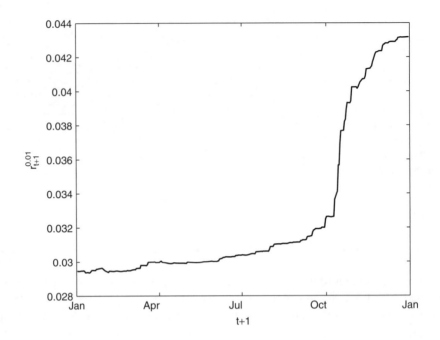

Figure 9.4   Exxon VaR, 02/01/08-31/12/08, DN (MA).

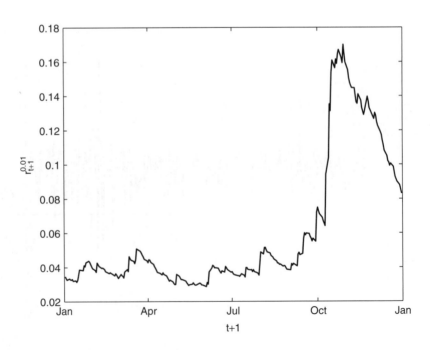

Figure 9.5   Exxon VaR, 02/01/08-31/12/08, DN (EWMA).

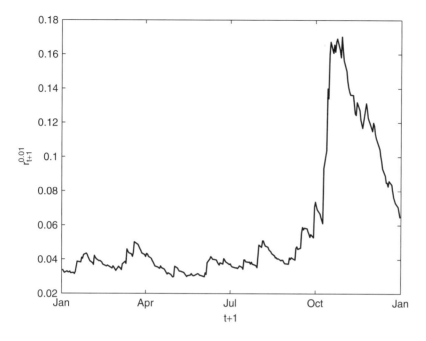

Figure 9.6   Exxon VaR, 02/01/08-31/12/08, DN (GARCH).

in the volatility of the Exxon returns. The MA conditional volatility forecasts do not forecast such a large increase in volatility and so the increase in the VaR in Figure 9.4 is much less significant.

Example 9.2:   Portfolio VaR, delta-normal

Using daily data on the price of General Electric Company (GE) stock and Microsoft Corporation (MSFT) stock for 31/12/97–31/12/08, compute the returns and graph the returns over the period 02/01/08–31/12/08. Using the returns data for GE and MSFT and the XOM data from Example 9.1, and employing the DN approach with an EWMA conditional volatility forecast (with $\lambda = 0.94$), compute the one-day VaR for an equally weighted portfolio of the three stocks (XOM, GE, MSFT) at the 99% confidence level over the period 02/01/08-31/12/08.

The relevant MATLAB® program is E92.m. A portion of E92.m is given in Box 9.2. The returns for General Electric and Microsoft are graphed in Figure 9.7 and Figure 9.8. The VaR is graphed in Figure 9.9.

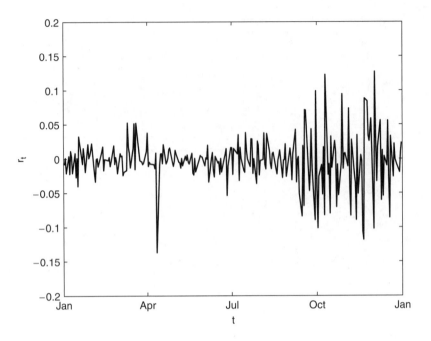

Figure 9.7   General Electric returns, 02/01/08-31/12/08.

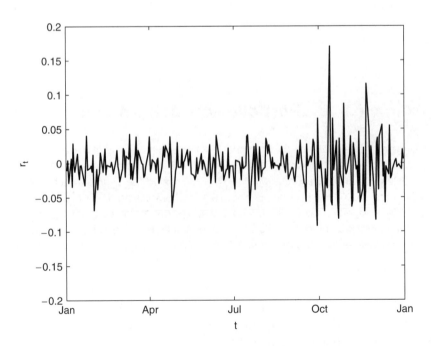

Figure 9.8   Microsoft returns, 02/01/08-31/12/08.

Box 9.2 E92.m

```
clear;
%Load the data.
D=xlsread('C9stocks');
%Define the variables.
P=flipud(D);
date=P(:,1);
P=P(:,2:4);
nr1=size(P,1);
ret=log(P(2:nr1,:))-log(P(1:nr1-1,:));
date=date(2:nr1,1);
MATLABDate=x2mdate(date);
nr2=size(ret,1);
%Use a loop to compute the VaR.
ind=1;
nl=nr2-253;
while nl<=nr2-1;
%Redefine a returns matrix for the loop
nret=ret(1:nl,:);
%Define a vector of weights.
w=1/3*ones(3,1);
%Compute the EWMA conditional variance forecast.
cv=c9ewma(nret);
wcvw=w'*cv*w;
%Compute the EWMA conditional volatility forecast.
vfor=sqrt(wcvw);
%Compute the z quantile.
zq=norminv(0.01,0,1);
%Compute the VaR.
rq=zq*vfor;
%Convert to >0 and collect in fvar.
fvar(ind,1)=-rq;
ind=ind+1;
%Update the loop.
nl=nl+1;
end;
```

By comparing the graphs of the returns in Figures 9.3, 9.7 and 9.8 it can be seen that, as with the Exxon returns, there is a huge increase in the volatility of the General Electric and Microsoft returns towards the end of 2008. Compared with the results for Exxon alone given in Figure 9.6, the VaR for the three-stock portfolio is only slightly lower over this period, demonstrating that, over the same period, risk was only reduced by a small amount by this degree of diversification (due to the positive correlation of the stock returns over this period).

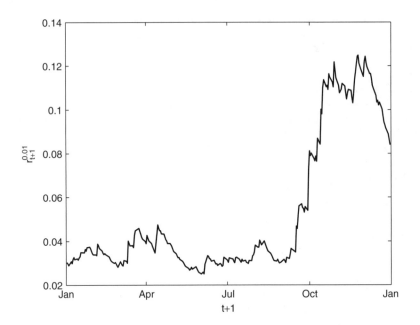

Figure 9.9   Portfolio VaR, 02/01/08–31/12/08, DN (EWMA).

Example 9.3:   Portfolio VaR, historical simulation

Repeat Example 9.2 using the HS approach employing a two-year rolling window of data.

The relevant MATLAB® program is E93.m. The VaR is graphed in Figure 9.10.

Note that in Figure 9.10 the rise in VaR towards the end of 2008 is much smaller than in Figure 9.9 when the DN approach with an EWMA conditional volatility forecast is used. Note also how, in contrast to Figure 9.9, the VaR in Figure 9.10 does not fall in December of 2008.

Example 9.4:   VaR Monte Carlo simulation

Repeat Example 9.2 using the MCS approach employing 100 000 replications. Assume that returns are conditionally multivariate-normal random variables where the conditional covariance matrix each day is equal to the sample covariance matrix estimated using a two-year rolling window of data (i.e. use the MA approach to compute the conditional covariance matrix each day).

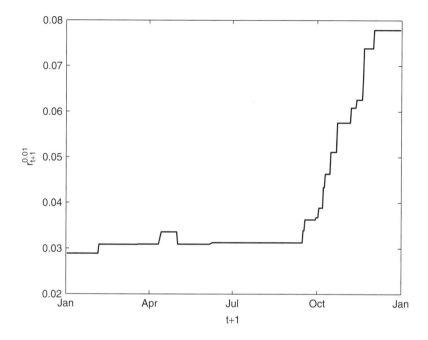

Figure 9.10   Portfolio VaR, 02/01/08-31/12/08, HS.

The relevant MATLAB® program is E94.m. A portion of E94.m is given in Box 9.3. The VaR is graphed in Figure 9.11.

Box 9.3   E94.m

```
clear;
%Set the random seed to give the same pseudo-random numbers.
rand('seed',1972);
randn('seed',1972);
%Load the data.
D=xlsread('C9stocks');
%Define the variables.
P=flipud(D);
date=P(:,1);
P=P(:,2:4);
nr1=size(P,1);
ret=log(P(2:nr1,:))-log(P(1:nr1-1,:));
date=date(2:nr1,1);
MATLABDate=x2mdate(date);
nr2=size(ret,1);
%Use a loop to compute the VaR.
ind=1;
nl=nr2-253;
while nl<=nr2-1;
```

```
%Redefine a returns matrix for the loop.
nret=ret(nl-252*2:nl,:);
%Simulate multivariate normal pseudo-returns.
cv=cov(nret);
ccv=chol(cv);
mz=randn(3,100000);
newr=ccv'*mz;
%Compute the portfolio returns.
w=1/3;
wnret=w*newr;
pnret=sum(wnret,1);
%Compute the order statistics.
spnret=sort(pnret);
%Compute the VaR.
rq=prctile(spnret,1);
%Convert to >0 and collect in fvar.
fvar(ind,1)=-rq;
ind=ind+1;
%Update the loop.
nl=nl+1;
end;
```

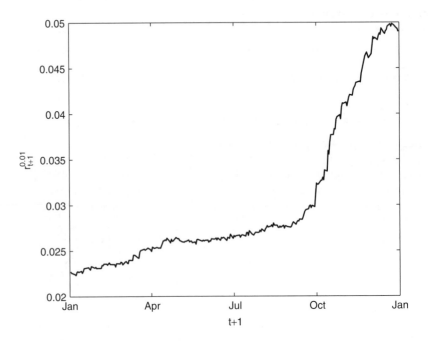

Figure 9.11   Portfolio VaR, 02/01/08-31/12/08, MCS.

Clearly the increase in VaR here is much less pronounced than for the DN approach with an EWMA conditional volatility forecast (Figure 9.9). This is to be expected because the MA approach is used in E94.m to estimate the conditional covariance matrix for simulating the pseudo-returns, which is known to be slow to capture rapid changes in the true conditional covariance matrix.

Example 9.5: Call option VaR, delta-gamma approach

Assume that it is 1 November 2007 and a US investor buys a call option on XOM stock which expires on 21 December with a strike price of $80. The current price is $88.50. Assume for simplicity that no dividends are paid and that the annual risk-free rate is 3%. Compute the option price and the one-day VaR at the 99% confidence level using the basic DG approach.

The key parameters when pricing the option are,

   (i) $P = 88.50$
  (ii) $K = 80$
 (iii) $T = 0.139$
 (iv) σ
  (v) $r = 0.03$

The annual conditional volatility of the underlying index σ is an unknown and a forecast $\hat{\sigma}$ has to be computed in order to compute the option price. The other relevant parameters δ and Γ can be estimated using (9.55) and (9.56). Here $\hat{\sigma}$ is computed by first computing $\hat{\sigma}_{s,t+1}$ using daily data on Exxon returns for 02/01/98–31/12/08 and an EWMA approach with $\lambda = 0.94$ and then applying the square-root-of-time rule, $\hat{\sigma} = \hat{\sigma}_{s,t+1}\sqrt{252}$.

The relevant MATLAB® program is E95.m, a portion of which is given in Box 9.4.

Box 9.4   E95.m

```
%Load the data.
D=xlsread('xom');
%Define the variables.
P=flipud(D(:,5));
nr1=size(P,1);
```

```
ret=log(P(2:nr1-293,1))-log(P(1:nr1-294,1));
nr2=size(ret,1);
%Compute the EWMA conditional variance forecast.
cv=c9ewma(ret);
%Compute the option price and the Greeks.
assetp=P(nr2+1,1);
strike=80;
riskfree=0.03;
time=35/252;
avol=sqrt(cv)*sqrt(252);
[bscp,bspp]=blsprice(assetp,strike,riskfree,time,avol,0);
[delta,pdelta]=blsdelta(assetp,strike,riskfree,time,avol,0);
[gamma]=blsgamma(assetp,strike,riskfree,time,avol,0);
%Compute the volatility forecast for the change in value.
dvol=sqrt(cv);
callv=delta^2*assetp^2*dvol^2+0.5*gamma^2*assetp^2*...
dvol^4;
vfor=sqrt(callv);
%Compute the z quantile.
zq=norminv(0.01,0,1);
%Compute the VaR.
fvar=-zq*vfor;
```

Running E95.m gives an option price of $9.40, and a one-day VaR of $2.93.

Example 9.6:   Call option VaR, partial Monte Carlo simulation approach

Compute the one-day VaR at the 99% confidence level for the option in Example 9.5 but using the partial MCS approach with 100 000 replications. Simulate the underlying Exxon returns assuming they are zero mean and conditionally normally distributed with the conditional volatility set equal to the conditional volatility in Example 9.5.

The relevant MATLAB® code is given in the file E96.m. A portion of the code from E96.m is given in Box 9.5.

The one-day VaR computed using E96.m is $2.81. Recall that when computing VaR for call options the basic DG approach ignores the positive skewness of the conditional distribution of the value changes, hence the VaR in Example 9.5 is larger than the VaR here.

Box 9.5   E96.m

```
%Set the random seed to give the same pseudo-random numbers.
rand('seed',1972);
randn('seed',1972);
%Load the data.
D=xlsread('xom');
%Define the variables.
P=flipud(D(:,5));
nr1=size(P,1);
ret=log(P(2:nr1-293,1))-log(P(1:nr1-294,1));
nr2=size(ret,1);
%Compute the EWMA conditional variance forecast.
cv=c9ewma(ret);
%Compute the Greeks.
assetp=P(nr2+1,1);
strike=80;
riskfree=0.03;
time=35/252;
avol=sqrt(cv)*sqrt(252);
[delta,pdelta]=blsdelta(assetp,strike,riskfree,time,avol,0);
[gamma]=blsgamma(assetp,strike,riskfree,time,avol,0);
%Simulate the stock returns.
sret=sqrt(cv)*randn(100000,1);
%Simulate the changes in value.
dv=assetp*delta*sret+0.5*gamma*assetp^2*sret.^2;
%Compute the order statistics for the simulated changes in value.
odv=sort(dv);
%Compute the VaR.
fvar=-prctile(odv,1);
```

Example 9.7:   Backtesting portfolio VaR

(a) Using the data from Example 9.2 and the DN approach with an EWMA conditional volatility forecast (with $\lambda = 0.94$), compute the one-day VaR for an equally weighted portfolio of the three stocks XOM, GE and MSFT at the 99% confidence level over the period 03/01/06–31/12/08. Backtest the results by computing the proportion of exceptions $\hat{p}_x$ and the LR_x, LR_{ix} and LR_{cc} tests. Graph the indicator of VaR exceptions over this period.

(b) Repeat (a) using the HS approach employing a two-year rolling window of data.

Table 9.2 Backtesting results at the 99% confidence level: DN approach

$\hat{p}_x$	0.024
LR_x	10.525***
LR_{ix}	0.929
LR_{cc}	11.453***

Note: ***denotes statistical significance at the 1% level.

The relevant MATLAB® code is given in the files E97a.m and E97b.m. Graphs of the indicator of VaR exceptions are given in Figures 9.12 and 9.13. The results are given in Tables 9.2 and 9.3.

It can be seen from Figure 9.13 that for the HS approach there appears to be a cluster of exceptions towards the end of the sample period – corresponding to the peak of the 2007–2009 financial crisis. It can be seen from Table 9.2 and 9.3 that the proportion of exceptions is closer to the desired 1% target for the DN approach than for the HS approach. However, in both cases the null hypothesis that the VaR approach generates the correct proportion of exceptions is rejected at the 1% level of significance by the LR_x test. The null hypothesis of independence is not

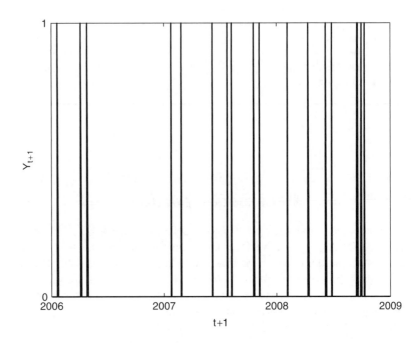

Figure 9.12   Indicator of VaR exceptions, 03/01/06-31/12/08, DN (EWMA).

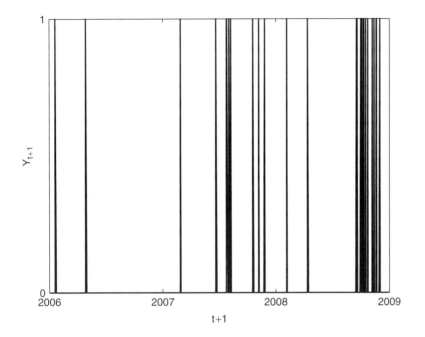

Figure 9.13   Indicator of VaR exceptions, 03/01/06-31/12/08, HS.

Table 9.3   Backtesting results at the 99% confidence level: HS approach

$\hat{p}_x$	0.034
LR_x	27.860***
LR_{ix}	1.173
LR_{cc}	29.033***

Note: ***denotes statistical significance at the 1% level.

rejected by the LR_{ix} test for either of the approaches. The LR_{cc} test rejects the null hypothesis of correct conditional coverage at the 1% significance level for both approaches.

9.10 Summary

This chapter has focused on the statistical risk management technique VaR. The main approaches to computing VaR for portfolios containing assets and derivatives have been discussed. For assets these are the delta-normal (DN) approach, the historical simulation (HS) approach and the Monte Carlo simulation (MCS) approach; for derivatives, these are the delta-gamma (DG) approach and the partial and full MCS approaches. We have explained how to compute VaR using these approaches and have discussed their strengths and weaknesses. This chapter has also focused on evaluating the performance of VaR models using backtesting, and the role of VaR and backtesting in international financial regulation. The empirical examples in this chapter demonstrate how to compute VaR for stocks and options and how to backtest a VaR model.

When computing VaR on a regular basis the majority of large investment banks tend to rely on the DN, HS and DG approaches. These approaches have the advantage of being straightforward to compute even for large portfolios. The 2007–2009 financial crisis and subsequent discussions of the role of VaR have highlighted many of the weaknesses of the DN and HS approaches (e.g. the assumption of conditional normality in the DN approach, the sensitivity of the HS approach to the sample size used). As a consequence, one might expect that in the future, banks will begin to move away from these traditionally popular approaches towards more flexible approaches to computing VaR, such as the Monte Carlo simulation approaches discussed here. Furthermore, the 2007–2009 financial crisis has stimulated new research in this area. Hence further improvements to the existing techniques discussed here will undoubtedly be proposed in the near future and new market risk management techniques will emerge.

9.11 End of Chapter Questions[35]

Q1. Download daily data on the price of one stock for 31/12/03–31/12/08.[36]
    (a) Using this data, compute the one-day VaR at the 99% confidence level over the period 02/01/08–31/12/08 employing the DN approach with an MA conditional volatility forecast.
    (b) Repeat part (a) using an MA conditional volatility forecast computed employing a smaller rolling window of data and compare with your results from part (a).

---

[35]A guide to answering these questions and relevant MATLAB® programs are given on the companion website (www.wileyeurope.com/college/sollis).
[36]Yahoo! Finance is one possible source of these data (www.finance.yahoo.com).

Q2. **(a)** Using the data for Question 1, compute the 10-day VaR at the 99% confidence level over the period 02/01/08–31/12/08 employing the DN approach with an EWMA conditional volatility forecast with $\lambda = 0.94$.

(b) Repeat part (a) using a GARCH(1,1) conditional volatility forecast and comment on any differences or similarities.

Q3. Download daily data on the price of three stocks over the period 31/12/03–31/12/08.[37]

(a) Using this data, compute the one-day VaR at the 99% confidence level over the period 03/01/06–31/12/08 for an equally weighted portfolio of the three stocks employing the DN approach with an EWMA conditional volatility forecast with $\lambda = 0.94$.

(b) Repeat part (a) using the DN approach employing an EWMA conditional volatility forecast with $\lambda = 0.97$. Compare with your results for part (a).

Q4. Download daily data on the level of the FTSE 100 stock market index for 31/12/03–01/11/07. Assume that on 01/11/07 a UK investor buys a single call option on the FTSE 100 index which expires on 21 December with a strike price in index points of 6500. Assume that no dividends are paid and that the annual risk-free rate is 3%. Compute the one-day VaR at the 99% confidence level using the DG approach employing an EWMA conditional volatility forecast for the underlying stock index returns.

Q5. **(a)** Using the data for Question 3, backtest the VaR model by computing the proportion of VaR exceptions $\hat{p}_x$ and the LR_x, LR_{ix} and LR_{cc} tests. Graph the indicator of VaR exceptions over this period and comment on any clusters of exceptions that occur.

(b) ''The banking sector's over-reliance on VaR was to blame for the 2007–2009 global financial crisis.'' Critically discuss this statement.

9.12 Appendix

9.12.1 Data

Example 9.1

xom.xls

Daily data on the price of Exxon Mobil Corporation (XOM) stock for 31/12/97–31/12/08 from Yahoo! Finance (www.finance.yahoo.com).

---

[37]Yahoo! Finance is one possible source of these data (www.finance.yahoo.com).

Example 9.2

C9stocks.xls

Daily data on the price of Exxon Mobil Corporation (XOM), General Electric Company (GE), and Microsoft Corporation (MSFT) stock for 31/12/97 – 31/12/08 from Yahoo! Finance (www.finance.yahoo.com).

Example 9.3

C9stocks.xls

See above.

Example 9.4

C9stocks.xls

See above.

Example 9.5

xom.xls

See above.

Example 9.6

xom.xls

See above.

Example 9.7

C9stocks.xls

See above.

9.12.2 MATLAB® Programs and Toolboxes[38]

Example 9.1

(a) E91a.m

---

[38]See www.wileyeurope.com/college/sollis for the programs E##.m.

(b) E91b.m

(c) E91c.m, Oxford MFE Toolbox

Example 9.2

E92.m

Example 9.3

E93.m

Example 9.4

E94.m

Example 9.5

E95.m, MATLAB® Financial Toolbox

Example 9.6

E96.m, MATLAB® Financial Toolbox

Example 9.7

(a) E97a.m

(b) E97b.m

9.13 References

Acerbi, C. and D. Tasche (2002) On the coherence of expected shortfall, *Journal of Banking and Finance*, 26, 1487–1503.

Altman, E.I. and A. Saunders (2001) An analysis and critique of the BIS proposal on capital adequacy and ratings, *Journal of Banking and Finance*, 25, 25–46.

Artzner, P., Delbaen, F., Eber, J.-M. and D. Heath (1997) Thinking coherently, *RISK*, 10, 68–71.

Artzner, P., Delbaen, F., Eber, J.-M. and D. Heath (1999) Coherent measures of risk, *Mathematical Finance*, 9, 203–228.

Basel Committee on Banking Supervision (BCBS) (1988) *International Convergence of Capital Measurement and Capital Standards*. Basel: Bank for International Settlements.

Basel Committee on Banking Supervision (BCBS) (2006) *International Convergence of Capital Measurement and Capital Standards: A Revised Framework, Comprehensive Version*. Basel: Bank for International Settlements.

Basel Committee on Banking Supervision (2010a) A new regulatory landscape. Remarks of Nout Wellink at the 16th International Conference of Banking Supervisors, Singapore, 22 September, 2010.

Basel Committee on Banking Supervision (2010b) Basel III: towards a safer financial system. Speech by Jaime Caruana at the 3rd Santander International Banking Conference, Madrid, 15 September, 2010.

Basel Committee on Banking Supervision (2010c) *The Basel Committee's Response to the Financial Crisis: Report to the G20*. Basel: Bank for International Settlements.

Black, F. and M. Scholes (1973) The pricing of options and corporate liabilities, *Journal of Political Economy*, 81, 637–654.

Christoffersen, P.F. (1998) Evaluating interval forecasts, *International Economic Review*, 39, 841–862.

Christoffersen, P.F. (2003) *Elements of Financial Risk Management*. San Diego, CA: Academic Press.

Cornish, E.A. and R.A. Fisher (1937) Moments and cumulants in the specification of distributions, *Review of the International Statistical Institute*, 5, 307–320.

Danielsson, J., Jorgensen, B.N., Samorodnitsky, G., Sarm, M. and C.G. de Vries (2005) Sub-additivity re-examined: the case for Value at Risk, EURANDOM Report 2005-006.

Hull, J. (2005) *Options, Futures and Other Derivatives*, 6th edn. New York: Prentice Hall.

Jorion, P. (2006) *Value at Risk: The New Benchmark for Managing Financial Risk*, 3rd edn. New York: McGraw-Hill.

Kupiec, P.H. (1995) Techniques for verifying the accuracy of risk measurement models, *The Journal of Derivatives*, 3, 73–84.

Perignon, C. and D.R. Smith (2010) The level and quality of Value-at-Risk disclosure by commercial banks, *Journal of Banking and Finance*, 34, 362–377.

Pritsker, M. (1997) Evaluating value at risk methodologies: accuracy versus computational time, *Journal of Financial Services Research*, 12, 201–241.

RiskMetrics: Technical Document (1996) New York: JP Morgan/Reuters.

RiskMetrics, Return to: The Evolution of a Standard (2001) New York: RiskMetrics Group.

RiskMetrics 2006 Methodology (2006) New York: RiskMetrics Group.

Rodriguez, L.J. (2003) Banking stability and the Basel capital standards, *Cato Journal*, 23, 115–126.

Tasche, D. (2002) Expected shortfall and beyond, *Journal of Banking and Finance*, 26, 1519–1533.

Turner, A. (2009) *The Turner Review: A Regulatory Response to the Global Banking Crisis*. London: Financial Services Authority.

Yamai, Y. and T. Yoshiba (2005) Value-at-risk versus expected shortfall: a practical perspective, *Journal of Banking and Finance*, 29, 997–1015.

Appendix
Statistical Tables

Table A.1 Areas under the standard normal distribution

An entry in the table is the proportion under the entire
curve that is between z = 0 and a positive value
of z. Areas for negative values of z are obtained by symmetry.

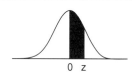

z	.00	.01	.02	.03	.04	.05	.06	.07	.08	.09
0.0	.0000	.0040	.0080	.0120	.0160	.0199	.0239	.0279	.0319	.0359
0.1	.0398	.0438	.0478	.0517	.0557	.0596	.0636	.0675	.0714	.0753
0.2	.0793	.0832	.0871	.0910	.0948	.0987	.1026	.1064	.1103	.1141
0.3	.1179	.1217	.1255	.1293	.1331	.1368	.1406	.1443	.1480	.1517
0.4	.1554	.1591	.1628	.1664	.1700	.1736	.1772	.1808	.1844	.1879
0.5	.1915	.1950	.1985	.2019	.2054	.2088	.2123	.2157	.2190	.2224
0.6	.2257	.2291	.2324	.2357	.2389	.2422	.2454	.2486	.2517	.2549
0.7	.2580	.2611	.2642	.2673	.2703	.2734	.2764	.2794	.2823	.2852
0.8	.2881	.2910	.2939	.2967	.2995	.3023	.3051	.3078	.3106	.3133
0.9	.3159	.3186	.3212	.3238	.3264	.3289	.3315	.3340	.3365	.3389
1.0	.3413	.3438	.3461	.3485	.3508	.3531	.3554	.3577	.3599	.3621
1.1	.3643	.3665	.3686	.3708	.3729	.3749	.3770	.3790	.3810	.3830
1.2	.3849	.3869	.3888	.3907	.3925	.3944	.3962	.3980	.3997	.4015
1.3	.4032	.4049	.4066	.4082	.4099	.4115	.4131	.4147	.4162	.4177
1.4	.4192	.4207	.4222	.4236	.4251	.4265	.4279	.4292	.4306	.4319
1.5	.4332	.4345	.4357	.4370	.4382	.4394	.4406	.4418	.4429	.4441
1.6	.4452	.4463	.4474	.4484	.4495	.4505	.4515	.4525	.4535	.4545
1.7	.4554	.4564	.4573	.4582	.4591	.4599	.4608	.4616	.4625	.4633
1.8	.4641	.4649	.4656	.4664	.4671	.4678	.4686	.4693	.4699	.4706
1.9	.4713	.4719	.4726	.4732	.4738	.4744	.4750	.4756	.4761	.4767
2.0	.4772	.4778	.4783	.4788	.4793	.4798	.4803	.4808	.4812	.4817
2.1	.4821	.4826	.4830	.4834	.4838	.4842	.4846	.4850	.4854	.4857
2.2	.4861	.4864	.4868	.4871	.4875	.4878	.4881	.4884	.4887	.4890
2.3	.4893	.4896	.4898	.4901	.4904	.4906	.4909	.4911	.4913	.4916
2.4	.4918	.4920	.4922	.4925	.4927	.4929	.4931	.4932	.4934	.4936
2.5	.4938	.4940	.4941	.4943	.4945	.4946	.4948	.4949	.4951	.4952
2.6	.4953	.4955	.4956	.4957	.4959	.4960	.4961	.4962	.4963	.4964
2.7	.4965	.4966	.4967	.4968	.4969	.4970	.4971	.4972	.4973	.4974
2.8	.4974	.4975	.4976	.4977	.4977	.4978	.4979	.4979	.4980	.4981
2.9	.4981	.4982	.4982	.4983	.4984	.4984	.4985	.4985	.4986	.4986
3.0	.4987	.4987	.4987	.4988	.4988	.4989	.4989	.4989	.4990	.4990

Source: Pearson, E.S. and H.O. Hartley (eds) (1966) *Biometrika Tables for Statisticans*, vol. I. New York: Cambridge University Press.

Table A.2   Critical values for Student's *t*-distribution

The first column lists the number of degrees of freedom (v). The headings of the other columns give probabilities (P) for t to exceed the entry value. Use symmetry for negative t values.

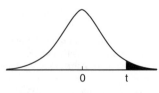

v \ P	.10	.05	.025	.01	.005
1	3.078	6.314	12.706	31.821	63.657
2	1.886	2.920	4.303	6.965	9.925
3	1.638	2.353	3.182	4.541	5.841
4	1.533	2.132	2.776	3.747	4.604
5	1.476	2.015	2.571	3.365	4.032
6	1.440	1.943	2.447	3.143	3.707
7	1.415	1.895	2.365	2.998	3.499
8	1.397	1.860	2.306	2.896	3.355
9	1.383	1.833	2.262	2.821	3.250
10	1.372	1.812	2.228	2.764	3.169
11	1.363	1.796	2.201	2.718	3.106
12	1.356	1.782	2.179	2.681	3.055
13	1.350	1.771	2.160	2.650	3.012
14	1.345	1.761	2.145	2.624	2.977
15	1.341	1.753	2.131	2.602	2.947
16	1.337	1.746	2.120	2.583	2.921
17	1.333	1.740	2.110	2.567	2.898
18	1.330	1.734	2.101	2.552	2.878
19	1.328	1.729	2.093	2.539	2.861
20	1.325	1.725	2.086	2.528	2.845
21	1.323	1.721	2.080	2.518	2.831
22	1.321	1.717	2.074	2.508	2.819
23	1.319	1.714	2.069	2.500	2.807
24	1.318	1.711	2.064	2.492	2.797
25	1.316	1.708	2.060	2.485	2.787
26	1.315	1.706	2.056	2.479	2.779
27	1.314	1.703	2.052	2.473	2.771
28	1.313	1.701	2.048	2.467	2.763
29	1.311	1.699	2.045	2.462	2.756
30	1.310	1.697	2.042	2.457	2.750
40	1.303	1.684	2.021	2.423	2.704
60	1.296	1.671	2.000	2.390	2.660
120	1.289	1.658	1.980	2.358	2.617
∞	1.282	1.645	1.960	2.326	2.576

Source: Pearson, E.S. and H.O. Hartley (eds) (1966) *Biometrika Tables for Statisticans*, vol. I. New York: Cambridge University Press.

Table A.3 Critical values for the F-distribution: upper 10% points

ν_2 \ ν_1	1	2	3	4	5	6	7	8	9	10	12	15	20	24	30	40	60	120	∞
1	39.86	49.50	53.59	55.83	57.24	58.20	58.91	59.44	59.86	60.19	60.71	61.22	61.74	62.00	62.26	62.53	62.79	63.06	63.33
2	8.53	9.00	9.16	9.24	9.29	9.33	9.35	9.37	9.38	9.39	9.41	9.42	9.44	9.45	9.46	9.47	9.47	9.48	9.49
3	5.54	5.46	5.39	5.34	5.31	5.28	5.27	5.25	5.24	5.23	5.22	5.20	5.18	5.18	5.17	5.16	5.15	5.14	5.13
4	4.54	4.32	4.19	4.11	4.05	4.01	3.98	3.95	3.94	3.92	3.90	3.87	3.84	3.83	3.82	3.80	3.79	3.78	3.76
5	4.06	3.78	3.62	3.52	3.45	3.40	3.37	3.34	3.32	3.30	3.27	3.24	3.21	3.19	3.17	3.16	3.14	3.12	3.10
6	3.78	3.46	3.29	3.18	3.11	3.05	3.01	2.98	2.96	2.94	2.90	2.87	2.84	2.82	2.80	2.78	2.76	2.74	2.72
7	3.59	3.26	3.07	2.96	2.88	2.83	2.78	2.75	2.72	2.70	2.67	2.63	2.59	2.58	2.56	2.54	2.51	2.49	2.47
8	3.46	3.11	2.92	2.81	2.73	2.67	2.62	2.59	2.56	2.54	2.50	2.46	2.42	2.40	2.38	2.36	2.34	2.32	2.29
9	3.36	3.01	2.81	2.69	2.61	2.55	2.51	2.47	2.44	2.42	2.38	2.34	2.30	2.28	2.25	2.23	2.21	2.18	2.16
10	3.29	2.92	2.73	2.61	2.52	2.46	2.41	2.38	2.35	2.32	2.28	2.24	2.20	2.18	2.16	2.13	2.11	2.08	2.06
11	3.23	2.86	2.66	2.54	2.45	2.39	2.34	2.30	2.27	2.25	2.21	2.17	2.12	2.10	2.08	2.05	2.03	2.00	1.97
12	3.18	2.81	2.61	2.48	2.39	2.33	2.28	2.24	2.21	2.19	2.15	2.10	2.06	2.04	2.01	1.99	1.96	1.93	1.90
13	3.14	2.76	2.56	2.43	2.35	2.28	2.23	2.20	2.16	2.14	2.10	2.05	2.01	1.98	1.96	1.93	1.90	1.88	1.85
14	3.10	2.73	2.52	2.39	2.31	2.24	2.19	2.15	2.12	2.10	2.05	2.01	1.96	1.94	1.91	1.89	1.86	1.83	1.80
15	3.07	2.70	2.49	2.36	2.27	2.21	2.16	2.12	2.09	2.06	2.02	1.97	1.92	1.90	1.87	1.85	1.82	1.79	1.76
16	3.05	2.67	2.46	2.33	2.24	2.18	2.13	2.09	2.06	2.03	1.99	1.94	1.89	1.87	1.84	1.81	1.78	1.75	1.72
17	3.03	2.64	2.44	2.31	2.22	2.15	2.10	2.06	2.03	2.00	1.96	1.91	1.86	1.84	1.81	1.78	1.75	1.72	1.69
18	3.01	2.62	2.42	2.29	2.20	2.13	2.08	2.04	2.00	1.98	1.93	1.89	1.84	1.81	1.78	1.75	1.72	1.69	1.66
19	2.99	2.61	2.40	2.27	2.18	2.11	2.06	2.02	1.98	1.96	1.91	1.86	1.81	1.79	1.76	1.73	1.70	1.67	1.63
20	2.97	2.59	2.38	2.25	2.16	2.09	2.04	2.00	1.96	1.94	1.89	1.84	1.79	1.77	1.74	1.71	1.68	1.64	1.61
21	2.96	2.57	2.36	2.23	2.14	2.08	2.02	1.98	1.95	1.92	1.87	1.83	1.78	1.75	1.72	1.69	1.66	1.62	1.59
22	2.95	2.56	2.35	2.22	2.13	2.06	2.01	1.97	1.93	1.90	1.86	1.81	1.76	1.73	1.70	1.67	1.64	1.60	1.57
23	2.94	2.55	2.34	2.21	2.11	2.05	1.99	1.95	1.92	1.89	1.84	1.80	1.74	1.72	1.69	1.66	1.62	1.59	1.55
24	2.93	2.54	2.33	2.19	2.10	2.04	1.98	1.94	1.91	1.88	1.83	1.78	1.73	1.70	1.67	1.64	1.61	1.57	1.53
25	2.92	2.53	2.32	2.18	2.09	2.02	1.97	1.93	1.89	1.87	1.82	1.77	1.72	1.69	1.66	1.63	1.59	1.56	1.52
26	2.91	2.52	2.31	2.17	2.08	2.01	1.96	1.92	1.88	1.86	1.81	1.76	1.71	1.68	1.65	1.61	1.58	1.54	1.50
27	2.90	2.51	2.30	2.17	2.07	2.00	1.95	1.91	1.87	1.85	1.80	1.75	1.70	1.67	1.64	1.60	1.57	1.53	1.49
28	2.89	2.50	2.29	2.16	2.06	2.00	1.94	1.90	1.87	1.84	1.79	1.74	1.69	1.66	1.63	1.59	1.56	1.52	1.48
29	2.89	2.50	2.28	2.15	2.06	1.99	1.93	1.89	1.86	1.83	1.78	1.73	1.68	1.65	1.62	1.58	1.55	1.51	1.47
30	2.88	2.49	2.28	2.14	2.05	1.98	1.93	1.88	1.85	1.82	1.77	1.72	1.67	1.64	1.61	1.57	1.54	1.50	1.46
40	2.84	2.44	2.23	2.09	2.00	1.93	1.87	1.83	1.79	1.76	1.71	1.66	1.61	1.57	1.54	1.51	1.47	1.42	1.38
60	2.79	2.39	2.18	2.04	1.95	1.87	1.82	1.77	1.74	1.71	1.66	1.60	1.54	1.51	1.48	1.44	1.40	1.35	1.29
120	2.75	2.35	2.13	1.99	1.90	1.82	1.77	1.72	1.68	1.65	1.60	1.55	1.48	1.45	1.41	1.37	1.32	1.26	1.19
∞	2.71	2.30	2.08	1.94	1.85	1.77	1.72	1.67	1.63	1.60	1.55	1.49	1.42	1.38	1.34	1.30	1.24	1.17	1.00

Table A.3　Contd: upper 5% points

v_2 \ v_1	1	2	3	4	5	6	7	8	9	10	12	15	20	24	30	40	60	120	∞
1	161.4	199.5	215.7	224.6	230.2	234.0	236.8	238.9	240.5	241.9	243.9	245.9	248.0	249.1	250.1	251.1	252.2	253.3	254.3
2	18.51	19.00	19.16	19.25	19.30	19.33	19.35	19.37	19.38	19.40	19.41	19.43	19.45	19.45	19.46	19.47	19.48	19.49	19.50
3	10.13	9.55	9.28	9.12	9.01	8.94	8.89	8.85	8.81	8.79	8.74	8.70	8.66	8.64	8.62	8.59	8.57	8.55	8.53
4	7.71	6.94	6.59	6.39	6.26	6.16	6.09	6.04	6.00	5.96	5.91	5.86	5.80	5.77	5.75	5.72	5.69	5.66	5.63
5	6.61	5.79	5.41	5.19	5.05	4.95	4.88	4.82	4.77	4.74	4.68	4.62	4.56	4.53	4.50	4.46	4.43	4.40	4.36
6	5.99	5.14	4.76	4.53	4.39	4.28	4.21	4.15	4.10	4.06	4.00	3.94	3.87	3.84	3.81	3.77	3.74	3.70	3.67
7	5.59	4.74	4.35	4.12	3.97	3.87	3.79	3.73	3.68	3.64	3.57	3.51	3.44	3.41	3.38	3.34	3.30	3.27	3.23
8	5.32	4.46	4.07	3.84	3.69	3.58	3.50	3.44	3.39	3.35	3.28	3.22	3.15	3.12	3.08	3.04	3.01	2.97	2.93
9	5.12	4.26	3.86	3.63	3.48	3.37	3.29	3.23	3.18	3.14	3.07	3.01	2.94	2.90	2.86	2.83	2.79	2.75	2.71
10	4.96	4.10	3.71	3.48	3.33	3.22	3.14	3.07	3.02	2.98	2.91	2.85	2.77	2.74	2.70	2.66	2.62	2.58	2.54
11	4.84	3.98	3.59	3.36	3.20	3.09	3.01	2.95	2.90	2.85	2.79	2.72	2.65	2.61	2.57	2.53	2.49	2.45	2.40
12	4.75	3.89	3.49	3.26	3.11	3.00	2.91	2.85	2.80	2.75	2.69	2.62	2.54	2.51	2.47	2.43	2.38	2.34	2.30
13	4.67	3.81	3.41	3.18	3.03	2.92	2.83	2.77	2.71	2.67	2.60	2.53	2.46	2.42	2.38	2.34	2.30	2.25	2.21
14	4.60	3.74	3.34	3.11	2.96	2.85	2.76	2.70	2.65	2.60	2.53	2.46	2.39	2.35	2.31	2.27	2.22	2.18	2.13
15	4.54	3.68	3.29	3.06	2.90	2.79	2.71	2.64	2.59	2.54	2.48	2.40	2.33	2.29	2.25	2.20	2.16	2.11	2.07
16	4.49	3.63	3.24	3.01	2.85	2.74	2.66	2.59	2.54	2.49	2.42	2.35	2.28	2.24	2.19	2.15	2.11	2.06	2.01
17	4.45	3.59	3.20	2.96	2.81	2.70	2.61	2.55	2.49	2.45	2.38	2.31	2.23	2.19	2.15	2.10	2.06	2.01	1.96
18	4.41	3.55	3.16	2.93	2.77	2.66	2.58	2.51	2.46	2.41	2.34	2.27	2.19	2.15	2.11	2.06	2.02	1.97	1.92
19	4.38	3.52	3.13	2.90	2.74	2.63	2.54	2.48	2.42	2.38	2.31	2.23	2.16	2.11	2.07	2.03	1.98	1.93	1.88
20	4.35	3.49	3.10	2.87	2.71	2.60	2.51	2.45	2.39	2.35	2.28	2.20	2.12	2.08	2.04	1.99	1.95	1.90	1.84
21	4.32	3.47	3.07	2.84	2.68	2.57	2.49	2.42	2.37	2.32	2.25	2.18	2.10	2.05	2.01	1.96	1.92	1.87	1.81
22	4.30	3.44	3.05	2.82	2.66	2.55	2.46	2.40	2.34	2.30	2.23	2.15	2.07	2.03	1.98	1.94	1.89	1.84	1.78
23	4.28	3.42	3.03	2.80	2.64	2.53	2.44	2.37	2.32	2.27	2.20	2.13	2.05	2.01	1.96	1.91	1.86	1.81	1.76
24	4.26	3.40	3.01	2.78	2.62	2.51	2.42	2.36	2.30	2.25	2.18	2.11	2.03	1.98	1.94	1.89	1.84	1.79	1.73
25	4.24	3.39	2.99	2.76	2.60	2.49	2.40	2.34	2.28	2.24	2.16	2.09	2.01	1.96	1.92	1.87	1.82	1.77	1.71
26	4.23	3.37	2.98	2.74	2.59	2.47	2.39	2.32	2.27	2.22	2.15	2.07	1.99	1.95	1.90	1.85	1.80	1.75	1.69
27	4.21	3.35	2.96	2.73	2.57	2.46	2.37	2.31	2.25	2.20	2.13	2.06	1.97	1.93	1.88	1.84	1.79	1.73	1.67
28	4.20	3.34	2.95	2.71	2.56	2.45	2.36	2.29	2.24	2.19	2.12	2.04	1.96	1.91	1.87	1.82	1.77	1.71	1.65
29	4.18	3.33	2.93	2.70	2.55	2.43	2.35	2.28	2.22	2.18	2.10	2.03	1.94	1.90	1.85	1.81	1.75	1.70	1.64
30	4.17	3.32	2.92	2.69	2.53	2.42	2.33	2.27	2.21	2.16	2.09	2.01	1.93	1.89	1.84	1.79	1.74	1.68	1.62
40	4.08	3.23	2.84	2.61	2.45	2.34	2.25	2.18	2.12	2.08	2.00	1.92	1.84	1.79	1.74	1.69	1.64	1.58	1.51
60	4.00	3.15	2.76	2.53	2.37	2.25	2.17	2.10	2.04	1.99	1.92	1.84	1.75	1.70	1.65	1.59	1.53	1.47	1.39
120	3.92	3.07	2.68	2.45	2.29	2.17	2.09	2.02	1.96	1.91	1.83	1.75	1.66	1.61	1.55	1.50	1.43	1.35	1.25
∞	3.84	3.00	2.60	2.37	2.21	2.10	2.01	1.94	1.88	1.83	1.75	1.67	1.57	1.52	1.46	1.39	1.32	1.22	1.00

Table A.3 Contd: upper 1% points

ν_2 \ ν_1	1	2	3	4	5	6	7	8	9	10	12	15	20	24	30	40	60	120	∞
1	4052	4999.5	5403	5625	5764	5859	5928	5981	6022	6056	6106	6157	6209	6235	6261	6287	6313	6339	6366
2	98.50	99.00	99.17	99.25	99.30	99.33	99.36	99.37	99.39	99.40	99.42	99.43	99.45	99.46	99.47	99.47	99.48	99.49	99.50
3	34.12	30.82	29.46	28.71	28.24	27.91	27.67	27.49	27.35	27.23	27.05	26.87	26.69	26.60	26.50	26.41	26.32	26.22	26.13
4	21.20	18.00	16.69	15.98	15.52	15.21	14.98	14.80	14.66	14.55	14.37	14.20	14.02	13.93	13.84	13.75	13.65	13.56	13.46
5	16.26	13.27	12.06	11.39	10.97	10.67	10.46	10.29	10.16	10.05	9.89	9.72	9.55	9.47	9.38	9.29	9.20	9.11	9.02
6	13.75	10.92	9.78	9.15	8.75	8.47	8.26	8.10	7.98	7.87	7.72	7.56	7.40	7.31	7.23	7.14	7.06	6.97	6.88
7	12.25	9.55	8.45	7.85	7.46	7.19	6.99	6.84	6.72	6.62	6.47	6.31	6.16	6.07	5.99	5.91	5.82	5.74	5.65
8	11.26	8.65	7.59	7.01	6.63	6.37	6.18	6.03	5.91	5.81	5.67	5.52	5.36	5.28	5.20	5.12	5.03	4.95	4.86
9	10.56	8.02	6.99	6.42	6.06	5.80	5.61	5.47	5.35	5.26	5.11	4.96	4.81	4.73	4.65	4.57	4.48	4.40	4.31
10	10.04	7.56	6.55	5.99	5.64	5.39	5.20	5.06	4.94	4.85	4.71	4.56	4.41	4.33	4.25	4.17	4.08	4.00	3.91
11	9.65	7.21	6.22	5.67	5.32	5.07	4.89	4.74	4.63	4.54	4.40	4.25	4.10	4.02	3.94	3.86	3.78	3.69	3.60
12	9.33	6.93	5.95	5.41	5.06	4.82	4.64	4.50	4.39	4.30	4.16	4.01	3.86	3.78	3.70	3.62	3.54	3.45	3.36
13	9.07	6.70	5.74	5.21	4.86	4.62	4.44	4.30	4.19	4.10	3.96	3.82	3.66	3.59	3.51	3.43	3.34	3.25	3.17
14	8.86	6.51	5.56	5.04	4.69	4.46	4.28	4.14	4.03	3.94	3.80	3.66	3.51	3.43	3.35	3.27	3.18	3.09	3.00
15	8.68	6.36	5.42	4.89	4.56	4.32	4.14	4.00	3.89	3.80	3.67	3.52	3.37	3.29	3.21	3.13	3.05	2.96	2.87
16	8.53	6.23	5.29	4.77	4.44	4.20	4.03	3.89	3.78	3.69	3.55	3.41	3.26	3.18	3.10	3.02	2.93	2.84	2.75
17	8.40	6.11	5.18	4.67	4.34	4.10	3.93	3.79	3.68	3.59	3.46	3.31	3.16	3.08	3.00	2.92	2.83	2.75	2.65
18	8.29	6.01	5.09	4.58	4.25	4.01	3.84	3.71	3.60	3.51	3.37	3.23	3.08	3.00	2.92	2.84	2.75	2.66	2.57
19	8.18	5.93	5.01	4.50	4.17	3.94	3.77	3.63	3.52	3.43	3.30	3.15	3.00	2.92	2.84	2.76	2.67	2.58	2.49
20	8.10	5.85	4.94	4.43	4.10	3.87	3.70	3.56	3.46	3.37	3.23	3.09	2.94	2.86	2.78	2.69	2.61	2.52	2.42
21	8.02	5.78	4.87	4.37	4.04	3.81	3.64	3.51	3.40	3.31	3.17	3.03	2.88	2.80	2.72	2.64	2.55	2.46	2.36
22	7.95	5.72	4.82	4.31	3.99	3.76	3.59	3.45	3.35	3.26	3.12	2.98	2.83	2.75	2.67	2.58	2.50	2.40	2.31
23	7.88	5.66	4.76	4.26	3.94	3.71	3.54	3.41	3.30	3.21	3.07	2.93	2.78	2.70	2.62	2.54	2.45	2.35	2.26
24	7.82	5.61	4.72	4.22	3.90	3.67	3.50	3.36	3.26	3.17	3.03	2.89	2.74	2.66	2.58	2.49	2.40	2.31	2.21
25	7.77	5.57	4.68	4.18	3.85	3.63	3.46	3.32	3.22	3.13	2.99	2.85	2.70	2.62	2.54	2.45	2.36	2.27	2.17
26	7.72	5.53	4.64	4.14	3.82	3.59	3.42	3.29	3.18	3.09	2.96	2.81	2.66	2.58	2.50	2.42	2.33	2.23	2.13
27	7.68	5.49	4.60	4.11	3.78	3.56	3.39	3.26	3.15	3.06	2.93	2.78	2.63	2.55	2.47	2.38	2.29	2.20	2.10
28	7.64	5.45	4.57	4.07	3.75	3.53	3.36	3.23	3.12	3.03	2.90	2.75	2.60	2.52	2.44	2.35	2.26	2.17	2.06
29	7.60	5.42	4.54	4.04	3.73	3.50	3.33	3.20	3.09	3.00	2.87	2.73	2.57	2.49	2.41	2.33	2.23	2.14	2.03
30	7.56	5.39	4.51	4.02	3.70	3.47	3.30	3.17	3.07	2.98	2.84	2.70	2.55	2.47	2.39	2.30	2.21	2.11	2.01
40	7.31	5.18	4.31	3.83	3.51	3.29	3.12	2.99	2.89	2.80	2.66	2.52	2.37	2.29	2.20	2.11	2.02	1.92	1.80
60	7.08	4.98	4.13	3.65	3.34	3.12	2.95	2.82	2.72	2.63	2.50	2.35	2.20	2.12	2.03	1.94	1.84	1.73	1.60
120	6.85	4.79	3.95	3.48	3.17	2.96	2.79	2.66	2.56	2.47	2.34	2.19	2.03	1.95	1.86	1.76	1.66	1.53	1.38
∞	6.63	4.61	3.78	3.32	3.02	2.80	2.64	2.51	2.41	2.32	2.18	2.04	1.88	1.79	1.70	1.59	1.47	1.32	1.00

Source: Pearson, E.S. and H.O. Hartley (eds) (1966) Biometrika Tables for Statisticans, vol. I. New York: Cambridge University Press.

Table A.4   Critical values for the chi-square distribution

P \ v	0.995	0.990	0.975	0.950	0.900	0.750	0.500
1	392704.10^{-10}	157088.10^{-9}	982069.10^{-9}	393214.10^{-8}	0.0157908	0.1015308	0.454936
2	0.0100251	0.0201007	0.0506356	0.102587	0.210721	0.575364	1.38629
3	0.0717218	0.114832	0.215795	0.351846	0.584374	1.212534	2.36597
4	0.206989	0.297109	0.484419	0.710723	1.063623	1.92256	3.35569
5	0.411742	0.554298	0.831212	1.145476	1.61031	2.67460	4.35146
6	0.675727	0.872090	1.23734	1.63538	2.20413	3.45460	5.34812
7	0.989256	1.239043	1.68987	2.16735	2.83311	4.25485	6.34581
8	1.34441	1.64650	2.17973	2.73264	3.48954	5.07064	7.34412
9	1.73493	2.08790	2.70039	3.32511	4.16816	5.89883	8.34283
10	2.15586	2.55821	3.24697	3.94030	4.86518	6.73720	9.34182
11	2.60322	3.05348	3.81575	4.57481	5.57778	7.58414	10.3410
12	3.07382	3.57057	4.40379	5.22603	6.30380	8.43842	11.3403
13	3.56503	4.10692	5.00875	5.89186	7.04150	9.29907	12.3398
14	4.07467	4.66043	5.62873	6.57063	7.78953	10.1653	13.3393
15	4.60092	5.22935	6.26214	7.26094	8.54676	11.0365	14.3389
16	5.14221	5.81221	6.90766	7.96165	9.31224	11.9122	15.3385
17	5.69722	6.40776	7.56419	8.67176	10.0852	12.7919	16.3382
18	6.26480	7.01491	8.23075	9.39046	10.8649	13.6753	17.3379
19	6.84397	7.63273	8.90652	10.1170	11.6509	14.5620	18.3377
20	7.43384	8.26040	9.59078	10.8508	12.4426	15.4518	19.3374
21	8.03365	8.89720	10.28293	11.5913	13.2369	16.3444	20.3372
22	8.64272	9.54249	10.9823	12.3380	14.0415	17.2396	21.3370
23	9.26043	10.19567	11.6886	13.0905	14.8480	18.1373	22.3369
24	9.88623	10.8564	12.4012	13.8484	15.6587	19.0373	23.3367
25	10.5197	11.5240	13.1197	14.6114	16.4734	19.9393	24.3386
26	11.1602	12.1981	13.8439	15.3792	17.2919	20.8434	25.3365
27	11.8076	12.8785	14.5734	16.1514	18.1139	21.7494	26.3363
28	12.4613	13.5647	15.3079	16.9279	18.9392	22.6572	27.3362
29	13.1211	14.2565	16.0471	17.7084	19.7677	23.5666	28.3361
30	13.7867	14.9535	16.7908	18.4927	20.5992	24.4776	29.3360
40	20.7065	22.1643	24.4330	26.5093	29.0505	33.6603	39.3353
50	27.9907	29.7067	32.3574	34.7643	37.6886	42.9421	49.3349
60	35.5345	37.4849	40.4817	43.1880	46.4589	52.2938	59.3347
70	43.2752	45.4417	48.7576	51.7393	55.3289	61.6983	69.3345
80	51.1719	53.5401	57.1532	60.3915	64.2778	71.1445	79.3343
90	59.1963	61.7541	65.6466	69.1260	73.2911	80.6247	89.3342
100	67.3276	70.0649	74.2219	77.9295	82.3581	90.1332	99.3341

Source: Pearson, E.S. and H.O. Hartley (eds) (1966) *Biometrika Tables for Statisticans*, vol. I. New York: Cambridge University Press.

Table A.4 *Contd.*

ν \ P	0.250	0.100	0.050	0.025	0.010	0.005	0.001
1	1.32330	2.70554	3.84146	5.02389	6.63490	7.87944	10.828
2	2.77259	4.60517	5.99146	7.37776	9.21034	10.5966	13.816
3	4.10834	6.25139	7.81473	9.34840	11.3449	12.8382	16.266
4	5.38527	7.77944	9.48773	11.1433	13.2767	14.8603	18.467
5	6.62568	9.23636	11.0705	12.8325	15.0863	16.7496	20.515
6	7.84080	10.6446	12.5916	14.4494	16.8119	18.5476	22.458
7	9.03715	12.0170	14.0671	16.0128	18.4753	20.2777	24.322
8	10.2189	13.3616	15.5073	17.5345	20.0902	21.9550	26.125
9	11.3888	14.6837	16.9190	19.0228	21.6660	23.5894	27.877
10	12.5489	15.9827	18.3070	20.4832	23.2093	25.1882	29.588
11	13.7007	17.2750	19.6751	21.9200	24.7250	26.7568	31.264
12	14.8454	18.5493	21.0261	23.3367	26.2170	28.2995	32.909
13	15.9839	19.8119	22.3620	24.7356	27.6882	29.8195	34.528
14	17.1169	21.0641	23.6848	26.1189	29.1412	31.3194	36.123
15	18.2451	22.3071	24.9958	27.4884	30.5779	32.8013	37.697
16	19.3689	23.5418	26.2962	28.8454	31.9999	34.2672	39.252
17	20.4887	24.7690	27.5871	30.1910	33.4087	35.7185	40.790
18	21.6049	25.9894	28.8693	31.5264	34.8053	37.1565	42.312
19	22.7178	27.2036	30.1435	32.8523	36.1909	38.5823	43.820
20	23.8277	28.4120	31.4104	34.1696	37.5662	39.9968	45.315
21	24.9348	29.6151	32.6706	35.4789	38.9322	41.4011	46.797
22	26.0393	30.8133	33.9422	36.7807	40.2894	42.7957	48.268
23	27.1413	32.0069	35.1725	38.0756	41.6384	44.1813	49.728
24	28.2412	33.1962	36.4150	39.3641	42.9798	45.5585	61.179
25	29.3389	34.3816	37.6525	40.6465	44.3141	46.9279	52.618
26	30.4346	35.5632	38.8851	41.9232	45.6417	48.2899	54.052
27	31.5284	36.7412	40.1133	43.1945	46.9629	49.6449	55.476
28	32.6205	37.9159	41.3371	44.4608	48.2782	50.9934	56.892
29	33.7109	39.0875	42.5570	45.7223	49.5879	52.3356	58.301
30	34.7997	40.2560	43.7730	46.9792	50.8922	53.6720	59.703
40	45.6160	51.8051	55.7585	59.3417	63.6907	66.7660	73.402
50	56.6636	63.1671	67.5048	71.4202	76.1539	79.4900	86.661
60	66.9815	74.3970	79.0819	83.2977	88.3794	91.9517	99.607
70	77.5767	85.5270	90.5312	95.0232	100.425	104.215	112.317
80	88.1303	96.5782	101.879	100.629	112.329	116.321	124.839
90	98.6499	107.565	113.145	118.136	124.116	128.299	137.208
100	109.141	118.498	124.342	129.561	135.807	140.169	149.449

Source: Pearson, E.S. and H.O. Hartley (eds) (1966) *Biometrika Tables for Statisticans*, vol. I. New York: Cambridge University Press.

Table A.5   Cumulative distribution function for the Dickey–Fuller test

Sample size T	Probability of a smaller value							
	0.01	0.025	0.05	0.10	0.90	0.95	0.975	0.99
$\hat{\tau}$								
25	−2.66	−2.26	−1.95	−1.60	0.92	1.33	1.70	2.16
50	−2.62	−2.25	−1.95	−1.61	0.91	1.31	1.66	2.08
100	−2.60	−2.24	−1.95	−1.61	0.90	1.29	1.64	2.03
250	−2.58	−2.23	−1.95	−1.62	0.89	1.29	1.63	2.01
500	−2.58	−2.23	−1.95	−1.62	0.89	1.28	1.62	2.00
∞	−2.58	−2.23	−1.95	−1.62	0.89	1.28	1.62	2.00
$\hat{\tau}_\mu$								
25	−3.75	−3.33	−3.00	−2.63	−0.37	0.00	0.34	0.72
50	−3.58	−3.22	−2.93	−2.60	−0.40	−0.03	0.29	0.66
100	−3.51	−3.17	−2.89	−2.58	−0.42	−0.05	0.26	0.63
250	−3.46	−3.14	−2.88	−2.57	−0.42	−0.06	0.24	0.62
500	−3.44	−3.13	−2.87	−2.57	−0.43	−0.07	0.24	0.61
∞	−3.43	−3.12	−2.86	−2.57	−0.44	−0.07	0.23	0.60
$\hat{\tau}_\tau$								
25	−4.38	−3.95	−3.60	−3.24	−1.14	−0.80	−0.50	−0.15
50	−4.15	−3.80	−3.50	−3.18	−1.19	−0.87	−0.58	−0.24
100	−4.04	−3.73	−3.45	−3.15	−1.22	−0.90	−0.62	−0.28
250	−3.99	−3.69	−3.43	−3.13	−1.23	−0.92	−0.64	−0.31
500	−3.98	−3.68	−3.42	−3.13	−1.24	−0.93	−0.65	−0.32
∞	−3.96	−3.66	−3.41	−3.12	−1.25	−0.94	−0.66	−0.33

Standard errors of estimates vary, but most are less than 0.02.
Source: Fuller, W.A. (1976) *Introduction to Statistical Time Series*. New York: John Wiley & Sons.

Table A.6   Response surfaces for critical values of cointegration tests

n	Model	Point (%)	ϕ_∞	SE	ϕ_1	ϕ_2
1	No constant, no trend	1	−2.5658	(0.0023)	−1.960	−10.04
		5	−1.9393	(0.0008)	−0.398	0.0
		10	−1.6156	(0.0007)	−0.181	0.0
1	Constant, no trend	1	−3.4336	(0.0024)	−5.999	−29.25
		5	−2.8621	(0.0011)	−2.738	−8.36
		10	−2.5671	(0.0009)	−1.438	−4.48
1	Constant + Trend	1	−3.9638	(0.0019)	−8.353	−47.44
		5	−3.4126	(0.0012)	−4.039	−17.83
		10	−3.1279	(0.0009)	−2.418	−7.58
2	Constant, no trend	1	−3.9001	(0.0022)	−10.534	−30.03
		5	−3.3377	(0.0012)	−5.967	−8.98
		10	−3.0462	(0.0009)	−4.069	−5.73
2	Constant + Trend	1	−4.3266	(0.0022)	−15.531	−34.03
		5	−3.7809	(0.0013)	−9.421	−15.06
		10	−3.4959	(0.0009)	−7.203	−4.01
3	Constant, no trend	1	−4.2981	(0.0023)	−13.790	−46.37
		5	−3.7429	(0.0012)	−8.352	−13.41
		10	−3.4518	(0.0010)	−6.241	−2.79
3	Constant + Trend	1	−4.6676	(0.0022)	−18.492	−49.35
		5	−4.1193	(0.0011)	−12.024	−13.13
		10	−3.8344	(0.0009)	−9.188	−4.85
4	Constant, no trend	1	−4.6493	(0.0023)	−17.188	−59.20
		5	−4.1000	(0.0012)	−10.745	−21.57
		10	−3.8110	(0.0009)	−8.317	−5.19
4	Constant + Trend	1	−4.9695	(0.0021)	−22.504	−50.22
		5	−4.4294	(0.0012)	−14.501	−19.54
		10	−4.1474	(0.0010)	−11.165	−9.88
5	Constant, no trend	1	−4.9587	(0.0026)	−22.140	−37.29
		5	−4.4185	(0.0013)	−13.641	−21.16
		10	−4.1327	(0.0009)	−10.638	−5.48
5	Constant + Trend	1	−5.2497	(0.0024)	−26.606	−49.56
		5	−4.7154	(0.0013)	−17.432	−16.50
		10	−4.4345	(0.0010)	−13.654	−5.77
6	Constant, no trend	1	−5.2400	(0.0029)	−26.278	−41.65
		5	−4.7048	(0.0018)	−17.120	−11.17
		10	−4.4242	(0.0010)	−13.347	0.0
6	Constant + Trend	1	−5.5127	(0.0033)	−30.735	−52.50
		5	−4.9767	(0.0017)	−20.883	−9.05
		10	−4.6999	(0.0011)	−16.445	0.0

Source: MacKinnon, J.G. (1991) Critical values for cointegration tests. In Engle, R.F. and C.W.J. Granger (eds) *Long-Run Economic Relationships: Readings in Cointegration*. Oxford: Oxford University Press.

Index

Note: Italicized page numbers refer to figures and tables